AF322731

Integrating Ethics with Strategy

Selected Papers of Alan E Singer

Integrating Ethics with Strategy

Selected Papers of Alan E Singer

Alan E Singer

University of Canterbury, New Zealand

World Scientific

NEW JERSEY · LONDON · SINGAPORE · BEIJING · SHANGHAI · HONG KONG · TAIPEI · CHENNAI

Published by

World Scientific Publishing Co. Pte. Ltd.

5 Toh Tuck Link, Singapore 596224

USA office: 27 Warren Street, Suite 401-402, Hackensack, NJ 07601

UK office: 57 Shelton Street, Covent Garden, London WC2H 9HE

Library of Congress Cataloging-in-Publication Data
Singer, Alan E.
    Integrating ethics with strategy : selected papers of Alan E. Singer / by Alan E. Singer.
        p. cm.
    Includes bibliographical references and index.
    ISBN-13 978-981-270-145-9 -- ISBN-10 981-270-145-1
    1. Business ethics. 2. Strategic planning. I. Title.

    HF5387.S573 2007
    174'.4--dc22

                                                            2006048909

British Library Cataloguing-in-Publication Data
A catalogue record for this book is available from the British Library.

Typeset by Stallion Press
Email: enquiries@stallionpress.com

Printed in Singapore by World Scientific Printers (S) Pte Ltd

CONTENTS

Introduction

Since the late 1970s, the political trend towards global capitalism and increased corporate power has been thought of by detractors as a temporary aberration in a broader historic movement to a technologically-enabled revitalisation of communities, social justice, humane ideals and the natural environment. Since then, the visible hand of governments almost everywhere have been pre-occupied with military-type security and supporting international business, with only modest efforts being directed towards compensating for the known imitations of market based systems.

During that same era, however, the business ethics movement has gained momentum, especially in North America and Europe (although similar movements existed long before, particularly in the UK). The first issue of the *Journal of Business Ethics* was in 1980 and the ensuing 30 years of steady growth represents a triumph for its founding editor, Alex Michalos. Soon after, *Business Ethics Quarterly* and other journals followed, as many philosophers turned their attention towards applied ethics and business ethics. These have provided a mixture of critical and supportive perspectives on business-as-usual and the academic management literature (e.g. *Administrative Science Quarterly, Strategic Management Journal, Academy of Management Review, Journal of Management Studies, Journal of International Business Studies*, etc.) but they have also come to represent a kind of parallel intellectual universe.

Slowly but surely, the mainstream journals began to admit a trickle of ideological, moral or "values-based" challenges to their dominant discourse. Articles on the relationship between economics and ethics, or on corporate social responsibility, or business and society, globalisation and international business, critical management and accounting, sustainable business, social entrepreneurship, social and green marketing, ethical investment, accounting ethics, social accounting, multi-bottom-line reporting and so on, all became more numerous and more prominent.

Several management science and systems journals were also involved. Journals such as *Human Systems Management* (US) and *Systems Practice* (UK) broadly advanced the scientific, the technical and the ethical, rather than any particular ideology or methodology.

This book records a sustained attempt by the author to bridge and inter-relate the parallel "discourses" or "universes" of business-as-usual and ethical business. It is comprised of 18 chapters, each being an adapted, updated and cross-referenced version of previously published work (with cited co-authors, in some cases) that has appeared since 1984 in various conference proceedings and business journals (full references are given in the chapter abstracts).

Summary of the Chapters

Part I of the book "Strategy and Ethics" is comprised of eight chapters, as follows: Frameworks (Chapter 1), Correspondences (Chapter 2), Synergies (Chapter 3), Limitations (Chapter 4), Ideals (Chapter 5), Ecology (Chapter 6), Wisdom (Chapter 7) and Conscience (Chapter 8). Each chapter elaborates on specific aspects of the relationship (e.g. corporate and collective moral agency, in Chapter 2 and Chapter 8). Part II then focuses upon the many available conceptual models of strategic and ethical decision making. Accordingly, there is more of a management science or systems flavour to this part. There are four chapters: Recursivity (Chapter 9), Games (Chapter 10), Optimality (Chapter 11) and Systems (Chapter 12). The final part of the book then investigates some contexts within which the preceding ideas can be applied, assessed and developed. It is comprised of six chapters, as follows: Poverty (Chapter 13), Health (Chapter 14), Knowledge (Chapter 15), Disinvestment (Chapter 16), Corruption (Chapter 17) and Justice (Chapter 18).

Another useful way of partitioning the contents of the book concerns the likely appeal of each chapter (article) to the general reader versus the technical reader. It is suggested that the general reader or student might be well served by turning first to Chapters 1, 4, 5, 9, 12, 13, 14, 16 and 18 (see Table I). The remaining chapters should be skimmed at first (there are plenty of diagrams and tables to assist this) with a view to re-visiting them, later.

Table I Chapters suited to general versus technical readers.

General	Technical
Part 1: Strategy and Ethics	
1. FRAMEWORKS: An Organising Framework for Strategy and Ethics	2. CORRESPONDENCES: Strategy as Moral Philosophy
4. LIMITATIONS: Market Limitations as Strategic Problems	3. SYNERGIES : Competitiveness as "Hyper-Strategy"
5. IDEALS: Managing Human Systems and Advancing Humane Ideals	6. ECOLOGY: An Ecological Understanding of Global Business
	7. WISDOM: Towards Wise Enterprise
	8. CONSCIENCE: Consciousness and Conscience as Emergent Properties
Part 2: Models	
9. RECURSIVITY: Strategy-Models are Self- Referential	10. GAMES: Game theory and the Evolution of Strategic Thinking
12. SYSTEMS: Management-Science and Business-Ethics	11. OPTIMALITY: Optimisation and Strategy
Part 3: Contexts	
13. POVERTY: Business Strategy and Poverty Alleviation	15. KNOWLEDGE: Meta-Theory and Intellectual Property
14. HEALTH: Curing Strategic Myopia	17. CORRUPTION: Management Decision and Political Action
16. DIVESTMENT: Corporate Conscience and Foreign Divestment Decisions	
18. JUSTICE: Preferential-Hiring and The Dualism	

Part I

In the opening chapter, the dispersed academic literature that has dealt with the relationship between business strategy and ethics is classified into 16 distinct themes (e.g. trust, performance, stakeholders, market limitations, etc.). An organising framework is then set out, based upon the classical idea of a dualism; but one that has many specified components (involving values-priorities, ethical theories, language, etc.). Contributions to strategy and ethics can then be further classified as (i) separating, (ii) spanning or (iii) synthesising selected components of the dualism. Experience suggests that this simple organising framework is very helpful indeed for contemporary researchers and students, as they encounter the ever growing but controversial set of readings in the area.

Chapter 2 then develops the "correspondence" thesis, which is one of the above-mentioned "themes". A mapping is constructed from a set of about 40 distinctively defined concepts in the general theory of rationality to another set of commonly used but independently-defined strategic management (strategy) concepts. Other more specific "correspondences" have been proposed in the literature from time to time (such as local-responsiveness as a form of caring); but these can all be placed within this over-arching and integrative framework. Then (in Chapter 3), following a brief overview of the concept of synergy as used in management theory, the above correspondence framework of strategy-as-moral-philosophy is expanded to incorporate the abstract and previously neglected notion of synergies amongst forms of rationality. This results in a different way of conceptualising the competitiveness of industrial systems or strategic entities.

Chapters 4 and 5 examine the "limitations" of markets, or market-failures component of the strategy–ethics dualism. It is suggested that many companies have attempted to lead ethically by example, yet have nonetheless operated quite uncritically within a global market despite that systems' known limitations. As a result, corporate communications that refer to the "common good" often lack credibility amongst informed listeners (irrespective of their level of authenticity). A simple methodology is then proposed for augmenting enterprise strategies and communications in this respect. It is applied from a distance to a well-known profitable Japanese company that has an expressed social and environmental mission. Finally (in Chapter 4) some related cultural issues are discussed. Chapter 5 then described several variants of capitalism: Human Systems Management (HSM) and Humane Ideals Management (HIM). They are compared with Financial-Market-Capitalism (i.e. the Anglo-US version, or business-as-usual). HSM and HIM both embody distinctive ways of thinking about the relationship between strategy and ethics, with the latter placing more emphasis on the possibility that business corporations can play an active role in advancing universal humane ideals.

Dialectical tensions (i.e. the dualism) are very evident in almost all international business episodes. These are discussed in Chapter 6, along with the varied perceptions and conflicting value-priorities of different groups. Although "dialectics" has hardly ever been mentioned in management education, and never in the mainstream business media, the highly related subjects of business-ecology, product-ecology and knowledge-ecology have been popular. Yet, the latter ideas, together with the sciences of life and mind that support biotechnology and information technology, are all very closely related to dialectics (intuitively, historically and formally). Accordingly, it is argued that much greater emphasis should now be placed upon dialectical reasoning in contemporary business analysis and political calculation.

The recognition that almost all issues in business and politics involve some understanding of significant opposites is but one aspect of human wisdom. In Chapter 7 several distinctive components of "wisdom" are identified and then placed in correspondence with various personal characteristics and business practices commonly associated with entrepreneurship and entrepreneurial behaviour. This particular application of the "correspondence" thesis turns out to be productive: it yields several prescriptions for "wise-enterprise", including (i) the selection of good purposes, (ii) the need to remain mindful of the business and personal lifecycles, (iii) the importance of authentic prioritisation, and especially (iv) strategic explication: the demonstration as well as the explanation of authentic enterprise purposes and plans. The final chapter in Part I is a brief follow-up to the earlier discussion (in Chapter 2) of corporate or collective moral agency. It develops the argument from an evolutionary perspective against the notion of collective moral agency, which is a component of the "dualism" framework.

Part II

Part II of the book focuses upon the many available conceptual models of strategic and ethical decision making. Accordingly, it is within the management science and systems stream of literature linking strategy with ethics. In Chapter 9, it is shown that conceptual models of business strategy can themselves be depicted and described in a variety of ways, such as objects-of-choice in a meta-modelling decision, as patterns that replicate in managers' minds, or as end-states of a transition process. Discussions of these models and their various uses then typically invoke exactly the same categories of meaning that are found in the discourse on strategy itself. Accordingly, self-reference is pervasive within the general theory of strategy. This, in turn, indicates a potential synthesis of strategic with ecological ways of thinking.

The related idea that the study of game theory could help managers to "think better" about strategic problems is re-interpreted (in Chapter 10) with reference to various extensions and adaptations of that theory. An adapted conceptual model of strategic interaction, called an Ultra-game, is set out. Players in such a game are (thought of as) plurally-rational and synergy-seeking strategic-entities. In contrast with game theory as it is usually studied, conceptual models of this type can help managers to augment their language, their ideology and their integrity. Compared to the formal mathematical representations and extensions of game theory, which have found but a few business applications, the adapted conceptual models are more directly relevant to contemporary business problems such as those involving the players' boundaries and identities, their likely future problems, as well as others' problems.

Chapter 11 of the book further extends the correspondence component of the dualism, by focussing on the widely used notions of optimality and optimisation. It is first noted that strategy concepts such as "management-without-tradeoffs" implicitly challenge conventional notions of optimality. The challenge is broadened when one also considers the many defined forms of "optimality", across the spectrum of the behavioural and managerial sciences (economic and evolutionary forms, systemic-ethical forms, optimisation when criteria or representations are yet-to-be constructed, and so on). As in "strategy as rationality" it is then argued that each form of optimality corresponds with an identifiable concept within the general theory of strategy. Although the meta-optimality arguments remain ambiguous or incomplete, they can play a role similar to meta-rationality and meta-ethics in informing strategic management theory. Once again, it is implied that we need to adapt methodologies and adjust ideologies.

The last chapter of Part II provides something of an overview of the above three chapters. It is noted that for several decades, many prominent management scientists and systems thinkers (as distinct from strategy scholars) have been advocating "ethicalism": the incorporation of social and ethical concerns into the traditional "rational" or "maximising" mindset of operations-research and management-science (OR/MS). In fact, elementary forms of decision-analysis can readily be augmented in ways that sweep in ethical issues. Alternative conceptual models of this type already exist, in areas of decision-analysis, game-theory and optimisation (as indicated in the above chapters). These have all brought about a closer alignment of management science (including its "science" of strategy) with business ethics.

Part III

The final part of the book investigates several contexts within which the preceding ideas might be applied, assessed and developed. In Chapter 13 it is noted that corporations typically justify their strategic priorities with reference to wealth creation and innovation. They do not normally view the alleviation of global poverty as an explicit strategic goal. It is then argued that if large multinationals are going to contribute to the reduction of global poverty, their deliberate strategies will in future need to systematically take into account the known limitations of market based systems, many of which compound the effects of poverty in parts of the world. To make the necessary adjustment, existing strategies can be augmented in ways that involve partnership with NGOs, governments and trans-governmental networks.

Then (in Chapter 14), various elements of pharmaceutical corporate strategies are described and evaluated, in accordance with the preceding observation. Dialectical reasoning is applied to the formulation and evaluation of corporate strategies in general, but it is shown to be especially relevant to strategies involving health (i.e. life and mind). Dialectical reasoning not only points to the suitability of business-government partnerships, it also yields several specific suggestions for augmenting corporate strategies and communications involving health.

The ethics and strategies of pharmaceutical companies are very much called into question when one considers the fact that leading players in this industry have lobbied successfully, in international forums, for strong intellectual property rights regimes, including patents on the life-saving drugs used to treat epidemics in less developed countries. Chapter 15 discusses the wider dilemma and controversy concerning the nature and enforcement of intellectual property rights (IPR), particularly copyrights and patents. It is shown that this well-rehearsed two-sided debate can be further informed by various meta-theories. Policy and strategy in the area can be depicted as a resultant of narrowly-defined interests of stakeholder groups, including corporations. It can also be described in terms of rational deliberations that span scenarios and strategies, but these are further informed by particular social science theories. When all is considered, the case for weaker IPR regimes (e.g. shorter patents) with suitably adjusted business strategies becomes quite compelling. There also seems to be some possibility of further contributions from meta-theories to the appraisal of business strategies and public policies.

In Chapter 16 it is shown how the content of any strategic decision by a major corporation can be seen in practice as comprising commercial, strategic and ethical factors. The relevant factors in any strategic decision can be identified then classified on the basis of commercial, strategic and ethical decision principles to which they relate: egoism, enlightened self interest, or deontology. The exercise of moral imagination then enables the full set of strategic alternatives to be identified, but also described in ways that clarify their moral relevance. This approach to strategic and ethical decision making is illustrated with reference to the paradigm case of corporate strategic divestment or disinvestment: MNCs operating in South Africa, during the era of Apartheid.

Continuing with "international business" issues, Chapter 17 then sets out some approaches to structuring corruption-related decisions. The generic consequences of bribery are identified and a prescriptive decision-model is set out, involving a range of business situations from fairly benign facilitating payments through to extortion. The philosophical principle of double effect is seen to provide an ethical justification for a strategy of ongoing support for NGO anti-corruption initiatives (i.e. a partnership), as a way of ameliorating the moral effects of making facilitating payments, under some specified conditions. There is a brief consideration of ways of reducing corruption, as seen from each side of the dualism (i.e. left-leaning versus right leaning politics). It is hinted that a global political consensus or compromise might eventually be achievable on this major issue.

The final chapter looks at another rather prominent political issue in some jurisdictions. Preferential selection based on ethnicity or gender has proven to be highly divisive, when mandated in educational and business contexts. Some studies were conducted several years ago to examine peoples' perceptions of the fairness of preferential selection. Using questionnaires and scenarios, it was found that it was widely perceived as unfair, and that the level of this "unfairness" was directly related to the discrepancy in merit (i.e. scores on job-relevant tests) between a selected minority candidate and a higher-scoring majority candidate. Significantly in the present context, the provision of either an "ethical" or "legislative" justification for these preferential selection decisions increased the perceived unfairness and feelings of injustice.

Conclusion

That last chapter arguably has wider implications for the entire book and the practical project of integrating ethics and strategy. The observed psychological "reactance" to attempts at justification exemplifies a wider tendency towards extremism. It is symptomatic of a failure to rationally accommodate good reasons into political and moral judgments. On the surface at least, this seems to render hopeless the mission of the entire book, as expressed in its title. Although the "dualism" is proposed in Chapter 1 as an "organising framework" for strategy and ethics, it is also implicit throughout the book that detailed arguments on both sides of the political divide will move any reasonable person towards a more moderate position, away from any blinding passion for profit, or for justice.

This higher-level contrast between moderation versus extremism (i.e. one either moves to the centre, or else towards one of the poles of each component of the dualism) is surely a function of the amount of time spent on seriously considering the arguments, with the integrative conceptual frameworks. In an experimental questionnaire context, not to mention the global media treatment of these issues one almost always observes hurried or breathless responses to incomplete information, or narrow and provocative framing. Whereas these tricks attract peoples' attention and elicit emotional audience responses, they also apparently tend to provoke a "psychological reactance" and produce polarisation where consensus and settlement was once possible.

Therefore, in order for the ideas and frameworks in this book to have any practical value, it is necessary that they be considered or discussed slowly and carefully, over a long period of time. To the extent that any ideology involving production and distribution is simply "a framework of ideas used to explain values" (see Chapter 4) any such protracted study is bound to result in a shift towards the centre, or, in the context of business management, the formulation of genuine intentions to integrate business ethics with strategy in the future.

Part I: Strategy and Ethics

Chapter 1

FRAMEWORKS: An Organising Framework for Ethics and Strategy

Abstract: This chapter is adapted and developed from (i) Introduction to *Business Ethics and Strategy*, Ashgate, England, 2007 (Edited reference collection, in the series The International Library of Private and Public Ethics) and (ii) "An organising framework for strategy and ethics," Proceedings of *ANZAM*, Rockhampton, Australia, December 2006. The growing literature dealing with the relationship between strategy and ethics is classified into 16 distinct themes (e.g. trust, performance, market-limitations, etc.) with various sub-themes (e.g. types and levels of trust, etc.). A comprehensive organising framework is then set out, based upon the classical notion of a dualism. Experience suggests that the new framework is very helpful for researchers and students in these areas.

1.1 Introduction

Most readers will start out with their own ideas about the central issues of business ethics in relation to strategy. For some, it centres upon the stakeholder versus shareholder debate; for others, it all boils down to reducing corruption in practice; still others see that this relationship is precisely what is being analysed in the utmost detail in formal game theory and its interpretations. When considering any such issues or themes, it seems to be well worth reflecting upon a rather basic and pervasive binary divide, or dualism in human affairs. In a memorable scene from the James Bond-007 movie "*Tomorrow Never Dies*": a British navy captain throws a simple switch on a control panel from "peace" to "war". There is no middle ground. It is often said that business and ethics is just like that: "strategy" is war (Sun Tzu's *Art of War* being the classic text), whilst ethics is broadly associated with peace: goodwill, love, harmony and human rights. Put differently, strategy is for winning and for the powerful, whereas ethics is for helping and caring. Perhaps, as Nietzsche thought, it is also for the weak and the losers.

It often seems that the entire literature involving business ethics and strategy can be read as an elaboration of this dualism. Accordingly, in this chapter, a framework based upon dualism is set out, for the specific purpose of organising that disparate literature. Although the notion of a dualism is classical and ancient, experience so far suggests that such a framework is very helpful for contemporary readers who confront a bewildering literature in several related domains. Not only in Strategic Management, Business Ethics and Economic Ethics, but also in Corporate Social Responsibility, Business and Society, Globalisation and International Business, Critical Management and Accounting, Sustainable Business, Social Entrepreneurship, Social and Green Marketing, Ethical Investment, Accounting Ethics, Social Accounting, Multi-Bottom-Line Reporting, and so on.

The following section of this first chapter briefly discusses commonly identified strategy and ethics topics or themes (i.e. stakeholder versus shareholder, corruption, game theory, etc.) with some of their sub-themes. Then (in Section 3) various components of the organising framework are identified (e.g. values, ethics, rationalities, market limitations, etc.). Each of the "components" is represented here as a bi-polar construct (e.g. efficiency versus justice; exploitation versus compensation, etc.) This is followed (in Section 4) by an identification of several distinct spanning themes in the literature (e.g. character, intention, emotion, persuasion, etc.). All these spanning themes can be applied in principle to either side (e.g. virtue indicates selflessness, etc.) or to both sides. It is then noted that many contributions to "strategy and ethics" attempt to synthesise the two sides (with reference to selected components). A final type of contribution to ethics and strategy effectively separates the two sides (Section 6). Such articles typically reinforce the ideas and language on one side only, in effect challenging or downplaying the other side.

1.2 Main Themes

The main themes or topics in the available literature on the strategy–ethics relationship are listed in Table 1.1 (first column). A few sample references are cited in each case, with a very brief description given below, in this section.

Table 1.1   The main themes linking business strategy with ethics.

Theme	Sample Contributions	Sample Sub-Themes
Integrative Frameworks	Robertson and Crittenden (2003), Reynolds (2003), Quinn and Jones (1995), Singer (1994a)	correspondences, domains, dependencies
Economics and Ethics	Narveson (2003), Hosmer (2001), Sen (1997)	invisible hand, rationalities, co-determination
Globalisation	Dobson (2001), Logsdon and Wood (2002), Collier (2000)	co-existence of views, business citizenship, property rights
Market Limitations	Prakash Sethi (2003), Haksever *et al.* (2003), Singer (2003/2006), Quinn and Jones (1995)	accountability for distribution, monopolistic tendencies
Environment	Starkey and Crane (2003), Rugman and Verbeke (1998), Shrivastava (1995)	narratives, levels of regulation, advantages, sustainability
Stakeholders	Jones and Wicks (1999), Freeman (1999), Jawahar and McLaughlin (2001)	normative, instrumental, empirical, narratives, timing
Models	Calori (1999), Davis *et al.* (1997), Donaldson and Preston (1995)	epistemology, biases, choices
Game theory	Solomon (1999), Binmore (1999), Gilbert (1996)	metaphor, duty, rationality, emotions, rhetoric
Trust	Brenkert (1998), Hosmer (1995), Barney and Hansen (1994)	market and social, types and levels, normative and empirical benefits
Lobbying	Oberman (2004), Brooke-Hamilton and Hock (1997)	contestability, private and public interests
Corruption	Robertson and Watson (2004), Schnatterly (2003)	crime, performance, effects of FDI
Poverty	Singer (2006), Prahalad and Hammond (2002), Freeman (1998)	BoP markets, intentions, attitudes
Philanthropy	Saiia *et al.* (2003),	strategy, altruism, ideology
Knowledge	Zeleny (2005), Resnick (2003)	wisdom systems, IPR
Holistic Themes	Soule (2002), Werhane (1998), Dobson and White (1995)	ambiguity, beneficence, moral-principles and imagination, gender
Performance	Margolis and Walsh (2003), Orlitsky *et al.* (2003), Simpson and Kohers (2002), McWilliams and Siegel (2000)	meta-analysis, industry-specific, ambiguity and controversy
Implementation	Waddock (2004), Rossouw and van Vuuren (2003)	global compact and TI etc., modes, alignment

Many of these themes are discussed further at various points, throughout this book.

1.2.1 Existing Integrative Frameworks

Several integrative frameworks for strategy and ethics have already been proposed. (All of these are quite different from the organising framework set out here). Most interactive frameworks involve the idea of a correspondence between categories of meaning in strategy and ethics. Reynolds (2003) placed the strategy concept of integration relative to the ethical concept of justice; whilst "responsiveness" was likened to caring. Robertson and Crittenden (2003) related ethical categories to the strategic "social and economic macro-environment". A comprehensive rationality-based correspondence framework of this type is set out in Chapter 2. Such approaches are in the tradition of philosophical pragmatism. In contrast, Quinn and Jones (1995) adopted a deontological approach to integration, when they claimed to have identified several "logically necessary priorities" for business managers.

1.2.2 Economics

Several leading economists have debated "business ethics". For example, according to Sen (1997) the economic way of thinking does indeed downplay the role of ethics. Ethical conduct can deeply influence an economy, whilst "social concern in private enterprise" is an important phenomenon. In any case, he noted, the study of "business principles and moral sentiments" has now become "a rich source of understanding". Hosmer (2001) also argues that economics, ethics and business strategy can richly inform each other, as domains of knowledge. A contribution from Narveson (2003), in contrast, "separates" the two sides, by arguing from Economics that "the morality of the market... does not require people to benefit others".

1.2.3 Globalisation

In the context of the globalisation debate, Dobson (2001) noted that many WTO policies are based upon the notion of the economy as a "wealth creating machine". An alternative of business as a "community of excellence" is derived from virtue ethics and is essentially the view adopted and propagated by international NGOs. Logsdon and Wood (2002) noted that in the choice of corporate strategies, worldwide human rights are very much at stake. The category of "citizenship" for individuals has minimalist (libertarian), communitarian and universalist interpretations, but these "correspond" to profit maximisation, multi-domestic and global integration business strategies, respectively. Collier (2000) is particularly concerned about the damaging effect of intellectual property regimes on distributive justice and she has emphasised the imperative to preserve "the basic human dignity of those disadvantaged by (globalisation)".

1.2.4 Market Limitations

According to Quinn and Jones (1995) the strategic management literature "turned the insights of (industrial) economics upside-down, by proposing that exploiting (and even creating) market barriers... are legitimate corporate strategies". Prakash Sethi (2003) noted in similar spirit that some corrective mechanism is needed in order to overcome the tendency towards exploitation of market power by corporations, with the associated lack of any guarantee of distributive justice. He argued that "corporations should be held accountable for a more equitable distribution of above-normal profits...". Haksever *et al.* (2003) further reinforced this idea when they explained how the decisions of corporate managers can "destroy value" for some stakeholders. More generally (see Chapters 4 and 5) corporations can (ought to?) systematically augment their strategies, in order to compensate for all the known limitations (or failures) of market-based systems.

1.2.5 Environment

Starkey and Crane (2003) cast the strategy–ethics dualism (see below) in terms of competing "narratives". They suggested (like many others before them) that ecological understanding (see Chapter 6) can be an impetus for change and for green strategy. Rugman and Verbeke (1998) examined global environmental regulations, with their likely influence on corporate strategy (assuming business–as–usual). Shrivastava (1995) explained how environmental technologies can sometimes be used to gain competitive advantage (i.e. a win-win strategy and a synthesising contribution to the debate).

1.2.6 Stakeholders

Jones and Wicks (1999) reviewed several versions of stakeholder theory, particularly the instrumental (doing well by doing good) and the normative versions (just do good). They then proposed the development of a "convergent" or hybrid stakeholder theory. Freeman (1999), whose works have been at the centre of much of the debate about stakeholders in business, then reminded us that the term "stakeholder" is an "obvious literary device, meant to call into question the emphasis on stockholders" (i.e. it is a form of persuasion, just like the economic-right try to persuade us to accept shareholder primacy). Jawahar and McLaughlin (2001) have recast the shareholder–stakeholder debate in terms of timing: during the start-up stage of a business, for example, managers will be pro-active towards stockholders, creditors and customers; but this can change at other stages of the life cycle. ("Ethics now versus later" is a component of the dualism, "persuasion" is a spanning theme, as discussed below)

1.2.7 Models

The existence of rival stakeholder and shareholder theories or models raises a larger question about the status and interpretation of all strategic management "models" (see Chapters 9–12). Calori (1999) offered a wide-ranging critique of "orthodox" models, whilst Davis *et al.* (1997) specifically contrasted the agency "model" (shareholder value) with the stewardship (stakeholder) model. Donaldson and Preston (1995) also discussed managers "choosing" between an input-output model of the firm and the stakeholder model.

1.2.8 Game Theory

This "model choice" debate is especially lively in the case of formal game-theory applied to business decisions (see Chapter 10). At the heart of the controversy is the distinction between a model per se and its likely effects on the behaviour of those who understand or study it. Aligning with Freeman's "narratives", Gilbert (1996) pointed out that "on a post-modern view, the PDG is not a fact of nature, it is a rhetorical device". Solomon (1999) then argued that the theory is "dangerous and demeaning", whilst Binmore (1999), a pre-eminent game theorist responded that the principles of game theory are in fact "ethically neutral", like $2 + 2 = 4$, whilst they also happen to generate exquisite rational explanations for many types of behaviour that are often considered moral, or ethical.

1.2.9 Trust

The concept of trust is prominent, both within game theory (or its meta-theory) and the wider strategy–ethics nexus. Brenkert (1998) noted that "in the market, trust requires special efforts and commitments that it does not require in ordinary social life". Barney and Hansen (1994) then distinguished several types of trust that effect the optimal strategy for profit. At the level of research paradigms, Hosmer (1995) noted that the definitions of "trust" found in empirical psychology and organisation theory both incorporate moral values, so that the theme "trust" per se necessarily lies at the confluence of normative and empirical theories of business behaviour.

1.2.10 Lobbying

In strategic lobbying, powerful corporate players disproportionately influence the rules of society. This seems unjust and unethical. However, Brook-Hamilton and Hock (1997) noted that lobbying by businesses can promote the public interest, not just corporate self-interest; but it does need to be "restrained by ethical standards". Oberman (2004) argued (from the economic-right) that so long as politics remains "contestable", corporate lobbying of any type is "legitimate".

1.2.11 Corruption

From a practical point of view, corruption is the major theme linking business strategy with ethics, although it is not given much consideration in the strategic management literature. One exception is Robertson and Watson

(2004) who related perceived corruption in a country to inward foreign direct investment (FDI). Another study by Schnatterly (2003) noted that white-collar crime affects business performance, but it is also affected by organisational structures and processes.

1.2.12 Poverty

The disputed role of business enterprises in poverty reduction nicely characterises the "dualism". A mainstream view sees that profit-maximising businesses create wealth, but they do not have an interest in re-distribution. Prahalad and Hammond (2002) are amongst those (leaning to the economic-right) who have told a persuasive story of a benevolent global capitalism-as-usual, in which bottom-of-pyramid (poverty) markets are "served" with consumer goods and micro credit for enterprise, women are duly honoured and involved, whilst high-tech infrastructures spread rapidly through the deliberate strategies of private enterprise. Freeman (1998) is amongst those (leaning to the left) who also see that business as usual is not the solution. The stakeholder idea "has substance", he wrote, and it can lead to the necessary changes in peoples' general attitudes. More generally, the alternative view sees that businesses must have mixed motives that include the reduction of poverty, if poverty is to be reduced (see Chapter 13). Business-as-usual is not enough.

1.2.13 Knowledge

The link between ethics and knowledge strategy is at least twofold. Zeleny (2006) has re-described knowledge as the "purposeful co-ordination of action" and wisdom as "socially accepted or experience-validated explication of purpose". If we are wise, our actions will automatically communicate our purposes, although the language of ethics and politics can be deployed to reinforce that message. The other part of the link centres on Intellectual Property Rights (see Chapter 15). Like Collier and many others, Resnick (2003) has referred to the widespread "sense that intellectual property increases disparities". In (legal) practice, he says, the best approach to resolving this dilemma between justice and efficiency is pragmatic; that is, to "assess and balance the competing moral values" case by case.

1.2.14 Holistic Approaches

Several contributions to ethics and strategy have adopted holistic approaches. For example, Soule (2002) appealed for "a few good moral principles" to help managers. Werhane (1998) has written on managers' lack of "moral imagination". It is often necessary to "break out of ones own schema" in order to properly assess any strategic situation. Dobson and White (1995) have re-cast the strategy–ethics relationship in terms of gender differences. They saw a strong male gender-bias in business theory and practice, but they linked the stakeholder model with the grand theme of "nascent economic woman".

1.2.15 Performance

Many empirical studies on the relationship between corporate social and financial performance have been conducted (see Table 1.1). Margolis and Walsh (2003) noted that the findings have been quite ambiguous; but this "reinforces rather than relieves" the tension surrounding ethics in relation to strategy. Then, again in the spirit of pragmatism, they suggest that the empirical ambiguity should be treated as "a starting point for inquiry". This book closely follows that advice.

1.2.16 Implementation

Finally, many contributions have focused on the implementation of ethical strategy (Table 1.1 last row). Rossouw and van Vuuren (2003) identified five distinctive "modes of managing morality", the highest level being a "seamless integration of ethics into corporate strategy". Waddock (2004) identified several "forces" that are making corporate citizenship "real". They include the UN's "Global Compact", the OECD, the ILO, the Fair Labour Association, the Triple Bottom Line Reporting movement and Transparency International, to mention but a few. The push towards social responsibility in business is supported by many specific laws at the national level, not to mention the intellectual and grassroots movements mentioned at the outset (e.g. Critical Management, Social-Entrepreneurship, and so on).

1.3 Components of the Dualism

As mentioned at the outset, the "organising framework" has several main components including values, ethical theories and forms of rationality, limitations of market based systems, political leanings, issues of timing (i.e. ethics now versus later), systems (i.e. shareholder versus stakeholder), individual versus collective moral agency and use of language. These are listed in Figure 1.1 and briefly described in this section. Further discussion of many of the "components" can also be found at various points throughout the book.

Each component can be thought of as essentially bi-polar. Although this might appear at first to an unwarranted simplification, any loss of complexity or detail is more than compensated for by the revealed usefulness of the framework. The dualism framework greatly facilitates the organisation of diverse contributions to business ethics and strategy. Werhane recently[1] put it thus: "While framing these mindsets (i.e. strategy and ethics) in terms

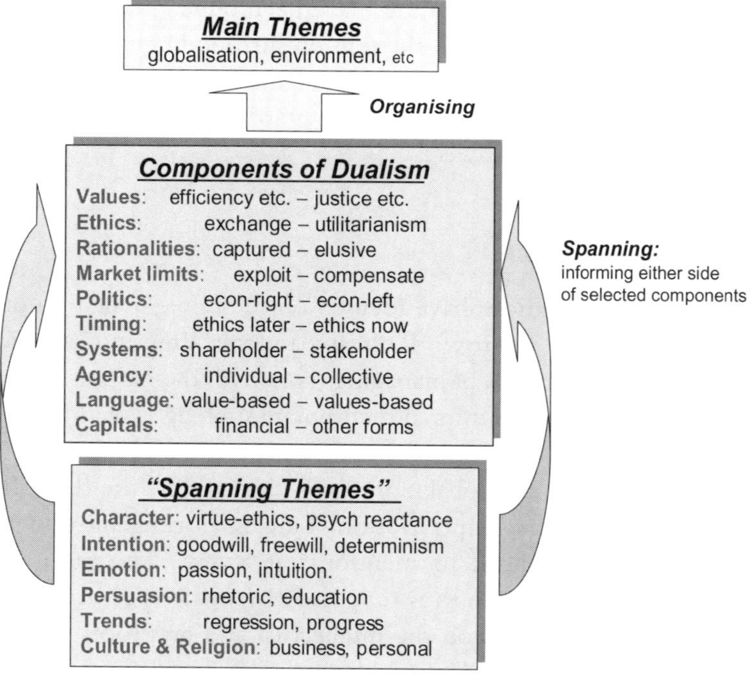

Figure 1.1   An organising framework.

of a series of dualisms may be a bit exaggerated, this technique serves to focus and force a careful analysis of each (contribution) in the context of the others" (parentheses added). Such an "analysis" and "contextualisation" of work in the area is precisely what the "organising framework" is intended to facilitate.

1.3.1 Values

Most people agree that the set of all human values can be (at least roughly) partitioned, with one sub-set or side generally associated with efficiency, craftsmanship and free-exchange; the other "side" with justice, care, avoidance of harms and the protection of human rights (refer to Figure 1.1). The former sub-set of values are also embodied in what Sen (1987) has called the "engineering view" of economics, whilst they are often associated with the male gender, in contrast to the latter which are equally "female" (e.g. Dobson and White, 1995).

1.3.2 Ethical Theories

In almost every textbook on business ethics, together with several recent strategy books, one finds an account of the major ethical theories, or forms of moral reasoning. These forms can also be partitioned. On the same side as the efficiency-related "values" one finds the economic principle of utility maximisation arising from exchange, as well as normative ethical egoism. On the other side of the dualism one finds utilitarianism: the "greatest good for greatest number of people". This resembles in important respects the multi-stakeholder model. Deontological ethics (Kantian capitalism) also belongs on this second "side" of the dualism. Contractarian moral and political theory is something of a special case here, although its central idea of agreements amongst free and properly self-interested individuals would place the theory on the "exchange and efficiency" side of the dualism.[2]

1.3.3 Rationalities

These (and other) theories of moral reasoning are interwoven with the many distinctive forms of rationality, defined across the entire spectrum of the social sciences (see Chapter 2). Again, the rationality-set of all such "forms" can also be partitioned. Put simply, one sub-set involves forms that can be formally reduced to preference relations. The second set involves higher level meta-preferences; that is, some kind of moral reflection and deliberation on those lower level desires. Many issues in marketing ethics swing on this partitioned or "bi-polar" component of the dualism, as does the comparison of betterness with goodness (see Chapter 11).

1.3.4 Market Limitations

The distinction between preference and well-being belongs on the long list of known limitations (and failures) of market based systems. Others include negative-externalities, monopolistic-tendencies and distributive justice. As mentioned previously (Section 1.2), business entities are often in a position to either exploit the various limitations (as they are generally not held accountable for doing that) or else to take the authentic moral high ground and try to deliberately compensate for them (see Chapters 4 and 5).

1.3.5 Political Leanings

The more exploitative type of competitive business behaviour (or hyper-competition) is in turn associated with right-leaning political ideology. It tends to champion the interests of the powerful and to endorse a purely instrumental approach to productive relationships. The left (liberal-democrat, social-democrat, socialist) place more emphasis upon universal empowerment and distributive justice, care-based ethics and the interest of communities (variously conceived). The left also broadly tend to favour social and environmental policies that are based upon currently available scientific understandings (e.g. the sustainability and stewardship views, or "ethics now").

1.3.6 Timing

As indicated previously (see Section 1.2.6) "timing" is also a bi-polar component of the dualism: "ethics-now" versus "strategy-now, with ethics later". Many believe that "strategy" (profit maximisation, efficiency) provides the means to accumulate financial capital, enabling ethical "ends" such as redistribution or environmental restoration to be pursued later.

A related phenomenon was described by the economist Knight (1936) who observed that unethical business is more likely when competitive intensity is very high (i.e. survival now, ethics later), or else when it is too low, due to monopoly power or undue secrecy (no accountability), as was described circa 2500 years ago in Plato's *Ring of Gyges*.

1.3.7 Systems (Stakeholder versus Shareholder Revisited)

Several components of the dualism can be brought together into "dual" descriptions of real or hoped-for business "systems". In "System 1" stakeholder relations are viewed instrumentally as a means to create wealth. NGOs are worthy adverseries, governments are lobbied in pursuit of narrow interests. This is business–as–usual, as many see it. In "System 2", strategic entities (e.g. management teams) have authentically mixed motives. Benevolent ruler-managers believe they can protect themselves from dissenting shareholders by arguing that the strategy is at least consistent with commercial goals. Socially conscious NGOs and good governments become genuine partners with business in joint missions (see Chapters 13 and 14). Variants of "System 2" are created whenever any of its elements are enshrined in law (cf. Margolis and Walsh, 2003; Waddock, 2004).

1.3.8 Moral Agency

The difference between the above two "systems" has sometimes been linked to the philosophical question of individual versus collective moral agency (i.e. can groups be morally responsible, or have moral duties). Milton Friedman (1970), for example, famously linked his claim that "the social responsibility of business is to increase its profits" (i.e. System 1) to the idea that ethics and morality are exclusively the qualities of individuals, not companies. Several others (e.g. Pruzan, 2001; French, 1984) have argued to the contrary, thus implying that collective responsibility for harms, or a collective duty of beneficence are well-founded ideas that do apply to businesses (see Chapters 2 and 3).

1.3.9 Language

A final "main component" of the dualism framework involves the use or misuse of language in ways that often involve trans-valuations (i.e. good becomes bad). The term "value based management", for example, often refers to shareholder wealth creation; but it has also been used to refer (perhaps more obviously) to the care-based "values" embodied in the stakeholder and stewardship models. In a sense, this type of consultant-speak is reminiscent of the Cold War when the Soviet Union claimed to exemplify freedom. Other examples involve terms such as "intellectual" and "property" (see Chapter 15) as well as the term "capital" which has been granted several non-traditional meanings (see Chapter 3), basically for ideological purposes (or to make political capital!). Many believe that this type of trans-valuation is itself a bad thing, not a game but a "slaughter" (Roy, 2005).

1.4 Spanning the Dualism

As mentioned at the outset, several other common themes in the literature on strategy and ethics span the dualism. The spanning themes (which should be distinguished from the commonly-identified strategy and ethics "themes" such as globalisation, listed in Section 2) can potentially inform both sides of the dualism (refer to Figures 1.1 and 1.2) and in some cases they point towards a possible unification or synthesis of component-poles. The spanning themes include psychological matters, such as human character, virtues, emotions and intentions, as well as social matters such as persuasion, trends, culture and religion. Each is very briefly considered in this section.

1.4.1 Character

The philosophy of virtue emphasises the characteristics of the individuals involved in any business activity (e.g. Solomon, 1999). This theme of character spans the dualism, because it is associated with the particular values most prominently embodied in any given business activity. For example, the motive to excel (excellence and efficiency in business) is generally seen as a sign of virtue. However, virtue ethics also sees that a caring attitude and a commitment to human ideals is an important virtue, or an indication of good character. Therefore, if an article (contribution) invokes virtue ethics to support business-as-usual, it is literally telling one side of the story.

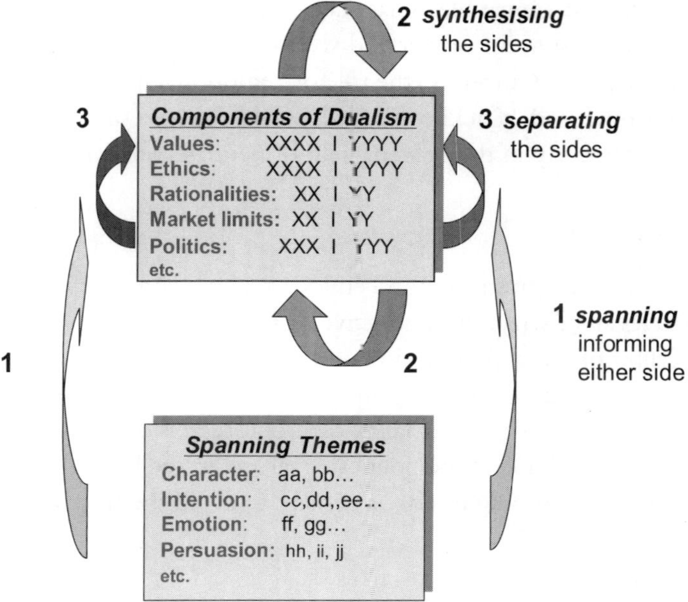

Figure 1.2   Three types of contribution to the relationship.

1.4.2 Intention

Theories of business strategy and business ethics each attach considerable importance to business goals and intentions. Thus intention per se is another noteworthy "spanning theme". In both strategy and ethics it is recognised (in separate contributions) that the outcomes of any plan or a project might not match those intentions. In ethics, Kant emphasised only the quality of individual human intentions. To be ethical, he argued, a person's strategy or plan must be based upon genuine goodwill towards others. Whether it succeeds is then of much lesser moral significance. In business strategy, that Kantian emphasis is typically reversed.

1.4.3 Emotion

It is often assumed, particularly within traditional economics, that the theory and practice of business strategy is based upon reason (e.g. Calori, 1999) whereas ethics is a matter of emotion. However, there are many important ways in which emotions can enter into strategy, whilst reason and ethics are far from being incompatible. Classically, for example, Plato identified a megalothymic passion for power and wealth, but also an isothymic passion for justice, or ethics. Currently, the role of "emotional intelligence" in business has become widely acknowledged, while the role of emotions is also being taken seriously in the nascent field of neuro-economics.

1.4.4 Persuasion

The entire literature on strategy and ethics is replete with assertions anecdotes and narratives all of which have selective or very partial empirical support. As a result, claims of moral progress in business (next section) often appear to be more like recruitment appeals: "join our business ethics movement and go with the flow", so to speak. Claims of moral regression likewise read like appeals for urgent action at the political level and in the boardroom, in order to reverse some disturbing trend, or perhaps to avoid the next apocalypse.

1.4.5 Trends

The final "spanning theme" in the organising framework concerns long-term social and political trends. Optimistic commentators write of a long term trend of moral progress in business (usually invoked to add weight to the "ethics" side of the dualism), whilst pessimists see a deterioration, or moral regression. Amongst the former, Hosmer (2001) for example described "a definite movement towards an expanded view that includes the interest of other persons," at least in economic theories. Logsdon and Wood (2002) predicted that "global corporations are likely to join the ranks of enforcers (of human rights)..." (emphasis added). Yet at the same time, many corporate executives have been developing an impoverished vision that effectively stops with anti-terrorism measures. Also, the great wave of corporate scandals has broken; corporate philanthropy (in the US at least) turned towards the "strategic" or instrumental (e.g. Saiia *et al.*, 2003), whilst the worldwide human rights situation appears to many observers to be regressing.

1.5 Synthesising

Many contributions to strategy and ethics have discussed notions of synergy, or somewhat similar notions, such as synthesis and complementarity (see Chapters 3, 6, 9 and 15). These sometimes positioned synergy per se as a specific "spanning theme", but they more usually involve some selected bi-polar "components" (see the arrows labelled 2 in Figure 1.2). Such contributions often explain how the "poles" can be combined, or how the assumed tradeoffs can in fact be overcome.

Contributions of this type occupy a rather distinctive place, within the organising framework. This is because the many ecological or evolutionary models for strategy (not to mention evolutionary ethical theories) can also be located at this point. Accordingly, we would locate at this point any contributions to ethics and strategy that emphasise the interdependency of communities and networks of stakeholders (e.g. Chapter 4), or articles that deploy organic metaphors (new paradigm: your business is alive). This implied association of "synthesis" per se with ecology and ecological thinking simply accords with ancient and modern observations that dialectical reasoning (thesis–antithesis–synthesis) characterise the sciences of life and mind.

1.6 Separating

Despite the many attempts to forge a synthesis between selected aspects of strategy and ethics, such as shareholder and stakeholder models, many contributions "in" strategy, or "in" ethics continue to effectively separate these two sides. Such articles typically invoke selected component-poles from within only *one* side of the dualism (refer to Figure 1.2). Thus, in strategy articles that "separate", the overarching concern in the narrative (even when alluding to ethical issues) is with efficiency, resource-exchanges, exploiting market power and shareholder wealth creation. Rugman and Verbeke (1998), for example, considered the effect of global environmental regulations in purely "strategic" terms. In similar spirit, McGee (1998) claimed that a "proactive social responsiveness mode of operating" in business would encourage managers to "focus on distributive equity rather than micro-level efficiency".

In contrast, many "separating" articles in Business Ethics tend to invoke selected poles from the ethics side of the dualism only, even when they are referring to strategic issues. In such contributions, imperatives such as justice and "ethics now" are mutually reinforced. They are often embedded into persuasive accounts of management obligations to stakeholder groups, or the need for pluralist ethics in business decision making, and so on. Quinn and Jones (1995), for example, argued that the business system itself "logically" depends upon several moral principles, so these ought to be obeyed and upheld by business strategists. The articles tend to avoid the categories and terminology of mainstream strategic management and industrial economics, as if they were written for a different audience, or intended to engage with a different mindset amongst readers.

1.7 Conclusion

As mentioned at the outset, many readers will have started out with their own ideas about the central issues of business ethics in relation to strategy. There is a good chance that those "ideas" were mentioned in Section 1.2 which referred to 16 "main themes". The organising framework (Figures 1.1 and 1.2) can then be used to place those preliminary "ideas" on the subject relative to all published contributions. By first expressing one's own ideas then shaping them within a framework, understanding is advanced. Throughout, there have also been some references made to other chapter numbers where the themes, sub-themes and bi-polar components of the framework are discussed further. It is hoped that the "organising framework" will continue to be helpful as an aid to comprehending and interrelating a growing and rather disparate literature, but also that it will itself stimulate further inquiry and work in the area.

Notes

1. See the prologue to the cited Ashgate (2007) collection of reprints on *Business Ethics and Strategy*, which has many contributors.
2. Contractarian "ethics" (moral and political theory) occupy a distinctive position, within the organising framework. The central idea of agreements amongst free and properly self-interested individuals places this theory on the "exchange and efficiency" side of the dualism. On the other hand, its principles of distributive justice based on liberty occupies a position on the other side. Accordingly, one might argue that the entire Contractarian theory is an elaborate "spanning theme", informing both sides, as does the general philosophical theory of intentionality.

Chapter 2

CORRESPONDENCES:
Strategy as Moral Philosophy

Abstract: This chapter is extracted and abridged from *Human Systems Management* 11(1), pp. 7–22, 1991; *Strategic Management Journal* 15, pp. 191–213, 1994 and *Strategy as Rationality*, Ashgate Series in Philosophy, 1996. It develops the "correspondence" thesis mentioned in Chapter 1. A mapping is constructed from a set of about 40 distinctively defined rational-moral concepts to another set of commonly used but independently-defined strategy concepts. Several more specific "correspondences" that have been proposed in the business ethics literature from time to time (such as local-responsiveness as a form of caring) can be placed and evaluated within this overarching conceptual framework.

2.1 Introduction

Throughout the 1980s there was a growing body of opinion, expressed most forcefully in the business ethics literature (e.g. Freeman, 1984; Goodpaster, 1988; Hosmer, 1991) that moral philosophy could somehow inform strategic management in ways that complement or even supplant the traditional contribution from economics. Many corporate managers expressed similar views. At a conference on the Ethics of Business in a Global Economy (in Columbus, Ohio, 1992) several CEOs were openly competing with each other to express their social and environmental concerns. For example, Georges-Yves Kervern, of UAP, France, argued quite forcefully that a synthesis of corporate strategy with ethics is "*Une thera-peutic — la moins violente possible — des maladies de la societe*". Akio Morita, chairman of Sony, similarly argued (on another occasion) that "Japanese corporations must start to think differently" not only increasing dividends but also "treating employees more humanely, whilst contributing more to the community and environmental protection".

In the US, celebrated companies like Ben and Jerry's have publicly attributed their US$1 billion per annum turnover to very high rates of new product introduction combined with egalitarian management policies of comparatively narrow salary differentials, day-care, family leave and round-table decision-making. At the same time, private sector managers in many other countries are actively seeking ways of blending social justice with their quest for economic efficiency. One manager in New Zealand has hired new staff only from the long term unemployed, another public company has spent $50,000 on local public schools, in addition to paying tax. Finally, in the UK, the successful policies and practices of the Body Shop are not only well known and respected, they are also widely copied. Most significantly, the Body Shop is said to be one of the most studied and discussed HBS cases ever.

Some believe that this sort of direct social action by corporate entities is a mistake, because it reduces international competitiveness of business and often adds to costs. Many economic and political theories would imply that this trend as naive and mistaken, unless the socially oriented policies and practices really reflect nothing other than a public-relations or marketing ploy (e.g. Friedman, 1970). Others (e.g. Sen, 1977 and 1987; Goldman, 1980; Buchanan, 1985; Etzioni, 1988; Kuhn, 1992) have sought to justify such policies and missions indirectly, within a critical but rigorously argued meta-theory of conventional economics. In this chapter, a conceptual framework of strategy-as-rationality (Singer, 1991b) is extended, in order to offer a justification of direct social and ethical engagement beyond what is demanded by the market, but still falling within a prescriptive theory of strategic management.

2.1.1 Sweeping Ethics In and Out

To date, ethical concerns have not had much of a presence in the mainstream theory of strategic management. There are several possible explanations for this, as follows:

- Strategy is about self-interest: To the extent that strategy is "how one goes about seeking personal gain" (Schendel, 1991) ethical-egoism constitutes the definitive moral foundation for strategy. To the extent that moral philosophy then offers alternatives to egoism, or is critical of it, it becomes irrelevant.

- Strategy targets the powerful: Strategy, as a discipline, targets the upper echelons (e.g. Hambrick and Mason, 1980) or those seeking power. In contrast, ethical concerns are sometimes seen as "an affliction of the weak" (e.g. Nietzsche, 1886).
- Strategy is practical: The discipline addresses the expressed concerns of practitioners, which are primarily commercial, legal and managerial; but not ethical.
- Strategy is modern: Strategy addresses distinctively modern managerial problems; whereas moral philosophy is an ancient discipline.

All of these proposed justifications for an a-moral, or economically-rational conception of strategy have been cast into doubt by developments over the last couple of decades. First, stakeholder, environmental and other social concerns have already entered many practical strategy frameworks (e.g. Andrews, 1980). These concerns could reflect a significant extension of the "rational self-interest" component of strategy. Next, as described above and elsewhere (e.g. Moss-Kanter, 1991) many practicing CEOs have expressed social, environmental and ethical concerns, in their words and actions. Finally, the fact that moral philosophy is indeed an ancient discipline, does not mean that it should be forgotten.

2.2 Strategy as Rationality

The role of rationality per se in strategic management is often identified with the contribution from economics and then contrasted with the perspective from administrative and organisational theories (e.g. Hitt and Tyler, 1991). When the strategy–rationality relationship is viewed via economics, its characteristics and limitations are well known (e.g. Rumelt *et al.*, 1991). On the positive side, economics has yielded strategy techniques and prescriptions such as Porter's industrial attractiveness model, while empirical management studies have challenged some tenets of economic theory (Figure 2.1). More critically, formalisation and

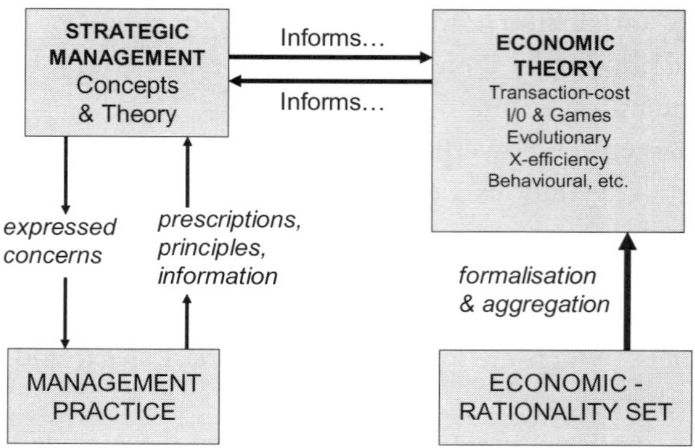

Figure 2.1 Economics and strategy.

aggregation have created a gap between economic theory and business practice (e.g. Kay, 1991; Grubel and Boland, 1986; Rumelt *et al.*, 1991). Whereas economists seek and often find rationality-based understandings of industrial systems, strategic management as a discipline seeks to respond more directly to the expressed concerns of practicing corporate managers (Schendel, 1991).

In addition to the strategy–rationality linkages via economics, it is also productive to view the same relationship in a quite different way. The various distinctive forms of rationality (e.g. bounded, systemic, selective, etc.) that are defined and utilised within the many branches of economic theory each captures the essence of a simple but important strategy prescription. Put differently, there is a set of economic-rationalities that inform strategy quite directly, without having to invoke the details of the associated formalised and aggregated economic theory (Table 2.1).

To the extent that the economic-rationality set informs strategy it might also be asked whether or not other forms of rationality could do the same. Other forms have been defined in the wider spectrum of the social and cognitive sciences, but also in ethics and moral philosophy. For example, the linkage between ends-rationalities and "strategic" goals

Table 2.1 Economic rationalities and strategy prescriptions.

Branch of Economic Theory	Form(s) of Rationality	Prescription for Management Practice (Managers Should ...)
Transaction cost	*bounded, weak*	... take into account the costs of information search and processing (in decisions about strategy and structure).
Industrial–organisation and game theoretic	*strategic*	... consider the reactions of other entities to your moves and others' moves. Hence take into account reputations, beliefs, signals, etc.
Evolutionary	*systemic, adaptive*	... learn from past mistakes. discover rules in the environment. Use experience to refine beliefs.
X-efficiency	*selective, ratchet*	... seek motivational devices that improve capabilities and develop potential. Allow for organisational inertia or status quo bias.
Behavioural	*cognitive, quasi*	... take into account systematic biases, heuristic use, costs of search and processing for self (meta-cognition) and for others.

can be informative for management theory, as described in the next section.

2.2.1 Strategic Goals

Many apparently ethical concerns, involving the well-being of other entities, are already firmly incorporated within the general theory of rationality. This is part of a larger idea that the rationality of the individual has an important evaluative dimension, concerning the choice of goals, or ends. However, compared to economically-oriented theories, moral philosophy and other social sciences have paid much more attention to the precise nature and optimal specification of individual's goals (e.g. Etzioni, 1988;

Rawls, 1972; Rescher, 1988). This particular evaluative or moral dimension of rationality has not been ignored in strategic management theory: indeed it is already quite clearly and comprehensively mirrored in the mainstream. The specific correspondences concerning goals, or ends, are as follows:

(i) Rational-egoism — shareholder-value-creation. Egoism involves satisfying one's own preferences (i.e. utility maximisation). If this is placed in carefully specified market contexts, it formally yields Pareto-optimal outcomes. This result, in turn, is at the heart of the normative theory of shareholder value-creation. Assuming appropriate managerial reward and incentive structures are in place (e.g. stock options and other performance incentives) the concepts of egoism for individuals and value-creation for other strategic entities, such as firms and corporations, are very similar in terms of their origin, their behavioural implications and their ethical justification (e.g. Hosmer, 1991).

(ii) Rational-sympathy — stakeholders-as-constraints. Extended forms of ends-rationalities correspond with stakeholder approaches in strategy. Both flow from the idea that it is rational (right, good) to have other goals in addition to self-interest, or shareholder value-creation, respectively. The "sympathy" form of extended individual rationality (Sen, 1977) corresponds precisely to Ansoff's (1965) stakeholders-as-constraints position. Both see that serving others interests is a prudential and pragmatic part of striving to achieve egoist goals in the longer term.

(iii) Rational commitment — not-for-profit. In contrast, Sen's rational commitments by the individual involve counter-preferential choice, genuine utility loss, or altruism. This corresponds to the special ethos of a not-for-profit organisation. In these cases, there is an over-riding (but nevertheless rational) commitment to a non-financial cause (e.g., health provision, providing employment, aesthetics, etc).

These forms of ends-rationality progressively increase in sophistication. The next level of increasing complexity moves beyond attempts to merely specify rational goals, towards an emphasis on the processes of goal formulation, as follows:

(iv) Deliberative rationality — formulating goals. The Rawlsian notion of a rational individual deliberating on goals corresponds to the concept of a policy dialogue, or the political and organisational process of goal formulation under ambiguity (e.g. Quinn, 1977). This in turn involves processes of relationship formation, or substantive forms of rationality (e.g. Dobson and White, 1995).

(v) Expressive rationality — continuous goal processes. In the absence of a definitive goal, the search for individuals' goals is continuous and important, or rational, in its own right. It underpins a person's sense of autonomy (self management) which is of ultimate value, beyond what is normally considered as economic wealth. This applies to the expressively rational individual (Hargreaves-Heap, 1989) as it does to "rational" organisations.

(vi) Systemic (posterior) rationality — emergent strategic vision. Just as a rational person's goals emerge over time, as a function of historical experience and capabilities, so does the strategic vision of the firm. In contrast with calculated forward-looking means-ends logic, posterior rationality (e.g., March, 1978) refers to the emergence of individual goals, over time, as a historical process. This form or rationality (also referred to as systemic) corresponds to the "ways-means-ends logic" or recipe for competitive organisational strategy (Hayes, 1985).

(vii) Ethical reasoning categories — strategic typology. Finally, each of the major approaches to ethical reasoning lends itself directly to a distinctive corporate policy. Utilitarianism in ethics corresponds to the use of social cost-benefit analysis in strategic choice, whereby policies are considered to provide the greatest good for the greatest number. This criterion has been used at times by many health enterprises required to operate "like businesses". Contractarian or Rawlsian strategies, on the other hand are ultimately driven by concerns of fairness and justice (Rawls, 1972; Freeman, 1984). Some organisations exist specifically to promote these ideals. Deontological or Kantian strategies recognise corporate duties, or simply doing what

Table 2.2 Strategy and ends-rationalities.

Strategic Goal Concept	Rational-Moral Concept
Objectives, goals	*value, substantive*
Shareholder-wealth	*self-interest egoism*
(with incentives for managers)	
Stakeholder approach	*extended*
Stakeholders as constraints	*sympathy, interdependent*
Not-for profit service ethos	*commitment, (altruism)*
Value-uncertainty	*goal ambiguity in rational choice*
Formulating objectives	*deliberative, reflective*
Policy dialogue	*expressive concern for autonomy*
Social cost-benefit-analysis	*utilitarianism*
Fairness-goals, rights-policies	*contractarianism*
Strategic duty	*deontology*

is right, even in situations where this runs counter to mainstream commercial considerations (Goodpaster, 1988; Singer and Van der Walt, 1987).

In sum, it appears that the language of goals in strategic management theory has simply been copied from an equivalent discourse on rational-morality found within a general philosophical theory of (individual) rationality. As with other elements and relations within the rationality set, this is surely no coincidence. Once again, it is explained by the simple observation that the three subjects, strategy, rationality and ethics are all grappling with quite universal problems of action, decision and behaviour of strategic entities in their social, economic and cultural contexts.

2.3 Strategy as Moral Philosophy

Although ethical theory tends to emphasise ends or goals, whilst the subject of rationality per se has focused more closely on best-means, the distinction is somewhat opaque because means, ends and beliefs are always finely intertwined. This is well-recognised within the general theory of rationality and in much of ethical theory (see for example the notion of cognitive equilibrium in Chapter 4). The many forms in the rationality set are intertwined with almost all of the major approaches to ethical reasoning, such as teleology, deontology and contractarianism. Developments in game-theory continue to reveal these connections and to chart new pathways from the rationality of game players to their de facto morality (see below and Chapter 12).

2.3.1 *Teleology and Deontology*

Consequentialist (teleological) ethics are closely associated with instrumental rationality, that is, choosing means to achieve known goals. These goals include the pursuit of self-interest (egoism) and the greatest good for the greatest number (utilitarianism). The rationality–ethics linkages in this case are quite transparent (e.g. Fumerton, 1990). Moreover, according to De George (1990, p. 44) utilitarianism simply "describes what rational people do in making moral decisions". It is also a description of what businesses do when they conduct a full cost-benefit analysis taking into account the interests of multiple stakeholders. Such utilitarian analysis could be conducted under the umbrella of legal or policy guidelines (i.e. rule–utilitarianism), or to facilitate a specific one-off decision (act–utilitarianism). In contrast, "a rationally operated company tries to maximise its good and minimise its bad" (De George, 1991). Thus, it is rather obvious that descriptions of various forms of moral reasoning also apply to the "rational" behaviour of a

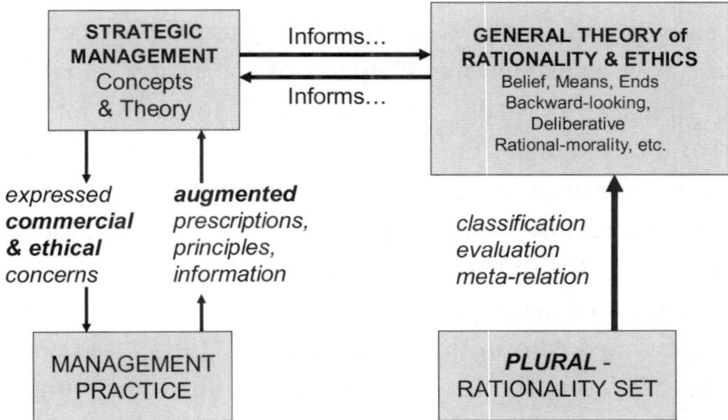

Figure 2.2 Strategy and the general theory of rationality.

variety of strategic entities. Just as we speak of corporate strategy, so we also have corporate-utilitarianism, or corporate-egoism, etc.

The role of rationality in an alternative deontological ethics is even more crucial. According to De George (1990, p. 66) the deontological tradition considers that "being moral is the same as being rational" and that "by analysing reason … we find the key to morality". In this context "reason" and "rationality" are seen as incorporating conscious reflection and analysis. Moreover, such reflection leads us inevitably to the categorical imperatives of the Kantian ethical tradition (i.e. the realisation that a moral agent should act according to universalisable principles). A similar concept of intra-personal "reflection" is also to be found in Rawls' concept of deliberative rationality which underpins some principles of distributive justice, or fairness in society. Such deliberation and reflection within the minds of individuals corresponds directly to the processes of discussion and consensus found within collectivities and other strategic entities (e.g. Boland *et al.*, 1994). Indeed, processes of consensus-seeking in general lie at the heart of an emerging post-modernist conception of contextual rationality (e.g. Habermas, 1981) but they also find expression in contractarian principles of morals-by-agreement (Gauthier, 1990). In sum, we see once again that what is good for individuals, according to philosphical traditions, can be considered as "good" for all types of strategic entity.

2.3.2 Game Theory

More recently, a variety of developments in game theory (strategic belief rationalities) have explained many aspects of apparently moral behaviour, using the language normally associated with forms of rationality (see Chapter 10). For example, the prisoner's dilemma game provides a clear and unambiguous rationale for obeying the Kantian categorical imperative, recasting this apparently "moral" principle as a form of rationality (e.g. Rapoport, 1991). Related work by Mackie (1978) offers rational game theoretic accounts of many principles of everyday observed morality such as returning favours. Also in this spirit, Axelrod (1984) used computers to explore the vast complexities of dynamic gaming, uncovering rational foundations for being nice and forgiving (typical moral language) as well as provocable and clear. In Axelrod's analysis, the game players themselves were disembodied, yet once again they have been repeatedly honoured elsewhere with a dual interpretation: as individuals (in Axelrod's own commentary) and as business firms, in the strategy literature (e.g. Nielsen, 1988; Singer, 1988).

Experimental gaming research at the interface of economics and psychology has forged yet other pathways between rationality and moral reasoning. In these games, players' pay-offs depend on the beliefs of the other players (as distinct from their strategy). This has allowed the effects of guilt and gratitude to be introduced to the calculus of game-playing (e.g. Geanakoplos and Pearce, 1989). In sum, as Williams (1985) has noted: "It might turn out (that) we are committed to an ethical life … because we are rational agents." As new game-theoretical developments steadily unfold (e.g. McLennen, 1990) this remark becomes increasingly salient. Moreover, it quite plainly applies with equal force to the "ethical life" of the rational corporation or any strategic entity. It is invariant with respect to the definition of the agent, since it refers only to the many shared characteristics of rationality and morality.

2.3.3 *Overarching Framework*

An overarching framework of strategy as morality may now be set out. First the structured set of strategic management concepts can be placed in an isomorphic correspondence with the set of plural-rationalities. Next, the overall inter-woven fabric of the plural rationalities has become sufficient to wrap up much of the logic of practical morality and a very large part of a wider ethical theory. Together, these propositions describe the framework of strategy as morality, depicted in Figure 2.3, in which all strategic entities are re-cast as moral agents.

The notion of corporate (or collective) rational agency (CRA) is implicit in the "strategy as rationality" framework, yet it has often been questioned and challenged by philosophers, economists and other social scientists (but always with specific forms of rationality, a subset, in mind). Arguments levelled against CRA have involved social-choice, cognitive-limits, systems theoretic considerations, and the politics (refer to Table 2.3). Each of these arguments, in turn, has been countered by pro-CRA arguments (Table 2.3, right-hand column).

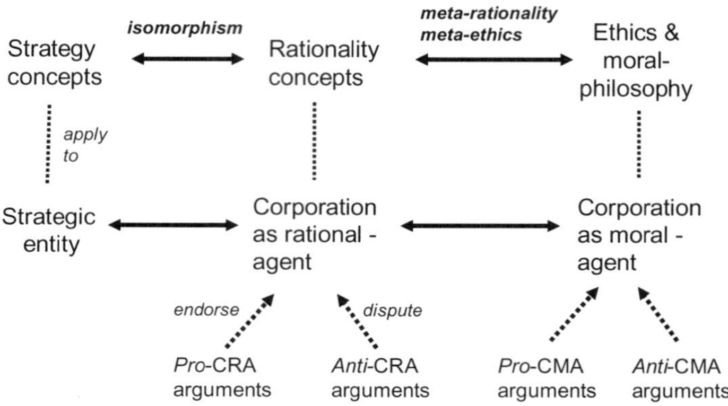

Figure 2.3   The conceptual framework of strategy-as-moral-philosophy.

2.3.4 Corporate Moral Agency

This tension between opposing camps on the question of collective rational agency has been equalled or surpassed only by the tensions involving the related notion of collective or corporate moral agency (CMA). This question of individual versus collective moral agency was identified in Chapter 1 as a component of the wider "dualism" framework embracing ethics and strategy. The philosophical arguments that oppose the concept of collective (and corporate) moral agency are summarised in Table 2.4 (left column), where they are listed alongside with their counter-arguments (i.e. on the right column and from the other side of the "dualism"). The latter anti-CMA arguments involve the machine metaphor, descriptive ethics, diversion of attention, compensatory-justice principles, intentionality, emergence, acquisition, as well as all the above mentioned arguments against corporate rational agency that are linked with CMA via various meta-rational and meta-ethical arguments (see Figure 2.2 and Section 2.4).

However, like their counterparts within the general theory of rationality, all of the philosophical challenges to the notion of corporate moral agency can now be seen as "roadblocks" in the path of inquiry, that ought to be confronted or circumvented systematically, as indicated in Figure 2.3. They do not necessarily imply that business ethics, or strategy-as-moral-philosophy is some kind of massive edifice built upon a fractured or broken foundation (of falsified CMA). This alternative idea of anti-CMA

Table 2.3   Corporate rational agency.

Argument	Anti-CRA	Pro-CRA
Social choice	Arrow's (1963) theorem (neoclassical economics) shows that it is impossible to combine individual preferences (for social outcomes) into a mathematically well-defined collective preference structure.	Levi (1986) constructed a theory of "hard" rational choice that is based upon unresolved value conflicts (inconsistent preferences) within the agent. The effective management of value conflict is central to this distinctive form of rationality.
Cognitive limitations	The necessary level of knowledge about the objects of choice is too high for consistent choices (Simon, 1987).	Many have noted correspondences between bounded rationality and collective (organisational) planning (e.g. Schwenk, 1984).
Systems theory	Purposeful subsystems (goal-choosing) exist within organisations but not within rational individuals. This distinction is definitive (Ackoff and Emery, 1972).	Rational individuals do have autonomous psychological sub-systems or multiple-selves (Elster, 1986). So the individual is like a complex institution.
Political perspective	The basis for strategic (collective) action of organisations is power, not rationality (e.g. Allison, 1971).	Many apparently political concepts (value-conflicts, identity, knowledge-access, realisation of potential, etc) are also at the core of distinctive defined a forms of rationality (e.g. Singer 1994).

arguments as roadblocks to inquiry (alluded to by Levi, 1986) might be considered as radical and maverick, or else simply pragmatic: it undoubtedly opens the way to useful insights, as well as practical methodologies (see Table 2.3). More importantly, it enables strategic management and

Table 2.4 Corporate moral agency.

Argument	Anti-CMA	Pro-CMA (counter)
Machine metaphor	Organisations are like machines controlled by individuals who must therefore accept moral responsibility (Danley, 1984).	Organisation is not machine-like, it "is" an organism (e.g. Zeleny, 1977), or at least a plurally-rational agent (this chapter).
Descriptive ethics	Group moral judgements are in fact distorted relative to individual consciences (e.g. Janis and Mann, 1977).	This is anti-CMA only if one argues from "is to ought". Pragmatically, it actually strengthens the case for a conceptual integration of ethics with strategy.
Diversion	Philosophical arguments for CMA are harmful diversions from the moral campaign whose proper target is the soul of the individual managers (Rankin, 1987).	Arguments and techniques based on CMA (like all correspondence frameworks) direct managerial attentions towards ethical concerns and they are intended to be persuasive (e.g. Freeman, 1999).
Compensation	The (legal-ethical) principle of compensatory justice requires that compensation should be paid by those (i.e. individuals) who caused the harm.	When corporate acts (e.g. serving unhealthy fast food) cause harm, it is generally unjust and impractical to blame individual(s). The corporation should pay.
Intentionality	That "structure" is a mere façade. Corporate acts actually express the intention of powerful individuals, particularly the CEO, specific senior managers aka a "corporate brain".	The existence of an "internal decision structure" is the key to a meaningful description of corporate acts as intentional" "hence carrying moral responsibility (French, 1984).

Table 2.4   (*Continued*)

Argument	Anti-CMA	Pro-CMA (counter)
Emergence	A diffuse complex planning process is seemingly incapable of assimilating and pursuing ideals. "Conscience makes cowards" so does not mix with productive activity (cf. Chapters 5 and 8).	Consciousness is an emergent property, leading towards conscience by an "unknown distance" (e.g. Engleberg, 1972). Productive entities are now at a critical stage where conscience is emerging.
Acquisitions	Under the assumption of CMA corporate acquisitions would become the "moral equivalent of murder", but this is "counter-intuitive" (Manning, 1984).	These involve disengaged deals with "dead capital" (e.g. Zeleny 2005) and have also been described (elsewhere) as killing the spirit of (or in) the target entity (implying there was a collective life-form with spirit).
Rational agency	CMA is an even stronger requirement than collective rational agency (CRA) but there are already several anti-CRA arguments (Table 2.3).	Each of those anti-CRA arguments can be countered separately (Table Y), but also jointly by strategy-as-rationality (this chapter).

business ethics to be seen and understood as not only inter-related, but as essentially the same subject.

2.4 Prescription in Strategic Management

The framework of strategy as moral philosophy projects the plural rationalities and rational morality directly into a general prescriptive theory of strategic management. In particular, within the framework, strategy concepts may be evaluated (for goodness, integrity, usefulness, etc) with reference to various known meta-rational and meta-ethical criteria, i.e. criteria for choosing amongst the rationalities and ethics. Next, the framework underpins a practical strategic decision making methodology. Finally, there are some broader implications for routine strategic management practices.

2.4.1 Choosing Rationalities and Ethics

When managers use particular ways of thinking, concepts, techniques and models in formulating and implementing strategy, they are also at the same time making their implicit choices between rational-moral principles. For example, a focus on such strategy concepts as stakeholders-as-constraints, continuous goal processes, etc., corresponds, within the framework, to an implicit choice of rationalities (sympathy, expressive) in the rationality set. This give rise to a rather salient question:

> "Which rationalities and ethics should be used to prescribe or guide corporate strategy?"

In seeking an answer to the corresponding question about individual rationality, philosophers and social scientists have developed several meta-rational and meta-ethical criteria and arguments that classify, evaluate and inter-relate the elements of the rationality set, as follows:

(i) Aggregate versus agent orientation: Some rationalities have served as foundations of formal aggregate-level economic theories, associated with public-policy prescriptions (e.g. Thaler and Sheffrin, 1981; Russell and Thaler, 1985). These are the economic rationalities. In contrast, some others, e.g. expressive, resolute, contextual, are primarily oriented towards a localised decision-theory, more at the level of the individual (or corporate) agent. These forms emphasise some of the more subtle dimensions of rationality, involving identity and co-ordination. These "agent-oriented" forms are, *prima facie*, at least as relevant to problems of strategy at the level of the firm as are the elements of the economic-rationality set.

(ii)   RUM-captured versus elusive: Some forms may be "captured" by arguments that identify them, for at least some purposes, as special cases of rational utility maximisation (RUM), or formal rank-ordering of preferences (e.g. Hirshleifer, 1976). Sen's sympathy or Etzioni's (1986) interdependent utility are partly captured within this net, as is bounded rationality, after allowing for the costs of information and computation. In terms of the present framework, raional utility maximisation is simply an umbrella-term, covering a subset of the rationality-set. The precise membership of this (fuzzy?) set is itself a matter to be settled through meta-rational argument. Other forms in contrast, are more "elusive". Examples include, commitments, expressive, contextual forms (Table 2). Within the present framework, the existence of these elusive forms implies that strategy should involve occasional (corporate) self-sacrifice; expression of (corporate) values; or the creation and maintenance of institutions and (corporate) traditions.

(iii)   Temporal-orientation (forward-looking versus backward-looking): The forward-looking rationalities are another subset, are defined without reference to the past, whilst for their complement (all other forms) there is at least some explicit historic reference. The latter include: posterior, adaptive, quasi, selected, resolute, and contextual forms, amongst others. This partition of the rationality set is the ultimate foundation of the more familiar strategy prescription of adapting to the past whilst, at the same time integrating with possible futures (Mintzberg, 1990; Ansoff, 1991; Kervern, 1990).

(iv)   Meta-ethical scope: Several other meta-ethical criteria critically evaluate the scope of any given form of rationality, as follows:

Globally versus locally-optimal (Mclennen, 1990). A globally-optimising form maximises total lifetime utility for the agent, after taking into account the impact of current decisions on the agent's future preferences, learning, habit-formation and co-ordination with others (resolute is global, narrow egoism is local).

Universalisable versus exclusive (Kant, 1956). A universalisable form is one that the "rational" agent prefers other agents to adopt (Kantian is universalisable, by definition, self-interest as RUM is not, in Prisoners' Dilemma Games).

Self-supporting versus self-defeating (Gauthier, 1990). A self-supporting form hypothetically chooses itself when used to select a form of rationality (as in Figure 2.3). Whilst Kantian and commitment are self-supporting, in this sense, formal-RUM is self-defeating in the Prisoners' Dilemma.

Collectively, these and several other meta-criteria (perfect-imperfect; precision-of-definition, etc.) characterise the prescriptive gap that now separates the assumptions of mainstream economic theory from several other normative principles of rationality and ethics. Put differently, whilst the axioms of RUM models in economics undoubtedly have a powerful normative appeal, so also do various meta-criteria that RUM fails. Now, with strategy-as-moral-philosophy in place, these same meta-criteria could also be used to evaluate the corresponding concepts in the strategy set.

For example, the strategy set concept of stakeholders-as-constraints, corresponds to rational sympathy in the rationality set. The latter is: agent-oriented, RUM-captured (utility could be maximised after allowing for the impact on others), also forward-looking, local, non-universalisable, and self-defeating. "Stakeholders as constraints" is thus characterised as a component of a general prescriptive theory of strategy in exactly the

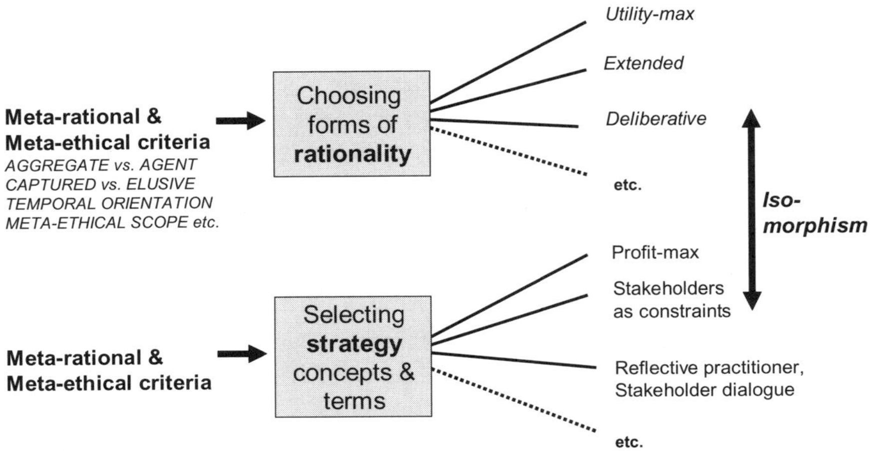

Figure 2.4   Choosing rationalities and strategy concepts.

same way. Put differently, it makes good sense to say that corporate strategy should be predicated on a view of stakeholders-as-constraints, but this sense of "should" is explicitly and critically qualified by the meta-criteria.

2.4.2 The SCIO Method

In practical strategic thinking, these complexities and ambiguities surrounding the various meta-criteria, meta-relations and incomplete meta-rational arguments can be avoided, simply by appealing to all of the principles of rationality and ethics. To foster this sort of integrative pluralistic approach, a strategic decision model or methodology is needed, which implicitly assumes all the (plural-) rationalities. Finding such a "model" is simple: it is nothing other than a checklist, or an inquiry procedure, structured directly upon plurally-rationality and the strategy–rationality correspondence. The acronym "SCIO" is used to refer to this technique (Appendix 2.1). It stands for "specifying canonical issues and options", with "canonical" meaning important and clear (like the canonical form of a matrix). Scio also means "I know", in Latin, thus conveying the idea of strategic entities as knowledge systems or and wisdom systems (see Chapter 7).

SCIO is a structured inquiry methodology, similar in some ways to cognitive mapping (e.g. Rosenhead, 1989). However, it is more oriented towards available reasons than to shared beliefs. SCIO seeks to improve strategic analysis by directing attention to each distinctive dimension and form of rationality. In this way, factors such as histories and traditions, co-ordination with others, identities, rights and duties all take their place in an expanded framework of strategic thinking, alongside the more conventional economic and commercial considerations. Put differently, SCIO supports "strategic thinking without boundaries" (Singer, 1996b) in what is often referred to as a "boundary-less" world. It also responds directly to a recent appeal by Margolis and Walsh (2003) for theoretical and practical approaches that see "the tension between economic objectives and broader social objectives as a starting point for inquiry".

If answers to all the rationality-based questions (listed in Appendix 2.1) are pursued systematically, the resulting decision reflects awareness (at some level within the collective strategic entity) and potential accommodation of the full range of normatively relevant issues. With SCIO, the answers to the rationality-based questions do not really matter very much! What does matter is the overall process of moving towards a more balanced *Gestalt*, or wisdom (Chapter 7) when deciding what to do. This notion has compelling theoretical rationale, precisely because those underlying meta-rational arguments are not complete, they are not solid, so there is no analytic or calculable optimal solution to the strategic problem of the firm. In contrast, conventional approaches to strategic the evaluation of strategic options are really quite naïve, in this respect. Managers and planners using conventional strategic and financial techniques are in effect choosing narrow form(s) of rationality, perhaps without ever realising it; that is, without realising that they are implicitly accepting and acting on the basis of highly questionable and disputed meta-rational and meta-ethical arguments.

2.5 Discussion

It is apparent that social scientists investigating individuals' schemes of action have developed many categories of meaning that have been shared, re-invented or borrowed (often unknowingly and without acknowledgment) by the strategic management discipline. The framework of strategy-as-moral-philosophy, with the corporation cast as a rational-moral agent, now make this "sharing" quite explicit. There some broad implications for management theory, practice and education.

2.5.1 Implications for Theory and Research

Prescriptive theories of strategic management (strategy) should more fully take into account progress in the general theory of rationality and ethics. Equally, empirical and conceptual progress in strategy should be carefully reviewed for its potential ability to advance descriptive and normative ethics. Several earlier observations to this effect are consolidated, by the present framework. These include the "striking congruence" between administrative and ethical problems (Goodpaster, 1985), the "uncanny" parallels between planning concepts and cognitive psychology (Hogarth and Makridakis, 1981) and the rather mysterious "reverse logic" of planning described by Hayes (1985). The conceptual framework of strategy as moral philosophy also provides a counterpart, at the level of business strategy, to the emerging synthesis of ethics and economics at the aggregate level.

2.5.2 Implications for Education

At present the subject of strategy is often taught separately from business ethics. Students can attend courses that greatly elaborate upon means for seeking gain for themselves (or on behalf of shareholders), while other courses prescribe an obviously different set of principles and values. Interaction then becomes part of the hidden curriculum. The present framework, like the wider organising framework in Chapter 1, places this conflict and its resolution directly onto the formal agenda of the business school, yielding a counterpart, at the level of strategy, to the proposed re-orientation of economics education (or mis-education) that was advocated earlier by Etzioni (1988).

2.5.3 Implications for Managers

In practice, the SCIO technique is but one of the potential spin-offs from the framework. There are also implications for the design of control systems and the articulation of corporate missions. The overall decision making philosophy implicit in SCIO could quite readily be coupled to multi-criteria performance evaluation and incentive systems, rewarding behaviours such as learning from past mistakes (open, systemic), preparedness for a crisis (minimising harm), strong stakeholder relationships (sympathy, commitments), or the level of development of an identity (expressive), in addition to conventional *ex post* financial measures. The conceptual framework also offers a rationality-based justification for authentic social and environmental corporate missions, as well as a more general corporate duty of beneficence (e.g. Margolis and Walsh, 2003).

2.6 Conclusion

Strategy as moral philosophy has broad implications for the type of socially engaged business policies that were described at the outset. To see this more clearly it is helpful to draw a distinction between an old-game of strategy and a new-game. The "old game" assumed (for good reasons) rational utility maximising behaviour and it was properly analysed (or squarely based upon) managerial-economics. Profit-maximising "firms", competed against each other, subject to laws of a government of a reasonably benevolent or far-seeing nation state, or empire.

In the 21st century (which began around 1975, according to Peter Drucker) with its trans-national entities, industrial networks, virtual-corporations, and stateless cyber-funds, the old game seems unrealistic and dangerously naïve as a set of assumptions. In the "new game", multiple types of productive entity cross boundaries of many language communities and co-exist alongside highly mixed governments. If such entities simply pursue narrow interests, unrestrained by effective authority, we have something very much like the Hobbesian state of nature on a global scale. In the "new game", in contrast, the moral role of business seems different and might be summarised as follows:

> "As a strategic manager, acting on behalf of any type of productive strategic entity, you should do precisely the things you would do as an integrated and balanced person, or as someone with moral character".

Strategic entities should therefore learn, develop capabilities and consider how their actions might evoke a response from others. Their ambition or "strategic intent" should takes into account the interests and values of all other entities. In many cases, it should embrace an ethic of service to other entities, at least partly in accordance with needs, but often beyond their ability to pay. This is precisely what some enlightened businesses have already been doing, for some time. Welfare states (of the old game) thus become supplemented by multiple types of welfare-entities, in the context of a multi-faceted approach to economic and social development. Optimists suggest that "private" companies will indeed eventually learn to play this new game, but this of course requires a belief or faith in the underlying moral progress of humanity.

Appendix 2.1

*The SCIO Inquiry-Based Method of Strategic Analysis**

1. Belief rationalities

1.1 *Belief*: Has **A** checked and verified all its relevant beliefs? ("**A**" denotes any strategic entity).

1.2 *Strategic*: Do **A**'s beliefs about future events allow for the reactions and interactions of other entities?

1.3 *Parametric*: Has **A** developed a myopic plan, assuming an un-reactive environment?

1.4 *Extensive*: What are **A**'s expectations based upon historic and current data with extrapolation?

1.5 *Scientific, intensive*: What are **A**'s expectations or forecasts as determined by a formal model, or simulation, etc.?

1.6 *Perfect*: (i) How complete or comprehensive is **A**'s knowledge? (ii) How reliable are **A**'s predictions?

1.7 *Minimal*: Are **A**'s currently activated beliefs all mutually consistent?

2. Means rationalities

2.1 *Instrumental*: Does **A** have a conventional means-ends plan, with an implementation program?

2.2 *Perfect, strong*: Has **A** calculated an optimal course of action?

2.3 *Minimal (inference)*: Has **A** actively searched for new inferences from the current beliefs?

2.4 *Intensive*: Has **A** developed and used a formal model-based strategy-selection system?

2.5 *Imperfect, procedural*: Has **A** developed decision-procedures and acceptability-criteria?

2.6 *Selective*: Is **A** achieving its current potential (e.g. with existing assets)?

2.7 *Bounded*: Has **A** explored ways of (i) improving the allocation of attention, (ii) reducing the costs of information search and processing?

2.8 *Quasi*: What would the majority of **A**'s decide if they were in this situation?

---

*For definitions of the forms of rationality (listed here in italics) refer to Singer (1991a, b and 1994a, b).

2.9   *Adaptive*: Does **A** carry out means-ends planning iteratively, continually learning and revising goals?

2.10 *Pre-commitment*: What action could **A** take now to prevent a possible and foreseeable change of goal or loss of commitment?

2.11 *Excess-of-will*: Has **A** identified any subgoals whose direct pursuit could be counter-productive or impossible?

2.12 *Rational-postponement*: Has **A** reflected upon the value of waiting and of keeping options open?

3. Backward-looking (systemic) rationalities

3.1   *Posterior*: What are **A**'s goals now? Should these be reformulated in the light of experience with past strategy.

3.2   *Resolute*: If current strategy fails to meet the updated criteria, was this situation foreseen in original evaluation of the strategy?

3.3   *Constrained*: (i) Is completion of current project or strategy a long-standing unfulfilled mission of **A**? (ii) Is continuation of a current questionable strategy an opportunity for **A** to develop lasting habits (of task-completion) conferring future benefits?

3.4   *Ratchet*: (i) What is the optimal timing and frequency of re-considerations? (ii) Does a change of strategy now imply damage to **A**'s reputation, or violation of trust in **A**, or loss of **A**'s co-ordination with others?

3.5   *Retrospective*: (i) If P+ (future of project) is changed, abandoned, will **A** be perceived (by **A** or others) as inconsistent? (ii) Can a justification of P− (past of project) be communicated? (iii) Have psychological biases (in forecasts for P+) been allowed for?

3.6   *Open*: (i) Have all mistakes in **A**'s past strategies been fully investigated and corrected? (ii) Has **A** thoroughly reviewed its past behaviour and taken all corrective steps, revising procedures (and beliefs) appropriately?

3.7   *Natural*: Have **A**'s beliefs been revised appropriately to reflect **A**'s experiences?

3.8   *Selective (systemic)*: (i) Will a habit and reputation of persistence (in similar situations) make **A** vulnerable to competitors with different strategies? (ii) Is there a risk to **A** of a war-of-attrition?

3.8   *Deliberative*: Does current and future strategy utilise to the full **A**'s newly-learned capabilities (competencies, capacities) developed during past strategies?

3.9   *Contextual*: Is future strategy part of a mission that involves "the creation or maintenance of traditions and institutions that express **A**'s vision of the good life with others"?

4. Ends rationalities

4.1   *Ends, value-rationality*: (i) What are **A**'s goals? (ii) Why does **A** have these (stated) goals? (iii) Are they the best goals?

4.2   *Egoism*: Is **A** pursuing its own interests?

4.3   *Extended ends-rationality*: Does **A** have goals other than self-interest?

4.4   *Sympathy*: Do **A**'s own "interests" include the interests of other entities?

4.5   *Rational-commitments*: Is **A** making some altruistic choices in pursuit of others interests?

4.6   *Expressive*: Has **A** achieved a sense of autonomy by systemically re-evaluating its own goals?

4.7   *Deliberative*: Has **A** set up a procedure or policy dialogue for assessing its goals and reducing doubt about its goals?

5. Rational ethics

5.1   *Utilitarianism*: Is **A** seeking and producing the greatest good for the greatest number (of other entities)? Is **A** using a social-cost-benefit approach?

5.2   *Contractarianism*: Does **A** have goals and policies involving fairness and protection of the rights of other entities (groups, individuals etc)?

5.3   *Deontology*: Does **A** fulfil all its duties and obligations?

6. Action and expressive rationality

6.1   *Action-rationality*: Is the strategy process in **A** conforming to the various principles of logical incrementalism (e.g. building awareness, overcoming opposition, partial solutions)?

6.2   *Expressive*: Is **A** taking actions that express its values and its own autonomous identity?

7. Other dimensions of rationality

7.1   *Interactive*: Does **A** look for possible rationales and patterns (over time) in its own and in other's decisions?

7.2   *Structural*: Has **A** determined the best structure of its own decision-making, with respect to: (i) the involvement of subsystems, (ii) identifying the issues, and (iii) distinguishing the phases?

Chapter 3

SYNERGIES: Competitiveness as "Hyper-Strategy"

Abstract: Parts of this chapter are based upon (i) "Competitiveness as hyper-strategy," *Human Systems Management* 14, pp. 163-178, 1995 and (ii) *Strategy as Rationality*, Ashgate, 1996. The first part briefly discusses the concept of synergy, as it applies to business strategy. It proceeds to a consideration of competition and cooperation amongst diverse types of productive entity. The strategy-as-moral philosophy correspondence framework (Chapter 2) is then expanded and adapted to incorporate the abstract notion of synergies amongst distinctive forms of rationality, or hyper-rationality (in the sociological sense first used by Ritzer and LeMoyne, 1991). The concept can be generalised to the full rationality-set, where it yields a general and integrative re-conceptualisation of the competitiveness of any strategic entity.

3.1 Introduction

Many previous writings have alluded to synergy, synthesis or complementarity involving selected components of the dualism (e.g. shareholders and stakeholders, social and financial capital, etc.). The term "synergy" has also been widely used in business literature and practice.

The following section of this chapter gives a brief overview of the synergy concept, in relation to business strategy. Then (in Section 3.3) the related idea of co-operation and competition amongst diverse types of strategic entity is considered. The strategy-as-moral-philosophy framework (Chapter 2) is invoked and expanded in order to incorporate the recently developed idea of the hyper-rationality of an industrial system (i.e. synergies amongst rationalities). This idea was first advanced in the Sociological (Neo-Weberian) study of Japanese industrial systems (Ritzer and LeMoyne, 1991). It can now be generalised (Section 3.4.1) in ways that yield potentially useful formulations of competitiveness.

57

3.2 Synergy

Classical moral philosophy (cf. Hosmer, 1995) is replete with prescriptions for people to act in all areas of their life in ways that reflect some kind of mixture of their short-term personal interest (or profit) with a:

> …vision of the future (Protagoras),
> …sense of self-worth (Aristotle),
> …goal of community (St. Augustine),
> …calculated benefit to society (Mill),
> …understanding of universal duty (Kant),
> …recognition of individuals' rights (Jefferson), and so on.

A similar "mixture" of economic and ethical motivation was also implicit in the inter-dependence of Adam Smith's *Wealth of Nations and Theory of Moral Sentiments*. The slightly more demanding idea of a "synthesis" of these "poles" (strategy and ethics) is of course also quite prominent in the earlier 20th century philosophy of Hegel, but also in much of the business ethics literature of the 1980s and 1990s (although Hegel's work is hardly ever mentioned there; cf. Chapter 5).

The more ambitious concept of real synergy $(2 + 2 = 5)$ became very familiar before that, in relation to business strategy in the 1950s and 1960s, when it was common practice to (i) adjust quantitative cash-flow projections in an attempt to predict (or advertise) "synergies" from business mergers and acquisitions (cost-savings, productivity gains, etc.), and (ii) to encourage managers "at" headquarters of multi-unit firms to identify and deliberately develop "synergies" between business units[1]. At about that time, the systems theorist Beer (1972) re-conceptualised any "viable" system as something necessarily more than the sum of its parts[2]. More recently, and with ethics once again prominently in mind, Sen (1997, *et seq.*) emphasised how "business principles and moral sentiments" must operate in combination, jointly determining economic and social outcomes. Now, in the 21st century, it is generally accepted that technocratic businesses can partner with other caring entities in ways that benefit both (e.g. Dobson, 2001). Creative "win-win" strategies involving the business and society, or business and the environment are widely touted and often achieved, under suitable market and political conditions (e.g. Rugman and Verbeke, 1998; Shrivastava, 1995).

3.2.1 *Synergy Orientation*

Synergy orientation refers to a generic pattern of three-stage (trinetarian) thinking that is evident in many streams of theory and research within management studies and the social sciences. A singular concept, such as utility maximisation (or economic capital formation, or shareholder-value, etc.) is typically challenged by an alternative pluralistic account, such as plural rationality (or the multi-capital framework, or the multi-fiduciary model, etc). Next, the relationships between those singular and pluralistic approaches (i.e. the meta-relations, as mentioned in Chapter 2) become the focus of further discussion and theory development. Typically, at this stage, tradeoffs amongst alternatives are explored. Finally, the "pattern" almost always culminates in specification or discussion of some type of mixture, synthesis or synergy. Four of these "synergy-oriented" streams of management theory are listed in Table 3.1 (left column). The basic categories or elements of each stream are identified, together with the labeling of the specific "synergy" component. Finally (right column) the general implication of that "component" for "strategy" is briefly described. The four streams are (i) the systemic and holistic, (ii) the multi-capital framework, (iii) multiple optimalities, and (iv) plural-rationality, as follows:

- **Systemic and holistic themes:** Several holistic approaches have referred to synergy-oriented processes. The dialectical-inquiry and devils-alternative "methods" proposed by Mason and Mitroff (1981) emphasised the need to consider opposites and seek out possibilities for synthesis in the context of business planning (i.e dialectics, as discussed in Chapter 5). The notion of moral imagination in business ethics (e.g. Werhane, 1998) similarly emphasised the deliberate construction of alternative descriptions or frames, in order to help managers break out of their entrenched mental schemas and hence to envision new possibilities. In the group context, stakeholder learning dialogues have been advocated (e.g. Isaacs, 1999; Calton and Paine, 1999) that incorporate "generative" discourses. In each case the emphasis is upon (i) the exploration of opposites, or re-descriptions of the strategic situation, and (ii) the creation and design of balanced or synergistic options or "truly optimal" business solutions (see below).

- **The multi-capital framework:** In this framework (a component of the dualism) distinctive forms of "capital" are identified. They include the human social and ecological forms, as well as the "economic" (financial[3] or manufactured) forms. The idea is to try to design business strategies that foster synergies amongst the forms, rather than trading them off against financial capital (Figure 3.1). A synergy-oriented approach seeks ways of adding simultaneously to all the forms of capital, especially in mutually reinforcing ways (e.g. Hawken, 1993 and 1999; Porritt, 2005). "Social capital" refers to communities, trust, and identity (e.g. Zeleny, 1995); human capital is the knowledge and capabilities embedded within individuals and collectivities; ecological capital refers to the nature-produced inputs to all types of productive processes. The dominant discourse of strategy has of course implicitly assumed that the goal of policy is to increase the level of "financial capital", although exactly how to do that remains contested, but it also appears to assume that the levels of the other forms of capital will eventually increase as a consequence, or afterwards (ie. the "timing" component of the dualism).

- **Multiple optimalities:** There are many distinctive forms of optimality, each of which can be associated with particular strategy concepts (e.g. Chapter 11). "Economically optimal strategies", that aim to maximise the financial value of the firm through forward looking activities, can be distinguished from systemic-ethical strategies that aim to directly increase the level of (classical) human-goods, such as health, friendship, justice

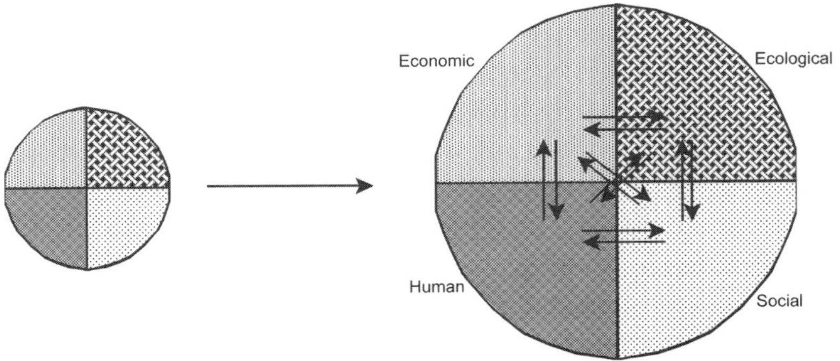

Figure 3.1   Synergy and the multi-capital framework.

Table 3.1

Synergy-Oriented Framework	Basic Components or Elements	Synergy or Synthesis Component	Implication for Strategy: Entities Should
Systemic and holistic themes and methods	Dialectical inquiry, Moral imagination, Stakeholder-synthesis, Generative discourse	*New synthesised possibilities, generated alternatives*	… explore opposites and re-descriptions, create and design balanced or synergistic options, use open discussion to discover new options.
Multi-capital framework	Economic, Human social, Ecological	*Designed multi-capital synergies*	… foster accumulation of all the forms of capital
Multiple optimalities	Economic and systemic–ethical forms of optimality, Alternatives, representations, values and criteria	*Optimal-design, cognitive-equilibrium, super-optimum*	… design ways to overcome perceived tradeoffs, co-produce profit, human-goods, future-self and future-system
Plural-rationality	Utility–max. Expressive, Reflective, Deliberative, Sociality and Weberian forms	*Hyper-rationality (i.e synergy-seeking, see text)*	… implant "hyper-strategy" (synergies amongst the forms of rationality). Integrate utility, identity, sociality and abstract ideas (science, ethics) etc.

and wealth. Other distinctive forms of optimality depend on the number of criteria in a problem and whether the alternatives (and values) are known (given) or are yet-to-be created or settled. The "synergy" component is then to be found in the specific notions of optimal design, super-optimum and cognitive-equilibrium.

- **Plural and "hyper" rationalities:** Within the general theory of rationality (Chapter 2) the trinetarian pattern and a distinctive notion of synergy are once again apparent; but these also have implications for the way we think about "competitiveness". In the general theory of rationality, detailed consideration of utility-maximising leads on to other distinctively defined forms (i.e. the rationality-set). The idea of "synergies" in this context was first referred to in sociological studies.

As elaborated below (Section 3.4.1) in their study of the competitiveness of industrial systems, Ritzer and LeMoyne (1991) were able to identify apparently synergistic interactions amongst the four defined Neo-Weberian forms of rationality: *formal, theoretical, practical and substantive-value* (see below). They described a hyper-rational entity as one that continually seeks out and designs ways of expressing or fostering synthesis or synergy amongst those "rationalities". This idea can now be extended to incorporate all the elements of the rationality-set, involving identity, duty and social relationships, as well as scientific understandings (see Section 3.4.1 below).

3.3 Competitiveness

Whilst synergy is often discussed, the notion of "achieving competitiveness" has become a mission and a mantra for many corporations and nations. Yet "competitiveness" per se is rarely defined in ways that carry coherent strategic implications, beyond cost reduction or differentiation. One difficulty or ambiguity concerns the distinction between competitiveness conceives as winning, or beating the opposition versus competitiveness as success or realisation of potential. Another definitional problem arises when one considers the diversity of type of strategic entity made possible by technological change. Accordingly, there has for some time been an increasing awareness of the desirability of re-examining traditional paradigms dealing with economic competitiveness and business competition.

The models and concepts of competitive strategy set out and popularised by Porter (1980, *et seq.*) and later by D'Aveni (1994) undoubtedly remain quite useful, but they also appear unsatisfactory, incomplete or even contradictory in many contemporary strategic management contexts. Earlier studies of the level of competitiveness achieved by Asian firms (Schutte, 1994; Ritzer and LeMoyne, 1991) contrasted their competitively successful strategies (and rationalities) of learning, co-operation and consensus, with the economic-rationality found in many Western firms, which emphasises measurement, control, efficiency and accountability.

This contrast becomes especially salient if one views "competitive" strategic entities not as traditional firms (fortresses) but as knowledge systems and learning systems that co-evolve, learn and share information across boundaries and borders. It can then be asked "Which form(s) of rationality are correct?" or equivalently, "Which form of strategy is really more competitive?". This article offers an answer to that question based upon the correspondence framework of strategy-as-rationality. First, however, it is necessary to discuss the concept of competitiveness as used in strategic management, in a little more detail. In the dominant paradigm, the term "competitiveness" has been used in various ways, to mean:

(i) The degree of cost-leadership of a firm, combined with the level of differentiation, or perceived quality, of its outputs (e.g. Porter, 1980).

(ii) The attractiveness of an industry as determined by the strength of the five "forces" in oligopoly models, such as the threat of new entrants. (e.g. Porter, 1985).

(iii) The combined strength, relative to a competitor, of several interrelated factors, e.g. production-capability; financial-capacity; marketing-effectiveness; political and economic environment, etc. (cf. Oral, 1986).

(iv) The ability of a firm to plan and carry out major moves in multiple arenas (cost-quality, stronghold protection and invasion, developing know-how, etc.) simultaneously and sequentially, thus increasing the level of rivalry amongst industry incumbents (D'Aveni, 1994).

(v) The relative costs and output capabilities of national economies (e.g. Porter, 1990).

Despite the fact that competitiveness is widely talked about, whilst its achievement has become a popular mission for corporations, nations and regions alike, the term "competitiveness" is rarely defined in a consistent way. When applied to nations, it usually means the same as productivity, or cost cutting, perhaps with some reference to economic infrastructure. When applied to corporations, however, it usually does not carry any specific and coherent strategic implications (e.g. Oral, 1986; Oral *et al.*, 1989). Generally, "competitiveness" is translated loosely as productivity and efficiency, an interpretation that is then put into practical effect as cost-reduction, process re-engineering, downsizing, re-sourcing and automation. Given current technologies, this leads in many cases to lower incomes for employees remaining within the boundaries of the more "competitive" strategic entity, or increased numbers of unemployed outside the boundary.

When many entities do this, the result is social inequity and dislocations. Yet, paradoxically, missions of achieving international competitiveness have been held up as quasi-moral-imperatives for management all over the world. If every strategic entity is trying to achieve competitiveness in the usual sense, then how many can truly succeed? In this regard, Zeleny (1992) recently noted that "the weak does not become stronger by freely competing with the strong: he is simply crushed". This is true for all "weak" entities, individuals, firms and nations, alike.

3.3.1 Ambiguities

Intertwined with the politics of competitiveness, there are at least two fundamental long-standing ambiguities in its conceptualisation. Corporate managers and politicians alike confront these twin ambiguities as they attempt to formulate or advocate "competitive" strategies. They concern:

(i) The very nature, scope or boundary of the "competitive" strategic entity itself, i.e. who or what is being "competitive" against whom? Put differently "who is crushing, or bashing whom?" (cf. Krugman, 1994), and

(ii) The relationship between winning, or victory, versus success, or realisation-of-potential. This distinction and relationship, in turn, is evocative of the plural rationality of the strategic entity, with meta-rationality.

These ambiguities are "twinned" because "achieving competitiveness" could simply be taken to mean overcoming limitations within a singular strategic entity, such a nation-state, or industrial system, rather than necessarily outperforming or defeating multiple other entities. Thus the question of an entity's boundaries and the appropriate rationality concepts, with their competitiveness measures, must be discussed jointly and co-determined. Accordingly, following a more detained discussion of these twinned ambiguities, a concept of competitiveness as the hyper-rationality (in the sociological sense of the term) of any strategic entity can be developed. This concept enables some resolution of the twin ambiguities within the conceptual framework of strategy as rationality. Competitiveness as hyper-rationality (or, equivalently, hyper-strategy) is then made operational as a new measure of the level of competitiveness of any entity.

3.3.2 *Rationalities and Competitiveness*

Many techniques of competitive strategy (e.g. Prescott and Grant, 1988) appear to implicitly assume that managers are engaged in ruthless game-playing for their own interests directly, or else indirectly on behalf of a firm. It is stretching credibility to argue, as some do, that they are behaving altruistically towards shareholders in this activity. In essence, economic entities and managers acting on their behalf are viewed as rational utility maximisers. Competitive strategy is then seen in terms of a barely contained conflict between warrior-like entities, an in-group, the firm, or "us" and an outgroup, the competition, or "them". These beliefs, when acted upon by many entities, or universalised, lead inevitably to a situation where: "Losers, and now even entire loser nations and states, are being... spawned... in abundance" (Zeleny, 1992b). A major alternative (or complementary) view sees a strategic-entity "competing" primarily against itself, or an imagined ideal version of itself, in a struggle to fully realise its own potential and develop its won capabilities. Traditionally, concepts like "potential" and "capability" have belonged in the domain of psychology, not economics; but their importance to economic analysis has slowly become more widely recognised (e.g. Leibenstein, 1976; Tomer, 1987; Oral, 1986; Sen, 1999).

The emphasis on "potential" in economics and strategic management is ultimately rooted in the idea that rational agents must not only have consistent preferences (utility) but they also have a duty to develop their own talents to the highest possible level and to put them to good use. This idea appears in many of the strands that have at times been woven into the overall fabric of plural rationality, including selective, systemic and expressive forms, as well as ethical utilitarianism. With these elements of an expanded rationality-set in place, "competitive" strategy also becomes oriented towards developing capabilities within the strategic entity (e.g. Hayes, 1985) rather than simply outgunning rivals. These forms of rationality are all quite close to meeting the various evaluative meta-rational criteria, such as universalisability, globality and self-support. In addition, whilst they may not be RUM-captured, they can be made consistent with RUM provided only that the latter is placed within a dynamic or evolutionary context (e.g. Axelrod, 1984; Neilsen, 1988). In such contexts it is now well understood that the global success of any strategic entity depends on the successful co-evolution of many other entities, not on their defeat.

3.3.3 Strategic Entities

Just as conceptions of rationality have become much more pluralistic, so too have forms of productive organisation, bringing with them attendant doubts about the traditional concepts of competitive strategy (e.g. Badaracco, 1991). In short, there is a persistent and troubling question of whose strategy and whose "competitive advantage" is being strategically managed. Who are "we" and whom are we playing against, or dis-advantaging, or "crushing" or "bashing"? To underscore the seriousness of this problem, it is simply necessary to note that contemporary strategic managers and politicians have frequently expressed their concerns about achieving the competitiveness of:

(i) **firms** ... in what is rapidly becoming a world of alliances, networks, flex-firms and multiple types of strategic-entity, many with permeable boundaries (e.g. Badaracco, 1991; Toffler, 1990; Moss-Kanter, 1991).

(ii) **national** economies ... in what is fast becoming an inter-national or global economy (e.g. Porter, 1990; Moss-Kanter, 1991).

(iii)   **traditional industries** ... in a what has already become a *post*-industrial society (e.g. Bell, 1973; Toffler, 1980; Zeleny, 1992) characterised by boundaryless productive entities, with convergent technologies and cultures.

The possible candidates for the "competitive" strategic entity in the several theories and models of competition could also be selected, from a rather long list that includes:

> Individuals or groups, a business segment or unit, a traditional firm or organisation, an alliance or coalition, an industry, a strategic-group, a set of players, a flex-firm, a hollow corporation, a network, a society, a nation, a region ...

or conceivably, the entire collective productive human enterprise viewed as a unitary whole (e.g. "*Metaman*", cf. Stock, 1993).

In addition to this long list of "competitive" entities, there are other more abstract candidates for the players referred to in abstract and formal theories of competition, such as: living-systems, cognitive-systems and psychological-selves. Particular theories and models of strategy, competition and competitiveness have, at times, been applied to each of these types of entity. Yet the proper scope, in this respect, of many of the models and theories is almost always ambiguous and it is often controversial to say the least (e.g. Singer and Brodie, 1990). For example, MIT economist Krugman has recently demonstrated that, insofar as one is concerned with the economic standards of living of the citizens of a large economic entity (e.g. US, Japan or Europe) where most of the entity's outputs are consumed within that same entity, the concept of competitiveness should then be taken to mean productivity. On the other hand, where corporations (e.g. Coke versus Pepsi) have become locked into a marketing war, so that one entity gains at the other's expense, competitive success takes on other meanings, such as relative market share.

This distinction (large nation-state versus traditional corporation) is by no means the only one. Smaller export-oriented national economies provide a third quite distinctive case, similar in many ways to large corporates. Unlike the latter, the political managers of small national entities remain quite directly concerned with the economic position of the entity's internal workforce, so to speak. Yet another, fourth distinctive case involves alliances and networks that are oriented towards co-operation, with the co-evolution of a set of entities (suppliers, customers and rivals, in Porter's terminology). Such strategies see corporate players, their employees and the competitor-set as co-evolving knowledge systems that come fully equipped with their own culture(s) or personality(s). As Richter (1994) has noted, if a set of competitors collectively fosters knowledge, they (or it) can more readily acquire the power to "dominate markets". Put differently, they develop a collective but still exclusionary form of sustainability.

3.4 Hyper-Strategy

Given these ambiguities and redundancies it seems time to ask whether we can have a single all-embracing but still useful concept of "competitiveness". The framework of strategy-as-rationality yields one such concept. It yields and accommodates the concept of the hyper-strategy of any strategic entity, which may then be operationalised as a generalised competitiveness measure. Hyper-strategy involves:

(i) a generalised **strategic entity** or agent,
(ii) the rationality-set or *plural*-**rationality**, and
(iii) a set of **synergies** between the forms of rationality.

The first two components have been already been elaborated. The third component (synergy amongst rationalities) emerges naturally from the framework, but has also been identified independently in empirical studies of the competitiveness of industrial systems, by Ritzer and LeMoyne (1991). From a perspective of Neo-Weberian theory, these researchers were able to identify synergistic interactions amongst the four Neo-Weberian rationalities: formal, theoretical, practical and substantive-value (see below) in the context of empirical studies of the Japanese industrial system. These synergies are the building blocks of their original concept of the hyper-rationality of industrial systems. It can now be extended easily to include (i) the entire rationality-set and (ii) the entire entity-set, thus yielding a more general "hyper-strategy". This provides a quite radical new conceptual model of competitiveness; one that avoids many of the difficulties mentioned earlier. The four distinctive forms of rationality as defined in Neo-Weberian theory of industrial systems are:

$$\{formal,\ practical,\ theoretical,\ substantive\}$$

Each of these forms is defined below, where the framework and terminology of strategy-as-rationality is used to extend the Ritzer and LeMoyne analysis.

3.4.1 Correspondence (Weberian Rationality–Strategy Elements)

The four Weberian rationalities each correspond with some concepts (or sets of concepts) that are observed within Japanese industrial policy and strategy, as follows:

(i)   *Formal* ↔ {*LRP, MITI*} Bureaucratic processes like formal long-range planning, along with formal structures like the Ministry of International Trade and Industry in Japan are manifestations of Weberian formal rationality, i.e. they are shaped around codified and generally applicable laws.

(ii)   *Practical* ↔ {*QCs, Brainstorming, Ringi*} The use of quality circles, brainstorming, and "bottom-up" suggestions, in order to meet the challenges of improved quality and new product development, are seen as examples of Weberian practical rationality, i.e. they are expedient ways of pursuing a given practical end, in ways characteristic of "merchants and artisans".

(iii)   *Theoretical* ↔ {*Knowledge acquisition, R & D-focus*} Commitments to research and development and the acquisition of knowledge and information, together with general education in mathematics and economics etc. in the wider society, are all seen as examples of Weberian theoretical rationality, i.e. mastery of reality by means of increasingly precise and abstract concepts, in ways characteristic of "intellectuals".

(iv)   *Substantive (Weberian)* ↔ {*systemic values*} Relative to individualism, the values of groupism, interpendence, harmony and obligation are seen as manifestations of Weberian substantive rationality, i.e. where economic choices are guided by a consistent set of ultimate human values.

In the highly "competitive" Japanese industry, these four distinctive forms of rationality are all observed to co-exist and to synergise, within the (socio-economic) system. In contrast, American industrial systems are, according to Ritzer and LeMoyne (1991) predominantly formally rational, with the other forms absent, or only weakly manifest.

3.4.2 Weberian Meta-Rationality in Japanese Industry

They also noted the following examples of meta-rational relationships involving the Neo-Weberian forms, as manifested in modern Japanese industrial systems. These relations involve the following pairs of forms:

(*Theoretical, Practical*) Abstract ideas help in the attainment of practical ends.
(*Substantive, Practical*) Practical living lays foundation for spiritual activity.
(*Practical, Formal*) Rules and laws are mindful of practical abilities and dispositions.
(*Theoretical, Substantive*) There is an intellectual input to the (historical) development of (religious) value-systems, directly and *via* the political authorities.
(*Formal, Substantive*) Particular "human" values exist within a formal legal or economic system, e.g. welfare provisions.
(*Formal, Theoretical*) There are scientific inputs to formal administrative procedures, like LRP, JIT, statistical methods, etc.

3.4.3 Synergies Within the Full "Rationality-Set"

With strategic entities now being viewed as knowledge systems (e.g. Chapters 5, 7 and 15) it has become quite natural to think of synergy in relation to the productive re-integration of fields of knowledge. New knowledge can be created by combining the knowledge that was previously embedded or sheltered within separated entities. It is but a small step from the creation of such knowledge-synergies, to a more specific search for rationality-synergies. Accordingly, the new concept of hyper-rationality refers to synergies emerging from the co-existence and combination of multiple rationalities. Weberian sociology and empirical observations of the Japanese industrial system have both indicated that different rationalities an potentially reinforce one another. The hyper-rationality of an industrial system is more than the mere co-existence of multiple forms of rationality within the strategic entity, it is an emergent (abstract) product of the entity's rationality-set. Ritzer and LeMoyne (1991) offered specific examples of synergistic relationships amongst the Neo-Weberian forms of rationality that they observed (or imputed to) Japanese industrial systems:

(i)   *{theoretical + practical}* An emphasis on knowledge increases the utilisation of lower-level skills.

(ii)   *{practical + substantive}* "Bottom-up" practical rationality is reinforced by the substantive rationality (ethic) of "groupism".

(iii)   *{practical + formal}* Bottom-up ideas improve the functioning of assembly lines and bureaucracies, e.g. quality circles.

(iv)   *{theoretical + substantive}* Values of groupism and harmony (*wa*) strengthen the commitment of scientists, researchers etc. to contribute to the success of the enterprise.

(v)   *{formal + substantive}* Values of groupism and harmony foster the development of the formally-rational permanent-employment system, which in turn reinforces the values.

The set of potentially identifiable synergies may now be extended (Figure 3.2) from the Neo-Weberian forms to the entire rationality-set, and from a Japanese "industrial system" to any strategic entity, as follows:

(vi)   *{RUM + expressive}* Financial successes could be used to reinforce a sense of identity (e.g. IBM in the 60s)

(vii)   *{contextual + RUM}* Financial success could be used to reinforce an entity's vision of the good life with others (e.g. B.P. supporting environmental groups)

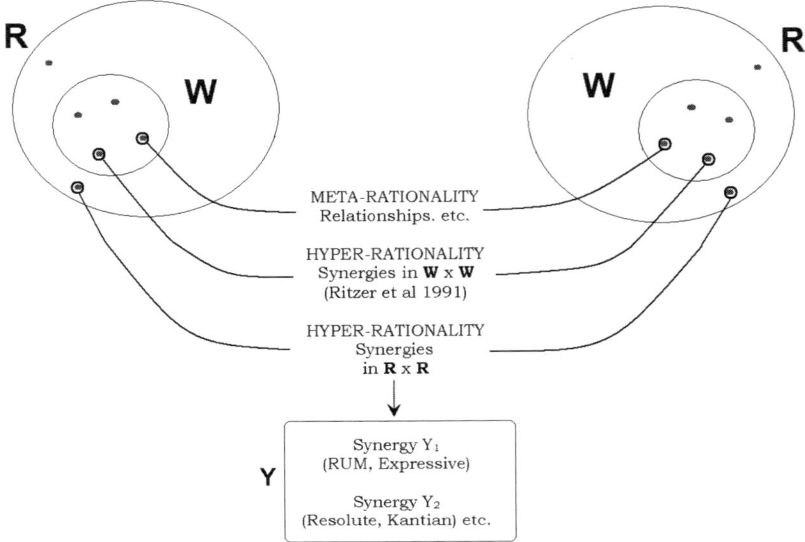

Figure 3.2　Competitiveness re-conceptualised as a set of synergies amongst forms of rationality.
Key: W = Weberian rationalities; R = Plural rationality; Y = Synergy-set (see Appendix 3.1).

(viii)　{*resolute +, Kantian*} A sense of duty and obligation could reinforce persistence with long-standing missions. (e.g. The United Nations Organisation)

(ix)　{*systemic +, expressive*} Lessons from the past could be used to reinforce a sense of identity and autonomy (e.g. Federal Express learning from failure of the Zapmail project).

(x)　{*strong or intensive + substantive-Weberian*} Formal models (e.g. market share models) may be used to reinforce the values of an entity (e.g. market share forecasting in American Standard Corporation).

Thus, implanting hyper-rationality (or equivalently, hyper-strategy) in any strategic entity simply means searching for ways of realising the synergies between elements of the entity's rationality set, identifying the absent synergies, then taking appropriate steps to implant or to strengthen those synergies. This is a new and comprehensive approach to increasing competitiveness.

3.5 Conclusion

It is often said that modern managerial practices are several steps ahead of management theory. Successful managers adapt their strategies to a rapidly changing environment, whilst abstract theories mature at a relatively slow pace. Therefore, to be useful, academics engaged in theory-building must sometimes look ahead and even jump ahead, in a spirit of pragmatic inquiry. They must also jump sideways, so to speak, breaking free from the more traditional discipline-based approaches to understanding strategy. In so doing, they might be able to lift their own level of competitiveness in the special new sense described here. This spirit has led to the new concepts of competitiveness with some suggested operationalisations (see Appendix 3.1). For academics and managers alike, the local details have been left deliberately sketchy, because they must be adapted by all thinking entities to their own unique situation and circumstance.

Finally it can be seen that this formulation of "competitiveness" as hyper-strategy is both universalisable and global. It hints at constructive, positive changes in human systems at all levels. Efforts directed at implanting hyper-strategy do not necessarily produce losers elsewhere in the system. Moreover, "achieving competitiveness" no longer means the same as seeking advantage and dis-advantage, rather it becomes concerned with what is more broadly rational, right and good for all strategic entities within a human system.

Appendix 3.1

Operationalisation and Measurement

There have been several attempts to measure synergy in strategic business analysis. As mentioned earlier, synergies are most commonly quantified as judgemental adjustments to sales and financial forecast parameters, such as cashflows, earnings-per-share, market-share, etc. in the context of investment and acquisitions planning. The International Competitiveness Model (Oral, 1986; Oral *et al.*, 1989) showed how to combine measures of a firm's actual and potential performance with macro-environmental measures for the firm and its competitors. [The particular concept of an organisation's "potential" was first measured in Beer's (1972) "Brain of the

Firm" framework, subsequently in the PARE methodology of Derkenderen and Crum, 1979]. The concept of hyper–strategy can also be developed (in principle) into a framework for measuring the level of competitiveness of any strategic entity, as follows:

(i) *Formalisation*

The notion of competitiveness as a set of synergies amongst elements of the rationality-set can at least be expressed in set and function notion, as follows. Define υ as a mapping of subsets of $\mathbf{R}$ onto particular synergies or hyper-rationalities $\mathbf{y}_i \,\varepsilon\, \mathbf{Y}$, i.e.

$$\upsilon: 2^{\mathbf{R}} \rightarrow \mathbf{Y}$$
$$\upsilon: [r_1, r_2, r_j] = \mathbf{y}_{i1}$$

Then for any given strategic entity A we have:

$$\upsilon: \; 2^{\mathbf{R}^{[A]}} \rightarrow \; \mathbf{Y}^{[A]}$$

where $\mathbf{R}^{[A]}$ is the set of rationalities co-existing in A. [A] is simply used as an identifier, and

$$\mathbf{Y}^{[A]} = \left[\mathbf{y}^{[A]}_{i_1}, \mathbf{y}^{[A]}_{i_2}, \mathbf{y}^{[A]}_{i_{n[A]}} \right]$$

where $\mathbf{Y}^{[A]}$ is the set of all the synergies realised in A amongst the set $\mathbf{R}^{[A]}$ and $n[A]$ = the number of distinctive synergies achieved or implanted in A.

(ii) *Measurement*

The level of competitiveness of the entity A is simply the combined magnitude of the synergies listed in the set $\mathbf{Y}^{[A]}$, as follows:

$$\text{level-of-competitiveness of } A = \sum_{r=1}^{n[A]} m(\mathbf{y}^{[A]}_{i_r})$$

where m (.) represents some constructed measure of the synergies.

Notes

1. Decades later, this practice is still being advocated by corporate strategists. "The multibusiness team can add value beyond the sum of the businesses" and this is partly because "the market cannot reproduce… the underlying social structure that enables effective collaboration…" (Eisenhardt and Galunic, 2006).

2. When mentioning Stafford Beer in the context of business strategy and ethics it should not be forgotten that he was engaged in the 1970s by the Allende regime in Chile to advise on the design of government systems (see his books, *Brain of the Firm* and *Heart of Enterprise*). Before that work was far advanced, however, the Allende regime was overthrown by Pinochet's forces, reportedly backed by right-leaning political entities (see dualism framework) including some MNCs. As is now well known, Pinochet was later convicted for many crimes, including widespread use of torture.

3. Within the field of finance, the phrase "multiple forms of capital" refers to the various types of financial instrument (e.g. debt, classes of equity, convertibles, etc). This is but one example of contrasting usages of vocabulary across business-related disciplines. It is very common and can be quite misleading.

Chapter 4

LIMITATIONS: Market Limitations as Strategic Problems

Abstract: This chapter is an abridged version of "Enterprise action for the common good: market limitations as strategic problems," *Journal of Enterprising Culture* 11(1), pp. 69–88, 2003. It is suggested that many companies have attempted to lead ethically by example, yet have nonetheless operated quite uncritically within the global market despite that systems' known limitations. As a result, corporate communications that refer to the "common good" often lack credibility. A framework and methodology is proposed for augmenting enterprise strategies and communications in this respect. It is then applied from a distance to a well-known profitable Japanese company that also has an expressed social and environmental mission. Finally, some related cultural issues are discussed.

4.1 Introduction

Many global corporations (Merck, Shell, Levi-Strauss, Canon, to mention just a few) have advocated ethical business, whilst also contributing directly to social and environmental projects. Many others (including the same entities in different times) have made no such claims, but have relied instead on the invisible hand of the market for any necessary ethical justification.

It is obvious that the latter entities could do much more to contribute directly to the common good. However, the same also applies, less obviously, to the "ethical" corporations. In the following section, there is a discussion of the low credibility and limited effectiveness of corporate ethics missions. The credibility problem (e.g. Higgins, 2002) is then seen as a strategic problem for all enterprises, one that is also related to political value-priorities. Then (in Sections 4.3 to 4.5) a framework for solving this problem is outlined. First, specific market limitations and possible strategic responses are described. Many of these responses involve benign partnerships with governments in which enterprises deliberately attempt to influence governments towards common good policies, rather than the more familiar vice-versa. The framework also yields a method for reviewing and augmenting strategy in this respect. In Section 4.6, it is applied (from a distance) to Canon corporation, on the basis of its very well documented history, strategy and expressed ethical mission. With this case study in mind, the framework is then further extended (in Section 4.7) to the strategic analysis of cultural values and perceptions.

4.2 Credibility

There are several reasons for the generally low credibility and widespread misunderstandings of expressed social and ethical enterprise missions. From a center-to-left political perspective, such missions might be seen (but perhaps misunderstood) as public-relations ploys that are deliberately designed to advance the cause of global capitalism and corporate power. Furthermore, with respect to rationality (rather than power) this same perspective sees that the "ethical" strategies do little to overcome the several specific limitations of markets and capitalism. Associated communications remain silent about these standard "limitations" that, for example, legitimise trades unions, challenge strong IPR regimes, create pressure for re-distribution of wealth and alleviation of poverty, and oppose the market positioning of corporate offerings in ways that create superficial desires, and so on.

From a center-to-right perspective, in contrast, the weak credibility of ethical missions rests upon a very different idea (one that is somewhat challenged by the available empirical evidence), that the associated strategies must surely involve tradeoffs against commercial goals, so they retard the accumulation of financial capital (e.g. Friedman, 1970). Investment fund managers who share Milton Friedman's highly-enduring view would be negatively pre-disposed towards any stated corporate ethics mission, seeing it as (i) an "affectation" (to use Adam Smith's classical description of those who claim to be trading for the public good), or as (ii) having the sole useful purpose (in the US at least) of reducing penalties imposed in any unforeseen legal proceedings, or as (iii) as undemocratic (as explained by Friedman), because enterprise managers dispensing philanthropy are not popularly elected representatives.

Accordingly, at both ends of the political spectrum, one finds that ethics missions fundamentally lack credibility. Claims by business enterprises to be working for the common good (e.g. Canon) or for the people (e.g. Merck), or for the natural environment (e.g Shell), simply do not ring true. This remains the case, even when the claims are substantiated by the efficient production of quality market offerings, or philanthropic programmes, or environmental restoration projects. For the same reasons, public statements by senior corporate officers along the lines of "the corporate assumption of global responsibilities", or that "it is now best to allow the private sector to take the lead" (e.g. Sandoz, 1997, p. 72) can often become further significant sources of concern by those who value freedom, rather than any cause for celebration.

Yet, as the latter statements suggest, there is also a third point of view that ought to be included in this assessment of strategy and communication. From the perspective of CEOs and corporate HQs messages of ethical leadership might actually feel completely benign and sincere. Put simply, if anyone wants to improve the human condition, they must first try to do this through example. From this perspective, it seems neither practical nor effective to rely upon others, whether they be NGOs, governments, or trans-national political entities. Accordingly, some influential managers might be completely sincere about their ethical, social and environmental missions, statements and commitments. Given the systemic limitations of capitalism and the nature of politics, it is quite unfortunate that they might very well be deceiving themselves and others, in this regard.

In the literature on ethics and strategy, discussions of conflicts between commercial doctrine and philosophical ethics are very common, particularly regarding Kantian ethics as it applies to business problems. For example, Kant's golden rule (act only according to universalisable maxims) can be understood as the very antithesis of competitive business strategy and the accompanying mindset. However, in the present context, the Kantian emphasis on goodwill (i.e. the intention to help others) is assumed to be enduringly relevant. That is, genuine aspirations for the common good still do count for a lot, in a world that is very far from perfect. Put differently, if these higher collective aspirations are routinely or cynically dismissed, there is little hope of general moral progress. Yet the such progress is needed, both as an end in itself and as a means to sustain the pre-requisites for the effective operation of markets and hence enterprise success.

Accordingly, the present situation, whereby ethics missions lack credibility, merits a strategic response by business enterprises. Not only should the common good be considered a legitimate mission, alongside profitability; enterprises should also (rationally) ensure that (a) their strategy fully reflects that expanded mission, and that (b) it is communicated publicly and credibly. Most enterprise strategies and communication would have to be substantially augmented in order to satisfy these conditions; but particularly at the political and ideological levels, where strategy involves business–government relations and mutual influences.

4.3 Limitations

In the absence of substantial government or other third-party involvement, markets and corporations alone cannot bring about much "common good". Historically, this was plainly emphasised by Adam Smith in *The Wealth of Nations* (1776). Here, the proper operation of markets was fully understood as depending on several social and moral pre-requisites. More recently, Amartya Sen, in *Development as Freedom* (1999) emphasised the need for a multifaceted approach to economic development (which is part of the common good), involving business, democratic government and other institutions working in concert. The known limitations of a "markets-only" approach, even one supplemented (in accordance with a popular contemporary variant of capitalism) with philanthropic and environmentally responsive businesses, can be summarised quite succinctly (Table 4.1). They are often called imperfections or failures[1] and they involve (i) public goods, (ii) distributive justice, (iii) monopolistic tendencies, (iv) economic externalities such as pollution,

Table 4.1 Market limitations and corporate strategies.

Limitation	Strategy
Public goods	Philanthropy
Justice (organisational)	HR policies
Justice (distributive)	Fostering WTMM's[2]
Monopoly	Patenting and SMIP[3]
Externalities	Environmental engineering
Preferences	Market orientation

and (v) the distinction between preferences and well-being (i.e. consumers often deceive themselves, harming themselves and others).

Any given enterprise strategy can be (and indeed ought to be) appraised systematically in relation to these limitations. Whenever this is done, it quickly becomes apparent that there are significant gaps in most corporate strategies, including those that explicitly claim to relate to the common good. There are corresponding doubts about the authenticity of the stated objectives and the credibility of the related corporate communications. However, once those "gaps" and sources of "doubt" have been clearly identified, several ways of overcoming them also quickly become apparent (Table 4.2), as follows.

4.3.1 Public Goods and Philanthropy

There are many noteworthy corporate programs of philanthropy, for example, donations of pharmaceuticals, scholarships, grants and support for various community activities. These can all be understood as direct action for the public good; but that understanding also has latent strategic and political components. For example, philanthropic expenditures often reduce corporate tax payments (whilst conferring other strategic benefits to the donor); but, when publicised, they also tend to influence voters' attitudes in any democracy, hence limiting the capabilities or re-ordering the priorities of governments. Once such systemic effects are fully taken into account, it is quite possible that corporate philanthropy programs (perhaps unintentionally) actually reduce the overall level of public goods in a society. It follows that enterprises that authentically pursue "common good" objectives ought to supplement or augment their philanthropy programs, with more active engagement in the political arena. That is, they should also endeavour to persuade governments to generously provide public goods (or at least to fund their provision). They should also aim to optimise tax payments within the context of a public-good oriented partnership with government, rather than simply minimise the payments.

4.3.2 Organisational Justice

Within many enterprises, management adopts a unitarist perspective; that is, they advocate a team approach, whilst also implicitly denying the existence of any fundamental labour-capital conflict. Accordingly, trades unions are often seen as a constraint on profits, condoning inefficiency, or as supporting particular socialist politicians. Yet trade unions can indeed serve the common good, by providing a counterbalance to the circuits-of-power inherent in capitalism. Like a good employer, they can protect and care for individuals at the lower end of the spectrum of wealth and power. It is a standard (and really obvious) critique of market-based systems (as well as many other political systems) that individual employees are often powerless, so that organised labour has a legitimate and ultimately valuable role in promoting a balance, which is part of the common good.

Organisational justice is frequently understood to involve matters of gender and race. These are explicitly addressed in many corporate policies, codes and practices. A recent critique by Bauman (1998) places all such practices in a much wider context; one that has considerable relevance to the present analysis. Bauman suggested that issues involving gender and race (often described as "political correctness" in the media) have for many years distracted the public mind. Such issues have been tacitly played up by the contemporary power elite, because the really "big issue", so to speak, is the stretching of pay scales, the disempowerment of unions and the growth of winner-take-most markets. The latter, in turn, are closely associated with the increasing well-documented gap between haves and have-nots and (arguably, contentiously) the growth of poverty in the world (see Chapter 14). So, for example, policies such as like affirmative action might very well be politically correct; but it is the stretching of pay scales and the power-shift to the executive suite that really needs to be "corrected" for the sake of the genuine common good.

4.3.3 Distributive Justice and Market Structures

Market offerings (products and services) and their promotion can have an marked effect on public attitudes and social relationships, that extends well beyond the satisfaction of individual desires and preference. This is especially the case with technologically advanced products, whose financial and social contributions are seemingly quite unstable. In general, one must consider the motives, patterns and contexts of the use of any technology, before claiming it makes a valid contribution to the common good. With regard to distributive justice, for example, some information technologies and products are potentially a source of empowerment and hence poverty-alleviation; yet they have also fostered the growth of winner-take-most and increasing-returns global markets (e.g. in movies, music, sports), which have in turn increased disparities of wealth, wasted much effort (of the many non-winners), but also (in large part through global media) encouraged passive public acceptance of a bad situation.

Corporate actions and communications that refer to the "common good" simply ought to recognize these effects and then seek ways of responding to them. For example, companies can openly support political ideals (see Chapter 5) like universal access to health services and education, progressive taxation policies and a diversity of political orientations in global media. To the extent that these ideals are approached, companies can then claim authentically to be co-creating, with governments, a much more trusting and secure society.

4.3.4 Monopoly and Patenting Strategies

Winner-take–most markets are a form of monopoly. "Winners" are able to exercise market power in ways that constrain aggregate benefits. Patent rights in particular grant temporary monopolies. Their economic justification also rests on balancing that cost against the benefits of increased financial incentives for innovation. Patents have been highly controversial since their inception; but in the pro-patent era of the last two decades, this controversy has greatly intensified (e.g. NRC, 2000; Watt, 2000). The era came about, historically, in large part as a result of corporate lobbying from the technology and entertainment sectors. A case against strong patenting regimes can now be made entirely within a technical economic analysis (i.e. the "balance" is wrong), but it can be further strengthened by separate consideration of some psychological, social and political aspects of the "common good", for example:

According to Watt (2000, p. 146), "foreign discrimination is built into the Western-invented (intellectual property) system and is still present, to some extent", whilst Vaver (2000) has noted that strong IPR regimes represent a threat to civil freedoms to talk, write, parody, and develop community cultures. In addition, some companies have patented human genetic material, implying that the common good is served by extending property relations over living systems, despite the implied prospects of new forms of slavery.

The more extreme consequences of strong IPR have already led to governmental and political-level responses. For example, the millions of avoidable deaths of AIDS patients, due in part to an inability to pay for the patent-protected pharmaceuticals, has resulted in a recent WTO ruling allowing the overriding of patents for drugs that treat infectious deadly diseases such as AIDS. Yet pharmaceutical corporations amongst others (including many that espouse ethics) have been generally reluctant to respond to various harms and un-kindnesses in which IPR regimes have obviously been a contributing factor. Accordingly, enterprises that are authentically concerned with the common good can now take several steps, including (i) re-designing and re-evaluating strategies in knowledge based industries so they do not depend on IPR, but instead use other ways of capturing revenue, appropriating profit and hence ensuring return on capital (see Chapter 16), and (ii) lobbying for weaker IPR regimes (shorter patents, conditional patents, override rights, and so on), and (iii) giving explicit recognition to the variety of non-pecuniary motives for innovation (aesthetic, altruistic, scientific), as for example, in a recent Shell advertising campaign.

4.3.5 Externalities and Environmental Strategies

Amongst all the economic externalities (i.e. costs imposed on those outside the immediate system of production and exchange), pollution of the environment is probably the most significant, politically and economically. There is a broad consensus about the potentially benign use of environmental engineering, with the new power of design, to overcome tradeoffs between profit and the environment (i.e. the race to the top). However, there remains several distinctive perspectives on the business-environment relationship (e.g. Werhane, 1999a) that reveal factors that tend to undermine any such progress. They include inter alia (i) the continuing existence of situations where immediate survival needs can only be met by damaging the environment, as well as (ii) the development of corporate-produced life forms, subject to ownership and control, through IPR. Accordingly, corporate environmental strategies that simply involve engineering and market positioning ought to be profoundly supplemented by political engagement strategies that promote joint action to reduce the negative effects of such "factors".

4.3.6 Preferences and market-orientation

In similar vein, enterprises can respond in many ways to the tendency inherent in capitalism to create desires and encourage excessive consumption (that is, beyond the point of optimal well being). In general, product attributes that confer genuine well-being can be designed and promoted, whilst marketing tactics that foster superficial desires or manipulate people's preferences can be avoided. This distinction (between preferences expressed by exchanges versus choices that create well being) is central to existing under-recognised theories of humanistic economics (e.g. Lutz and Lux, 1988). It was also emphasised by Sen (1987) as a key point of contrast between the enduring neoclassical paradigm and an ethical alternative. In humanistic economics, like humanism generally, preferences (as in neo-classical economic theory) are associated with the "lower self", but they are contrasted with meta-preferences that express the higher self. The former are often deliberately created and manipulated by promotional campaigns, whereas the latter are arrived at after critically and reflectively reviewing lower-level preferences, much like the review of corporate values and strategies being carried out in this chapter!

4.4 Augmentations

Systematic consideration given to all the main market limitations can enable thoughtful enterprise managers to design specific augmentations to strategy, in order to overcome the limitations and hence to contribute much more authentically and credibly to the common good. The above-mentioned generic examples are summarised in Table 4.2 and can be re-stated, as follows.

(i)   With regard to public goods, there is a need for political engagement and common-good oriented partnerships, with governments. Optimal tax policies, in the hands of good government, can fund a level of public goods in a society that more faithfully reflects the

Table 4.2   Elements of strategy with their ethical augmentations.

Strategy	Augmentation
Corporate philanthropy	Political engagement, human goods
HR policies	Unions, discuss distraction, pay-compression
WTM markets	Critique some applications
IPR and patent-wars	Lobby for weak IPR, strategies without IPR
Environmental engineering	Respond to the root causes
Market re-orientation	Ethical orientation, avoid deception

common will. This viewpoint is hardly ever articulated by business managers and entrepreneurs. Indeed, the opposite stance is usually adopted, with most executives arguing at every turn for lower taxes and less government, in accordance with more narrowly-construed personal and stakeholder interests.

(ii)   With regard to typical HR policies, there is a risk that these distract public attention away from the fundamental issue of distributive justice, as the extent of world poverty has increased. Accordingly, enterprises can moderate any tendency to stretch pay scales, whilst accommodating legitimate unions.

(iii)   Some technologies foster winner-take-most markets, making inequality worse. Accordingly enterprises can promote alternative contexts for the use of their market offerings and publicly critique some of the offending applications.

(iv)   Enterprises ought to be more forthright about the problematic relationship between strong IPR regimes and the common good. Rather than lobby for strong IPR, they should seek changes in IPR regimes, reflecting the idea of knowledge as a common heritage. Strategies can be re-designed so they do not depend upon IPR.

(v)   Environmental engineering and the use of environmental technologies for competitive advantage plainly contribute to the common good; but political partnerships are also needed to help eliminate the root causes of environmental degradation.

(vi)   The market-orientation of most enterprises can be augmented with a stronger ethical orientation, particularly involving practices and communications that minimise deception.

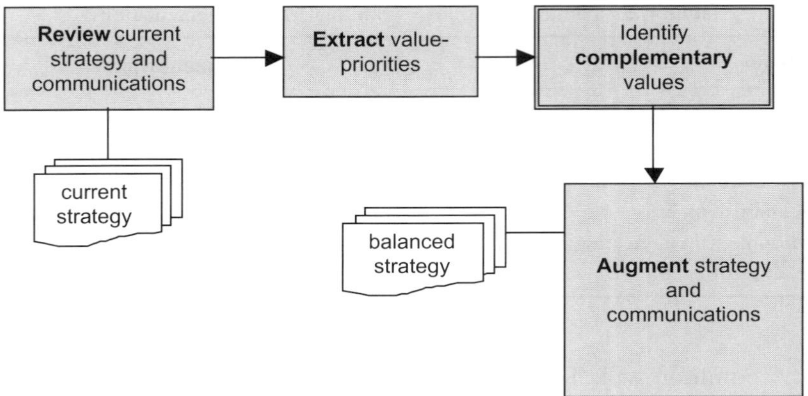

Figure 4.1 The process of augmenting strategy and communications.

The process of identifying these "ethical" augmentations can also be summarised conveniently and even presented as methodology of strategy formulation (Figure 4.1). First the current strategy and communications of any given enterprise must be described. In so doing, the implicit systemic (political) understandings and value-priorities (core values) can be extracted and made quite explicit (as in 1970s strategy techniques like assumptions-surfacing and testing). This can now be done with systematic and direct reference to the known limitations of market systems, as listed in Table 4.1. Consideration of these then inevitably leads to richer political understandings and to better appreciation of some implicit value-priorities and their complements (i.e. the two sides of the dualism). In each case, changes and augmentations of enterprise strategy can be creatively designed, with a view to overcoming the market limitations and cognitive biases, hence progressing towards the common good. Existing strategy is thereby expanded to quite fully incorporate a systemic–ethical dimension.

4.5 Partnerships

If business enterprises are to become effective and credible contributors to the common good, it is not only necessary to overcome the limitations of markets by augmenting enterprise strategy, it is also necessary to co-opt other entities in this mission, especially governments. Put differently, enterprises do not have to regard global capitalism based upon financial markets and minimalist government as a given immutable or even desirable condition; rather, they can assume the mantle of ethical leadership, thus influencing and re-shaping the entire system with the common good firmly in mind (see Chapter 5). This is a fundamental extension of the traditional strategic imperative to shape the market, with profitability in mind. A similar "multifaceted" approach to integrated economic and social development has recently been advocated by Sen (1999, p. 126). He called for simultaneous progress on several fronts, including different institutions that reinforce (rather than confront) each other in carrying out this mission.

These two main ideas, (i) the effect of normal enterprise strategy on the common good in the context of market limitations, and (ii) the influence of enterprises on governments, are brought together and illustrated in Figure 4.2. Enterprise activities typically produce positive and negative effects, as described in the previous sections. They also influence governments directly through lobbying, but also indirectly through communicating and propagating an ideology that in turn influences attitudes amongst electorates. This can all be done with the common good in mind.

The traditional conception of business–government relationships is much narrower and it is far more adversarial. Profit maximising enterprises traditionally delegate the task of overcoming market limitations to governments (the visible hand) yet at the same time they often quite intentionally tie that "hand", by avoiding tax payments, lobbying for tax reductions and

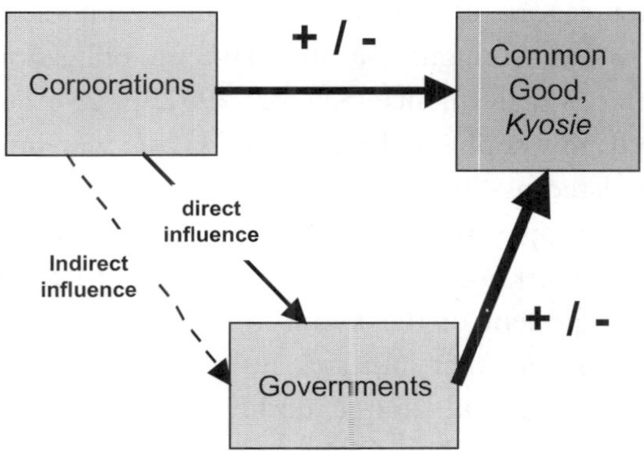

Figure 4.2 Enterprise–government partnerships for the common good.

generally influencing public attitudes to favour yet more tax reductions. With this approach, even political corruption can become quite acceptable to the philanthropic and environmentally aware enterprise, despite the fact that it often detracts greatly from the common good (for example, it is amongst the major known causes of poverty and famine).

4.6 Canon and *Kyosie*

The application of these integrative strategy frameworks can be richly illustrated with reference to Canon Corporation. There are several reasons why this is a pertinent example. First, the company is extremely well-known; secondly, it is a profitable producer of quality products. Thirdly, it has a stated social and environmental mission. Fourthly, it has a well-documented history that appears to indicate some instability and wavering in its orientation towards both profit and the common good (e.g. Kaku 1996; Sandoz 1997; Granstrand 2001; www.canon.com; *Business Week*, 2002). There is yet another reason: as a Japanese company that operates in global markets the case suggests the further possibility of applying the framework to the analysis of cultural values (see next section).

The corporate name "Canon" was originally derived from *Kwannon*, the Buddhist god of mercy, in conjunction with the usage of the word "canon" as an ethical standard to live by. Later, it was decided by executives that the company would "make a commitment to work for the betterment of the entire human race" (Sandoz, 1997). Around 1984, chairman Mitarai reportedly advanced the idea within Canon, that "profitability alone is not enough; we also have an obligation to lend our strength to society's betterment" (Sandoz, 1997, p. 25). Subsequently, in 1988, an explicit philosophy and mission of *kyosie* was announced. It has since been translated as "living and working together for the common good", or as "all people, regardless of race, religion and culture, harmoniously living and working together for many years to come".

The main proponent of the *kyosie* mission, Mr. Kaku, has a documented personal history that indicates authenticity and sincerity: he was a survivor of the Nagasaki atomic bomb; his childhood was spent in "straightened circumstances" in China, where he experienced a community "full of people sleeping on streets, but with empty homes with high rents". Most significantly in the present context, he is also said to "dislike empty words".

4.6.1 Philanthropy and Engagement

In apparent conformity with *kyosie*, this famous company has implemented an extensive philanthropy program that supports social, scientific and cultural activities in most countries where it operates (www.canon.com). This can be seen as direct action for the common good; but, as noted earlier, that perspective overlooks several systemic and political effects such as the influence of direct action on voters' attitudes, tending to reduce the pressure on governments to provide public goods.

4.6.2 HR Policies

According to Sandoz (1997, p. 6), at the entrance to Canon's HQ near Mount Fuji, there is an elevator on the left for general use, with a separate one "on the right" that travels to the "realms of the Gods". Yet Canon and its mission are both described as humanistic (1997, p. 45). As mentioned earlier, humanism (like Buddhism) emphasises higher-level preferences, which are in turn linked (via the concept of deliberative rationality) to questions of distributive justice; but especially the position of the least-well-off in society (e.g. Rawls, 1972). Such "justice" concerns have been directly expressed by Mr. Kaku, thus: "even if a deal is extremely profitable, unless the profit is shared, the benefits will be small" (p. 60).

Is this notion of "sharing" a credible element of strategy, at Canon (or anywhere)? The company has a stated goal to employ as many citizens as possible, expanding employment "throughout the world". It also appears to be quite progressive with respect to meritocracy and the avoidance of bias, in recruitment and promotion decisions (but Bauman's "distraction" critique applies). With regard to remuneration and the stretching of pay scales, Canon could better implement distributive justice by, for example, preserving the moderation of pay scales (as has been traditional in Japan and until recently in Continental Europe). Finally, Canon's management appear to have adopted a unitarist perspective, in that trade unions are reportedly seen as "nothing more than fund raising and support groups for politicians". *Kyosie* on the other hand, implies that the company ought to uphold the legitimacy of unions, perhaps even persuading them to fulfill their proper role of protecting individual employees. Such an approach would nicely complement the current emphasis upon employee's personal development, as expressed in the *3J* philosophies: *ji-hatsu, ji-kaku, ji-chi* (self-motivation, self-awareness and self-management).

4.6.3 Winner-Take-Most markets

Canon's core mission is "to strive for the very best in every product and activity and thereby contribute to society" (Sandoz, 1997, p. 37). This has remained unchanged for more than 40 years and is said to be "deeply ingrained" in Canon's employees. However the relationship between perfect products and social "contributions" is neither so deep, nor stable. Here, one must also consider the motives, patterns and contexts of use of products and technologies, before estimating any level of contribution to society and the common good (e.g. Buchholz and Rosenthal, 2002).

For example, Canon famously developed a retinal camera, enabling medical examination and diagnosis through patients' eyes. However, if such high-tech medical services become available only to a very small minority, then a society as a whole might even be harmed in the long run by rationed care that excludes those who lack the ability to pay and who probably are most in need (as mentioned earlier in relation to pharmaceuticals). Obviously one cannot associate any particular enterprise, nor even any one entire industry with these fundamental systemic and political problems; but, as has been emphasised throughout this chapter, single well-respected companies can be highly influential. In this case, for example, Canon could publicly support universal health services in all the countries in which it operates. Indeed it is that kind of "PR" that really relates to the public (cf. Zeleny 2005 and Chapter 5)

Developments in imaging technology often find major applications in the security and military industries. Yet the demand for these services is generated (at least in part) by a perceived need to protect "haves" from disenchanted have-nots. This situation, which must surely distress Mr Kaku and like-minded people everywhere, appears to be caused (again in part) by the very technologies that companies like Canon have co-created and developed. Digital technologies have fostered the growth of winner-take-most global markets. To set thing right, Canon could publicly support income redistribution through progressive taxation and privacy policies.

4.6.4 *Patenting Strategies*

Canon has responded very actively and adapted brilliantly to the international patent system. Indeed, the company is a leader in this aspect of knowledge strategy, being consistently at or near the top of the table for number of (US) patents granted to a corporation (e.g. Granstrand, 2000). Yet, this status of patent-warrior (i.e. in the economic and technological battle between companies and nations) does not fit at all squarely with an authentic *kyosie* philosophy.

On the company website, there is no mention whatsoever of IPR and its intensive strategic management (other than copyright of the site itself). It seems implausible that a world-beating performance in rates of patenting would be completely overlooked by a proud corporate communications department. It is far more likely that IPR is well-understood as being morally controversial. Accordingly, several steps could be taken: first, a full description of IPR strategies and policies, together with the general social "dilemma" (e.g. NRC, 2000) ought to be clearly and frankly communicated. Then, as mentioned earlier (Section 4.2), Canon could lobby with others for a relaxation of IPR regimes, whilst at the same time re-designing its strategies so they depend less upon IPR (i.e. initiate another race-to-the-top).

4.6.5 *Environmental Engineering*

In contrast to its strategic silence over IPR, Canon has been quick to advertise its major accomplishments in environmental engineering (e.g. Kaku, 1996; www.canon.com). However, as discussed previously, there are several unseen forces at work that undermine efforts at achieving the common good in this way. Political engagement is once again indicated in order to alleviate global poverty (that also damages the natural environment) and to uphold the ideal of knowledge as common heritage (also in relation to the environment). Canon might also respond to the "excessive consumption" critique of markets, by designing and promoting product attributes that create genuine well-being and by de-marketing attributes that pander to superficial desires.

4.6.6 *Market Orientation*

For many years, Canon has been a strongly engineering-oriented company. Its product development has plainly been driven by a quest for technological mastery and scientific understanding. However, it has also been suggested (Sandoz, 1997) that a stronger market-orientation is necessary. In this connection, one executive noted that one can "dream of the stars" (i.e. the technological possibilities or humane ideals) but the company "has to sell here on Earth" (the market).

Since Canon's major product theme is "image", the common-good effect of any stronger market-orientation depends in part upon the context in which these images are used. Neither the common good (nor the higher-self) is well served, if image-related products simply result in (i) people's privacy and dignity being replaced by intensive surveillance, or (ii) access to knowledge being displaced by gladiatorial entertainment, or (iii) education being transformed, by incremental steps, into edu-tainment. The costs and harms resulting from of these changes are potentially extremely high. Since any shift towards a market-orientation at Canon is likely to add to those costs, the company should seriously consider an alternative: retain its humanist ethos and "re-orient" towards ethics. In so doing it can maintain a focus upon profit (e.g. *BusinessWeek,* 2002) but be less myopic, gazing in other directions as well.

4.6.7 *Augmenting Strategy at Canon*

Currently Canon's website states that "it is the presence of imbalance in our world… (that) hinders the achievement of *kyosei.*" That very same notion, "balance", has been applied in this chapter to Canon's own strategy, resulting in the specification of several ways of augmenting it. These are summarised as follows.

(i) With regard to public goods, Canon can promote the idea of funding of public goods via an optimal level of taxation.

(ii)   With regard to HR policies, Canon can moderate the stretching of pay scales, recognise the legitimacy of unions and be forthright about distributive justice in societies.

(iii) Greater efforts are needed to promote alternative and humane contexts for the use of technologies, whilst also critiquing some applications.

(iv) Canon can end its strategic silence about the ambivalent relationship between strong IPR regimes and the common good. It can also lobby for greater global recognition of the common heritage principle, whilst re-designing strategies so they have less dependence upon IPR.

(v)   To make environmental engineering effective, political partnerships are needed. These can be aimed at alleviating poverty and discouraging excessive consumption, which are amongst the root causes of environmental degradation.

(vi)   Finally, Canon's engineering and market orientation should be augmented with a stronger ethical orientation.

Thus, there are several specific ways in which the company can respond openly and fully to the known limitations of market based systems, including the gross imbalance of power and wealth in the world that has been explicitly mentioned in its own communications. This would give much greater authenticity and credibility to the *kyosie* mission and it would be a superb example for others to emulate. Accordingly, management should consider all of the above prescriptions, but they can also assume the mantle of leadership in encouraging others to do likewise.

4.7 Culture

According to Sandoz (1997), Mr. Kaku can best be described "not as a businessman, but as the soul and conscience of Canon". Yet business and conscience need not be mutually exclusive (see Chapters 2 and 8). The notion that enterprising activities can be both economic and ethical (i.e. complements) must be highly acceptable to anyone familiar with East Asian philosophical traditions, not to mention a complete history of Western economic and scientific ideas. Mr. Kaku was reportedly influenced by Western philosophy, but particularly the works of Immanuel Kant. Accordingly, like Kant, he has probably paid much more attention to universal ideals (like the common good in *Kyosie*) than to the ideas of complementarity, synergy and the dialectic (see Chapters 1, 6 and 13). Kant accepted the idea of dialectics of the mind (as in the dualism of Chapter 1 and the "+" *and* the "−" influences in Figure 4.2). In contrast to many other political philosophers (e.g. Hegel), he did not particularly consider dialectics as a basis for Worldly action. Canon's ethics mission (like that of many other corporations) now seems to reflect precisely this Kantian doctrine. There seems to be an expression of universal ideals, but at the same time a reluctance to accept and act in the world in ways that are based upon dialectical oppositions, like the augmented strategy elements outlined here.

This analysis hints at the possibility of extending the above framework beyond political values (markets and their limitations), to include some related cultural value-priorities (of the type that any global company, like Canon inevitably encounters in its global operations). For example, basic political concepts such as "public" and "good" (Table 4.1, row 1; Table 4.3, rows 1 and 2) are understood in quite diverse ways across cultures. In Japan "public" is reportedly often associated with an attitude of "who cares?" (Sandoz, 1997, p. 35), whereas "private" reportedly indicates the existence of "recognizable responsibility". In the UK and European context, "public" is still (fortunately) associated with "responsibility" for others, not to mention community awareness and a degree of political maturity. The basic concept of "good" is also open to contrasting interpretations across cultures. First, there is the idea already discussed that goodness (like well-being) need not correspond to revealed preferences (e.g. Shanks, 1993; Broome, 1993); but there are also generic empirical differences in preferences across cultures. "Western goods" such as open spaces, freedom, equality and fraternity; have been contrasted with "Japanese goods", such as small private gardens, the aesthetic of rice cultivation (e.g. Shiogi and Nakano, 1999).

This idea, of "difference" in cultural values itself often becomes an "opposite" in the mind (i.e. dialectics). Value-priorities (or forms of goodness) that have at times been associated with given cultures, or styles of business, have at other times become re-described with an exactly opposite emphasis (i.e. good becomes bad, a trans-valuation). For example,

Table 4.3   Complementary cultural value-priorities.

Value	Trans-Value
"Public" = no responsibility	"Public" = civic responsibility
"Good" = preference	"Good" = well-being
Attachment to family	Nepotism
Personal relationships	Cronyism
Respect for authority	Rigidity
Consensus and settlement	Justifying corruption
"Wait and see"	Lack of leadership
Network of suppliers	Monopolistic practices
Gift giving	Bribe, grease payment

according to an article in *The Economist* (1998) about East Asian values in general, written shortly after the Asian stock-market collapse:

> "Attachment to family (now) becomes nepotism, the importance of personal relationships becomes cronyism, consensus become corrupt politics, conservatism and respect for authority becomes rigidity and an inability to innovate" and so on.

In a similar vein (Table 4.3), a propensity to "wait and see" becomes lack of leadership; networks of trusted suppliers become re-cast as collusive practice; gift-giving becomes bribery, and so on. Such complementary values and understandings plainly arise from distinctive histories and institutional frameworks. As with markets and their limits, once the values and trans-values are made explicit, enterprise strategies and communications can be augmented to respond to them, to accommodate them and to communicate them globally.

4.8 Conclusion

At present, there is a widespread need to respond much more openly and fully to the several known limitations of market based systems, not to mention perceived contrasts in cultural value-priorities. This is especially the case for limitations, values and perceptions associated with a gross imbalance of power and wealth in the world. Accordingly, enterprise management ought to consider the various prescriptions for actions and communications set out in this article, whilst also encouraging others to do likewise. As any Kantian would say, simple aspirations for the common good still count for a lot in a far-from-perfect world; but they must first be authentic, hence credible.

Note

1. Heath (2006) recently referred to the "market failures" model or perspective on business ethics, as an alternative to the stakeholder model (see the dualism framework in Chapter 1). He wrote (p. 551) that "what so often upsets people about corporate behaviour... is the exploitation of one or another form of market imperfection" and accordingly advocated a "willingness to refrain" from this type of exploitation. In Chapters 4 and 5, the stronger remedy of actively compensating for the various limitations (failures or imperfections) is considered. This might be achieved in several ways, including through partnerships with other institutions.

2. Winner-take-most markets.

3. Strategic management of intellectual property.

Chapter 5

IDEALS: Managing Human Systems and Advancing Humane Ideals

Abstract: This chapter is extracted and adapted from "Global strategy and ethics: managing human systems and advancing humane ideals," *Business Ethics Quarterly*, 2006. That paper reviewed and constructively critiqued Milan Zeleny's recent book: "Human Systems Management: Integrating Knowledge, Management and Systems," World Scientific Publishing, Singapore, 2005. In the critique, two variants of capitalism are described: Human Systems Management (HSM) and Humane Ideals Management (HIM). They are compared with Financial-Market-Capitalism (i.e. the Anglo-US variant, or business-as-usual). HSM and HIM both embody distinctive ways of thinking about the relationship between business strategy and ethics.

5.1 Human Systems

A recent book by Zeleny (2005), the long-standing journal HSM (IOS Press), and many other journal articles by Zeleny have offered a seemingly comprehensive set of prescriptions for running contemporary state-of-the-art competitive enterprises in service of society: the normative principles of meso-level business strategy and ethics. The HSM book has also provided a very distinctive viewpoint on micro-level managerial ethics, as well as macro-level social and political systems. It also advances some distinctive ways of thinking about familiar philosophical and social science constructs, by placing them squarely within the context of contemporary technological enterprise. These constructs include knowledge, wisdom, purposes, ethics, capital and synthesis (where contributions by Zeleny to the theory of trade-offs are well-known) as well as culture and ideology. The contributions in these areas are summarised in Table 5.1.

Table 5.1 Selected constructs with HSM contributions.

Construct	HSM Contributions
Knowledge	Coordination of action
Wisdom	Explication of purpose
Purpose of enterprise	Self-production, service to society
Ethics	Mastery of micro-contexts
Synthesis	Cognitive-equilibrium, *de novo* programs
Capital	Multi-form, live and dead
Organisation	Autopoeisis, organism, boundaries
Culture	Productive practices, convergence
Ideology	Capitalism with HSM is not an ideology

5.1.1 Knowledge

Taking its cue from FA Hayek (1945), HSM starts by identifying the central problem of contemporary management as the division and re-integration of knowledge; or more precisely, the "co-ordination of complementary complexes of specific skills". In this context, knowledge should be thought of, indeed *is* the coordination of action. Put simply, knowledge equals know-how. It is not … a justified belief, or knowing-that. Managers of productive enterprises should now think of all knowledge as tacit knowledge, the rest (encoded, explicit, externalised, etc.) is simply information, or data; yet "it is the greatest truth of our age: information is not knowledge".

5.1.2 Wisdom

The action-emphasis in HSM is extended to a distinctive notion of management wisdom. It is "knowing-why" things are so. Implicitly adopting a Buddhist tenet, "know-why" is identified as a component of a larger wisdom of enterprise. In Buddhist writing (e.g. Dhammananda, 1999), it is said that "the knowledge of how things work is quite different from… wisdom, which is insight as to *why* it works, or *why* it is done". Similarly, in HSM, the wisdom of enterprise refers to management understandings of why things work (the science), why particular activities are being carried out (the strategy) and especially, why particular purposes or missions have been adopted. Elsewhere, several other components of wisdom have been identified, but they also include the selection of suitable purposes (see Chapter 7).

The other component of wisdom is "the explication of purpose". The wise entity fully communicates all its "know-why", but it does this primarily through its actions. Elsewhere, Zeleny has quoted Sir Fletcher Jones: "what a man says whispers, what he does thunders". If we are wise, our actions will automatically communicate and explicate our purposes. Furthermore, to be self-sustaining in the current environment, the purposes of an entity must be socially accepted and "validated by experience"; they must be credible and aligned with enterprise actions. Corporations can be informed; they can be knowledgeable; but in the global era "they must also become wise".

5.1.3 Purposes

HSM endorses the established idea in the field of strategic management (and long before that, in philosophy, cf. Burrell, 1989) that an entity is not completely free to select or compose its purposes and goals. To some extent these emerge from its current circumstances and activities, so they reflect its capabilities. Accordingly, the logic of business strategy includes not only the traditional (ends → ways → means) sequence, but also its reversal (means → ways → ends), and one has to search for the right goals or ends to "validate and enhance" the existing means.

To the extent that an enterprise can still freely choose its purposes, Zeleny has argued that these should not be looked for in the financial markets. The Milton Friedman maxim that the social responsibility of business is to increase its profits is rejected. On the contrary, managers of productive enterprises should *not* concern themselves with either share prices that are based upon speculative trades and deals, nor the influence of quarterly financial reports on this type of speculation. Economic institutions should absolutely not encourage such a focus. Many prominent Western industrialists and entrepreneurs have shared this rather negative view of financial markets: "a business that exists to feed profits to people who are not engaged in it stands on a false basis" (Thomas Bata, a Czech entrepreneur); "the stock market is just a little show on the side" and it "has nothing to do with business" (Henry Ford), whilst according to JF Lincoln, "the stockholder should have the lowest priority".

HSM is therefore siding firmly with the stakeholder model of enterprise, or stakeholder capitalism. The purpose of enterprise is to serve customers, employees, and society, certainly not to facilitate the accumulation of financial capital from a distance, through speculative trades. With regard to customers as stakeholders, HSM quotes JF Lincoln that "The proper responsibility of business is to build a better and better product at lower and lower price". Modern enterprises (do and should) strive to be agile and kinetic. They should strive to deal with "markets of one" (one customer, that is, not one stock-trader) just as medical doctors have always tried to respond to each individual patient and each episode.

5.1.4 Ethics

Recently, Zeleny has also proposed a "4E spine" of enterprise, in somewhat similar vein to the clichéd 4Ps of marketing and 5Ps of strategy. The "spine" is "efficiency, effectiveness, explicability (as mentioned)… and ethics". Modern managerial action should possess all four qualities. The proposed "ethics" component of the 4E spine is distinctive, and it integrates with strategy in a new way. It is a mixture of virtue ethics, pragmatism and egoism, in which ethics in business is held to be observable only at the micro-level. In general, ethical behaviour is seen to be a spontaneous inclination (rather than a planned response), and it stems "naturally" from a desire for gain. To be ethical, one simply "acts good". Accordingly, business ethics becomes a property of micro-level human behaviour, and it operates in real time (or "online", to quote Ken Goodpaster *circa* 1983). By implication, one need not attempt to obey explicitly encoded (and imposed) ethics rules. Ethics committees that struggle to compose even a few good principles (cf. Soule, 2002) are really not needed. Still more controversially, Zeleny argues that, to be "truly" ethical (i.e. act good) one cannot be intentionally "ethical" (i.e. obey official rules). One should simply act spontaneously out of an "informed sense of the good".

5.1.5 Capital

HSM endorses a multi-dimensional view of the concept of capital. There are several distinct forms of capital (Chapters 3 and 14), including human, social and ecological as well as manufactured and financial (which in turn has many sub-forms). To create prosperity at the national level, Zeleny believes that social capital is usually the most critical one, although in reality it has often been the most neglected and ignored. Social capital is "the enabling infrastructure of institutions and values" in a society. In line with Sen (1996), Zeleny also noted that Japan's wealth is primarily due to its human and social capital investments and that "strong cultures with high levels of civic trust tend to produce higher economic performance… not the other way around". Social capital cannot be engineered, but it can be deliberately cultivated. Furthermore, trade-offs in which the level of social capital is reduced in a system in order to maximise the manufactured form of capital "are rarely sustainable". Instead, enterprise strategies and national policies should both aim to achieve a balance or a harmony between the four forms, essentially by creating the right amounts of each one, rather than destroying one in order to create the other. In contrast, financial–economic models routinely incorporate or subsume the distinctive forms of capital into a single overarching formal utility (wealth or profit) function. Although this is done strictly for the purposes of formal analysis, Zeleny claimed that the different forms of capital "cannot" be subsumed into a single measure in this way; that is, such models mislead managers and policy makers (see Part 2: Chapters 9–13).

The distinction between the "manufactured" and "financial" forms of capital is important in HSM. It can be refined or recast as a distinction between "live capital" which is the re-invested monetary earnings of a productive enterprise, versus "dead" capital, which is the accumulated financial profit gained from speculative trades and deals. (Under generally accepted accounting principles within FMC, the item "retained-earnings" combines these "live" and "dead" forms. Also, human capital is reflected to some extent in the judgement-based valuation of intangibles, whilst triple bottom line reporting also incorporates the social and ecological forms.) Put simply, live capital is a very good thing: it refers to the assets used by an enterprise to produce its valued market offerings *and* future-self. It takes its place within a *natural* productive cycle:

Production → Capital → more Production

"Dead" capital is not so good. It "has as its main purpose the production of payments for owners", and it can be represented as

$$\textbf{Capital} \rightarrow \textbf{Production} \rightarrow \textbf{more Capital}$$

Although it may be obvious that both of these sequences are embedded in a recurring means-ends chain (and are modelled in financial-economics as dynamic dividend and investment decisions), the "accent" and implications for business strategy differ, under the two different representations, or frames. The first sequence coheres with the Japanese management tradition in which manufacturing and marketing are accorded a much higher priority than financial-market deals. Also, within the Anglo-US critical scholarship, one can find plenty of references to the notions like "dead" capital. For example, Manning (1988) noted that under the assumption of corporate moral agency, acquisition becomes the moral equivalent of murder, although she found that "counterintuitive" (Chapter 2). At about the same time Burrell (1989) wrote trenchantly on "linearity and death" in his broad critiques of the engineering view of economics. All such references tend to reinforce the underlying point that the "live" action-sequence is good, whilst the second sub-sequence (or frame) seems lifeless.

5.1.6 Synthesis

The development of all four forms of capital (social, human, etc.) in harmony exemplifies the ethos of "management without tradeoffs" (MWT), which is in turn a component of a larger Global Management Paradigm (GMP). GMP combines ideas such as open-books, customer and supplier integration, mass-customisation, horizontal (flat) organisation, within a mindset that continually focuses upon the elimination of trade-offs. In managerial decision making, nothing should be thought of as fixed or given (like the "given" constraints in mathematical programming problems). All trade-offs are "perceived" or "apparent", and everything can be reframed and potentially redesigned. One should always try to "*dis*-solve" any given problem, through innovation.

5.1.7 Living Organisation

The term "synthesis" is also, of course, suggestive of dialectics. Ever since that latter notion was first articulated (by Plato) it has been associated with the sciences of life and mind (see Chapters 6 and 13). Accordingly, in the HSM thesis where synthesis is a major theme, there is also a persuasive thesis on living organisation. It is also claimed that productive enterprises answer directly to a particular description of living: one that involves the biological concepts of *autopoiesis* and a "natural" life-cycle of production, bonding and degradation. The Amoeba system of Kyocera Corporation is used to illustrate and affirm this notion. The corporate entity consists of autonomous agents (associates) and teams (amoebae), linked by intra–company markets. The "amoebae" are embedded within inter-company networks of suppliers and communities of customers who are integrated into the production process and thereby extend the internal network into a functional and competitive whole, or a competitive complex.

The challenge for "strategic" managers of such a system (if any) is not "how we can sustain the system" but how we can help it to sustain itself, with its sub-systems (i.e. again like a good doctor helping a patient). In the contemporary context, Zeleny believes that these (*quasi-* or actual) biological principles continue to yield a natural, spontaneous and gainful way to arrange human affairs. He notes that "humans like change… so long as it preserves the support network that they are part of ". In contrast, the radical disruptions of productive organisation that can occur under the dictates of bureaucratic (e.g. socialist) hierarchies and under financial market capitalism (by virtue of M and A activity) are unnatural, undesirable and unnecessary. Whilst these critiques of bureaucracy and financial markets may be rather familiar, they have always been evaded or suppressed by power seekers and ideologues.

5.1.8 Ideology

According to the HSM thesis, hierarchical management is ideological and "hopeless"; its consequences are decline and corruption. Top-down state involvement in enterprise operations and ownership is especially counter-productive, along with the historically related notion of social class. Zeleny has argued that each employee or citizen should be thought of as a repository of know-how and certainly not as a representative of a class that is in need of solidarity. By implication, trade unions are no longer necessary (but see next section). Yet HSM also objects to the mainstream Anglo-US variant of financial-market capitalism (FMC), where there are too many "swindles" and too much dead capital. Accordingly, it is essentially advocating a variant of capitalism, a kind of Third Way, in which (i) enterprises are structured and viewed as self-sustaining and learning entities, (ii) stakeholders and "live capital" are fully integrated into the network and (iii) an individual's education is for enterprise, but with substance. A startling claim is then made that, unlike both socialism and FMC, such a system "is not an ideology". Zeleny insists that he has simply described and depicted a natural and spontaneous system: one that "comes to life when ideological pressures and limitations cease".

5.2 Humane Ideals

Despite that insistence, HSM moves unambiguously into the political arena when it argues against state ownership and suggests that "the state is least equipped to promulgate morality" (for an opposing view on that see for example Casson, 1998). On such a reading, there is a risk that the thesis might then become fuel for the political far right: the modern day Spencer or Hegel. Not only are enterprises modelled as social and biological systems, but their core dynamic is "human striving" to become a valued member, or a "master". The domain of HSM is effort, earning and the struggle to achieve.

The problem with these notions when viewed as components of a political doctrine (or variant of capitalism) is that only those individuals who can "earn" (or who can pay) will be able to sustain. This ethic of care comes under pressure, and the idea of moral minima applied to global society as a whole is implicitly challenged, or at best neglected. Accordingly, there remains another pressing question for contemporary managers, concerning humane ideals: can enterprises also play a role in influencing governments so that they jointly promote all aspects of morality more effectively? Modern enterprises might be able to act autopoietically and heteropoietically, co-producing not only the future enterprise and it market offerings, as was specified in HSM, but *also* fostering moral progress in a much wider sense. To do this credibly and effectively, it is surely not enough (as HSM implies) to aim only for a culture of enterprise. It is *also* necessary to

(i)   know (i.e. know-that) all market-based systems confront specific limitations regarding the ways in which they can "serve society" and "benefit all", and then

(ii)   try to compensate systematically for those known limitations.

5.2.1 *Market limitations*

The standard set of known limitations of market-based systems can be considered one at a time in relation to the HSM prescriptions, as well as business strategies within the mainstream financial market capitalism (FMC), or business-as-usual. As discussed in the previous chapter (Chapter 4) these limitations include *inter alia* the monopolistic tendencies of producers, distributive justice concerns, the inability to pay, the availability and credibility of market information, the difference between consumers' revealed preferences and their well-being, together with various forms of social alienation (Table 5.2, column 1). As a matter of strategy, most FMC-type companies routinely try to exploit all of these limitations. For example, they not only attempt to maximise their market power (see below), but also try to create desire (e.g. Crisp, 1987), to conceal information, to glamourise social alienation, and so on. As described above, HSM sets out several elements of a more enlightened strategy that can have the effect of overcoming some of those limitations (e.g. by catering honestly to markets-of-one, by re-integrating price and value, etc.). However, it has remained silent on several other limitations, especially those where the compensatory strategies of enterprise would involve an ethic of care, the protection of rights, or an assurance that all peoples' needs for income and opportunity are met to a reasonable level (refer to Table 5.2, columns 3 and 4).

It has often been noted that businesses are able to exploit market limitations as a matter of strategy. However, what has hardly ever been stated clearly and explicitly is the simple idea that all types of enterprise might now be able to serve society much better by strategically *compensating* for all of these limitations, especially if they are willing and able to act jointly in

Table 5.2 Limitations of market based systems and compensatory strategies in three variants of capitalism.

The Known Limitations	Financial Market Capitalism	Human Systems Management	Humane Ideals Management
Monopolistic tendencies	Anti-trust	Knowledge as power, hyper-competition,	Rights and empowerment through unions
Distributive justice and fairness	Government policy	Individual contribution and community needs, educate to self-sustain	Individual needs, public goods, educate to help
Ability to pay	Government policy	No handouts, paying-customer is king	Expand the network, Keynesian approaches
Information	Speculative trades positioning, PR	Authentic conversations, open books	Same
Preference versus well-being	Creation of desire, framing	Products incorporate human goods	Same
Alienation	Production for market	Re-integration of labour, knowledge and price	Integrate non-valued members
Associations	Democracy and markets, mechanistic	Democracy and markets, biological	Care, rights, moral-minima

partnership with governments, to this end.[1] Accordingly, an alternative system of enterprise (Humane Ideals Management or HIM) can be envisaged, in which this type of "compensation" strategy becomes the norm for ethical business. HIM is a hypothetical (but arguably achievable) way to arrange human affairs, and it can be thought of as a potential augmentation or adaptation of HSM and FMC (Figure 5.1). Its elements are briefly outlined in the remainder of this chapter.

5.2.2 Monopolistic tendencies

In FMC-type companies, it is standard practice to consider the strategic uses of market power that knowingly deny benefits to others (e.g. Boddewyn

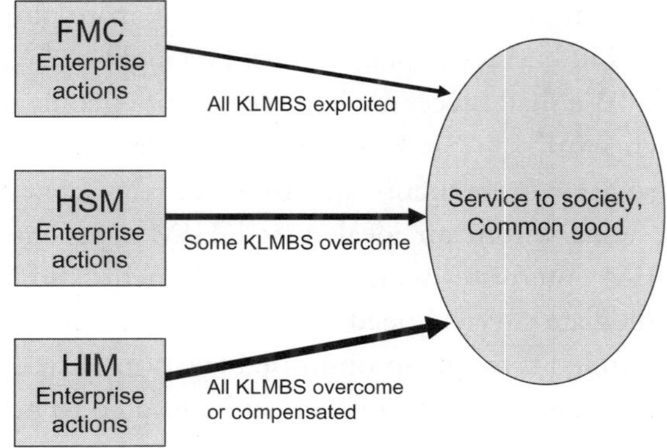

Figure 5.1   Variants of capitalism and enterprise service to society.

and Brewer, 1994). As Quinn and Jones (1995) and Prakash Sethi (2003) have all noted, this implies that there is little concern for others' rights.[2,3] To compensate for this (refer to Table 5.2, row 1), ideals-based HIM strategies would work within the spirit of anti-trust laws, but they would also work with governments to help ensure (for reasons of social service) that there is an adequate dispersion of market opportunities. The mainstream strategy literature has notably shied away from considering this type of "ideal" or ethical approach, but it has also neglected another obvious way of counterbalancing excessive corporate power;[4] that is, partnerships with trades unions. On this point, HSM sides strongly with FMC: trade unions are seen as the dysfunctional embodiment of a social class, rather than a way of building social capital. In contrast, the HIM enterprise would encourage a legitimate role for trade unions: the upholding of rights and the provision of security for those who are not yet valued members of any productive complex, or who lack the capacity to attain autonomy, or who need care.

5.2.3 Distributive justice

In HSM, enterprises strive to become valued members of a productive complex, whilst individuals who do not add value "should not take part". However, we do not find out what those people should do instead. Again and again, one hears a similar political message from those who have already succeeded in business: "people must be taught to help themselves" (Thomas Bata); "We shall succeed when we educate people to manage and direct their own work…" (Sir Fletcher Jones). One hears this much less from medics, social entrepreneurs and those on the front line of global social welfare, with whom an ideals-based HIM-type enterprise would tend to side. HIM enterprises work with governments and NGOs to help ensure that immediate survival needs are met to a reasonable level, public goods are well funded through an optimised taxation system and that people everywhere are generally encouraged and educated to help each other, directly.

5.2.4 Ability to pay

There have always been a variety of reasons why some individuals lack the "ability to pay" for at least a dignified standard of living. HSM makes no recommendation on overcoming this particular limitation (Table 5.2, row 3). Again, successful entrepreneurs do seem to know about what not to do: by dispensing gifts of money… "people become dependent on handouts and ignore their abilities of self reliance". (Zeleny, 2005) "Charity does not help people… the goal of philanthropy is to foster self-help", (Thomas Bata), and so on.

HIM, in contrast, sees that there are certain types of charitable actions that are consistent with many of the core principles of HSM, but that also endow more people with an ability to pay and to participate. Just as HSM has self-sustaining enterprises integrating customers into their production cycle, HIM enterprises attempt to integrate their employees more fully into the consumption cycle. They take direct and indirect actions (through stakeholder strategies, political lobbying and partnership) aimed at sustaining and growing the network of customers-who-can-pay. The most obvious direct action of this type is simply to lobby, to increase wages across a broad front. Recently, a senior executive of the (much criticised) Walmart Corporation mentioned this very notion: he said on TV that he was in favour of raising the national minimum wage "because minimum wage earners are our customers". A second approach to strategically expanding the customer network involves influencing governments to have more tax revenues channelled into poverty-alleviation programs. These include social safety nets (charitable social welfare) as well as bottom-of-pyramid micro-credit programs for enterprise.

5.2.5 Information

In both HSM and HIM, speculative trades and un-earned gains are associated with dead capital, and they are discouraged and regulated accordingly. This includes gains from playing the market from a distance, as well as the exploitation of insider information (Table 5.2, row 4). Under these variants of capitalism, people everywhere are encouraged instead to implement their tacit knowledge: the type that brings forth effective coordinated actions in the service of society. For example, accountants would ensure that the internal management accounts and external financial reports are as open and clear as possible, so that everyone can understand them and see how they relate to the explicated strategy of the enterprise. Similarly, marketers would ensure that "the product speaks for itself" (again, action, not encoded information). They would engage in authentic conversations with stakeholders and see to it that the company acts quickly (kinetics) in response to any revealed product weaknesses.

5.2.6 Preferences and Well-Being

Within FMC consumer markets, encoded information is routinely used to create desires, manipulate frames and obscure any known product weaknesses. Zeleny (2005) wrote that "Industrial-era" public-relations "PR" departments routinely provide spin that "no longer relates" to the public. Coupled with shock transitions from socialism to capitalism (in E. Europe), this type of abuse has already misled many young people into "flying around the flashing lights of empty promises of hope, until they end up totally exhausted with their wings already burned". In contrast, HSM (and HIM) enterprises do not try to trick people. Like Bata enterprises, they "endeavour to fulfil even the unexpressed wishes" of their customers. They produce artefacts (e.g. cars, cameras, clothing, etc.) that are infused with the human goods (beauty, quality, harmony, etc.) and that will immediately be recognised by customers as fostering their genuine well-being.

5.2.7 Alienation

Whilst they strive to meet customers' authentic requirements, HSM-type enterprises are also collectively laying to rest the 19th century Marxist idea of the alienation of the worker–producer. Under the conditions that prevailed when Marx was writing, factory workers might have been mentally numbed (made stupid) by the mechanical division of labor, whilst craftsmen might well have experienced a sense of alienation as a result of having their expressive values and identities subsumed into a singular monetary measure (price). However, as Zeleny has often remarked, in contemporary production we observe instead a *re-integration* of labour, task and knowledge. Labour is once again becoming a craft, a profession and a skill (think of *American Chopper*). Furthermore, in a spectacular inversion of Marxist thought, HSM-type enterprises think of price as an expression of their collective integrity. For them, price has become an integral part of the multi-attribute market offering. That is why Thomas Bata declared that "bargaining does not exist" and "our first word is our last". Put simply, in HSM (and in HIM) the product is always good, and so the price is always correct.

5.2.8 Political Associations

Finally, as a wider political generalisation, most variants of capitalism (Anglo-American, European, Japanese; FMC, HSM, HIM, etc.) have at times been linked with democracy and the upholding of individual freedom. In comparison with other systems (or ideologies), they are held to foster a negative freedom from state oppression, as well as the positive freedom associated with individual achievement. For FMC, such claims often confront documented episodes that attest to the contrary, involving extractor corporations and the tacit acceptance of human rights abuses. At the other end of the spectrum, these claims must be further moderated to take into account the contemporary situation in China (PRC), with its network of bilateral trade agreements.

HSM joins with proponents of FMC in making the strongest possible case for freedom, but it sees it as less dependent on national politics, but much more upon productive enterprises adopting integrator stakeholder

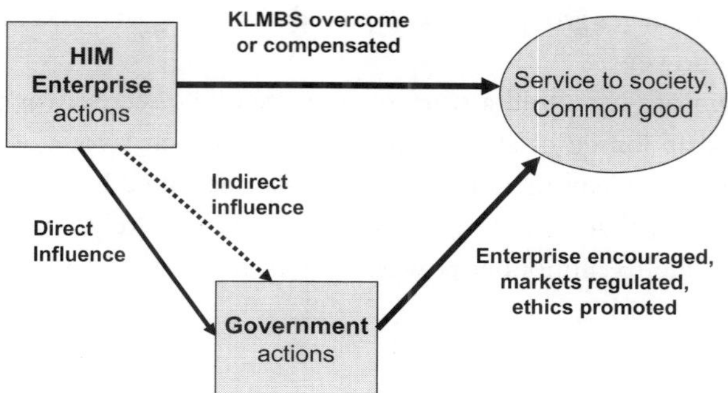

Figure 5.2 A framework for enterprise strategies that compensate for market limitations.

strategies. Zeleny (1988, *et seq.*) has appealed for a macro-level democracy "based on respect" (i.e. respect for every citizen, certainly not for authority derived from hierarchy and positional power), yet he has dismissed governments as being "least equipped" to improve the ethical or moral climate. In contrast (Figure 5.2), HIM enterprises attempt to engage and influence governments to this end, directly through lobbying as well as indirectly through their communications. This is in accordance with their explicated mission of service to society and their informed sense of the good: fully informed, that is, of the specific ethical limitations of market-based systems.

Notes

1. Strategies that compensate for market limitations implicitly recognise the moral duty for a company to act "when it co-creates bad conditions, or when there exists unjust conditions from which the company benefits" (Margolis and Walsh, 2003).
2. Like Quinn and Jones, HSM also challenges the I/O-economic framework for business strategy, but in a different way. HSM invokes elements of the hyper-competition framework (D'Aveni, 1994) such as agility, technical know-how and minimal government intervention. Unlike Quinn and Jones, neither D'Aveni, nor HSM, nor Boddewyn and Brewer considered the social and moral significance of the market power wielded by global hypercompetitive entities.
3. Prakash-Sethi (2003) argued for an accountability-based approach to this problem, suggesting that corporations should be "held accountable for a more equitable

distribution" whenever groups "were deprived… because of market imperfections and corporate power".

4. Plato's *Ring of Gyges* told a story of how excessive secrecy (or power) often results in the abandoning of ethics and moral scruples, in favour of self-gratification. A comparable phenomenon in business was identified by economist Knight (1936), who noted that "unethical" behaviour is more likely when the risks are very low (e.g. due to monopoly power) or very high, as when intense competition threatens survival.

Chapter 6

ECOLOGY: An Ecological Understanding of Global Business

Abstract: This chapter is based upon "Global business and the dialectic: towards an ecological understanding," *Human Systems Management* 21(4), pp. 249–265, 2002. It discusses the dialectical tensions that are still very evident in almost all international business episodes, as well as in the perceptions and value-priorities of once-separated civilisations. Although these have hardly ever been mentioned in the mainstream business media, as well as in professional education, much has been communicated (and replicated) on the related subjects of business-ecology, product-ecology, knowledge-ecology and ecology-of-mind. These latter ideas together with the sciences of life and mind that support biotechnology and information technology are all related to the principle of dialectic (intuitively, historically and formally). Accordingly, it is argued that much greater emphasis should now be placed upon dialectical reasoning in contemporary strategic business analysis and political calculation.

6.1 Introduction

In contemporary business and politics, it often seems that one person's considered description of a strategic problem is another's stunning reversal of the truth. For example, one media report of a recent WTO meeting, described "Citizens, who cared about the voiceless, hammering on the door of unaccountable moguls", whilst the same article depicted "Thugs trying to stop democratically elected world leaders from pondering the problems of the age". Accordingly, in international business, there are deep-rooted ambiguities, dualities, polarities and means–ends conflicts that have become very common currencies (cf. Chapter 1). Corporate communications speak enthusiastically of a global knowledge economy; yet those same economic forces relentlessly dumb-down the wider culture. Within that "knowledge economy", one again finds internal contradictions. For example, wealth is being created by restricting the circulation of ideas, but also by promoting ideas. Such dualities create dilemmas for thoughtful policy makers, but they also lie at the root of many social divisions.

6.1.1 Categories

Despite the dualities, tensions and contradictions,[1] conventional business analysis and strategy formulation continues to deal in seemingly straightforward un-conflicted categories of meaning, such as the "social, economic, ecological, political and technological" dimensions of the macro-environment (the SEEPT acronym). In this chapter, it is argued that a more useful and complete understanding might be achieved by first identifying the oppositions and contradictions that lie at the core of any such analysis, but also by giving priority consideration to the relationships between the categories (e.g. socio-political and socio-technical systems, environmental-technologies, etc.). To this end, an alternative approach to business analysis is indicated, linked to a new integrative theory of strategy. The discussion starts in the territory of economics and ethics, traverses the political and the technological, but comes to rest firmly in the ecological. The unifying theme is that of dialectical reason: the repeated articulation of opposites with their synthesis or resolution. It is indicated that most significant strategic problems, particularly those involving the knowledge economy, biotechnology and information technology (i.e. life and mind), can best be approached in this way. In fact, such an account is not at all new, but it certainly appears to have been forgotten.

6.1.2 Overview

In the following section, some international business case episodes are re-interpreted in two ways. The commercial logic of the cases, representing instrumental forms of rationality, is placed relative to the ethics associated with reflective and expressive forms of rationality. Conventional strategic analyses, media narratives and even educational texts almost always set out just one of these two interpretations, one side of the story, or one form of rationality. A similarly one-sided and incomplete view is often taken with respect to the wider macro-environment of the firm (Section 3 of this chapter). For example, in appraisals of the Left versus Right political divide, or Asian versus Western values, which are both pertinent to these case episodes, highly selective critiques and politicised rhetoric are often deployed.

Such rhetoric has been deployed before against the more general and central proposition of this chapter: that dialectical reason actually has a central place within strategic thinking. The principle of the dialectic is but one component of a larger bundle of ideas, or tenets, that is routinely ignored *in toto*. Dialectical understanding has been quite absent from the dominant discourse that has propagated the norms and rules of international business (e.g. Burrell, 1989). Yet, when it is viewed on its own merits (i.e. without political baggage) the dialectic *per se* has fantastic potential and quite obvious relevance. For example, ever since the idea was first articulated (by Plato, in 428–348 BC), it has been closely associated with development; but especially with progress in the sciences of life and mind. Given current environmental concerns, the association with "life" is timely. Given the talk about a knowledge economy, the association of the dialectic with "mind" simply demands further investigation. Accordingly, in Section 5 of this chapter, several pathways are mapped out that lead from "dialectic reasoning" to "ecological understanding" and the idea of an ecology of mind (e.g. Bateson, 1972). The final section of the chapter then briefly discusses in more general terms how philosophy might inform strategy.

6.2 Cases

Episodes of international business can be interpreted under the economic way of thinking, but *also* viewed as moral tales (Table 6.1). Indeed, it is rarely possible to determine which interpretation, the economic or the moral, is correct. Yet, contemporary reports, media accounts and educational texts (some say ideological texts) almost always offer just a singular interpretation. It can be either one, but overwhelmingly it is the economic. This persistent tendency to present just one side of a two-sided

Table 6.1 Conflicting descriptions.

Entities and Episodes	Reasons and Justifications	
	Thesis	**Anti-Thesis**
Honda, Rover and BMW	Trust building, mutual learning, "inexplicable" betrayal	Fiduciary duty mis-attribution, historical myopia
Levi Strauss	Terms of engagement, human rights concerns, clean hands, ethical leadership	Reputation, brand identity and image, free publicity, internal US politics, IPR concerns
Canon	*Kyosei* and common good, environmental-design	Aggressive patenting, nationalism, monopoly
Merck	Strategic philanthropy, spinoff products, emergent strategy, "medicine for the people", involvement of UN agencies, payments honour the culture	Lobbying for IPR, moral boundaries (e.g. AIDS), "medicine for the profits", payments devalue the culture

(or many-sided) story results in a considerable loss of practical insight, not to mention an impoverishment of learning. To illustrate, some episodes from well-documented international business case studies are briefly re-visited, in this section. They are the Honda–Rover alliance and the acquisition of Rover Ltd. by BMW, in the late 1980s (e.g. Potter, 1996; Earl, 1992); the decision of Levi Strauss to withdraw from China (e.g. Paine and Katz, 1999); the varied missions and strategies of Canon Corporation (e.g. Goodpaster, 1996; Granstrand, 1999) and finally the international activities of Merck and Co. in the 1990s (e.g. Donaldson and Werhane, 1999, p. 148–153; Kloppenberg and Gonzales, 1994). Two of the case episodes are described in economic and instrumental terms, followed by an alternative ethical account; in the remaining two, that order of presentation is reversed.

6.2.1 Honda

The first case indicates two different interpretations of a conflict involving Japanese managers' perception (of betrayal) versus the Anglo–US principle (of fiduciary duty). The first interpretation is cultural (E–W values), the second political (the ambivalent standing of "fiduciary" duty). To summarise the case very briefly, in 1988, British Aerospace (BAe) acquired Rover Ltd., from British Leyland (BLMC). Honda had been in an alliance with Rover, for some time (Appendix 6.1). From that point onward Honda's management had to do business with different entities representing different interests. They also became aware of possible further transfers of ownership of Rover. In 1993, BMW did indeed make a takeover bid for Rover and BAe decided to sell, since it needed cash for its own product development. The management of Honda reportedly viewed this sale of Rover as a "betrayal". Honda had always sought a strong association with the UK automotive industry, whilst in the US, BMW was a direct competitor of Honda.

When Earl (1992) further analysed this episode, he used the metaphor of personal relationships modelled as games of interests. For example, both parties were "mindful of the possibility of being used", and so on. However, according to Potter (1996) "the breaking (of) trust … was absolutely *inexplicable* to the management team within Honda" and "the reaction (of management on both sides)… underlined the cultural differences involved".

The inexplicable "betrayal" can be quite adequately explained with reference to the wider context: the social and political macro-environments within which all such games are played. To the English mind, the notion of a "betrayal" amongst corporate managers seems naïve and quaint. It is a throwback to a period before the European Enlightenment, before the tough rules of international trade had developed. The reported Japanese reaction, in contrast, appears to be rooted in a culture in which the fundamental conflicts inherent in capitalism seem not to have been made nearly so explicit, nor so widely recognised. In that culture, personal relationships, trust and loyalty had retained their prominence in all spheres of activity, productive as well as social. The systemic-level conflicts remained latent, unseen and unspoken.

In this case, the role of fiduciary duty, the ethic that drove BAe to sell to BMW, merits much more prominence as the locus, or site of the conflict and its explanation. Contrary to appearances, this "duty" has never been upheld as a moral principle, certainly not as a personal virtue, neither in the Western business nor in the East. It is very different from, say, trustworthiness, which might be economically prudent and morally praiseworthy, in both the East and West. The "duty" is far, indeed, from representing a cultural norm, held broadly throughout Western societies. It is not even uniformly upheld as a norm within Anglo-American businesses. Rather, it is nothing other than a temporary political settlement of the fundamental dialectical oppositions: capital versus labour; efficiency versus justice; self-interest-with-guile versus moral commitment and care, not to mention expressed preferences (e.g. for fast cars) versus genuine well-being.

It is obvious that any properly educated or reflective mind, anytime and irrespective of cultural inheritance, can quite fully comprehend these conflicts, together with any of the superficial differences amongst national cultures (e.g. Shiogi and Nakano, 1999). In practice, any "anger" displayed by a "betrayed" party might be calmed, or at least redirected, by a *dialogue* in which these systemic-level political matters are made much more explicit. Why is this political-ideological analysis of alleged "cultural" conflicts absent from practical business discourse, not to mention the many documented sources used to educate future managers? In the context of a developing global knowledge economy, this is a very serious omission. It is a dangerous and all-too-common form of dumbing-down.

6.2.2 Levi Strauss

Another well-documented episode involves Levi Strauss and Co (LS). This case illustrates a different type of conflict involving ethics, economics and politics. Like the Honda–Rover story, the episode also demonstrates the value of a dialectical reasoning in contemporary business. Here, the thesis "rational prudence" confronts its classical anti-thesis, "moral commitment" (i.e. captured versus elusive forms as indicated in the dualism of Chapter 1). Then, nested within this conflict lies another dualism: perception versus reality, or image versus substance. As in the previous example, strategic analysis becomes much more powerful when these opposites are surfaced and made explicit.

The decision of LS and Co. in the early 1990s, to withdraw completely from China has often been described and portrayed in ethical terms (Appendix 6.1). It is suggested that an individual, acting on behalf of a corporation, can make a potentially costly moral commitment to human rights (as documented in the UNHDR). Many managers at LS and other US based MNC's expressed surprise at the withdrawal, describing business opportunities in China as a "gold-rush". An alternative account of the same episode involves instrumental rationality and pragmatic considerations. Under this description, the withdrawal was based upon normal commercial criteria; it was not decided with ethics in mind (e.g. Preece, 1995). For example, other US companies were participating in the gold-rush, so a divestment decision would be quite conspicuous and hence likely to get free media attention. This would predictably support the LS brand and improve the reputation of the company. In addition, the highly publicised one-child policy in China, at that time, did not fit at all well with the LS brand image. By distancing itself from the controversy, LS was able to reinforce its quintessentially American image. By this account, it was the commercial logic, not rights concerns, that dictated the withdrawal.

This kind of analysis in terms of nested but abstract oppositions (e.g. prudence versus commitment; perception versus reality) has wider practical implications. For example, one can make a moral appeal to high-minded customers, about a policy that is actually arrived at through commercial calculations. Equally, one might make a commercial appeal to stockholders and directors and fund managers, in order to secure a policy that is really motivated by a commitment to humane ideals. From an external standpoint, such as an analyst or a stakeholder, one can never know for sure whether the communicated justifications are indeed the actual motivations for any particular business decision.[2] Making the correct call on that point, based on subtle behavioural cues, is the kind of character judgement that is the province of a true strategic and political analyst (see also Chapter 9).

6.2.3 Canon

This case (see Appendix 6.1 and Chapter 4) involves another common but fundamental dualism involving moral boundaries. It is essentially the tragedy of the commons, or the "co-operate versus defect" decision, in a Prisoners' Dilemma Game (Chapters 9 and 12). Nested within this dualism, one finds another dilemma concerning intellectual property rights, particularly patents (e.g. Granstrand, 1999; National Research Council, 2000; Watt, 2000).

Around 1994, the chairman of Canon Corporation, Mr Kaku, spoke and wrote of a corporate ethos known as *Kyosei* or "Living and working together for the common good". At the same time, Canon had been taking a leading role in the so-called "patent wars" that are still fought aggressively between Japanese and US corporations, separately and collectively. Researchers at Canon were told to "be prepared for the era to come when only some companies, strong in patents, will cooperate with each other and survive".

These two missions, "working together for the common good" and aggressive preparation for such a "new era", are in tension with one another. *Kyosie* indicates community and trust, like a "co-operate" decision in a PDG. Strategic patenting seeks unilateral advantage, like a "defect" decision. Moreover, in evaluating the latter policy, one quickly uncovers further oppositions and dilemmas. The economic case for IPR, even in terms of instrumental rationality, is famously contentious. Furthermore, Watt (2000, p. 146) has noted that "foreign discrimination is built into the (Western invented) patent system, and it is still present, to some extent". Such "discrimination" plainly conflicts with the idea of the "common good". The dilemma can be further deepened by any separate consideration of the moral, psychological and political effects of IPR regimes; that is, their overall consequences for human well-being and social justice (see Chapter 16). Once again, as analysis of this business strategy case probes to increasing depths, the nested dialectical oppositions become ever more apparent.

6.2.4 Merck

A final example in this chapter involves Merck Corporation (Merck, Sharpe and Dohme). Like the previous case, this episode also involves the historical dilemma of patenting policies, particularly the perceived trade-off between incentives for innovation versus monopoly power; but it also highlights the oppositions between means versus ends, or instrumental versus expressive forms of rationality.

The case starts with a narrative of corporate social responsibility: the development of a drug to cure a terrible illness amongst impoverished African communities, which could not be justified in conventional commercial terms. As is commonly the case, this philanthropic project over time yielded profitable by-products, including a new AIDS treatment. However, since the late 1990s, the price of AIDS drug cocktails have become conspicuously high, due to the market power created by the patenting system (often justified with reference to the perceived need for incentives for innovation and the systemic requirement for an expected return on capital). The patenting system (not to mention knowledge-capitalism in general) has been very strongly supported by the lobbying activities of the US pharmaceutical industry, of which Merck is, of course, a very prominent member.[3]

A related episode involves Merck's (1990) licensing agreement with *InBio*, of Costa Rica (e.g. Kloppenberg and Gonzales, 1994). *InBio* is a non-profit NGO, whose purpose is to protect bio-diversity. It obtains revenue by supplying organisms, under contract, to private companies. One deal with Merck reportedly raised USD1m, to be spent on protecting native species. This apparent win–win synthesis of economics with ecology (cf. Section 6.5.2) was praised by many but also criticised, by some, for completely ignoring another major stakeholder: the indigenous Talamanca Indians. It was their tribal land from which the various samples were taken. This critique is derived from the idea that the very act of placing a financial value on any resource or product actually de-values it (i.e. it becomes a lose–lose situation, rather than a win–win). Put differently, the intrinsic or expressive values of the resources remain so long as they are embedded in their cultural contexts, but this "value" is destroyed by commercialisation.

Not many corporate managers today have much patience for such ideas. Indeed, they are more likely to argue that the cultural values are upheld and honoured by becoming embedded in a global economy. Yet, tenets such as "lobbying opposes the public interest" or "price destroys value" are elements of a quite standard critique of capitalism, as a system (cf. Section 6.4). These ideas are quite absent from the contemporary business media and from most business literature. Yet, as the cases indicate, they can add to anyone's understanding of the political macro-environment of business, with its surprising dynamics. Strategists who are enlightened on this point might be able to forestall unwanted outcomes, whilst investment analysts might be better able to the kinds of threats that can arise, together with their probable effect on the shareholder wealth.

6.3 Values

In addition to the dialectical oppositions revealed in the above four episodes, one can also point to diametrically opposed understandings that involve entire national and regional cultures, particularly the so-called Eastern (Asian) versus Western "values". As many have noted (e.g. Mintzberg, 1988; Pucik and Hatvany, 1983; Fukuyama, 1992; Hampden-Turner and Trompenaars, 1997; *The Economist*, 1998; Sen, 1999, to mention but a few) cultural differences, along with the varied perceptions of those differences, can potentially effect the conduct of international business. These perceptions and descriptions have themselves been the subject of many disputes. Alternative interpretations have been offered, and forms of synergy or synthesis have been advocated.

6.3.1 Trans-valuations

More specifically, each and every one of the characteristics, value-priorities or principles that have at times been associated with Eastern (or Western) business conduct, has also been questioned, challenged and re-described with an opposite emphasis. As displayed earlier (in Table 4.3), the extent to which any given tenet or principle has been attributed to a particular culture evidently varies over time and site.

Other similar re-descriptions or trans-valuations are easy to find (see Chapter 4). For example, a cultural propensity to "wait and see" has been re-described as a lack of leadership (e.g. Shiogi and Nakano, 1999). A network of trusted suppliers, carefully cultivated over time, might be re-cast as proof of collusive practice; moral sentiments such as *Kyosie* quickly confront unspoken moral boundaries (i.e. How common is the "common" good?), and so on.

6.3.2 Synergies (re-visited)

Just as some have described and re-described cultural differences, others have advocated cultural synergy and synthesis (quite in accordance with Chapter 3 and the principle of the dialectic). For example, in Japan, Maruyama (1992) suggested that we should "figure out ways to make positive uses of the differences between the multiple logics that are present to varying degrees in different cultures", whist Yawata (1994) wrote that "every concrete case of (economic) capital operation in society is a synthesis, of social, institutional and cultural factors". More recently, Shiogi and Nakano (1999) suggested that "harmonisation (between global business and local cultures) has become the crucial factor in the internationalisation process". Meanwhile, in Korea, Don Ki Kim suggested (c.1995) that "the right way forward for Korean management is to develop a hybrid of Confucian thought and Western cultural factors".

From a European perspective (as described earlier in Chapter 3), Ritzer and LeMoyne (1991) described synergies within the Japanese (Eastern) industry in terms of (Western) Neo-Weberian rationalities. Trompenaars (1993, p. 174) wrote that "transnational structures allow us to synthesise the advantages of all cultures, while avoiding their excesses". Later, Hampden Turner and Trompenaars (1997) described many dynamic complementarities amongst Westerns and Eastern values (refer Section 5). Finally, with reference to China and America, both Goodpaster (1994) and Linstone and Zhu (2000) have contrasted "modes of understanding" and "frames of reference" for decision-making, whilst they have advocated the design of "bridges" and the creation of synthesis, respectively.

6.3.3 Political Interests

Many who emphasise cultural differences, rather than advocating and designing syntheses, appear to have personal and political interests in promulgating distinctive interpretations of the "Asian versus Western values", not to mention that other story of "Left versus Right" political orientations (e.g. Sen, 1999; Giddens, 1998). Sen, in particular, has noted that those who link "Asian values" to economic success are typically in powerful positions … in Asia. For them, it is rather convenient to talk up virtues such as "obedience and loyalty", whilst maintaining a strategic silence on the historical fact that the West has also had similar "traditions"… promulgated by Plato and St. Augustine (amongst others) but now thoroughly superseded and forgotten.

To further complicate matters, many documented descriptions of generic East–West value-differences appear to be somewhat self-reproaching. For example, Shiogi and Nakano (1999, p. 175) in Japan wrote of a "tendency to overlook evils, in order to preserve harmony". Yet, several years earlier, when there was a fear in the US of "Japan as #1" Mintzberg (1988, p. 351) described the typical Japanese corporation as having a "more developed, stylistically rich ideology" than its US counterparts. In similar vein, narrative comparisons of Western takeover activities (e.g. BMW and Rover) with the internal or "organic" development of Asian corporations (e.g. Canon) also seem to carry the same self-reproaching subtext … when they are written by Western authors: the other "culture" is superior in important respects. Such descriptions are especially common in articles that were written in the West, during the era of comparatively very rapid growth of some Asian economies.

6.3.4 Rhetoric

As indicated in the above account, discussions and considerations of regional value differences (and the Left–Right political divide) frequently deploy rhetorical devices. Language is used to promote interests, rather than to furnish objective descriptions. In the context of international business and political rhetoric, two such devices are especially common. They are

   (i)   criticising and then rejecting a big idea, by simply critiquing selected components or elements of that idea, and

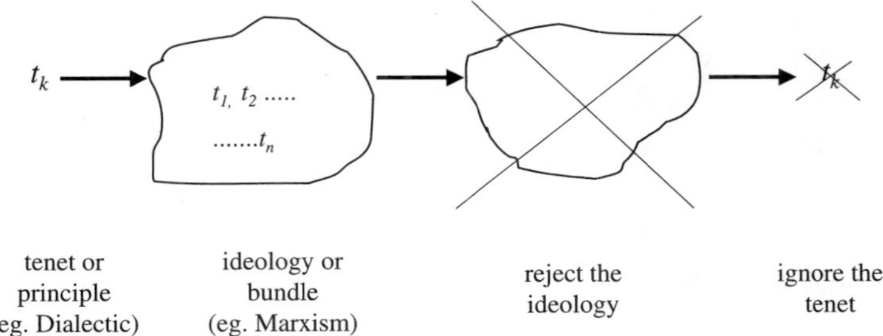

Figure 6.1 A rhetorical device.

(ii)   criticising and then rejecting a particular component of a big idea, by first *bundling* that component into the big idea, then *rejecting* the whole bundle, including the original component (Figure 6.1).

Sen (1999) mentioned the former device when deployed in relation to "Asian Values" in general; but it is the latter tactic that is most pertinent in the present context. A spectacular example of the "bundle then reject" political rhetoric concerns the very idea of the dialectic itself. This particular principle or tenet has been very thoroughly "bundled" into "bigger ideas" that are nothing less than anti-capitalist ideologies. The principle of the dialectic has thus become shunned, ignored and excluded from strategic analysis and the wider discourse of international business, both in the East and in the West, precisely because of those (unfortunate) anti-business associations. This phenomenon might be dismissed as a nothing more than a trivial example of faulty reasoning, or cognitive simplification in managerial decision making; but in the context of a knowledge economy and business ecology it has become a very costly error.

6.4 Dialectic

When the dialectic is viewed on its own merits, detached from the wider ideological and cultural baggage, it appears to have fantastic relevance to contemporary productive practices, strategic business theories and political confrontations. As already indicated, it can come to the fore whenever conflicting perceptions and principles exist and have the (unseen) potential to impact upon business valuation and success. In international business, this is almost always the case. In addition, there are many theoretical linkages between dialectical reasoning and ecological understanding (Section 5 of this chapter). This means that those who claim to display the latter out of political correctness, or out of genuine concern about the environment, can no longer lightly dismiss the former. At the very least, the complete absence and rhetorical exclusion of the dialectic from the dominant contemporary discourse of business and management requires some further explanation. It becomes understandable only when one reviews some of the ideas historically associated with the dialectic and with its main (infamous) proponents. These are outlined in the following sections.

6.4.1 History

The term "dialectic" originates from the Greek *dialektos,* meaning discourse or debate. In the writings of Plato (428–324 BC), it specifically referred to binary oppositions, tensions and contradictions amongst ideas (just like the dualism in Chapter 1). The principle was developed to include the idea that all levels of knowledge advance through a process of *Thesis*, or posit; *Antithesis* or counter-posit; then *Synthesis* (T–A–S). The history of the dialectic then reveals three main phases (Table 6.2). Up to *circa* 1900, there was repeated formulation, expression and recognition. In ancient Greece, Plato considered the dialectic to fully characterise the progress of reason. Much later, in Germany, Fichte (1762–1814) first expressed the principle explicitly as "T–A–S". Hegel (1770–1831) then identified this as "the required approach for all significant non-mechanical problems" (cf. Reece, 1980), whilst Engels (1820–1895) saw the dialectic as operating at all levels of reality and nature, where it embodies the "qualities of life and mind".

The 20th century saw ultimately destructive interpretations and enactments of the principle. It was used to afford an intellectual justification to monumental power struggles. It was invoked, by Vladimir Lenin in the context of the class struggle (labour versus capital), where the enacted "synthesis" was revolutionary violence and the forced re-distribution of power and property. The dialectic was also present at the other political extreme, within Nazi ideology. Here the enacted synthesis of "have versus have-not" nation states was to be nothing less than World War II.

Table 6.2   The principle of the dialectic in three eras.

Pre-20th century: recognition, formulation, expression

- Characterises the progress of reason
- Expressed as T–A–S
- Identified as the required approach for all significant non-mechanical problems
- Seen to operate at all levels of reality
- Especially operates in nature, concerning qualities of life and mind

20th century: re-interpretation, enactment

- Applied to power struggles (passions, appetites) rather than to reasons, morals and human ideals
- Applied to social classes, where the enacted synthesis is revolution (and re-distribution)
- Applied (indirectly) to have versus have-not nation states, where the enacted synthesis is warfare

21st century: resurrection, re-assertion

- Indicates and warns of potential for totalitarian *corporatism* (through use of reason to justify and apologise for power, as in the case re-interpretations)
- Draws attention to opportunities for synthesis created by technologies (synergy orientation, win–win, super optimisation)
- Re-established at the core of ecological thinking through (a) intuition, (b) design, (c) levels of analysis.

Despite this dismal track record, the 21st century now holds out the promise of a resurrection and re-assertion of dialectical reasoning in business and politics (cf. Fukuyama, 1992). It now comes in a different form. Social classes and nation states are no longer the most relevant entities to which the principle applies. Rather, in the contemporary context of shifting alliances and knowledge economics, it refers more directly (and usefully) to *abstract* propositions, or knowledge, such as the common-good versus patent wars; rights talk versus free publicity; monopoly power versus moral commitment, instrumental versus values-based actions, and so on. A dialectical analysis of any significant contemporary business problem simply sets out conflicting narratives and perspectives as its starting point (as indicated earlier, in Section 6.2). Typically, an elite-consensus view can be consciously juxtaposed with a critical account (see Chapter 16) perhaps expanded to include minority voices and other cultural-specific understandings (as noted in the Merck case). "Synthesis" then consists of the creation of a new and more inclusive narrative (e.g. Werhane, 1999a) with the co-production of new explicit knowledge.

The history of the dialectic also serves as a timely reminder of the future macro-environmental scenario of totalitarian corporat*ism* (e.g. MacPherson, 1985), as distinct from national social*ism* and commun*ism*. (Thomas Bata was quoted in Zeleny (2005, p. 288) as claiming that "No '-ism' ever helped anybody or resolved anything. And it never will"; but such statements do not make ideology vanish.) The last century amply demonstrated how political extremism becomes more likely whenever rhetoric is deployed in order to justify power; but many see that happening now, in the strategic behaviour of international corporations and especially private media corporations. Finally, the intuitive associations of the dialectic with "life and mind" can be re-expressed more formally and more completely, by revisiting some late 20th century discoveries (Section 6.5). To the extent that the dialectic is thus strongly associated with ecological thinking, it has yet another basis for inclusion in any contemporary global management paradigm.

6.4.2 Rejection

Despite these good prospects, there remains a great reluctance to consider dialectical reason in strategic analysis, or even when using a business case episode as a learning device. Instead, an engineering view of business strategy (and economics) undoubtedly prevails. Most managers and business educators adopt and deal with a singular elite-consensus view of reality, in much the same way as a mechanic works with a given troublesome engine. Their tendency to downplay or ignore the dialectic seems not to be entirely due to the qualities and attributes of the idea itself. Rather, it might be more fully explained by the rhetorical "bundling" of ideas referred to earlier (Section 6.3.4), that is also evident in contemporary discussions of regional cultures and politics.

As indicated in Figure 6.1, the principle of the dialectic certainly carries with it a great deal of political and ideological baggage, much like the ideas of "Asian values" and "Left-wing politics". This can be further illustrated with reference to ideas and principles associated with particular individual philosophers (i.e. Plato, Fichte, Hegel, Marx and Confucius) whose names are also most closely linked to the dialectic, as follows:

(i) Plato not only described the dialectic, but also advanced the idea that the leaders in a society should have as their goal the well-being of the people, with a primary focus on the human goods, such as health, justice and friendship. He further insisted that these "goods" were not to be confused with what the people may wish (Reece, 1980), that is, their market preferences.[1] This recipe for social advancement is the exact anti-thesis, of the commercial strategy of "giving the people what they want". Accordingly, libertarians and conservatives everywhere are well-armed: they can quickly dismiss Plato's ideas *in toto*, including the dialectic.

(ii) Fichte, subsequently, developed the idea of the dialectic, but he can similarly be condemned by association. He identified with Kant (1724–1804) whose categorical imperative, "behave only according to a *maxim* that one would wish to see universalised", is antithetic to most principles of competitive strategy (e.g. Koslowski, 2001). Moreover, a variant of that imperative requires every person (e.g. employers) to always treat other people at least partly as "ends in themselves", whereas commercial practices such as layoffs frequently violate this.[4] Once again, the dialectic can again be made to appear guilty by an association with apparently anti-capitalist and anti-business ideas.[5]

(iii) Hegel is perhaps most widely associated with the "T–A–S" form of the dialectic, although he never actually used that particular phrase (Reece, 1980). Hegel also wrote that "idea, or truth posits its opposite, and rises to synthesis over and over again". He saw the dialectic operating within and between social systems. Significantly, in this context, he was also "one of the first European philosophers to incorporate Asian (Indian and Chinese) ideas into his overall scheme" (Fukuyama, 1992, p. 60). Hegel was also influenced by Kant, whilst Hegelian teachings in turn were influential amongst Marxists philosophers. As Fukuyama (1992, p. 59) has also noted, such associations have led to "prejudice against Hegel" and have "blinded people to his (contemporary) importance".

(iv)   Marx (1818–1883) is widely associated with "Marx-ism", a "bundle" or ideology that has many contributors, but is anathema to the contemporary elite. In addition to embracing the dialectic, Marxism also claims, for example, that property divides people and that production for the market fosters alienation, or a "sense of void in inner life". Hence it appears to be the anti-thesis of capitalism. Yet several distinctive "claims" or tenets of Marxism remain relevant to business strategic analysis, such as (a) the decline in relative importance of (nation) states and (b) the powerful influence that the mode of production (e.g. IT, global media, etc.) can have on a society's culture, not to mention the dialectic itself.

(v)   Finally, Confucian and Neo-Confucian thought also contains a principle quite similar to the dialectic: "the rectification of the one and the many" (e.g. Wu, 1967, p. 140), with the further idea that "harmony is achieved by affirming both, in the here and now." Once again, on the surface, this Eastern philosophical tradition also appears to be a "bundle" of anti-business sentiments. Like the Kantian ethics, Neo-Confucianism is fundamentally humanistic. It upholds the importance of ritual over desire; administrative posts in government over "less government"; gentlemanly conduct (*Li*) over street-trading; "loving thy neighbour" (*Jen*) over competition; as well as filial piety (male loyalty) over consumer rage.

Since Confucianism and Marxism seem quite out of place in contemporary dumbed-down, consumer-driven, gender-conscious societies, it has become all too easy to completely dismiss and even mock the principle of the dialectic, as well. Yet, ironically, political conservatives and business planners in the East and the West now would almost certainly endorse many specific tenets of Neo-Confucianism,[6] together with quite a few Marxist principles, as already mentioned. Therefore, excluding the principle of the dialectic from contemporary business analysis, simply because of its wider anti-business associations, is quite like throwing out the baby with the bathwater. Although the dialectic is associated with corrupted historical movements and unpopular attitudes, a more careful account suggests that it can be resurrected and re-evaluated very positively, on its own merits. As already mentioned, any such re-evaluation would also include a contemporary account of the increasingly well-understood linkages between dialectic reason and ecological thinking.

6.5 Ecology

Ever since the dialectic was first articulated, it has been intuitively associated with progress in the sciences of life and mind. Yet, amidst all the contemporary talk about information technology, knowledge economy, biotechnology and environmentalism, the D-word itself is rarely, if ever, mentioned.[7] The ancient association can now be substantially updated and reinforced. Recently, several new pathways have been laid down, linking the "D-word" to ecology and hence to environmentalism (the "E-word").

To travel these pathways and see the linkages, one must first step back, re-casting the dialectic in terms of the more elementary idea of *difference*. From that starting point, thesis and anti-thesis (T–A) simply become perceived differences, or contrasts: the elementary building block of all perception and cognition. Examples include (a) the binary 0–1, (b) the moves C–D, in a Prisoners' Dilemma Game, and (c) the many–one distinction referred to in Confucian philosophies. Synthesis (S) then becomes any type of unification or resolution of those differences; some form of rectification of the "many and the one". It is any process whereby the different elements are brought together, into a new but temporary unity.

The following sections (6.5.2 and 6.5.3) give a brief account of two historical but intuitive associations and linkages between dialectic and ecology. Then, forms of unification or synthesis are outlined; first by design, then by the collapsing of distinct levels-of-analysis and description into a single level, through processes of self-reference and self-replication. The final linkage (Figure 6.2) involves repetition, expressed here as iterated or recursive computational procedures.

6.5.1 Intuitions

Two thousand years after Plato's early intuitions, Friedrich Engels (1820–1895) wrote that the dialectic operates especially in nature, where "matter gains the qualities of life and mind" (Reece, 1980). Half a century later, the great anthropologist, Gregory Bateson (1904–1980) characterised "ecological

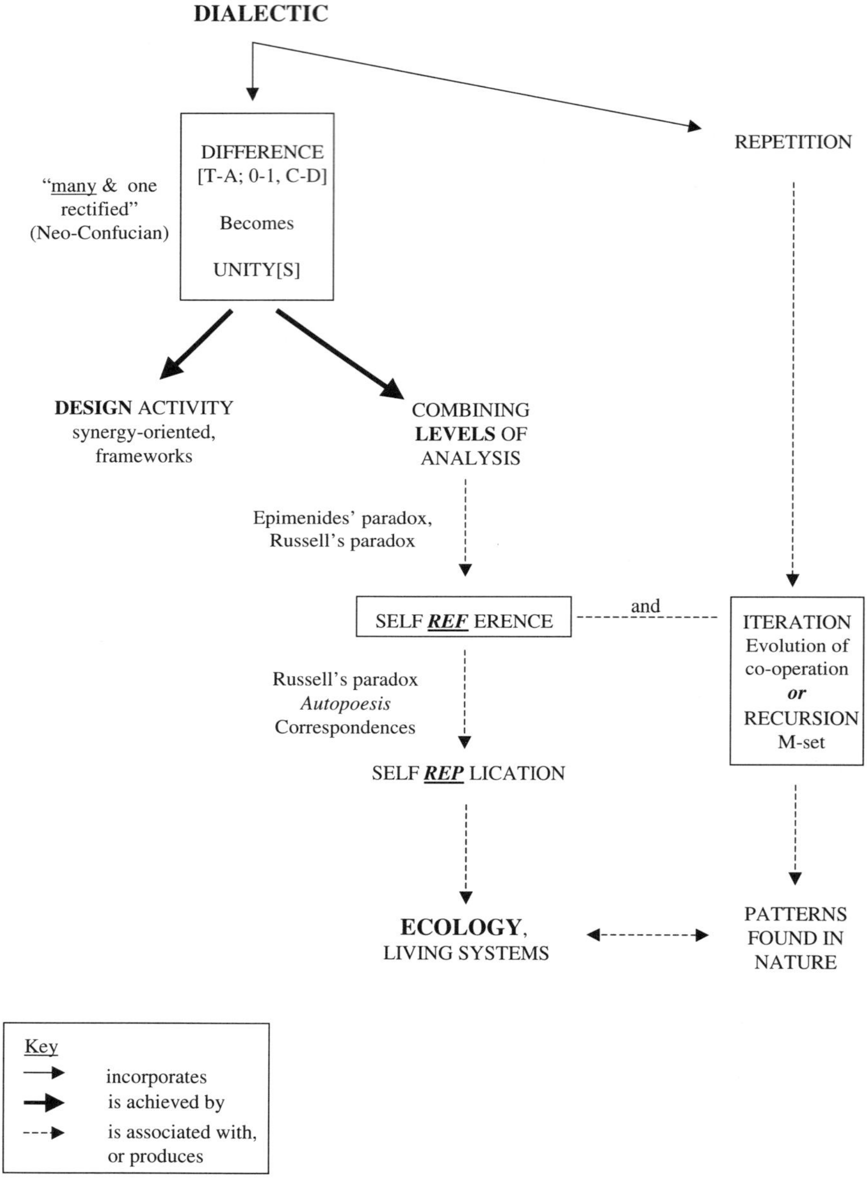

Figure 6.2 From dialectic to ecology.

understanding" in terms of differences, levels-of-analysis and repeated self-reference or recursivity (Bateson, 1972; Harries-Jones, 1995). Similar ideas were then incorporated by Laing (1969) into a formal theory of mind which became the basis for an applied psycho-therapy: a rectification of mental life. Laing particularly saw that emotional disturbances result from communications at different levels that conflict with one another. All these ideas were then further developed intuitively by Hofstadter (1979), as described below (in Section 6.5.3)

Almost 20 years after that, this time inspired by pragmatic business consulting (but, as is typical, without referring to any of the above ideas and sources), Hampden Turner and Trompenaars (1997, p. 234) described their own intuitions about the management of cross-cultural complementarities with their apparent similarities to biological processes. Addressing business audiences, they explicitly "borrowed the metaphor of the DNA molecule" whilst confessing that "value synthesis is not protein synthesis". They then depicted an infinitely recurring dynamic interaction of principles and practices, a virtuous circle, or "infinite game", which was finally depicted as a strand of DNA. Most significantly and predictably, in this context, they never mentioned the "D-word"!

6.5.2 Design

A second pathway from dialectic to ecology (i.e. other than intuition) is more concrete, as it involves actual synergistic designs,[8] particularly designs involving profit and the natural environment. As with the value-differences and synergies described earlier (Section 6.3), there are several contrasting narratives involving ecology and business. Many of these comprise a thesis and anti-thesis, such as development versus conservation; economics versus thermo-dynamics, or linear growth versus complex systems (e.g. Partridge, 1999; Simon, 1999). The narrative synthesis is then found in stories of green business success, profitable environmental restoration or the deployment of environmental technologies for competitive advantage and economic efficiency (e.g. Shrivastava, 1995; Hawken, 1993; Werhane, 1999a to mention but a few).

6.5.3 *Levels of Analysis*

A third way of linking the dialectic with ecology (i.e. after intuition and synergistic design) involves the bringing together (or the rectification) of different levels of meaning and representation (Figure 6.2). This can be done by appealing to various forms of self-reference. Like the dialectic, the idea of self-reference also has its origins in classical Greek thought, specifically, in Epimenides' paradox (cf. Hofstadter, 1979), as follows: in the natural language sentence "This sentence is false", the thesis that the sentence in the markers is true quickly generates in the mind the anti-thesis that it is false. There follows a search for a resolution of the contradiction and a reduction of the cognitive dissonance.

More than 2000 years later, the paradox was re-stated by Bertrand Russell in more formal set-theoretic language, as Russell's paradox. Given the notion of sets and membership, one can understand the meta-mathematical sentence "the set of all sets that are not members of themselves". The thesis that "this set contains itself" then yields in the mind its anti-thesis: that it does not. To resolve the uncomfortable contradiction, a more elaborate Theory of Types was "designed" and explicitly documented in *Principia Mathematica*. That theory made a clear distinction between levels of logic, between signs (e.g. sentences) and their referents (meanings, semantics).

The next step towards an ecological understanding of dialectics occurred when Russell's paradox was restated as a natural-language riddle involving self-production or self-transformation:

> "In a certain village, there is a barber who only shaves the men who <u>do not</u> shave themselves. Who shaves the barber?"

This time, the thesis that the barber shaves himself quickly generates in the mind the anti-thesis that he does not. Here, an entity (the barber) is producing a slight variant of itself (i.e. the shaved version). This distinctive idea of "production of future self", or *Autopoiesis*, has become well recognised as an important quality of "living" systems (Maturana and Varela, 1980). It was developed (and still is being expanded) into a theory of "living organisation" by Zeleny (1981). At about the same time, Hofstadter (1979, p. 535) independently reviewed "some of the mechanisms that create self reference" in various contexts and then went on to compare them

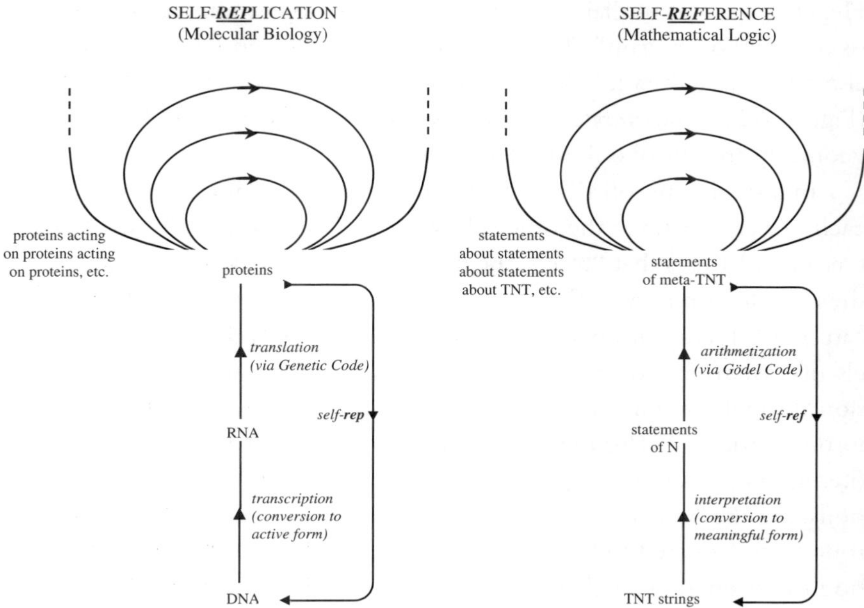

Figure 6.3   Hofstadter's self–ref and self–rep.

point-by-point with mechanisms that self-replicate. He identified some "remarkable and beautiful parallels" which are depicted in Figure 6.3 (adapted from Hofstadter 1979, p. 533).

At the base of the figure we find a string of symbols within a formal abstract system called typographical number theory, TNT, mapped onto a single DNA molecule. The interpretation of the string (i.e. its conversion to a meaningful form) is then placed in correspondence with the biological transcription of DNA to RNA (i.e. its conversion to active form), and so on. In this way, the "mechanism" of self-reference which has been viewed here as one way of unifying difference is seen to be the same (i.e. up to isomorphism) as the self-replication of a real living system.

6.5.4 Repetition

A final line of thinking that links dialectic and ecology involves repetition in conjunction with self-reference, that is, iteration and recursion. In the

Hegelian version of dialectic, the binary T–A opposition "rises to synthesis over and over again". This repetitiveness component of the dialectic can also be associated with "life and mind" when it is linked with self-reference (Figure 6.2). The *iterated* Prisoner's Dilemma Game (PDG) and fractal geometry are but two illustrative examples.

In a single one-off PDG, defection formally dominates; it is better for each player, whatever the other player does. This thesis famously encounters an anti-thesis that "to co-operate" is the correct rational move, due to the overall symmetry of the game. The famous and uncomfortable paradox can be explored within a theory of meta-games, which is an explicit levels-of-analysis approach; but it finds a more compelling dissolution (solution through design) in the iterated version of the PDG, as demonstrated in the work of Axelrod (1984 *et seq.*). By repeatedly selecting algorithms (i.e. abstract players) for participation in each round (of about 200 iterations) on the basis of their success in accumulating points from previous rounds, the iterated PDG was shown to be a rich metaphor for the evolution of co-operative behaviour, as it occurs in the natural world or in the new world of business.[9]

This connection of dialectic and ecology through iterative processes is further strengthened with reference to computational procedures in the contemporary field of fractal geometry. The link between repeated self-reference and ecological systems became much more apparent in the late 20th century when powerful computers (themselves using many levels-of-analysis) were deployed to explore particular mathematical relationships. As is now rather well known, given any point **C** in the complex number plane (Argand diagram), its membership of a particular set, the **M**-set, can be determined by a computer algorithm. The criterion for membership is whether or not a corresponding infinite sequence remains well behaved and bounded versus diverging to infinity (yet another binary difference) under repeated (i.e. recursive) applications of a simple algorithm. For the particular straightforward function: $Z_{k+1} = Z_k^2 + \mathbf{C}$ (and $Z_0 = 0$), this partitioning of the complex plane produces the **M**-set which unmistakably appears like a living object.[10] Similar recursive computations have subsequently produced many of the patterns that are found in nature.

6.6 Strategy

In contemporary strategic management theory, where the dialectic is ignored, phrases like business ecology, product ecology, knowledge-economy and the like are nonetheless frequently deployed. Many popular business books (and plans) are superficially adorned with pictures of forests and fractal ferns. Yet the fundamental contradictions, oppositions and dilemmas that lie at the core of real ecological systems and the capitalist business systems are hardly ever mentioned. These have been relegated to the far fringe of management literature and to the periphery of the business school curriculum.

According to the ideas set out in the preceding sections, however, this situation is due to change. If there is going to be some new global paradigm for managing the technologies of life and mind (Bio-technology, IT) it will inevitably bring with it a resurrection and renewed emphasis upon the dialectic. Put differently, if that principle continues to be excluded from the dominant discourse of business due to its weighty historical baggage (refer Section 6.4), the very foundations of any knowledge economy, not to mention natural capitalism and culturally appropriate economic development, will be quite hollowed out and undermined.

If one accepts instead that a new strategy paradigm should be developed that places the dialectic at its core, then Figure 6.2 (above) might be used as a crude map. It depicts some of the territory and some of the access routes. If such a theory were to develop and spread, it would quickly displace or at least complement theories based upon value-creating exchanges, which still remain at the core of business thinking. Marketing, for example, is still officially "the science of exchanges". Although the idea of exchange remains quite elemental, it is surely being joined by the ideas of self-reference and self-replication (e.g. replication of knowledge, copying of ideas, etc.). Put more technically, the formal preference relations that lie at the base of the Neo-classical economic paradigm will eventually become supplanted by, or at least augmented by, formal recursive relations in models of business strategy.

6.6.1 Trans-disciplinarity

New models and theories of the strategy of productive entities will not only have to incorporate recursive relationships, but also (like old theories)

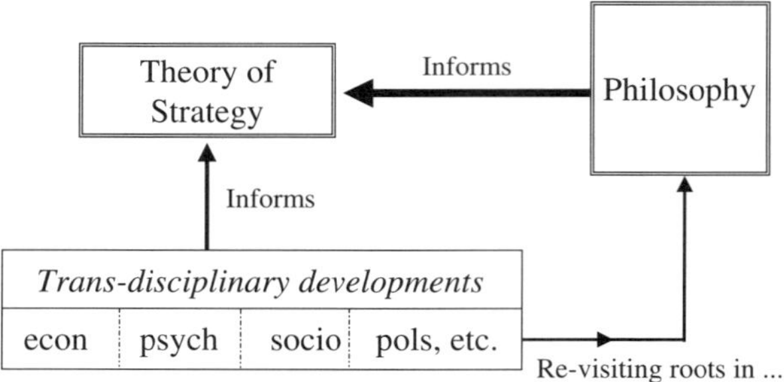

Figure 6.4 Philosophy and strategy.

actually have to be self-referential (see Chapter 9). They will compete, as theories, for a share-of-mind in much the same way as the competitive strategic entities (i.e. the firms and knowledge producers) that they claim to refer to (e.g. Singer, 2001b). At the same time, new theories of strategy are also bound to be *trans*-disciplinary. Indeed the very idea of a knowledge-economy has thoroughly problematised any lingering notions of separated source-disciplines for management theory.[11]

At the same time, within the remnants of each "source discipline" one finds a current tendency to revisit and re-examine the philosophical roots (Figure 6.4). As a result, comparative-philosophy, cognitive-science, epistemology and ethics have become identified as the new "sources". As indicated in Chapter 2, it is also becoming apparent that documented business episodes and consulting texts have the potential to guide and inform even these fundamental disciplines, for example, by documenting paths to human fulfilment or downfall under contemporary conditions. Put differently, philosophy can inform strategy and vice versa (e.g. Burrell, 1989; Singer, 1991b, 1994a; Calori 1999).

6.7 Conclusion

At the outset, dialectical tensions were observed between alternative accounts of contemporary events. Similar tensions are now very evident in most business episodes and amongst the wider value-priorities associated with civilisations and classes (e.g. East versus West, First World versus Third World, labour versus capital, one religion versus another, and so on). It is regrettable indeed that these tensions have hardly ever been mentioned in the mainstream business media and only very rarely in university based business education. At the same time, much has been written, reported and replicated on new business theories and paradigms, or economic transitions, not to mention environmental management and the ecology of business. Since all of the latter are associated intuitively, historically and formally with the principle of dialectic, the time has come to discard the baggage of the last century and to re-install dialectical reasoning as a central principle in strategic business analysis, as well as political calculation, indeed, when operating at all levels of reality. The need for this progressive step has never been more obvious.

Appendix 6.1

Summary of the Four Case Episodes

(i) Honda, Rover and BMW

Twenty years ago, in England, Rover was owned by the British Leyland Motor Corporation (BLMC) which was partly owned by the government. Rover needed a partner to help it "build a modern car in a hurry" (Potter, 1996). Meanwhile, in Japan, Honda needed to gain access to EEC markets. Accordingly, Rover management approached Honda, and a strategic alliance gradually developed. There were opportunities for Rover to learn about Japanese TQM and for Honda to learn about the styling of luxury interiors. Honda was to receive profits from supplied components, as well as royalties. Over several years, a higher level of integration was steadily achieved (Earl, 1992); however, many difficulties were encountered, such that Mr. Yokoyama, the MD of Honda R&D, spoke of a "basic difference in corporate cultures".

(ii) Levi Strauss

In the early 1990s LS and Co. was outsourcing sewing and finishing work to workshops and factories in Latin-America and Asia, including China (Paine and Katz, 1999; Preece *et al.* 1995). Media reports of harsh working conditions at a supplier based in Guam prompted the LS management to document "Business Partner Terms of Engagement", or acceptable employment practices for supplier firms. In Bangladesh, for example, LS paid for under-age employees to attend school. Later, a China Policy Group (CPG) was formed which recommended constructive engagement in China and other countries. However, the CEO overturned this recommendation, ordering a complete withdrawal from China within three years. The public justification of the decision referred to human rights issues.

(iii) Canon

Around 1994, the chairman of Canon Corporation, Mr Kaku, spoke and wrote of a corporate ethos known as *Kyosei* or "Living and working together for the common good" (see Chapter 4). During the 1980s, Canon developed efficient and recyclable photocopier drums, reducing pollution. It was said that "learning to tolerate diverse cultures and to accept their differences" was essential for happiness. US-based observers (e.g. Goodpaster, 1996; Donaldson, 1996a,b) subsequently compared *Kyosei* with the "moral point of view" in business which often involves a pluralistic combination of interests, rights and duties, whilst referring to the Platonic human goods such as well-being, prosperity, justice and community.

A few years later, another CEO, Mr. Yamaji, stated that at Canon, "we try to encourage the view that the company's value to society lies in developing new technology" (Granstrand, 1999, p. 266–267). Meanwhile, Canon had been taking a leading role in the patent wars fought aggressively between Japanese and US corporations, separately and collectively. Each year from 1987 to 1997 Canon took first, second or third place in the world for the number of US patents granted (1999, p. 4) and it became the highest ranked corporation with respect to total number of patents. Researchers were told to "be prepared for the era to come when only some companies, strong in patents, will cooperate with each other and survive".

(iv) Merck

During the 1970s, a new drug, *Ivermectin*, was developed and tested for veterinary use. It was then thought to be a potential cure for River Blindness, which at that time afflicted millions of Africans. Almost no one had the ability to pay for it, despite their dire need (this being a standard limitation of market economies). Nonetheless, the company proceeded with development of the drug in accordance with a stated mission that "medicine is for the people, it is not for the profits". The WHO supported the project which succeeded in its primary mission. Furthermore, spin-off products reportedly facilitated the development of treatments for AIDS. Yet, in the 1990s as tens of millions suffered with AIDS, effective drug cocktails were once again not affordable by those who desperately needed them.

Notes

1. There are many other dualities and tensions involving ethics and economics (Chapter 1). For example, efficiency versus fairness and distributive-justice. Revealed preferences (consumer choices) that express the lower self, versus meta-preferences that represent the higher self; deliberation and ethical commitment to a humane ideal versus prudence and utility-maximising choices. More generally an economically optimal strategy (Chapter 11) contrasts with a systemic-ethical optimum that involves co-production of the human goods. Under all these descriptions, Sen's imperative (1993, p. 19) to "take note of each" component is reinforced by dialectical and ecological thinking.
2. This is supported by a view that sees rationality and morality as "interactive", that is, involving observer and observed, or "in the eye of the beholder" (e.g. Ackoff, 1983).
3. Adam Smith wrote that such lobbying typically opposes the "public interest". At least one media company reported that the SA government "refused to pay for the drugs". The company did not criticise the IPR system. It is thus inevitable that the provision of medication to AIDS sufferers became a wider political project.
4. Psychological substitution of means for ends, or deriving psychic utility from the very pursuit of ends, is but one approach to synthesising ethics with economics (e.g. Koslowski, 2001, p. 99). See also Chapter 4
5. Kant actually rejected the application of the dialectic to the real world, indicating that whilst the dialectic regulates ideas within the human mind, it does not apply to "things in themselves" (Reece, 1980). That position has become more problematic, at least in relation to living things, as indicated in this chapter.
6. This also applies to the idea, echoed in Indian philosophies, that harmony in the lives of individuals and families is a pre-requisite for order in the city, the state and the federation.

7. The dialectical inquiry method of planning, which involves a plan and counter-plan is one exception (Mason, 1969).

8. This synthesis illustrates "management without trade-offs" (e.g. Zeleny, 1999), "synergy orientation" (e.g. Singer, 1999b; Singer and Calton, 2001), or "super-optimisation" (e.g. Nagel, 2001). Trade-offs such as those involving cost versus quality, information richness versus reach, local cultures versus global strategy are overcome by re-design of the system.

9. Games of interests (utilities) can also be dissolved in practice by engagement and transformation of the players themselves (e.g. Singer, 1997a).

10. Many other lifelike patterns can be produced from different mathematical seeds. In these patterns, the parts often resemble the whole, like the fronds of a fernleaf.

11. In practice, considerable trans-disciplinarity already exists. Traditional categories of meaning, such as "SEEPT", serve as mere triggers for reflective inquiries into relationships and boundaries. The social, economic, ecological, political and technological are no longer vantage points from which grand perspectives can be gained, or within which policy issues can be confined.

Chapter 7

WISDOM: Towards Wise Enterprise

Abstract: This chapter foreshadows a larger project by the author, with others, on "Wisdom and Entrepreneurship". The various personal characteristics and business practices associated with entrepreneurship are identified and placed in correspondence with some distinctive components of wisdom, including its ethical aspects. This new "correspondence" framework (cf. Chapter 1) indicates several prescriptions for "wise-enterprise", including (i) the selection of good purposes, (ii) a mindfulness of the business and personal lifecycles, (iii) authentic prioritisation, and (iv) explication: the demonstration as well as explanation of enterprise purposes and plans.

7.1 Introduction

As noted in Chapter 1, there have been several attempts to place terms from the management lexicon in correspondence with philosophical or social science categories, such as "rationality", "citizenship" and "justice", to mention a few (Chapters 1 and 2) . Currently, it is entrepreneurship rather than "management" that is especially being encouraged almost everywhere (e.g. Armstrong, 2005). At the same time, notions such as "corporate wisdom" and wisdom-systems have begun to emerge (Chapter 5).

In the following section of the chapter, the distinctive characteristics of entrepreneurship are summarised. Then (in Section 3) several components of "wisdom" are identified. Within a framework of correspondence, this approach yields several prescriptions for "wise enterprise". They include selecting good purposes and constructing a pattern of activity that is mindful of business and personal life cycles, but also entrepreneurial explication, that is, the demonstration and explanation of those purposes, plans and prospects. In the final section, it is argued that wisdom is an important new entrant into the business lexicon. It has obvious merit in educational contexts but it can also act as catalyst for wider moral progress.

7.2 Business Practices

Like wisdom, the idea of "entrepreneurship" embraces business practices as well personal attributes. The most salient known characteristics of entrepreneurial (and intra-preneurial) business include innovation, co-creation of the environment, co-ordination and selective internalisation (i.e. capturing benefits). To these one must add some more general activities such as tactical communication, stewardship of resources and creation of wealth (Table 7.1, left column).

7.2.1 Innovation

In his classic work on entrepreneurship, Schumpeter (1934, p. 74). referred to "the carrying out of new combinations" by "entrepreneurs". More recently, Casson (1982) has characterised the entrepreneur as an actor who recognises the opportunity to "establish a market for a new type of good", who "brings new markets to life through innovation" and "who specialises in identifying new opportunities". Karlsson *et al.* (2005) then described the entrepreneur as one who has endowments of new knowledge or new combinations of old knowledge. Throughout, these "new" business practices are associated with the personal creativity of the entrepreneur (refer to Table 7.1).

Table 7.1 Entrepreneurial business practices associated with personal capabilities.

Business Practices	Personal Capabilities
Innovation	Creativity, intuition, synthesis
Creating the environment	Uncertainty absorption
Co-ordination of action	Leadership, confidence
Internalisation	Ambition
Tactical communication	Shrewdness, persuasiveness
Wealth creation and stewardship	Selection and pursuit of goals

7.2.2 Creating the Environment

It is often noted that entrepreneurial innovation, like the strategies of powerful corporations, involves attempts to create new industry structures and rules. With regard to structure, Schumpeter (1934) wrote of elite entrepreneurs who have a vision of an industrial network (structure) that they plan to create. Relevant actions often involve forms of political lobbying (Chapter 1). This contrasts with a more static view of firms, where information flows and structures are considered to exist in a "given" market environment. It also contrasts with traditional utility-based economic and decision theories in which the market and the objects of choice are taken as "givens". At the level of corresponding personal characteristics, one can contrast psychological attitudes towards risk with the more adaptive individual capabilities to "absorb uncertainty".

7.2.3 Co-ordination

The notion of co-ordination is also prominent in descriptions of an entrepreneurial action. Casson (1982, p. 23) considered the entrepreneur to be "someone who specialises in taking judgmental decisions about the co-ordination of scarce resources". He also noted that the principle instrumental use of information in business is for this type of coordination. Later, Kao (1997) referred to a person who excels at "assembling resources and making things happen", whilst Bolton and Thompson (2004, p. 13) recently described someone "who knows the right people, can pick a good team, act quickly and make it all happen". This function of "coordination of action" now seems so important that Zeleny (2005) has (controversially) proposed it as a re-definition of the "knowledge" of enterprise (see Chapter 5). It also corresponds to a component of leadership, at the level of the individual.

7.2.4 Internalisation and Tactical Communication

When entrepreneurs envision "industrial networks", they typically involve a network of personal equity holdings, directly and through holding companies. In well-documented cases such as The News Corporation, the desire and ability of the entrepreneur to retain (i.e. internalise) control and ownership is plainly a major influence upon the strategic development of the enterprise. In microeconomic terms, the entrepreneur needs to "hold sufficient equity that loss of value (i.e. of the enterprise) will have a major adverse effect on his consumption plans" (Casson 1998, p. 38). Such a "loss" can take place at the incubation stage of a venture, through an imprudent communication of the new plan (or "new synthesis") to guileful parties. For example, potential financiers might pick up the idea and run with it themselves, thus behaving more like devils than angels. Accordingly, the shrewd entrepreneur normally considers alternatives to "internalising" a plan.[1] This is but one component of entrepreneurial wisdom (see Section 7.4), but it is far from the whole story.

7.2.5 Wealth Creation and Stewardship

The purpose of the entrepreneurial venture is of particular significance in the present context. In addition to "shrewdness", wisdom also refers to the pursuit of *good* ends. Kao (1997) has defined "the entrepreneur" entirely within a framework of business-as-usual, or Financial Market Capitalism, as "a person who undertakes a wealth-creating and value-adding process". This contrasts with but the social forms of entrepreneurship and with the stakeholder variants of capitalism. Even within business as usual, Casson (1998) is amongst those who have noted that the structure of goals in private firms is not so simple, because the profit goal is often diluted (or complemented) by concerns with dynasty, brand, "an ethic of stewardship", or "pride in reputation".

7.3 Personal Capabilities

Each of the above business practices is associated with distinctive personal characteristics and capabilities (Table 7.1, right column). Characteristics such as leadership (confidence, ambition and persuasiveness), shrewdness, and purposefulness have already been mentioned. Other distinctive "personal capabilities" of the entrepreneur include creativity (intuition, an ability to synthesise) and uncertainty absorption (tolerance of ambiguity), as follows.

7.3.1 *Creativity, Synthesis and Intuition*

Entrepreneurs are often regarded as having special psychological abilities involving intuition and synthesis (e.g. Doktor and Bloom, 1977). Recently, Doktor (2005) wrote that "This ability to see associations… and thus to integrate and synthesize… lies at the heart of successful entrepreneurship". He added that "the cognitive ability to perceive rare associations… is the great power of the entrepreneur, for (in this) lies the *innovation* that was emphasized by Schumpeter (1934)". Casson (1998) also noted this requirement for a distinctive type of "information synthesis" and suggested that the entrepreneur has a "personal advantage" in this respect.

7.3.2 *Uncertainty Absorption*

Schumpeter (1934) drew an enduring distinction between "risk", as understood in microeconomic analysis, and a more amorphous notion of uncertainty. He suggested that entrepreneurship has more to do with the latter: acting effectively in uncertain or ambiguous situations. The ability to "absorb uncertainty" has been linked to several other individual cognitive capabilities. The European Foundation for Management Development (EFMD, 2005, p. 19) wrote that, in business, "Many of the most creative impulses arise from… ambiguity and uncertainty". Doktor (2005, 1969) also noted that "it is successful decision making in the face of uncertainty that is the entrepreneur's special gift" and that "this requires an intuitive–synthetic style of thinking" that in turn lies "at the heart of creativity and innovation".

7.4 Wisdom

Classical and contemporary thinkers have identified several components of wisdom (Table 7.2). They involve special domains of knowledge, but they are also, like some aspects of enterprise, generally associated with an expansive mode of thinking. On the other hand, high risk activity is normally thought of as unwise (i.e. it is entrepreneurial, but not wise). Finally, in order to attain wisdom, there might be a need for some additional business practices and personal qualities. Accordingly, if we now place the several components of wisdom relative to the above-mentioned characteristics of

Table 7.2 Correspondences between components of wisdom, strategy and entrepreneurship.

Wisdom	Strategy	Wise Enterprise
Know depth	Strengths and weaknesses	Know limitations, avoid demagoguery
Know significance	Situation analysis	Know the circumstances
Know breadth	Design of alternatives	Re-frame, be mindful of ideology
Select means	Decision making and choice	Create new synthesis
Construct life pattern	Strategy as temporary pattern	Coordinate life pattern
Select good ends	Shareholder, stewardship goals	Adopt good (dual) purposes
Prioritise authentically	Purposes, mission	Timing, personal and business lifecycles
Communicate plans	Prudent disclosure	Explication
Explicate purposes	Develop ideology	Develop ideology

entrepreneurship, a more complete understanding of the *wisdom of enterprise* begins to take shape.

Various components of wisdom were identified in classical and renaissance works (Aristotle, Protagoras and Montaign). A few modern works have added to these (e.g. Rice, 1958; Kekes, 1983; Zeleny, 2005). The "components" fall into three classes. The first (Table 7.2; rows 1–3) involves dimensions of knowledge, as identified by Kekes (1983): depth, significance and breadth. A second class involves good means and ends, the selection of suitable goals and purposes. The last class of wisdom components involves communication: not just shrewdness but also explication: the demonstration (of the good purposes and plans) through action, as well as its explanation with words.

7.4.1 Knowledge of Depth

According to Socrates, wisdom requires awareness of one's own ignorance and the limits on one's capabilities. Similarly, for Protagoras, wisdom "licenses the possible but warns against the impossible". Accordingly, wisdom or knowledge of depth "guides commitments, by eliminating ideals (ultimate purposes) that are counter to human limits" (Kekes, 1983). Wise persons know what not to do, if they want a good life and they remain

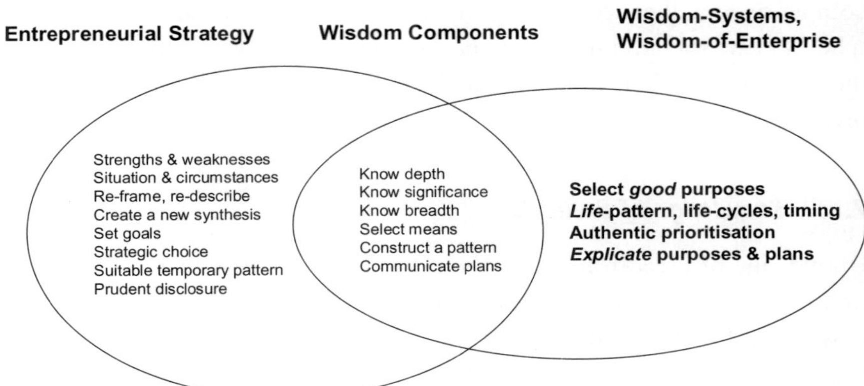

Figure 7.1   Entrepreneurial strategy and the wisdom of enterprise.

mindful of the "universal and unavoidable" conditions that determine human limitations and potentialities. Some limits are universal, some apply to a specific class of people (e.g. entrepreneurs) and some are specific to each individual. The wise entrepreneur constructs a pattern of life that takes all of these limitations into account.

In business strategy (Table 7.2 and Figure 7.1) this component of wisdom is reflected in any routine analysis of business strengths and weaknesses (i.e. a SWOT analysis). Managerial capabilities and potentials are also often assessed. The wisdom component of "depth" then generates an additional prescription (or warning) for the entrepreneur: one ought to be sensitive to universal and personal limitations. One should, for example, reject the popular slogan "no limits" and avoid the (media–endorsed) temptation to behave like a demagogue.

7.4.2 Knowledge of Significance

Interpretive knowledge refers to an accurate appreciation of the significance of "what is generally known" (Kekes, 1983). The wise person also knows that others might interpret public information (common knowledge) quite differently and they might draw different inferences (e.g. different forecasts from the same data). The corresponding component of business strategy is the "situation analysis" encompassing macro–environmental forecasts and competitive intelligence. In this context, the wise entrepreneur is someone who "knows the circumstances" (as Sun Tzu noted over 2400 years ago), including what others might "know" and how they might, in turn, interpret it.

7.4.3 *Knowledge of Breadth*

Knowledge of breadth involves the related appreciation that any description is just one possibility amongst many. It involves reflective self-awareness regarding the limitations of one's perspective and ideology (see below). Classically, Montaigne (1533–1595) wrote, "there is a plague on man: the opinion that he knows something". Much later, Kekes (1983, p. 279) added that the conscious acknowledgment of diverse perspectives "opens the way to a tolerant liberality of spirit that is essential to being cultivated and benign". This fully aligns with contemporary appeals to moral imagination in business (e.g. Werhane, 1999b). In contrast, many leaders and entrepreneurs "…deal with issues within the limited framework of their personal ideological assumptions" (Lodge and Vogel, 1987) even though interpersonal differences in ideology "effect the outcomes" of personal and business activities.

7.4.4 *Selecting Means (to Known Ends)*

Aristotle recognised that the ability to select means to given or known ends was also a basic component of wisdom. Since wisdom must guide action, it must involve the choice or design of suitable means. This notion corresponds to the idea of "strategic choice", in the managerial lexicon. However, for the entrepreneur, the "choice of means" particularly involves design or crafting of alternatives, not just choice. The entrepreneur creates a new synthesis which then becomes the "selected" means for achieving goals, whether personal, financial or social.

7.4.5 *Constructing a Pattern*

Kekes (1983) also associated wisdom with knowledge of "how to construct a pattern…" that leads to a good life (as discussed below). The notion of a person's life pattern corresponds to the idea of "strategy as a pattern", in business. Mintzberg (1987) offered this as nothing less than a definition of "strategy". Wise entrepreneurs will attempt to "construct a pattern" of action (put differently, they co-ordinate action); but wisdom dictates that this must incorporate a personal life plan, as well as a business plan.

7.4.6 Selecting Good Purposes

"Wisdom" also involves an ability to select the means to "*good*" ends. Montaigne (1533–1595) wrote that wisdom involves "arranging human affairs for the benefit of humanity" (Rice, 1958; also cited in Kekes, 1983). When this is coupled to the "patterns" of action, we obtain the wisdom problem of "How to construct a pattern... that is likely to lead to a good life". Unfortunately, notions such as "good ends", the "good life" and "the benefit of humanity" are all enduringly controversial, as indicated by the strategy–ethics dualism described earlier (in Chapter 1). One can, for example, compare the self-centred life of Robinson Crusoe with the more sociable or universalisable ideal of a good life with others.

7.4.7 Authentic Dynamic Prioritisation

Doktor *et al.* (2005) recently noted that entrepreneurs do indeed sometimes set aside their primary wealth-creation goal because of "competing obligations" such as family and other "non-economic considerations that outweigh transactions". More generally, wise entrepreneurs ought to carry out an authentic prioritisation of their activities, based on what they know to be truly important (e.g. Kekes, 1983, p. 280). They will not waste time with irrelevancies, but they will design and select projects in the full light of their self-knowledge, including their personal limitations and mortality.

Personal priorities naturally change over time. Wise persons must therefore balance their present satisfactions with their long range hopes and their anticipated future capabilities. Accordingly, wise entrepreneurs' goals will fit in with the "seasons" of life (Kekes, 1983), or else they will be "misguided" when the inevitable changes come. At the level of business strategy, this involves consideration of both the business lifecycle and the personal life pattern of the entrepreneur. One such "pattern" observed by Jawahar and McLaughlin (2001) has entrepreneurs giving priority to financiers and customers in the start-up phase of a business; but in the mature stages of the enterprise (and sometimes of the entrepreneur's life), priorities then shift towards philanthropic projects and non–market stakeholders.

7.4.8 Communication

Managers and entrepreneurs routinely explain activities in relation to stated targets, but they also explain aspects of their future plans to selected audiences (e.g. finance providers). As mentioned earlier, these "explanations" often involves calculated deception, or shrewdness. Start-up entrepreneurs face special challenges in this regard. They need to explain their novel synthesis to resource providers who are often conservative in disposition and analytic in their cognitive style (e.g. Doktor and Bloom, 1977). Second, they must judge character: who to trust and who to deceive. Third, entrepreneurs must persuade key stakeholders of their personal capabilities to "coordinate the action" and to make the plan succeed.

7.4.9 Explication

The remaining component of wisdom (Table 7.2, last row) augments these communications. It involves knowing why particular plans and purposes have been adopted, as well as an ability to explain and demonstrate that knowledge. Put differently, the wisdom of enterprise includes the explication of purpose (Zeleny, 2005). "Explication" demands a close match between the words and actions (as in the "totally aligned organisation" of Rossouw and van Vuuren, 2003). Wise entrepreneurs should strive to create a least distance between their actions and their explanations. They will accordingly avoid traditional planning, the linear approach:

$$\begin{matrix} \text{stated} \\ \text{purposes} \end{matrix} \rightarrow \begin{matrix} \text{alternative} \\ \text{strategies} \end{matrix} \rightarrow \begin{matrix} \text{choice of} \\ \text{strategies} \end{matrix} \rightarrow \text{implementation}$$

but will instead adopt an approach based upon the "wisdom cycle" of enterprise (e.g. Zeleny, 2006) which looks more like:

… **explained purposes** ↔ **demonstrative actions** ↔ **necessary adaptations**…

"Explanation of purpose" requires an ideology, whilst Lodge and Vogel (1987) observed that "a nation is successful" when its ideology (i.e. the ideas it uses to explain its purposes) is (i) "coherent and adaptable" and where (ii) there is "a least distance between its prevailing ideology and actual practice". A similar recipe for strategic success now plainly applies to non-national entities, particularly wise entrepreneurs.

7.5 Dualism and Wisdom

The "explication" and "good purpose" components of wisdom in turn require that the wise entrepreneur

(i)   understands the moral dimension, for "Without an ethical dimension one could perhaps be clever or astute, but not wise" (Zeleny, 2005).

(ii)   adopts some type of enterprise ideology, that is, a "framework of ideas used to explain values and purposes" (e.g. Lodge and Vogel, 1987).

The dualism framework (Chapter 1) can support both of these requirements. It is nothing other than a "framework of ideas" that can be "used" to explain, justify and or persuasively communicate values, purposes and plans. However, it specifically indicates the wisdom or goodness of adopting dual goals. Several classical and theological discussions of "wisdom" endorse this point. For example, Protagoras wrote (*circa* 480 BC) that "before any uncertainty, two opposing theses can be confronted" (antilogics, a precursor to dialectics). He went on to suggest that "it is *wise* to strengthen the weaker argument, because it might contain the best answer". Theological sources are also quite direct on the same point. The recorded sayings of Buddha, for example, state that "he who has great *wisdom* thinks of his own welfare, that of others, that of *both*... and the welfare of the whole world" (Dhammananda, 1999, p. 61).

Business ethicists have repeatedly pointed to the wisdom of a dualism framework.[3] For example, Hosmer's (1995) discussion of ethics and strategy evoked Protagoras and Aristotle: every "person" should act for a *mixture* of short term gain with... his\her vision of the future, or sense of self-worth. He mentioned the goal of community (St. Augustine), the calculation of social benefit (Mill), the understanding of universal duty (Kant), the recognition of individual rights (Jefferson). In addition, many other contemporary strategy scholars have prescribed dual purpose, win–win, or "balanced" enterprise strategies, at least in some circumstances.[4]

7.6 Conclusion

According to Zeleny (2006), corporations can be informed; they can be knowledgeable; but in the global era, they "must also become wise". Whilst the current trend is towards knowledge strategies, Zeleny suggests that "the next transition from knowledge to wisdom" is already taking shape. This viewpoint aligns with optimists who perceive a long term trend of moral progress in "human affairs". As a note of caution, it is perhaps worth recalling that fully 25 years ago Kenneth Goodpaster claimed that there was, at that time, "an evolution of moral consciousness in the executive suite", with more and more executives asking "what ought to go on". The actual record since then has been decidedly mixed. If executives and entrepreneurs have remained generally reluctant to embrace specific moral principles, it is possible that an appeal to the "wisdom of enterprise" might prove more persuasive, in future.

Notes

1. Such as quietly purchasing any specialised assets that are needed, like land for a real estate plan, then tactically divulging the plan or simply waiting for others to come up with the same idea.
2. Vogel (1987, p. 310), a sociologist, observed that each society harbours "contradictory ideological elements (that) coexist in a complex mixture".
3. Dobson (2001) noted that the "technical" view of enterprise (giving priority to efficiency and craftsmanship, etc.) can co-exist with the "moral community" view described in Etzioni's (1988) "Moral Dimension". See also Derry (2001).
4. For example, Rugman and Verbeke (1998); Shrivastava (1995).

Chapter 8

CONSCIENCE: Consciousness and Conscience as Emergent Properties

Abstract: This chapter is an adapted version of "Planning, consciousness and conscience," *Journal of Business Ethics* 1(3), pp. 113–117, 1984. It argues against the contested notion of corporate or collective moral agency, from a broad evolutionary perspective. This was briefly referred to in Chapter 2, where it was compared with several other arguments on either side of the issue.

8.1 Introduction

The Oxford English Dictionary defines Anthropomorphism as "the ascription of a human attribute to anything impersonal". Such ascriptions are generally regarded as philosophically unsound, an error in reasoning: yet many writers on Corporate Strategy and Policy have found the temptation to "anthropomorphise" to be almost irresistible. Moreover, most readers feel perfectly comfortable with such phrases as "The company expects, or wishes...", or acknowledge quite freely the coherence of ideas like the "Corporate Conscience".

Some theoreticians have claimed that organisations should be structured, so as to employ the very principles embodied in the human nervous system (e.g. Beer, 1981) or in the self-production of living systems (e.g. Zeleny, 1981), whilst others merely hint at the usefulness of comparing organisation with organism: when Mintzberg (1976) described how the human brain is divided into two hemispheres (the left is rational, analytic and sequential, whilst the right is intuitive, emotional and holistic), he casually observed that "... in a sense, the coupling of the holistic and sequential reflects how bureaucratic organizations themselves work...".

There does indeed seem to be a strong temptation to award human-like properties, particularly some form of consciousness, to non-human entities; but is this a temptation to err? Many non-human animals possess what is generally regarded as consciousness; moreover, corporations, by virtue of their planning processes, may be seen to possess a quality that is very close indeed to the modern concept of individual consciousness. However, it will be argued here that the subtle quality of human intuition and, particularly, the "higher" ideals of conscience cannot be rooted in an organisational process irrespective of the complexity; these remain the special preserve of the individual mind.

In order to develop and support this argument it is first necessary to indulge in the popular pursuit of trying to clarify what is meant by "Consciousness". A study of the relevant literature reveals that thinking on the issue is strongly influenced by the zeitgeist or the intellectual fashion of the period. For example, as physics displaced chemistry at the spearhead of scientific advance, so did conceptions of consiousness as an "analysable compound" give way to ideas of "particle interaction". More recently, post-Darwinian thought has shifted from an "anthropomorphic" position, which supposes that even microorganisms enjoy psychic life, to the contemporary and popular doctrine of Emergent Evolution:

> Its main idea is a metaphor: just as the property of wetness cannot be derived from the properties of hydrogen and oxygen alone, so consciousness emerged at some point in evolution in a way underivable from its constituent parts.... (The) new relations emergent at each higher level guide and sustain the course of events distinctive of that level. Consciousness, then, emerges as something genuinely new at a critical stage of evolutionary advance. When it has emerged, it guides the course of events in the brain and has casual efficacy in bodily behaviour. (Jaynes, 1976)

One influential supporter of this doctrine, it should be noted, is R. W. Sperry of the California Institute of Technology, the neuroscientist who has supplied us with much of the hard evidence for brain lateralisation of function. Sperry (1979) declares his support thus:

> I have already stated my belief that the organizational features of the brain which give rise to conscious processes are in large part genetically

determined. If this is true then consciousness must be subject to the evolutionary processes.

It may now be seen that this, contemporary, view of consciousness does indeed provide us with a very powerful metaphor for the process of corporate planning.

8.2 A Metaphor for Corporate Planning

Arguments that employ metaphor can be dangerous but may also promote new insights. Some of the features of corporate planning, as a process, are strikingly similar to those of human consciousness conceived of as an emergent property. For example, corporate planning, as an activity, "emerged" during the 1960s in response to the increasingly complex corporate function and structure. With regard to individuals, Sperry (1979) continues thus:

> From the standpoint of functional control, one may ask what benefits precisely are conferred by the introduction in evolution of subjective conscious effects? Thinking in regard to this question is still preliminary and speculative along lines like the following: consider the tactical difference between responding to the world directly and responding to inner conscious representations of the outside world.... The real world can hardly be manipulated as can inner images.... Further, the employment of implicit trial-and-error responses to inner mental models and the avoidance thereby of overt response commitments, with possible errors in the real world, is a central rationale in the evolution of thinking.

One may equally well ask "What benefits, precisely, are conferred by the introduction of a corporate planning function in a complex organisation?" The planning team do indeed employ some sort of model of the world, in order to evaluate various strategic options; by discarding strategic options which fail to deal with environmental threats and opportunities, the team intend to avoid those "overt response commitments" which might prove damaging to the corporation. In other words, like consciousness, corporate planning has survival value. Just like consciousness for the individual, planning confers operational advantages to the organisation:

> Older... concepts of brain organization... may be replaced by a model in which the brain is seen to be organized as a decision-making control system monitored with value priorities and in which conscious phenomena confer certain operational advantages over and above those obtainable in systems that lack consciousness.

If we simply substitute "corporate planning" for "conscious phenomena" and "corporation" for "brain", we obtain a convincing sales pitch for one's business planning consultant. On the other hand, by adopting a rather different philosophical position regarding the nature of consciousness, this metaphor might equally well be embraced with enthusiasm by the "anti-planners": the belief held by some that planning cannot significantly influence corporate destiny then corresponds to the epiphenomalist view of consciousness. Julian Jaynes has described this view:

> Consciousness can no more modify the working mechanism of the body or its behaviour than can the whistle of a train modify its machinery or where it goes ... the shadow that loyally walks step for step beside the pedestrain, but is quite unable to influence his journey.

This epiphenomenalist view, in turn, must contend with the fact that conscious awareness is seen to be heightened during moments when action is most hesitant (so, it is argued, consciousness can scarcely be a by-product of action). Equally, by extending the metaphor, one may re-establish the primacy of planning by referring to cases where existing strategies are floundering and new ones have yet to emerge.

All in all, it can be seen that the debate about the nature of individual consciousness nicely parallels that on the nature of corporate planning.

8.3 Organisations and Organisms

Metaphors can be dangerous: in no sense are consciousness and planning the same process: by considering both as "properties of complex systems", is it possible to say with any precision where the breakdown occurs?

Ackoff and Emery (1972) provide us with a potentially important clue. In their book "On Purposeful Systems", they explain a difference between organisations and organisms (including individuals) when viewed as decision making and control systems:

> Both organisms and organizations are purposeful systems, but organisms do not contain purposeful elements. The elements of an organism may be functional, goal-seeking or multi-goal seeking but not purposeful.

Most physiologists would agree. The "elements" or subsystems of an organism are indeed goal seeking as J. Z. Young explains:

> But we now find that every organism contains systems that literally embody set points or reference standards. The control mechanisms operate to ensure that action is directed to maintaining these standards.

However, these "control" subsystems are not purposeful in the Ackoff and Emery sense, whereby a purposeful (sub)system is one that "selects its goals as well as the means to pursue them" and is capable of changing its own goals in constant environmental conditions, thereby displaying what we might call a form of (free) "will". Acceptance of this thesis leads us to conclude that it is the existence of purposeful subsystems (divisions, departments or individual employees) in the corporations that precludes us from asserting that properties of the brain have direct counterparts in organisations. Indeed, Ackoff and Emery claim that

> This difference alone (i.e. the existence of purposeful subsystems) will be sufficient to justify the differences between biology and sociology.

It is productive to pursue this point. If the existence of purposeful subsystems is the essential distinction between organisations and organisms, in systems terms, then an organisation which is so structured as to deny the freedom of "selecting goals" to all its subsystems is closer to a complex organism. In such an organisation, the "consciousness" then becomes identified with that of the CEO who "uses" the organisation as a tool in pursuit of his or her own objectives. Conversely, the greater the degree of autonomy delegated to subsystems of the firm the less can one speak, even metaphorically, of "a (unified) corporate consciousness". In other words, where strategy formulation is shifted downwards, it becomes, as Andrews (1980) puts it, "a process of organization rather than the masterly conception of a single mind". This may appear self-evident, but there may be implications for the quality of the strategy that results from the process.

8.4 The Individual Strategist

Mintzberg, (1976) tentatively suggested that where a strategy is indeed the result of one individual's efforts it is often creative, integrated and "interesting": "Scratch an interesting strategy" he claims, "and you will probably find a single strategy formulator beneath it". If, however, "The organization goes the route of systematic planning... it will probably come up with what can be called a 'main line' strategy".

There is an implicit suggestion here that the individual is capable of excelling in the quality of his or her "strategic thinking" beyond that which can be achieved by organisational processes (by the Corporate Consciousness, that is). Moreover, this excellence may only be achieved through articulation of left and right hemispheres which enables a synthesis of intuition and rationality "in the same skull". The "corporate brain", it seems, either lacks a right hemisphere altogether or else cannot achieve the integration of right with left that would harness creative forces within the system to rational planning procedures.

It would then seem plausible that a "corporate brain", already deficient in balancing intuition with rationality, might be unable to achieve the higher form of consciousness that we think of as conscience. It then becomes unreasonable to expect that ethical behaviour would emerge from an organisational or collective process of strategic planning.[1] The overall structure of the argument so far is depicted in Figure 8.1.

8.5 Corporate Ideals

Ethical behaviour entails the existence of ideals. Ackoff and Emery have offered a definition of an ideal using the general language of systems theory: it is "an objective that cannot be obtained in any time period but can be approached without limit". This "approach" is being achieved through

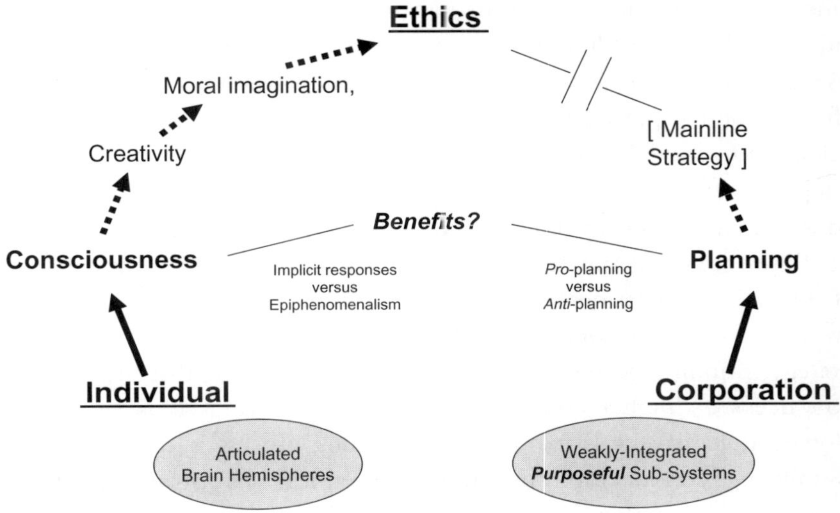

Figure 8.1 Overview of an argument against corporation-moral-agency.

regular re-formulation of lower level objectives. Corporate objectives undoubtedly exist; but does the concept of a "corporate ideal" have any substance? The corporation may be purposive, in that short term goals are amended in pursuit of longer term objectives (for example: sacrifice short term profitability to promote growth in market share); but is it an "ideal seeking system"?

Not if we accept Mintzberg's (1976, author's italics) idea that "strategy is the organization's conception of how to deal with its environment for a while". There is nothing here to support the thesis of an idealistic input to strategy. Indeed, the "systems" concept of ideal, a super-long range possibly unattainable goal, seems to be rather close in spirit to Heibroner's "grandiose image of society", which that philosopher claims is conspicuously lacking in business ideology. Short on ideals, corporate actions thus all too often seem to lack "higher consciousness" or conscience.

8.6 The Unknown Distance

In his book of this title, Engleberg traced the literary usage of the words "consciousness" and "conscience" in the writings of several great thinkers.

Once similar, the meanings drifted apart, reaching a critical stage of separation in the late 18th and 19th centuries, when conscience was largely associated with guilt. Yet this is the same period when "corporate policy" often advocated pursuit of profit with matters of conscience conveniently delegated to another institution altogether. Engleberg concluded that such a separation of meaning is untenable: the development of consciousness leads, via an "unknown distance", to individual conscience.

Sure enough, corporations now find that a planning procedure, devoid of ethical considerations, is likewise becoming "untenable": as external pressure groups blossom and place increasing constraints on acceptable strategy, planning becomes more demanding, indicating that the corporation needs a "higher consciousness" or conscience if it is to survive. However, it may be that no diffuse planning process is capable of fully assimilating consideration of ideals and ethical standards; the process becomes too complex; in other words, it is beyond corporate consciousness. Instead, ethical conduct may be brought about either through "public law", from outside the corporation, or else from the "private consciences" of individual policy makers. (In a free society, the preferred alternative is obvious.)

8.7 The Price of Conscience

Conscience, as Engleberg reminds us, has its price and risks. Heightened awareness of the effects of corporate actions on employees and society can be a big problem for strategy formulation. Ackoff (1974), for example, refered to the "Humanisation and Environmentalisation problems". As H. A. Simon might argue, having more goals is equivalent to having more constraints. Those who prefer a less technical statement of the theme might ponder the "most famous soliloquy in English":

> Thus conscience doth make cowards of us all;
> And thus the native hue of resolution
> Is sicklied o'er with the pale cast of thought,
> And enterprises of great pitch and moment
> With this regard their currents turn awry
> And lose the name of action. (Hamlet)

In other words, conscience and dynamism do not mix well, at least in most corporate contexts. A control system that rewards effective action in pursuit of corporate objectives all too often conflicts with individuals' ideals. Andrews (1980) makes the same point thus: "No system of control... can take the place of the individual who has a clear idea of right and wrong...". Whilst Appley (1963) asserts in his book "*The Management Evolution*" that "The highest standard for each individual is that which his conscience tells him is best".

Perhaps, then, those senior managers who are really serious about "Good Corporate Citizenship" might begin by staffing their organisations, right to the top, with "good citizens". As a result, emergent strategies are then more likely to be morally defensible and implementation relatively free from conflict. Perhaps the "unknown distance" can, at least, be diminished.

8.8 Conclusion

Contemporary perspectives on consciousness provide us with a metaphor for the corporate planning process; although, by some accounts, organisations ultimately differ in systems terms from organisms. Like consciousness, planning has survival value and confers operational advantages. Whereas individuals' actions may be guided by conscience in pursuit of ideals, corporate acts often lack these qualities. It may be that no diffuse planning process is capable of accommodating ideals and ethical standards. Put differently, ideals are "beyond" corporate consciousness. Therefore, the pursuit of corporate objectives will often conflict with individuals' ideals.

Notes

1. It is perhaps worth pointing out that this anti-CMA argument is in tension with the particular pro-CMA argument set out in French (1984). French claimed that the existence of an internal corporate decision making structure (procedures etc.) was sufficient to validate the notion of collective intention and hence also collective (or corporate) moral agency (see Chapter 2). These two arguments might be

reconciled by noting that French seems to be emphasising collective moral responsibility (or accountability, due to the intentionality and deliberate actions), whereas the present argument is pointing to the possible lack of capability of the corporation to act morally. If that capability is lacking, then the moral responsibility is undermined, accordingly.

Part II: Models

Chapter 9

RECURSIVITY: Strategy-Models are Self-Referential

Abstract: This chapter is an abridged version of "Strategy and recursivity," *Human Systems Management* 22, pp. 73–85, 2003. An argument is put forward that conceptual models of strategy can themselves be depicted and described in a variety of ways, such as objects-of-choice in a metamodelling decision, or as end states of a transition process, or as patterns that replicate in managers' minds. Discussions of the strategy models and their uses then typically invoke the same categories of meaning that are found in the general discourse on strategy itself. Accordingly, recursivity and self-reference are pervasive in the theory of strategy. This, in turn, indicates a potential synthesis with ecological thinking.

9.1 Introduction

The production and distribution of strategic management models has itself become a mature industry. Conceptual models such as those found in Porter (1980, 1985) complement and compete with many other models, such as hyper-competition (D'Aveni, 1994), co-opetition (Brandenburger and Nalebuff, 1996), stakeholder-management (Freeman, 1994), core-competence (Hamel and Prahalad, 1990) and de-construction (Evans and Wurster, 2000) to mention but a few. As a result of the variety and diversity, questions have been raised from time to time about the epistemological status of these models, as well as the nature of the relationships between them (e.g. Wensley, 1981; Prescott and Grant, 1988; Tsoukas, 1994; Donaldson and Preston, 1995; Calori, 1999).

The present chapter further explores these questions. It starts with a working definition of terms such as conceptual model and metamodel. Then (in Section 9.3) the idea of models as objects-of-choice and comparison is developed. This idea of "choice", in turn, is elaborated with reference to distinctive forms of rationality and optimality (e.g. Singer, 1994a, 1996a, b, d). Section 9.4 then outlines several other ways of thinking about conceptual models of strategy, including designed objects, end–points of transitions, catalysts of renewal, tools of influence and, especially, patterns that replicate.

It quickly becomes apparent that if we view conceptual models as abstract entities or objects that can produce cognitive and social effects, they are seen to behave in quite similar ways to the conventional units of strategic business analysis, such as knowledge-producing firms and organisational networks, whose behaviour they (the models) are supposed to depict. Put differently, models of strategic behaviour themselves behave strategically, in a sense competing for share of mind. This implies that there is a pervasive but latent recursivity in much of our contemporary thinking about strategy. "Recursivity", in turn, is a foundational concept in ecology and the ecological way of thinking (e.g. Bateson, 1972; Harries-Jones, 1995). Accordingly, in Section 9.5, several pathways are mapped out linking strategy with ecology via recursivity. The resulting conceptual framework underpins and lends substance to currently popular but intuitive phrases such as business-ecology and knowledge-ecology.

9.2 Conceptual Models

Any conceptual model can be defined as a set of images and natural language expressions that depict and describe a problem context or a perceived reality (e.g. Oral and Kettani, 1993). In business contexts such as strategy formulation, these "models" typically refer to a set of entities, or units of analysis (e.g. individuals, firms, networks, states, etc.), together with some subset of their behavioural repertoires. Any particular model can then be communicated in such a way that it fosters a particular way of thinking in the managerial mind. This simple description of models and what they do actually conceals many latent philosophical issues, some of which are alluded to and discussed throughout this chapter.

9.2.1 Metamodels

The preface "meta" literally means about. Accordingly, the term metamodelling in its broadest sense[1] refers to any discussion or conceptualisation of models and modelling processes (e.g. Van Gigch, 1991). "Meta" can also imply a higher level of understanding achieved by giving consideration to ultimate meanings, as, for example, in a meta-theory of representative practices, which identifies and contrasts distinctive approaches to knowledge-production (Alvesson and Deetz, 1998). The present chapter confines itself to consideration of conceptual metamodels within the field of strategic management, or strategy. Such a model can be defined as

A CONCEPTUAL-MODEL OF (a conceptual–model of
(aspects of reality)).

That is, a metamodel is a set of images and natural language expressions that describe and depict conceptual models per se. In this case, however, the relevant "aspect of reality" is the strategic behaviour of all types of productive entity within an environment composed of many other such entities. In the following section on comparison of models, strategy models are depicted as objects-of-choice in a static decision problem, analogous to the familiar idea of choice amongst strategic options. Five other conceptual metamodels are then outlined in Section 9.4 involving design, transition, renewal, influence and replication.

9.3 Comparison

A conceptual model can itself be described as an object of choice within a static decision problem (Figure 9.1). Various conceptual models of strategy (including those already mentioned) are listed in Table 9.1, with their acronyms (e.g. CSCA, etc.). As with all other taxonomies and comparisons of models (e.g. Prescott and Grant, 1988; Singer and Brodie, 1990; Donaldson and Preston, 1995; Evans and Wurster, 2000), the particular models or objects-of-choice have been selected primarily because they are well known and remain current, but also because each has a somewhat different focus and content so that taken together they span quite a wide range of strategic management issues.

It is quickly apparent that models like hyper-competition (CMHC) are depictions and descriptions of a competitive environment of a strategic entity, whilst others like CC and boundedly rational agent refer to internal

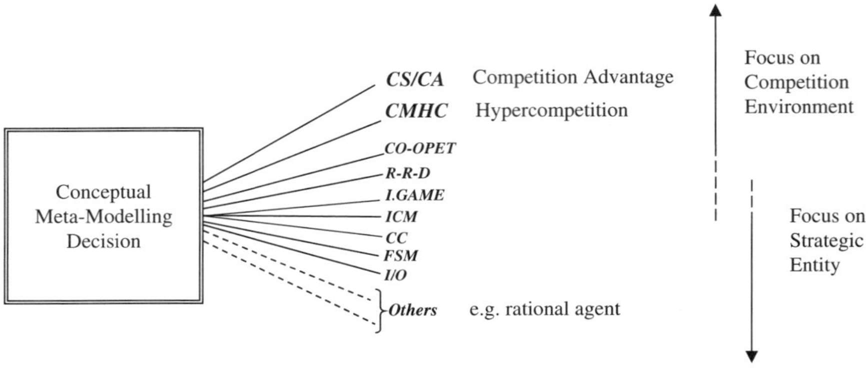

Figure 9.1   Static choice of strategy models.

potentials and processes of a typical entity. A third subset (e.g. R–R–D, I.game, FSM, etc.) consists of models that encompass some internal processes of a strategic entity, together with components of its proximal external environment (e.g. inputs, stakeholders, etc.). It might be said that only the latter strictly qualify as strategy models, as distinct from models more closely associated with other management disciplines such as marketing and OB/HRM; but the boundary between these three categories is not so clear.[2] Indeed, any given model of a strategic entity, with its effects, also furnishes a model of an environment that is made up of such entities.

9.3.1 Feature-Comparison

Within a static choice framework, pairwise comparison involves the identification of distinctive features of the given objects of choice (the models). This activity of feature extraction or detection of difference is quite fundamental to the psychology of perception and cognition (e.g. Harries–Jones, 1995, p. 173). It also facilitates the generation of clearer natural-language descriptions of the given objects–of–choice. In the special case of model-comparison, it also fosters new understandings or a greater sense of coherence concerning aspects of the modelled reality.

Table 9.1 Some conceptual models of strategic behaviour.

1. Competitive strategy/advantage (CSCA): This consists of five competitive forces; (i) the threat of new entrants; (ii) supplier power; (iii) the threat of substitute products; (iv) buyer power and (v) rivalry amongst incumbent players, together with several generic strategies for achieving sustainable competitive advantage (Porter, 1985)

2. Hypercompetition (CMHC): This model includes (i) four arenas in which a game with various types of move is played out over time; (ii) an escalation ladder, whose steps are the moves around the four arenas; (iii) a concept of competitiveness as sustaining a momentum of change and (iv) progress towards an end state (D'Aveni, 1994)

3. Co-opetition (CO-OPET): The external environment is a set of complementing entities, as well as competitors. A firm's customers value a given product more when they also have the complementer's product(s). Suppliers are more willing to supply the firm when they are also supplying the complementer. Strategic behaviour consists of searching for complements and creating markets (Brandenburger and Nalebuff, 1996)

4. Richness/reach/deconstruct (R-R-D): The apparent trade-off between information richness (customisation, bandwidth, etc.) and reach (number of entities using it) is continually being overcome, by advances in technology. At the same time, the physical and informational components of business activity are becoming separated, so that entities that depended on bundling these together are forced to dismantle or "deconstruct" and then try to re-construct (Evans and Wurster, 1997)

5. Infinite game (I.GAME): Win–lose competitions and trade-offs are re-conceived as potential win–win situations, or "trade-ons", whilst increased attention is paid to the future external and internal environments (Hampden-Turner and Trompenaars, 1997)

6. International competitiveness model (ICM): This is conceptual model with a formalisation for measurement purposes that distinguishes between the actual and potential profit performance of a firm and its competitor(s). "Competitiveness" is conceptualised as the combined strength, relative to a specified other firm, of several competencies and the political and economic environments (e.g. Oral *et al.*, 1989)

7. Core competence (CC): The key resources of an entity are a set of competencies that it should nurture. A corporate portfolio should contribute to and extract value from these internal resources (Hamel and Prahalad, 1990)

8. Full stakeholder model (FSM): Local communities and employees are stakeholders, alongside shareholders, customers and the managers. This conceptual model has a normative (ethical) core; for example, managers ought to act "to maintain and care for relationships and networks" and "care for the earth" (Freeman, 1994, p. 134)

9. Input/output (I/O): The entity processes inputs from its proximate environment, delivering outputs. A redesigned version of the model depicts strategic vision with ecological components (e.g. Shrivastava, 1995)

In the general strategy literature, it is quite common to find articles that make explicit pairwise comparisons of models. For example, Evans and Wurster (2000, p. 63) recently compared the R-R-D model with both CS/CA and CC. They identified some shared features, such as the competitive threat of substitute offerings and the level of competence necessary to overcome the richness–reach trade-off. They also identified contrasting features, most notably the units of analysis, or the productive entities. (These are corporations in CSCA and CC, but "much larger semantically rich communities", in R-R-D). Similarly, Donaldson and Preston (1995, p. 72) systematically compared FSM with the input–output (I–O) model of a firm, poignantly asking why the former should be "accepted or preferred" over the latter, or any of its alternatives. Another more detailed example set out in Table 9.2 and Figure 9.2 places CS/CA relative to CMHC. In this case, the new features of CMHC are identified first, then the shared features, then some of the disputed features (i.e. where the models or their underlying assumptions appear incompatible or contradictory). Finally, some missing features are identified: features that are found in some of the other strategy models, such as those listed in Table 9.1.

9.3.2 Complementarity

Similar comparisons of features can be carried out for any given pairs of models. Whereas CS/CA and CMHC have some "disputed" elements (Table 9.1), in other cases a pair of models can appear on the surface at least to act as natural complements, with no immediately apparent incompatibilities. To give a simple example (discussed subsequently in Section 9.4), the stakeholder model (FSM), in which governments and employees are depicted as "stakeholders" of a firm, can be literally superimposed upon the five-force Industry Attractiveness model (CS/CA), resulting in a more complete and complicated picture of an entity's environment (e.g. Lewis *et al.*, 1993).

However, on further reflection, or under other descriptions, mutual incompatibilities between models do frequently surface. For example, the FSM is sometimes interpreted as involving trade-offs of the shareholder wealth (or utility) against the interests of various stakeholder groups (e.g. employees, the natural environment, etc.); but this is not the case with

Table 9.2 Comparison of competitive advantage and hypercompetition.

(a) The new elements of the CMHC are

1. The rapid erosion of all entry barriers to all industries
2. The concept of the escalation ladder within and between the four arenas, with exhaustion and surprise (disruption) patterns of moves
3. The purely instrumental use and evaluation of strategic alliances
4. Prescribed moves that deliberately increase rivalry amongst incumbents

(b) The elements shared with CSCA are

5. Industry incumbents act to weaken the four external forces (I–IV)
6. Cannibalisation, destruction of one's own assets, or disruption
7. Players co-operate (partly) in order to compete more effectively
8. Players lobby to create a more favourable legal environment (in CMHC this is particularly against antitrust laws)

(c) The elements shared with some other models are

9. Strategy as a pattern of decisions (in CMHC, this involves the four arenas, depicted in the figure)
10. Ethos of profit maximisation despite the law, or with (civil) lawsuits as calculated risks
11. Time-based competition, with analysis of the timing of any strategic move (also partly in CSCA)
12. The end-state, with a few large (Global) players or alliances

(d) The disputed elements of CSCA are

13. The concept of a sustainable competitive advantage based on a specific competence in a stable state
14. The existence of industries with one or more weak "forces", with associated prescriptions from CSCA
15. The derived concept of a disruptive player as a "bad competitor"

(e) The missing elements of the CMHC, found in other models, include

16. Strategies of embeddedness (i.e. within a productive complex), and sustained partnering
17. Industry structures determined by tacit knowledge boundaries, information specificity and separability
18. Engagement strategies, involving customers and suppliers
19. Transformational strategies, involving employees and alliance partners, etc.

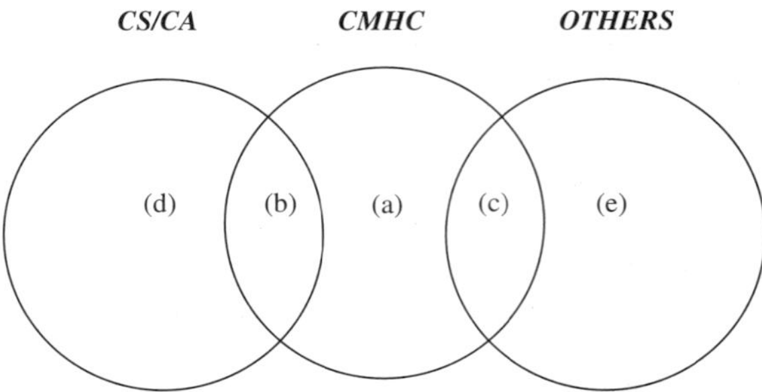

Figure 9.2   Feature comparison of conceptual models.

CS/CA. Similarly, for stewardship models of strategy or corporate governance, in relation to agency-theoretic models (e.g. Davis *et al.*, 1997). Many avenues for resolving these types of dispute can then be found within the general theory of rationality, where it is re-cast in terms of utility-maximisation versus rational-commitments, together with the several meta-rational arguments (expressed in natural and mathematical language) that place those distinctive forms of rationality relative to each other (Chapter 2).

9.4 Other Metamodels

Conceptual models can also be depicted and described in several ways other than as objects-of-choice and comparison. In this section, five other metamodels are briefly described (Table 9.3). They are design, transition, renewal, influence and replication, as follows.

9.4.1 Design

Technological advance has enabled all types of design to become better and cheaper. This heightened power of design extends beyond physical products, mental patterns and organisational structures to also embrace the wider cultural and ideological contexts within which all those minor productions occur. At the same time, technology has amplified the importance of many of the material and abstract things that are being designed (e.g. Werhane, 1999b), because these can have increasingly profound effects, for

Table 9.3 Metamodels and entities.

Metamodel	Depiction of CM	Role of Entity
Comparison	Object-of-choice	Analyser
Design	Trigger	Designer
Transition	End-state	Learner
Renewal	Trigger	Self-producer
Influence	Instrument	Political entity
Replication	Meme	Host

better or worse, on the human and natural environments (as discussed subsequently in Section 9.6). A conceptual model of strategy is not only a product of human design activity, but can also be an initiator, or a trigger, of a process of further design, or re-design. This happens whenever the psychological tension or dissonance caused by the differences between a new model and prior understandings motivates an entity to design some new combination or new synthesis, in order to reduce the dissonance or dissolve the tension.

This idea of the creative design of models and frameworks, in the context of strategic decision analysis, can be generalised to all levels of the strategic thinking process, as depicted in Figure 9.3. In meta-decision analysis (MDA), the activity of design extends beyond the generation of new strategic alternatives, to encompass new conceptual models and possibly even new forms of rationality or optimality (see Chapters 11–13). Put differently, in MDA, an entity reflects upon and re-considers its options or alternatives, its models and its rationalities. (The term "step back" contrasts saliently with the technical term "roll-back" as used in standard utility-based calculations involving decision trees.) This "stepping back" repeats and reflective thinking continues until a cognitive equilibrium is attained and the situation is resolved (e.g. Zeleny, 1989).

9.4.2 Transition

In addition to the outcome of design activity, a strategy model can also be depicted as an end-state of a psychological transition process (Figure 9.4). It is the final stage of a process of cognitive accommodation, variously described

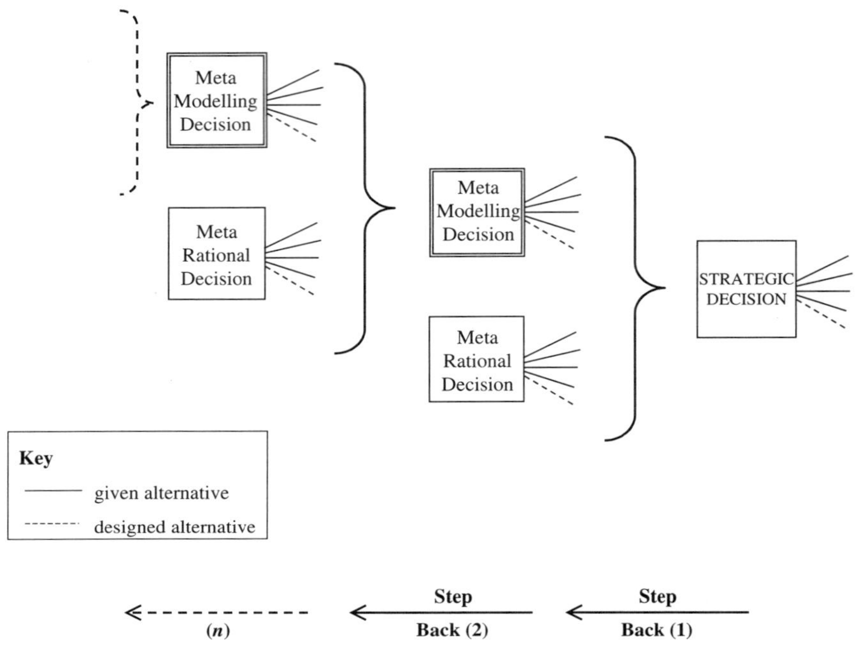

Figure 9.3   Meta decision analysis and design.

as the creation of a new schema, *gestalt,* mindset, or frame.[3] As mentioned previously, the "change" from one conceptual model to another might be accompanied by a simultaneous but much wider paradigm shift or ideological transition. For example, a utility-based game model can be transformed into a model of engagement (Chapter 10), or the I–O conceptual model can be transformed into a stakeholder model in the managerial mind (Donaldson and Preston, 1995), in several ways that are separate but mutually supporting. These "ways" include the incremental addition of features in a depiction of the model, but also natural language (or meta-language) arguments that are intended to persuade managers about the models and the systems that they represent.

The particular example of comparison of CS/CA versus CMHC can be reconstructed in terms of this "transition" metamodel (Singer, 1999a). The CS/CA model can indeed be transformed, by incremental steps, into the hypercompetition model (refer to Figure 9.5). As the transition takes

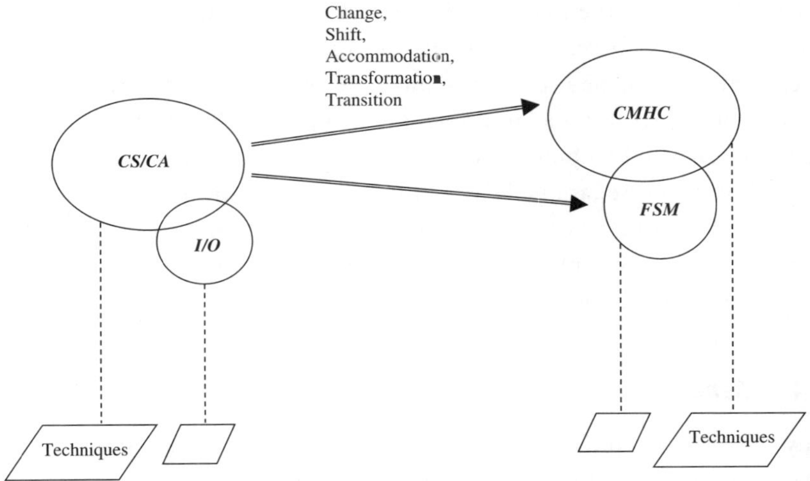

Figure 9.4 The transition metamodel.

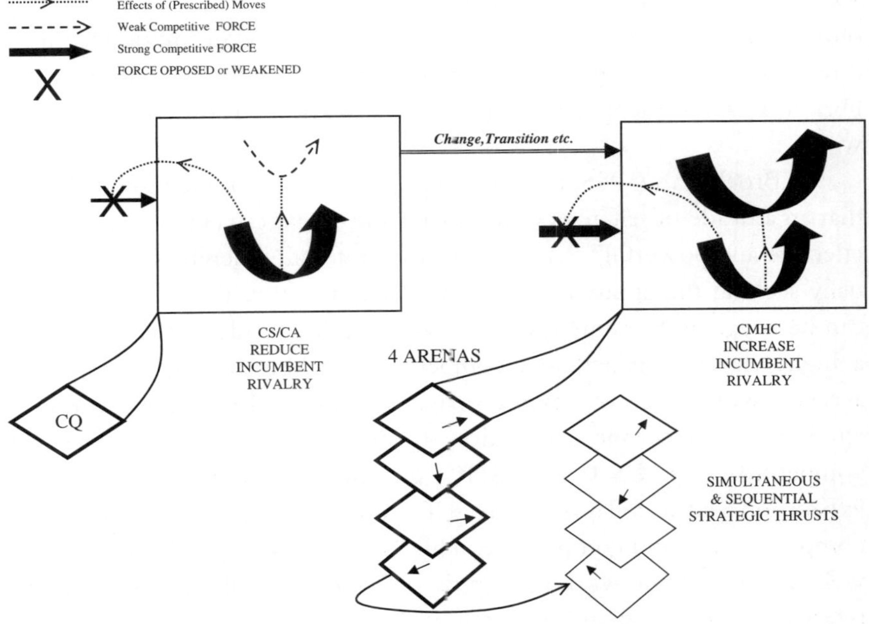

Figure 9.5 Transition from competitive advantage to hyper-competition.

place, elements of the first model (CS/CA) such as the existence of industries-with-weak-forces are deleted or forgotten. They are replaced or over-written with new elements and new features, such as the escalation of incumbent rivalry and multiple arenas (Table 9.2). At the same time, new model-based techniques of practical strategic analysis actually replace the old. In this case, as in all cases of transition, questions about choice and preference amongst models are re-cast as questions about timing (see Chapter 1). For example, one can ask how an entity knows when it should make these transitions.

9.4.3 Renewal

Any given conceptual model can act as a trigger of an inner-directed change process, or the psychological and cultural renewal of an entity. A model triggers an exploration of new alternatives, an examination of an entity's core values and its rationalities, resulting in a transformation of the entity itself, or a heightened sense of self (e.g. Taylor, 1989; Broekstra, 1998). Put differently, design activity, which is normally thought of as outer-directed, is now seen to be complemented by an important inner-directed transformation. The process of stepping back to a cognitive equilibrium in MDA (depicted in Figure 9.3) can also be re-interpreted in this way.

In Broekstra's (1998, p. 173), account of this phenomenon he claimed that an attitude of self-referral involving a deep experience of self is "more effective and powerful" than one of other-referral, whereby one is continually seeking the approval of others. Put differently, the self-referral that can be triggered by some given model potentially endows the entity with a higher level of generalised competence, making it more competitive across a wide range of environmental conditions. In contrast, continual attempts to understand a relentless stream of other-produced models of competition (e.g. CS/CA, CMHC) eventually culminates in saturation, exhaustion and a collapse of the self, ironically, with a probable loss of competitiveness and competence. This "renewal" metamodel also coheres well with the classic work of Argyris (1977) on mental models, because it refers to the personal and organisational benefits that can flow from what he called the double-loop learning and reflective practice.

9.4.4 Influence

Any strategy model can be deliberately deployed for political purposes. It can be endorsed by powerful entities such as a senior management team, or a state, whereupon the model influences others' decisions and actions. Specifically, an entity in a position of power can draw attention to a particular model or embed it explicitly in some formal institutional process, with the covert intention of influencing others' behaviour. For example, the CMHC model or the R–R–D model might be deployed in an organisation, ostensibly, in order to alert managers to new types of competitive threat, but with a covert purpose of reinforcing an ideology associated with the model. Strategy models like these two can deflect people's attention away from ethical issues such as distributive justice or the environment.

In contrast, models such as I–Game, or FSM, might be deployed in an authentic attempt by management to produce a more trusting or caring organisational climate. In either case (i.e. pro-ethics or anti-ethics), the individuals and groups being influenced by model deployment would in effect be in a position of deferring to others, or simply engaging in single-loop learning. Put differently, they are being encouraged to master a hidden curriculum of compliance and subservience. As described in the preceding section, this type of influence tends to block rather than foster reflective practice, hence also retard self-renewal and full self-realisation. Yet, to the extent that manufactured fictions can be made to prevail on the ground, model deployment amongst unreflective subordinates can be quite successful as a political tactic, in practice.

9.4.5 Replication

Finally, conceptual models can again be re-described as productive entities that co-produce ideas and copies of themselves in the minds of managers. Under this description, conceptual models of strategic behaviour replicate and compete for the share of individual and collective mind, as in Foucault's description of the competing discourses that, he says, characterise the contemporary global culture. This "replication" metamodel finds its sharpest expression in the quasi-scientific idea of a *meme* (Dawkins, 1976). Memes are chunks of information that lodge in minds in much the same way parasites lodge in biological organisms.[4] Their role in mental processes, or evolution of culture, or ecology of mind (e.g. Bateson, 1972) is then closely analogous to the role of genes in natural ecologies, or in microbiological systems. Specifically, every time an entity hosts a meme (i.e. something attends to, or evokes a model), a replication occurs. With this metamodel, a strategy model is recast as a particular type of producer-entity, so that the distinction between the producer (of an idea) and the product (the idea itself) collapses. This notion carries potentially quite profound implications for strategic thinking within a knowledge-based system of production and distribution, as discussed in the following sections.

9.5 Recursivity and Ecology

The replication metamodel incorporates the notion of a strategic entity (e.g. organisation or host) that does not freely select a conceptual model of strategy. Instead the model itself "lodges" within the entity. This quickly raises questions about whether or not a strategic entity can exercise that form of freewill in which it chooses to see the world in particular ways (e.g. Casti, 1994; Dennett, 1995; Ridley, 1999). In the strategy literature, similar questions have often been asked about the ability of a firm to freely choose and deliberately execute its own strategy (e.g. Mintzberg and Waters, 1985; Whittington, 1993). This significant "similarity" involves (i) a metamodel (i.e. replication) and (ii) a particular conception of strategy (i.e. emergent strategy and strategy-as-perspective). It is by no means the only such similarity. For example, questions about timing have already occurred in this chapter at these two quite separated levels of analysis: one can certainly question the timing of a firm's strategic move from one position to another, as done within the CMHC, but one can equally challenge the timing of an entity's transition from one conceptual model of strategy to another, such as from CS/CA to the CMHC.

More significantly, all of the various categories of meaning that have been developed and used to answer the vexed question of "What is strategy?" can now also be applied to the equally vexed question of "What is a conceptual model (of strategy)?". Specifically, a correspondence exists between the metamodels (i.e. comparison, transition, design, etc.) and several key concepts of strategic management, such as selecting strategic alternatives,

Table 9.4 Strategy and metamodels.

Metamodel	Strategy Concept
Comparison	Strategic choice, selection
Design	Generate options, overcome trade-offs
Transition	Management of change
Renewal	Develop competencies
Influence	Incrementalism, symbolism
Replication	Emergent

change-management and generating strategic options (Table 9.4). Thus, successive higher levels of strategic thinking and analysis simply reveal recurring categories of meaning, with repeating patterns of thought.

9.5.1 Fractals

At this point, a new and different way of associating strategic management with complexity and chaos theory becomes quite apparent, involving the metamodels of strategy. In fractal geometry (e.g. Casti, 1994; Harries–Jones, 1995), mathematical objects such as the Mandelbrot set are produced or computed by infinitely recursive mathematical operations. These patterns can be depicted in a two-dimensional complex plane (the Argand diagram). At the boundary of the M-set, the microstructure consists of patterns embedded within similar patterns that recur infinitely many times as one zooms through successively higher levels of image resolution. Furthermore, gradual zooming causes an archetypal pattern to become temporarily obscure but then to reappear in a very similar form to the original set (these are called the "baby M-sets").

Something strikingly similar has occurred in the above account of strategic metamodels. Starting at the object level of reality and practice, attention was re-directed to the set of conceptual models of strategy (Table 9.1), where a confusing multitude was encountered. At this level of thought, the ultimate meaning and epistemological status of the conceptual models remains quite obscure. However, by "zooming" to the level of metamodelling, not only did a more orderly set of categories re-appear, but these were observably similar to some more familiar practical strategy concepts that we started with (Table 9.4). Accordingly, the Mandelbrot set, which also exhibits this kind of zooming phenomenon and is derived from recursive operations, might be considered as a depiction and as a mathematical description of strategic metamodels.

The pattern of linkages described so far between strategy models, recursivity[5] and chaos is depicted on the left-hand side of Figure 9.6 (below). First, recursivity or self-reference is inherent in the very idea of metamodelling as defined earlier (in Section 9.2). Next, the self-referential nature of strategy models was revealed in a novel way (in Table 9.4), together with a specific similarity between metamodelling and fractal patterns (i.e. zooming). In addition, the mathematical description of the M-set also involves formal recursion (i.e. the repeated application of a mathematical function to its own outputs).

9.5.2 Ecology

The entire analysis and discussion thus far can be expanded into a wider framework that links strategy with ecology. First, a direct linkage between recursivity and ecology can be made via chaos theory, simply by noting that recursively produced fractal patterns are, or are perceived as, identical to the patterns found in nature. This link is depicted on the lower right of Figure 9.6.

Deeper theoretical linkages between recursivity, chaos and ecology can also be outlined, as depicted on the upper right of Figure 9.6. Recursivity essentially means self-reference, which typically involves some kind of unification of perceived differences or the bringing together of previously separated levels of description (refer to Chapter 6). This abstract notion was first expressed in Epimenides' classical paradox: "this sentence is false". More than 2000 years later, it was re-formulated as Russell's paradox: if we write that "the set of all sets that are not members of themselves", the proposition that "this set contains itself" quickly yields in the mind the idea that it does not. To resolve this version of the paradox, a more elaborate theory was designed (in *Principia Mathematica*) that distinguished between signs (e.g. sentences, conceptual models) and their referents (the semantics).

Finally, the link between mathematical logic and ecological systems becomes quite apparent when Russell's paradox is restated slightly as a riddle

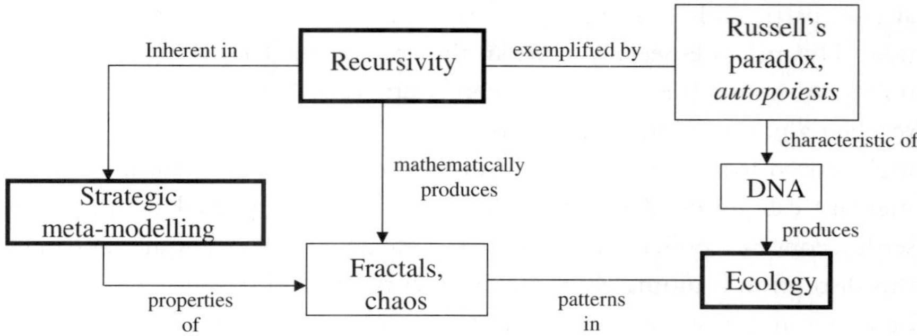

Figure 9.6 Recursivity and ecology.

involving self-production (refer to Chapter 6). At that point in the argument, something that was initially expressed a purely abstract idea of self-reference becomes transformed into a description of physical self-replication, much like a DNA molecule existing in the material and natural world. This molecule, in turn, is understood to be the building block or "producer" of ecologies.

9.6 Implications

It has often been observed in practice that models of strategy compete for share of mind in much the same way other intangible products like software, or tangible market offerings like the books in which they are written. It is perhaps less obvious that the models might behave like the very entities (i.e. firms, knowledge producers) to which they are referring. In either case, the full implications of self-reference in knowledge about the strategy of productive entities has not been very fully considered. It has been realised (e.g. Evans and Wurster, 2000, p. 5) that knowledge-related products are seemingly forcing existing businesses to deconstruct (i.e. to dismantle and perhaps re-configure their business processes and value chains). Yet, at the same time, managers' models of strategy also compete, and they too are being frequently disrupted.

More generally, it is not just businesses and strategy models that "deconstruct" in a world where a producer and a product answer to similar description and carry out similar functions; wider abstract understandings are also at risk, particularly concerning the social and economic contexts of business. This risk is especially acute in the area of intellectual property rights policy. Although this has always been controversial, it now appears to have reached a point of "intellectual crisis" (Vaver, 2000, p. 630). The increasingly varied forms and applications of IT again and again disrupt the elementary categories of meaning that were historically used to frame and settle economic policies and business strategies. As is now quite apparent, this disruption is ultimately rooted in recursivity and the related paradoxes of communication, yet its implications for social futures seem far from being fully appreciated (e.g. National Research Council, 2000; Watt, 2000; Singer and Calton, 2001).

9.6.1 Theory of Strategy

The theoretical strategy literature frequently refers to "evolutionary perspectives" (e.g. Whittington, 1993) as well as environmental or green strategies that seek competitive advantage (e.g. Hawken, 1993; Shrivastava, 1995; Rugman and Verbeke, 1998). Most contemporary theories and models ignore recursivity and its related ideas. In economic theory, the emphasis is upon utility-creating exchanges coupled with an analysis of incentives for production. Mainstream marketing theory duly focuses upon exchanges that create value. Indeed the American Marketing Academy defines marketing as "the science of exchanges". A great many strategy models and frameworks also emphasise creation of "value" (i.e. utility) for customers and for shareholders.

The present framework offers an additional deep-structure approach to linking strategy with ecology. It seems that the mainstream theories can be augmented to incorporate notions of recursivity and self-production (e.g. replication of software, copying a strategic business model, organisational autopoiesis, etc.). Put differently, the preference relations that constitute the axiomatic foundation of the Neo-Classical Economic paradigm can be augmented with some formal recursive relations. Accordingly, the value-creation goals associated with these preference relations can be augmented by goals of self-production and co-production, including the production of various moral and ideological effects on the wider business and social system.

Such a theoretical advance would not only further identify strategic thinking with ecological thinking, but also carry some ethical implications. The identification of strategic thinking with ecological thinking recasts the strategy–ethics interface in the most traditional of terms: strategic thinking can now be seen as either an intrinsic part of an ecology of mind, or else as a distinctively human, ethical or humane activity that transcends nature. The first viewpoint incorporates its own warnings: any idea (including this one) can lodge in minds, where its effects can be beneficial, neutral or destructive for its carriers. With the second interpretation, strategic managers are understood to be capable of transcending their material and natural circumstances, thereby operating, individually and collectively, at a higher level of moral consciousness and with humane ideals in mind.

9.7 Conclusion

The present study began with an exploration of strategic metamodelling. A conceptual framework was developed that further indicates how strategic thinking in business might come to be more closely identified with ecological thinking. It is certainly no longer necessary to see the fields of strategy and ecology as being in opposition, or incompatible. On the contrary, in a productive system where natural man co-operates and competes with artificial intelligence (as, for example, in the co-production of this chapter) it is difficult to see how they can ultimately be separated.

At the level of management practice, terms such as "business ecology", "product ecology" and "knowledge ecology" have all been deployed quite widely, indicating that many have already sensed the fundamental commonality between strategy and ecology. This understanding looks likely to endure. Knowledge from the new sciences such as ecology, chaos and complexity will probably become more fully incorporated into future theories and conceptual models of business and management. To the extent that this happens, studies of the latter might in turn provide an important platform for enriching and popularising understandings of the "New Sciences" whilst also clarifying their social and economic significance. Here, there appears to be a two–way symbiotic relationship within an even larger ecology of knowledge.

Notes

1. A different and more technical usage of the term has referred to statistical models of outputs, from large scale computer simulations (e.g. Kleinjen and Van Groenendaal, 1992).

2. This distinction corresponds roughly to marketing versus organisation versus strategy, as fields of study. It also evokes a classical *Janus*-image: looking inward and outward. All such distinctions are problematic. For example, in a game of strategy, the description of other player(s) determines what is rational and moral for the first player; yet it is also an outward projection: a reflection of the disposition and self-knowledge of the first player. Thus, a choice between, say, CMHC versus FSM influences an entity's perceptions of its external environment, but the choice itself is partly determined by its own behavioural pre-dispositions and moral propensities.

3. A compelling metaphor for the transition metamodel is found in the lithograph "*Liberation*", by artist M. C. Escher (1955). A row of triangles transforms incrementally into birds in flight (e.g. Hofstadter, 1979, p. 57).

4. As indicated in the discussion of "renewal", an entity that hosts any particular model is not necessarily advantaged, for memes, like genes, can be beneficial, or neutral, or destructive.

5. Taking a different approach, Beer (1972) examined the operation of recursive loops in the design of organisational control systems, but within a larger conceptual framework of organisation-as-organism. Beer's ideas have endured (e.g. Brocklesby and Cummings, 1996). Other commonalities between ecological and organisational systems have been discussed elsewhere (e.g. Zeleny, 1981).

Chapter 10

GAMES: Game Theory and the Evolution of Strategic Thinking

Abstract: This chapter is an abridged version of "Game theory and the evolution of strategic thinking," *Human Systems Management* 16, pp. 63–75, 1997. The idea that the study of game theory could help managers to think better about strategic problems is re-interpreted with reference to various extensions and adaptations of that theory. An "adapted" conceptual model of an Ultragame is then set out, in which the players are plurally rational strategic-entities. Conceptual models of this type can help managers to augment their language, their ideology and their integrity. Compared to the formal mathematical extensions of game theory, which have found but a few business applications, the adapted conceptual models are more directly relevant to contemporary business problems such as those involving the players' boundaries and identities, as well as their likely future problems and others' problems.

10.1 Introduction

It is often said that game theory can help managers to gain new insight, or to *think better* about problems of competition and business strategy (e.g. Howard, 1971; Chatterjee and Lilien, 1986; Saloner, 1994 to mention a few), but it is often not clear what "thinking better" really means, in contemporary management contexts.

If the phrase is simply taken to mean avoiding miscalculation or identifying an equilibrium point, then game theory and its various extensions (e.g. supergames, metagames, information-dependent games, etc.) provide an appropriate analytic framework. However, if "thinking better" is taken to imply an improved understanding of the world as it now really is, or improving creativity when finding and solving important problems, then the role of game theoretic models in business strategy becomes laid open to a rather significant critique. First, the players in games of business strategy are themselves often changing their structures, their boundaries and their identities, as all types of productive entity are re-configuring in novel ways, made possible by the new communication technologies. Second, while contemporary managers are undoubtedly confronting increased competition in the marketplace, they are also (often reluctantly) having to confront many social and environmental problems. In sum, formal game theory cannot be expected to yield practical solutions to many of the most important problems of contemporary "strategic" business management.

Despite the limitations, research in game theory could still help managers to "think better", especially if the theory itself is *adapted* to this purpose in ways to be defined shortly (in Section 10.2). As a first step, it may be noted that formal models in general (e.g. for forecasting, asset-valuation, or strategic-analysis, etc.) have often been observed to function in organisations (and in educational contexts) in unorthodox ways, that is, ways that are somewhat disconnected from the mathematical theories that gave birth to them. In particular, the formal models of game theory, as they have become more widely known and understood, have also tended to promulgate quite distinctive assumptions about business goals, competitive behaviour and the nature of rationality in management (e.g. Solomon, 1999). For this reason, game theoretic models do much more than merely represent or explain strategic behaviour; they also affect that behaviour and slowly change it. Put differently, the models themselves are like *memes* (Dawkins, 1976), which are the cultural equivalent of genes. The models or memes lodge in players' minds (individually and collectively) as they are copied, spread out and propagated through a community of thinkers, or players.

In Section 10.3, various extensions and adaptations of game theory are briefly described. The "extensions" involve mathematical developments of simple game models that are characterised by the fundamental assumption of Rational-Utility-Maximising (RUM) players and jointly determined outcomes. "Adaptations" in contrast involve extending the players' set of rationalities by including other distinctive forms, including those that are not captured by RUM. (For fuller accounts of but a few of the "elusive" forms of rationality see, for example, Schick, 1984; Rorty, 1986; Sagoff, 1988; Etzioni, 1988; Hargreaves-Heap, 1989; Cudd, 1993; Baier, 1995).

Examples of adaptations include the operationalised version of Metagames (e.g. Howard, 1971) and Hypergames (e.g. Bennett and Huxham, 1982) as well as the conceptual model of an Ultragame (Chapter 3 and Singer, 1993b, 1994a, 1995, and 1996b,c,d). Section 10.4 then discusses various ways of comparing and evaluating these extensions and adaptations. Finally, by invoking the conceptual framework of Strategy-as-Rationality (Chapters 2 and 3), this metatheoretic treatment of games and their rationalities can be placed at the core of strategic management theory and practice.

10.2 The Roles of Mathematical Models

Several studies have identified unorthodox roles of formal (quantitative or mathematical) models in organisations (e.g. Fischoff and Goiten, 1984; Rosenhead, 1989). These roles can be classified (Table 10.1) as (i) relating to the internal politics of organisations, such as conferring power to individuals based upon their expertise with the model, (ii) soft-OR applications, in which adapted models function as problem-structuring methodologies and (iii) ideological roles, in which formal models come to symbolise, promulgate, or propagate particular assumptions and beliefs about the organisation and its strategic problems (as in Solomon's critique). Each of the above "roles" is quite plainly *social*, as well as analytic and cognitive. Indeed, it has increasingly become recognised by Management Scientists (Landry and Oral, 1993, p. 162; Rosenhead, 1989) that the building and validating of all formal mathematical models are "not only cognitive activities, but also social activities". The present chapter explores this social dimension of game theory: its politics, its formulations and its ideologies.

With game theory, the consequences of ignoring the social dimension of model validation and model use, whilst attending to the traditional mathematics of optimisation, can indeed be rather serious. Twenty five years ago, Davis and Hersh (1981) suggested that mathematical modellers often "deliberately force... social aspects of the universe" into the "delightful (mathematical) patterns they have wrought", implying that they force out the more elusive social, ideological and moral aspects of the system being modelled. Later, Etzioni (1988) made a rather similar point in his book, *The Moral Dimension*. He also (like Solomon after him) noted that formal economic theories based upon RUM players and agents, often

Table 10.1 Some unorthodox roles of formal models.

(i) "Political" roles include models as

Status-symbols: when the managers who understand and operate the model acquire status and power based upon this expertise

Pliers: when the need to estimate model parameters enables managers to extract confessions, or assumptions, from subordinates, or to squeeze them into line

Batteries: when the participants in a detailed analysis tend to increase their psychological commitment to any resulting prescriptions (i.e. the illusion of control)

(ii) "Soft" roles include models as

Platforms: when models become an arena or platform for an organised discussion, or reflection

Socratic tutors: when models enable their users to learn, or to educate themselves, by means of structured inquiry. For example, presentation of the Prisoners' Dilemma Game sometimes evokes questions about possibilities for cooperation

Keys: when models become like a set of keys which will "open doors for the actors and allow them to proceed" (Landry and Oral, 1993)

(iii) "Ideological" roles include models as

Rituals: when the process of model building serves to reinforce a culture of profit maximisation (associated with RUM) in an organisation

Glue: when models bind or unite managers (or team members) together, behind a common set of goals, concepts and vocabulary

Filters and switches: when a model serves to direct (or re-direct) attention towards (or away from) particular aspects of a managerial problem, such as the social and moral aspects

Memes: when models function as units of cultural transmission. Like popular tunes, they leap from mind to mind and affect the behaviour of the "infected" entities

---

"miseducate" students of business management and tend to co-produce a future society or social system with all the "wrong" characteristics. For example, the students (and the society) become more comfortable with, or de-sensitised to the corresponding language of threat, fear, predation, opportunism and guile (all in the name of fiduciary duty); but they remain relatively impatient, careless or ignorant about words such as fairness, justice, dignity and moral rights.

It is not that only neo-classical and evolutionary economics, with their corresponding perspectives on strategic management (e.g. Whittington, 1993), that have successfully propagated the language of Jungle-Warfare throughout many business and political communities: in his book *Darwin's Dangerous Idea,* philosopher Dennett (1995, p. 491) has also specifically warned of the risks associated with "doing good work in Evolutionary Ethics" (which is based upon game theoretic models), nonetheless remaining "dismayingly heedless of the misuses to which (these models) might be put, by ideologues of one persuasion or another".

10.2.1 Models as Memes

Formal models quickly "leap from mind to mind", like memes, in effect generating copies of themselves, changing or infecting individual and collective minds and slowly influencing the zeitgeist. Accordingly, the general characteristics of memes become relevant to ethics. First, like genes, memes help themselves: once they have been created, they tend to disable any opposing or hostile forces in their environment. This dynamic was clearly illustrated in the success of the Tit-for-Tat algorithm (a meme) in Axelrod's (1984) evolutionary competition. In the case of game models (like the Prisoners' Dilemma Game regarded as a meme), this "disabling" capability has historically taken on the form of RUM-capturing: the many attempts (some Nobel prize winning) to disable the more traditional notions of morality and sociality, by capturing them in terms of the players' interests and utilities.

Second, successful memes (like genes) are not necessarily advantageous to the society or total system that hosts them. They do not confer success upon the system as a whole. As Darwin himself wrote, "I cannot persuade myself that a beneficent and omnipotent God would have designedly created the *Ichneumonidae* (a type of wasp) with the express intention of their feeding within the living bodies of caterpillars". Put differently, some of the genes (or memes) that are generously hosted by a system (or culture) can turn out to be highly destructive. In this sense, there are good memes and bad memes (e.g. Dennett, 1995).

Is game theory "good" or "bad"? Those who see something distinctive and elusive (i.e. not "captured") in their notions of morality, sociality and ethics, something that cannot be adequately represented or expressed in terms of mere interests, preferences and desires, must also see something correspondingly "bad" about game theory... its ideological overtones, with its potentially corrosive social impact. More constructively, despite the occasional claims by some economists of the theory's capability for generating "good advice" for managers and strategists (Camerer, 1994), or of its complete ethical neutrality (Binmore, 1999), it would seem that it is also capable of improvement through adaptation, brought about by conscious human intervention aimed at promoting and communicating ethical ideals.

10.3 Adaptations

During their 50 year history, the so-called "simple" game models (Howard, 1971) have been extended in various ways (Figure 10.1 and Table 10.2). An "extension" of a formal model is defined for present purposes as a mathematical development which yields a deeper or more comprehensive analysis. Such extensions characteristically retain the implicit assumption of RUM players. As Von Neumann (1959, p. 13) himself put it, this means that "the behaviour (of each of the players) is (assumed to be) motivated by the same selfish interests as the behaviour of the first player". Examples of this type of formal extension include Supergames (Luce and Raiffa, 1957), Games-with-imperfect-information (Harsanyi, 1968), Metagames (Howard, 1971) and Psychological or information-dependent games (Geanakoplos and Pearce, 1989; Gilboa and Schmeidler, 1988).

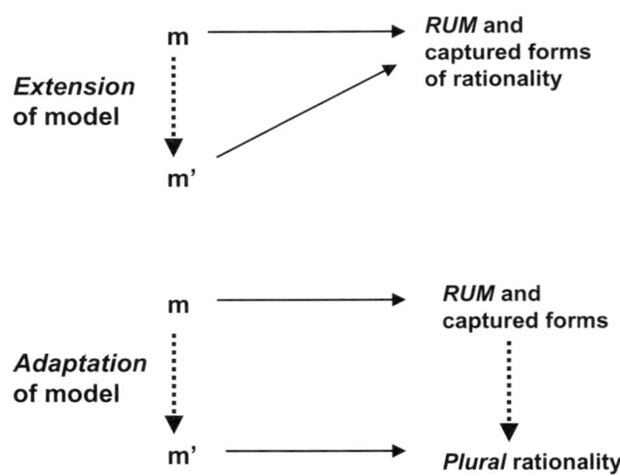

Figure 10.1 Extensions versus adaptations of formal models.

Table 10.2 Extensions of formal games with some properties.

Model m	Decision-function rationality is ...	Objects-of-choice are ...	Type of *prescription*	Rigour-relevance	Purpose(s)	Players are homo ...	Decision error is to ...
m_1 Simple game (normal or extensive form)	*RUM* (strategic)	Given and probabilistic	Choose a pure or mixed or probabilistic strategy, or make side-agreements	High rigour	Improve under-standing, provide insight, prescribe, guide and hypothesise	*economicus*	Choose a dominated strategy, etc.
m_2 Supergame	*RUM* (evolutionary)						
m_3 imperfect-info-game	*RUM* (with Bayesian revision)				To uncover the objectively rational behaviour in a game		Miscalculate
m_4 Metagame (I) (1971)	*RUM* (meta-rationality$_1$)	Constructed algorithmically from the given objects of choice	Choose a metastrategy or conditional strategy, etc.	Hardly ever used as technique			
m_5 Info-dependent or psychological games	*RUM* (psychic utility)	Given, incorporating psychological states	As in m_1–m_4		To capture hopes, fears, disappointments, etc.		

These "extensions" are labelled m_1 to m_5 in Table 10.2, where some of their more salient properties are also listed.

In contrast with extensions, the term "adaptation of a formal model" suggested here refers to potential developments of the model itself, or actual methodological operationalisations of the model, that incorporate or sweep in some other distinctive form(s) of rationality. These could include the elusive forms (refer back to Section 10.1) that are not fully captured, or reducible to RUM. When a model is "adapted" in this sense, its image under the mapping decision-function-rationality (Singer, 1991a, 1994b) becomes extended, but not necessarily the model itself (Figure 10.1). Examples of the so-called "adaptations" of simple games include Metagames in their operational form (Howard, 1971), Hypergames as a "methodique" (Bennet and Huxham, 1982) and Ultragames (as described in Chapter 2 and below). These adaptations are labelled m_6 to m_9 in Table 10.3.

10.3.1 The Ultragame Model

The conceptual model of an Ultragame is the result of pursuing the process of adaptation of formal game models to its ultimate conclusion. An Ultragame (m_8 and m_9 in Table 10.3) is a methodology that simply sweeps in all the distinctive forms of rationality, the entire rationality-set, into a conceptual model of strategic interaction amongst multiple types of entity, each of which is plurally rational. In this "model", it is implicitly assumed that each player is not only engaged in a competitive battle to further its "selfish interests" or utilities (even when broadly defined). But also seen to be engaged in a search for competitive success with reference to plural rationality (as explained previously, in Chapter 3). Put differently, all of the players in an Ultragame are assumed to have significant concerns for society, morality, ecology and autonomy that mediate their behaviour, but that cannot be fully captured as preferences over a set of well-defined strategic action alternatives.

Despite its incomplete formal exposition, the conceptual model of an Ultragame can readily be made operational as a structured *inquiry*, framework or "method" for strategic thinking (Singer, 1993b). This can be used in practice to support internal strategic analysis, where players basically direct questions at themselves, or for understanding the behaviour of other

Table 10.3 Adaptations of game, with some properties.

Model m	Decision-function rationality is …	Objects-of-choice are	Type of *Prescription*	Rigour-Relevance	*Purpose*(s)	Players are *homo* …	Decision error is to …
m_6 Metagame (1987)	Meta-rationality, with belief forms	Actions (given or generated) perceived as means of control of issues	Inquiry, incorporating promises, fears, hopes, etc	Moderate rigour, used as tool and technique	Problem-structuring, facilitating agreements, understanding conflict, arming oneself, exploring scenarios	*economicus* and *cogitans*	Overlook possible cutcome scenarios
m_7 Hypergame	RUM with belief forms	Perceived hypothesised (assumed)	As for (meta-)game but with reconsideration of the identity of other players and their preferences				Misperceive other players' perceived game
m_8 Ultragame (1)	Plural-rationality	Vaguely perceived, partially defined constructed, symbolic hyper-real	Inquiry based upon plural-rationality	Low rigour, relevant to problem-owner, other's problems and future problems	Redirect attention, propagate ideology, re-make players	*economicus* and *cogitans* and *civicus*	Poor choice of rationality as evaluated by meta-criteria
m_9 Ultragame (2)	Hyper-rationality	Designed strategies	Engage in optimal design, with synergies		As above, motivate synergies and optimal design	*creans* and *designans*	Failure to design synergistic alternatives

entities, as in traditional business "competitor" analysis methodologies. Various questions in ordinary natural-language flow directly from each distinctively defined form of rationality. For example, there are questions rooted in the *cognitive* and *instrumental* forms of rationality (Walliser, 1989), but also associated with simple games such as "What are the competitors' expectations about our behaviour? What are its internal incentive structures?". Other questions are then based upon the more *elusive* forms of rationality such as "Does the entity... have a history or policy of treating others fairly?... avoiding or minimising harm?... preserving traditions?... contributing to the development of institutions that symbolise a good life with others?... protecting the rights of others?... fostering autonomy and positive freedom?". In the World today, there are many people who think that contemporary corporate managers and network participants should be asking all of these questions, then seeking or designing some answers, not to mention openly discussing these questions whilst encouraging others to do so. Indeed, it is the primary purpose of the Ultragame model to re-direct the players' attention accordingly.

10.3.2 Synergistic Design

A further adaptation of game theory, an Ultragame-2 incorporates the idea of *synergies* amongst the distinctive forms of rationality (see Chapter 3). In this adaptation of game theory, each strategic entity is re-conceptualised as being hyper-rational, in the sociological sense (see Glossary). Hyper-rational entities seek to implant synergies amongst their plural forms of rationality (Ritzer and LeMoyne, 1991; Singer, 1995). Additional questions for strategic analysis then follow quite naturally from various forms of rationality synergy, for example, does the entity (or player)

> ... apply scientific knowledge to increase the utilisation of its lower-level practical skills? (i.e. the theoretical and practical Weberian forms)

> ... forge links with benevolent institutions in ways that *strengthen* its sense of identity? (i.e. the contextual and expressive forms)

> ... creatively seek new ways of producing wealth for exchange, that also promote social justice, further democratic aims and *also* help to restore vital ecosystem? (i.e. the deliberative and RUM forms)

There are indeed a great many people who now think that managers should be asking precisely these questions, then actively seeking or designing some positive solutions, much more often (e.g. Drysek, 1995; Hawken, 1993; Hosmer, 1994, to mention a few). Neither the simple game theory nor its formal extensions can possibly help to cultivate or propagate this type of strategic-ethical thinking. Only the adaptations can do this.

10.3.3 Illustration

Despite the prevailing competitive ideology associated with extended games, some contemporary strategic-entities already do behave as if they were players in an Ultragame. For example, in 1992, the famous clothing company Levi Strauss reportedly broke off its relationship with some of its international garment suppliers, because the suppliers' business practices were deemed to be socially or environmentally unacceptable. The company then documented its "business-partner terms of engagement" that set out some hard questions to be asked about its suppliers, thus encouraging all the players involved to adopt more socially responsible business practices. In this episode, Levi Strauss were not searching for some optimal price-quality vector amongst some given alternatives. Like many other business players, they had committed themselves to a process of persuasion, assistance and co-operative re-design of the system in ways that reflect a larger rationality-set.

This kind of socially responsible business practice involves active "partner engagement" or persuasion (with words as well as money). Dialogue and morality play a distinctive role in bringing about creative change. It can be modelled (described, depicted, conceptualised) as an Ultragame. Yet it cannot be fully captured as a formal extended game, nor by the "supplier as a competitor" conceptual model of business strategy. As many have pointed out (e.g. Shrivastava and Scott, 1992), the latter models completely fail to capture the spirit and rationale of the progressive "partner engagement" doctrine, or the associated ethic of stewardship and care.

This rationality-based contrast between the simple game model and an Ultragame is illustrated further in Figures 10.2 and 10.3. In the figures, player 1 is a supplier company (a workshop, or sweatshop) located in a less-developed country. Its owner-managers (not to mention the employees) can perceive an alternative to the *status quo*: to become a progressive business. However, this would require some further investment leading to a higher unit cost, at least in the short term. These costs could be passed on, as a higher supply price. The *status quo* choice is simply to continue as an oppressive employer, paying very low wages for long hours, but enjoying relatively low unit cost. Player 1's preference then depends upon what player 2, the overseas buyer, is expected to do. Player 2 might prefer to renew the contract, or go elsewhere. When the strategic problem is thus *formulated* as a simple game, the plausible preference rankings for both players are as shown in the matrix (Figure 10.2).

With this formulation, the calculated (RUM) solution is to close the deal at the lower price $(1^=, 1)$. When implemented in the real world, this "solution" helps perpetuate and reinforce *habits of oppression*. Casual observation of many global sourcing policies readily confirms that this is not

PLAYER 2
Buyer

		Give contract to supplier	Find another supplier
PLAYER 1 Supplier	Progressive (higher cost & price)	$(1^=,\ 4)$	$(3,\ 2^=)$
	Oppressive (lower cost & price)	$(1^=,\ 1)$	$(4,\ 2^=)$

RANKINGS
(1 is best, 4 is worst)
PLAYER 1
1= becomes progressive and gets contract.
1= remains oppressive and gets contract
3 becomes progressive but loses contract and is consoled by conscience
4 loses contract, remains oppressive

PLAYER 2
1 buyer gets low-price supply
2 buyer finds another cheaper supplier but incurs costs of search
4 buyer gets high-price supply

FORMULATION:
As game of ranked interests

OUTCOME:
Deal closed, oppression perpetuated

Figure 10.2   A sourcing decision as a simple game.

such a rare outcome. Indeed, and this is the major point of the present paper, the outcome is rather inevitable, so long as one persists in formulating strategic business problems psychologically or mathematically as games-of-selfish-interests. Therefore, from a human system perspective, this formulation is itself a major part of the problem.

The Ultragame model now offers an explicit alternative formulation of the strategic interaction of producers. Rather than calculating joint interests, Ultragame players engage in inquiry, persuasion, reflection and creative re-design of their strategic possibilities. This process continues until the strategic problem is settled, resolved or dissolved (e.g. Zeleny, 1994a). More specifically, the supplier (player 1) asks some hard questions about player 2 and about itself (Q and Q′ in Figure 10.3). Some examples are

Q1. Does this entity (i.e. buyer and self) have a reputation or policy emphasising fairness in the treatment of stakeholders?
Q2. Are the entity's routine practices in line with its expressed values?
Q3. Does the entity utilise experience at all levels of operation in a process of continual improvement and re-design?, etc.

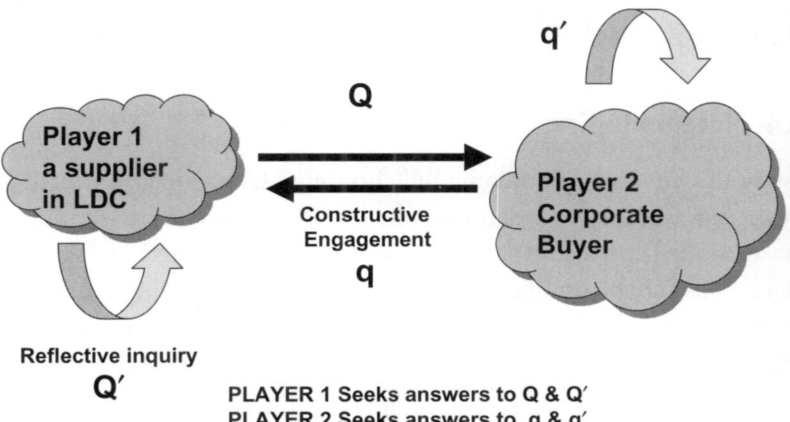

Figure 10.3 Sourcing policy as an Ultragame.

At the same time, player 2 (the buyer) seeks answers to another set of questions as they apply to player 1 and to itself (q and q′), as follows:

q1.   Does the entity have programs in place to develop its internal capabilities (e.g. training, education, etc.)?

q2.   Is there a pattern over time in this supplier's decisions? (e.g. delays, quality problems, poor treatment of staff, broken agreements, etc.)

q3.   Is our own situation (e.g. cash flow problems) unduly influencing our current dealings with the supplier? (e.g. inclining us to overlook the bad working conditions, etc.)

All of these questions (for a complete list see Appendix 10.1) flow readily from considerations of plural-rationality and hyper-rationality (in the synergy-seeking sense described in Chapter 3), that is, entities ask whether each particular form of rationality and which rationality-synergy is manifest in each of the other entities within the system being modelled. When this type of conceptual modelling occurs amongst multiple players, the outcome in the real world is likely to tend towards increased levels of trust and openness, as well as health, or competitive fitness. Put differently, the adapted conceptual model, in which with the strategic problem is re-formulated as an Ultragame, is itself part of the solution.

10.4 Metamodelling

Despite this envisioned outcome of "choosing" Ultragames as a method of strategic analysis, they are not universally preferred. If one were selecting from various models listed in Tables 10.2 and 10.3 (as depicted in Figure 10.4 and in Chapter 9), one could ask the metamodelling question: "Which model is best?" The column headings of these tables then provide a framework for structuring an evaluation of the models, as follows.

10.4.1 Rigour Relevance

All of the extensions of simple games (m_1 to m_5 in Table 10.1) are mathematically rigourous, but, for various reasons (e.g. Camerer, 1994), they are hardly ever used to solve real managerial problems. (However, almost 50 years after

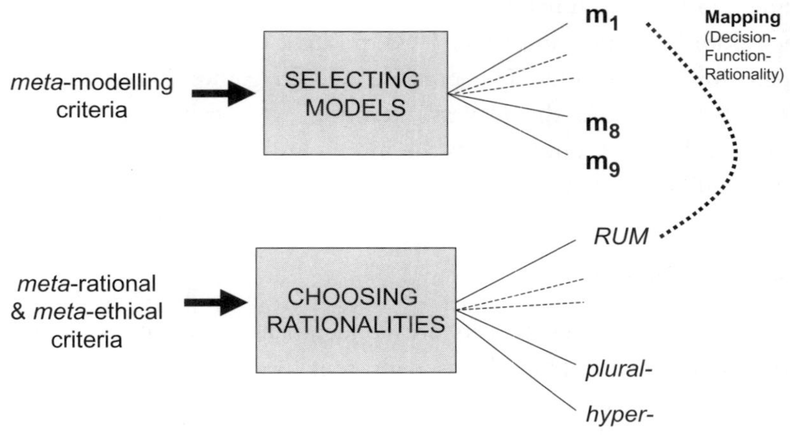

Figure 10.4   Selecting game models as choosing rationalities.

the original work, some business applications have been found to problems such as the setting of "fair" user-pay fees for privatised airport runway facilities.) In contrast, the soft-OR adaptations (m_6 and m_7 in Table 10.3) have been used in practice to facilitate problem-solving in a variety of organisations (e.g. Rosenhead, 1989). Ultragames (m_8 and m_9) occupy a rather special position on the rigour-relevance spectrum (e.g. Oral and Kettani, 1993). They are plainly conceptual rather than mathematical, but they are particularly relevant to problems that the players themselves may not even consciously perceive. These include problems associated with the players' integrity, ideology and language, as well as future problems and others' problems.

10.4.2 The Purposes

The mathematical extensions of game theory were developed partly out of intrinsic curiosity (e.g. Davis and Hersch, 1981) but also to yield potentially useful insights into utility-maximising behaviour. They have been used to prescribe action accordingly (e.g. by first finding an equilibrium point). In addition, the models have yielded many testable experimental hypotheses (e.g. Colman, 1982). In contrast, the adaptations of game theory were designed in order to function as *platforms, tutors* and *keys* (Table 10.1), to "open doors" (Landry and Oral, 1993, p. 163), to explore scenarios, or to prepare for negotiations. The purpose of Ultragames is also to act as a *switch* that re-directs the players' attention away from their immediate interests and desires, but towards the more elusive forms of rationality and the possibilities for creative re-design.

10.4.3 The Players

In extended games, the players are conceptualised as utility-maximising *homo economicus.* They have consistent preferences amongst given well-defined objects-of-choice (moves or strategies). In the soft-OR adaptations, however, the players are *homo economicus* and *homo cogitans.* The strategic alternatives are constructed percepts, whilst beliefs are accessed and revised as the game is played (i.e. the belief-oriented, or cognitive forms are swept in, becoming decision-function-rationalities). In Ultragames, the players also become *homo civicus* (Drysek, 1995), that is, they are mindful of the elusive forms of rationality and the importance of remaining open to persuasion by social dialogue and reflective deliberation. The objects-of-choice in the game might be partly defined, partly constructed or vaguely perceived. For example, they could be hyper-real symbols and signs (e.g. Goldman and Sapson, 1994), or prototypes of synergistic designs, envisioned and experienced in virtual worlds. In the latter case, the players have also become *homo creans* (creator) and *homo designans* (designer).

10.4.4 Decision-Errors

In extensions of games, an "error" takes the form of a miscalculation, or a player's choice of a formally dominated strategy. For example, in the one-off, two-player Prisoners' Dilemma Game, "co-operate" is sometimes called an "error", because it is dominated by "defect". In games of imperfect information, errors are normally associated with miscalculations involving probabilities. (In the metatheory, these are sometimes further interpreted in misapplications of players' cognitive heuristics.) In psychological games, errors can also involve the overlooking of some of the outcome-related influences on the psychic-utilities of the players (see Chapter 11). In metagame and hypergame analysis, the notion of "error" is yet further expanded to include the overlooking of important possibilities, the misconstruing the other players' perceived games, or even wrongly identifying the other players (e.g. Howard, 1971; Rosenhead, 1989).

An error in an Ultragame is much more fundamental: it is a poor choice of rationalities by the players (Figure 10.4). In this context "poor" specifically relates to known evaluative metarational criteria, such as *globality-universalisability* and *self-support* (see Chapters 2 and 12). Ultragame players can make errors-of-omission whenever they ignore the elusive forms of rationality, or when they fail to design and implant rationality-synergies. It is becoming increasingly apparent that this type of "error" leads to disparity, resentment, frustration and oppression when it becomes widespread in human systems.

10.5 Implications for Managers

This analysis of game models with their rationalities can be placed at the heart of strategic management theory and practice, simply by invoking the conceptual frameworks of Strategy-as-Rationality or Strategy-as-Moral-Philosophy (Chapter 2). These consist of (i) a strategy-set whose elements are the major concepts and components of the various theories of strategic management, (ii) an entity-set whose elements are the multiple types of player or strategic-entity (e.g. individual, firm, network, virtual-corporation, etc.) and (iii) the full rationality-set. The frameworks set out an isomorphic correspondence between the strategy-set and the rationality-set. The frameworks extend the "individual metaphor" for the firm, widely employed in the mainstream theory of strategic management (e.g. Barney, 1994). It is noteworthy that objections to that extension have been described elsewhere as "roadblocks in the path of inquiry" (e.g. Levi, 1986).

When the Ultragame model is placed within these strategy frameworks, it carries some rather fundamental implications for managerial policies and practices. In addition to the methodology of inquiry (set out in the previous section), there are several other prescriptions concerning (i) the enrichment of the language of "strategic management", (ii) the propagation of an augmented ideology and (iii) the prospects for attaining individual and collective integrity within business systems.

10.5.1 Enriched Language

The problem of choosing models depicted in Figure 10.4 corresponds (via the isomorphism in strategy–as–rationality) to a selection of concepts in a manager's strategic-thinking, as well as a choice of language for the strategy-discourse (Figure 10.5). Thus, for example, the choice of the RUM-captured forms of rationality, with extended (but not adapted) game models, corresponds to the deployment of the traditional language of economic competition. Words like threat, fear, predation, sanctions, monitoring and control then become the norm. In comparison, the "choice" of the Ultragame model, with the corresponding (metarational and metamodelling) choice of plural and hyper forms of rationality, leads quickly to an enriched discourse, with an augmented vocabulary. This includes words like co-existence (*Kyosei* in Japanese), sociality, civility, openness, creativity and synergistic design. Many people think that such words should be heard much more often in contemporary business and politics, at all levels.

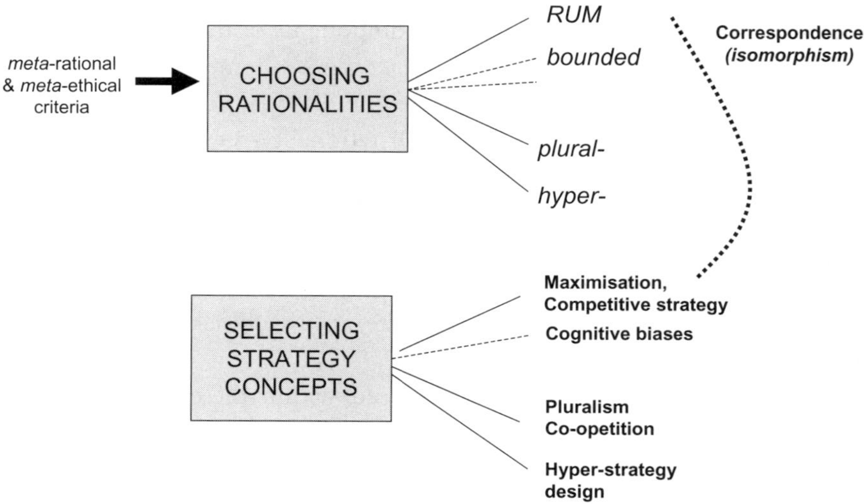

Figure 10.5 Choosing rationalities as selecting strategy concepts.

10.5.2 Ideological Transition

The traditional language of competitive strategy is often associated with a relentless and guileful pursuit of essentially selfish interests by the stronger and more powerful players. For many people this has now come to symbolise a negation of freedom: unacceptable levels of subjugation, disempowerment and marginalisation. They have slowly become trapped within the "descending iron cage" that Max Weber associated quite directly with the instrumental and calculated forms of rationality. Put differently, they have become victims of an economisation of society (G. Ritzer calls this "McDonaldization").

It is possible that new models like Ultragames, with other similar ethical decision making techniques (e.g. Goodpaster, 1985; Singer, 1994a, Zeleny, 1995b) could take on the role of *keys,* (refer to Table 10.1) enabling all types of entity to prise open the doors of this "cage". To amplify and communicate this point, the three notions discussed so far, adaptation of models, extensions of the rationality-set and augmentation of language, are brought together into a unified schema in Figure 10.6. As simple game models are adapted to become like Ultragames, their set of decision-function-rationalities becomes extended, whilst the corresponding language of strategic management becomes augmented and enriched. Put differently, as the adapted models and the augmented language spread throughout individual and collective minds, the ideology of strategic management, the framework of ideas used to express its values, is slowly transformed until it is quite indistinguishable from Business Ethics.

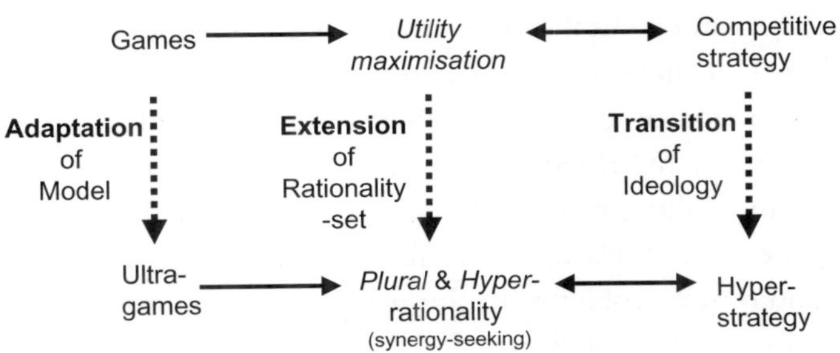

Figure 10.6 Adaptations and transitions.

10.5.3 Integrity

This notion of ideological transition (the right-hand side of Figure 10.6) can also be expressed in more personal and practical terms, literally closer to home. The ideology of economic competition (the top part of the figure) has encouraged countless individuals to strongly differentiate their work life from their personal or family life. When such people enter an office or a factory, they become fighters, warriors or slaves; but when they physically leave the workspace, they transform themselves into discussants, mentors, friends or lovers. Despite the growth of working-at-home (and in transit), many continue to defend this way of life, i.e. they endorse and demonstrate the principle of role-differentiation.

Strategy-as-rationality with Ultragames fosters an alternative principle: that of role-integration. The ideology of Ultragames, plural-rationality and hyper-strategy (bottom of Figure 10.6) seeks to encourage all entities, including individual managers, into becoming integrated and balanced persons, at all times. Such a fostered re-integration of personal and managerial (or productive) life-roles seems timely. It is especially well suited to the many new forms of production made possible by technological advance (e.g. the virtual firm or network), not to mention the many new types of family arrangements.

10.6 Conclusion

The idea that game theory can help managers to "think better" about their strategic problems has now been given a much broader and universalisable interpretation. Traditional game theory and its extensions have certainly yielded many mathematical insights, with several testable hypotheses. The methodologies of metagames and hypergames have also helped managers to explore scenarios, or to arm themselves more thoroughly for negotiations; but, when they are re-armed with the concept of an Ultragame, or similar ethical decision making methodologies, managers quickly become capable of thinking better and talking better about their strategic problems, others' problems and future problems. In this way, the adaptations of game theory could now be used as platforms for designing, discussing and reflecting upon new strategies and structures, whose purpose is living and working together, or service to society (Chapters 3 and 4). Put differently (Dennett, 1995, p. 510), the adapted game theory could become one of "the mind tools we need to design and redesign ourselves, ever searching for better solutions to the problems we create for ourselves and others".

Glossary

Metagame

A metagame is the game that would exist if one of the players in a simple game chose his strategy after the others, in full knowledge of their choices.

Hypergame

A hypergame is a game-like model of conflict in which each "player" can have a distinctive perception of what the "game" is. Specifically, Player 1 might think that player 2 has a particular set of preferences for the outcomes of a simple game, but these could differ from player 2's actual preferences, and vice versa.

Hyper-rationality

A hyper-rational entity (in the sense used throughout the book) is one that seeks out, creates, designs and achieves synergies amongst the distinctive forms of rationality. This usage of the term "hyper-rational" which differs from the better-known economic usage of extreme-calculatedness (e.g. Barney, 1994), or strong-instrumental rationality (e.g. Binmore, 1987; Wallisser, 1989) owes its origin to a recent study of the Japanese industrial system by sociologists G Ritzer and T LeMoyne (1991) who identified synergies amongst the Neo-Weberian forms of rationality in that system (practical, substantive-value, etc.). The concept readily generalises to the entire rationality-set and entity-set.

Metarationality$_1$

The philosophical and mathematical arguments and criteria that have been used to classify, evaluate and inter-relate the distinctive forms of rationality in the rationality-set, or to place them relative to each other.

Metarationality$_2$

This is utility maximisation in the special context of a metagame, where the objects of choice are the conditional strategies. (If player 1 chooses this, then player 2 prefers that.)

Plural-rationality

The rationality-set, whose elements are the many (about 50) distinctively defined forms of rationality, within the broad spectrum of the social sciences, including economics and philosophy.

Ultragame-I

A conceptual model of strategic interaction amongst multiple types of strategic entity, in which each entity is plurally rational.

Ultragame-II

A conceptual model of strategic interaction amongst many strategic entities, in which each entity is hyper-rational (in the above synergy-seeking sense).

Appendix 10.1

SCIO Applied to Competitive Intelligence Analysis, Including Synergies or "Hyper-Strategies"

(a) Competitor's beliefs (belief rationalities)

1. What are **A**'s expectations about our moves?
2. Does **A** use extrapolatory forecasting?
3. Does **A** use conventional template planning?
4. Does **A** use sophisticate model-based forecasting system?
5. Does **A** conduct routine ex-post reviews of operations?
6. Are any of **A**'s apparent beliefs (or statements) inconsistent?
7. Do **A**'s recent actions indicate "blind-spots"?

(b) Competitor's calculations (means rationalities)

8. Does **A** have a record of actions based on non–obvious inferences? (e.g. successful first moves)
9. Is **A** using a model-based strategy-selection system?
10. What are **A**'s policy rules and established procedures?
11. Is flexibility evident in **A**'s strategic position?
12. Has **A** postponed strategic moves (i) to permit clarification of environmental trends and (ii) to correct internal deficiencies?
13. Is there internal disagreement over goals or objectives?
14. Does **A** use adaptive planning?
15. What are implications of **A**'s use of (a) specific cognitive heuristics (e.g. availability, representiveness, anchoring) and (b) heuristic planning guides?
16. What are **A**'s capabilities?
17. What is **A**'s actual and potential level of performance?
18. Does **A** use "PARE" analysis, i.e. assessing potential, resilience?
19. How strong is **A**'s strategic momentum (*status-quo* preference)?

(c) Competitor's goals, motivations (ends rationalities)

20. What are **A**'s stated goals or objectives?
21. What goals are implicit in **A**'s actions?
22. Are these goals well chosen, suitable?
23. Can **A**'s (a) current actual goals and (b) strategic vision be inferred from **A**'s past behaviours, patterns and statements?
24. What is **A**'s internal incentive structure?
25. Does **A** balance shareholder value-creation against stakeholder interests in (i) actions, (ii) statements and (iii) justifications?
26. Does **A** have an ideological commitment, "hot spot", or mission?
27. By what process or procedure does **A** formulate goals?
28. How much importance does **A** attach to this process of goal formulation?

(d) Competencies: practical, expressive, systemic rationalities

29. Is **A** competent at implementation, "spiralling"?
30. Does **A** have internal programmes of capability development, in various functional areas?

31. Is **A** skilled at matching capabilities to strategies?
32. Does **A** have a corporate (or brand) (i) identity? (ii) reputation? (iii) niche?
33. Do **A**'s past moves have symbolic value, reinforcing identity?
34. Does **A** maintain traditions?
35. How similar is the past and current context, for triggering the traditional responses?

(e) Competitor's ethical policies

36. Does **A** use (i) social cost–benefit analysis and (ii) utilitarian public justifications?
37. Is there a record or policy emphasising fairness in the treatment of stakeholders?
38. Does **A** recognise strategic duties and obligations? How are these interpreted?

(f) Competitor analysis and interactive rationality

39. Is there a pattern over time in **A**'s actions or decisions?
40. How does (the analyst's) own situation affect the analysis of **A**? What are (the analyst's) biases?

(g) Synergies (hyper–strategies)

41. Does **A** apply its abstract knowledge to *increase* the utilisation of its own lower-level skills?
42. Are **A**'s routine practices fully *supported* by its expressed and cultivated values?
43. Does **A** utilise experience at all levels of operation to continually re-design and *improve* its own procedures?
44. Do the values and culture of **A** foster the advancement of scientific knowledge in ways that are *fully integrated* into **A**'s systems and outputs?

Chapter 11

OPTIMALITY: Optimisation and Strategy

Abstract: This chapter is adapted from "Optimality and strategy," *International Journal of Operations and Quantitative Management* 2(2), pp. 111–126, 1996. The original paper was prompted by conversations with Arnold Reisman of Case Western Reserve University. It is argued that conceptual models of strategy-without-trade-offs challenge conventional notions of optimality and optimisation. This challenge is broadened by the several distinctively defined forms of optimality within the behavioural and managerial sciences. It is then shown that each form of optimality corresponds with an identifiable segment of the strategic management theory. Although the metaoptimality arguments remain ambiguous or incomplete, they can play a role similar to the general theory of rationality in informing the theory of strategic management, particularly with respect to its systemic and ethical dimensions. Once again, the resulting prescription is for methodological adaptations, with their associated ideological transitions.

11.1 Introduction

According to the editor of *Journal of Economic Psychology*, "optimality is not worth arguing about" (Lea, 1991, p. 225). Moreover, according to some perspectives on strategic management, strategy does not matter, either: it is a "futile distraction" (Whittington, 1993, p. 39). Why, then, should anyone bother with an essay on optimality and strategy? The answer lies with alternative perspectives that see a need to revise our traditional concepts of optimality, in order to create more powerful tools for solving the challenging problems we will surely face, as we step into the 21st century (e.g. Churchman, 1994; Mason, 1994; Schoemaker, 1993; Zeleny, 2005). At the same time, business and corporate strategies are assuming a more dominant role as co-producers of that problematic future (e.g. Hosmer, 1994; Weber, 1996). Therefore, the two ideas optimality and strategy remain rather important. Moreover, it will be argued here that the relationship between them matters a great deal; indeed, it is fundamental.

The chapter starts with a brief discussion of the distinctive forms of optimality associated with *de novo* programming (Zeleny, 1995a,b,c; Shi, 1995) and trade-offs-free strategic-thinking (e.g. Hayes and Pisano, 1994); it then goes on (in Section 11.3) to consider the often neglected systemic and ethical perspectives on optimality (e.g. Boulding, 1978; Casti and Karlqvist, 1994; Levi, 1986; Shanks, 1993). It becomes apparent that there are now two distinct classes of optimality concepts with corresponding strategy elements (Section 11.4). They are referred to here as Economic-Optimal-Strategy (EOS) and Systemic-Ethical-Optimum (SEO). Since the metaoptimal arguments linking the two classes remain essentially unresolved or unsettled (Section 11.5), it is appropriate and necessary (in the sense of being intellectually honest) to work with both classes, that is, with the multiple forms of optimality. This, in turn, involves the adaptation of decision making methodologies (Section 11.6), together with a corresponding augmentation of management ideologies (Section 11.7).

11.2 Strategy Without Trade-Offs

The very first article to appear in the new *International Journal of Operations and Quantitative Management* showed how the redesign of a formal system of linear-programming constraints (*de novo* programming) could be used to help "modern businesses aspire to trade-offs-free thinking" (Zeleny, 1995b, p. 3). This type of thinking places great emphasis on design and creativity and is becoming an increasingly prominent part of the contemporary business and managerial ethos, or the zeitgeist (e.g. DeBono, 1992; Hayes and Pisano, 1994; Huysmans, 1994; O'Keefe, 1995). Over the last two decades, many productive systems and even whole industries have been creatively re-designed in ways that have eliminated trade-offs. Some simple examples of trade-offs-free thinking involve cost in relation to quality, as well as environmental engineering, as described below.

11.2.1 Production Cost and Quality

In the late 1970s, it was becoming increasingly obvious that many businesses and whole industries in the US and elsewhere were strategically stuck-in-the-middle. That is, costs were not particularly low, while product quality, differentiation or value-added were not especially high. With the technology of that time, any prescription to put right both of the deficiencies would probably have been unworkable. Competitiveness considerations dictated the practical choice of a single generic strategy: either cost-leadership or differentiation (Porter, 1980).

Figure 11.1 depicts the style of the 1970s of strategic-thinking as involving optimisation (i.e. maximisation of competitiveness). The prescription to choose just one of the generic strategies implicitly assumed that quality, or differentiation, was costly, although it reduced the risk of failure in the marketplace. Furthermore, the shape of the graphs in the conceptual model reflects the old thinking that the best (i.e. optimal) strategy was either cost-leadership or differentiation, but not both.

During the 1980s, however, the situation depicted in Figure 11.1 changed in a significant way (Figure 11.2). Advances in product and process designs prompted a re-think of the cost–quality relationship, while consumer

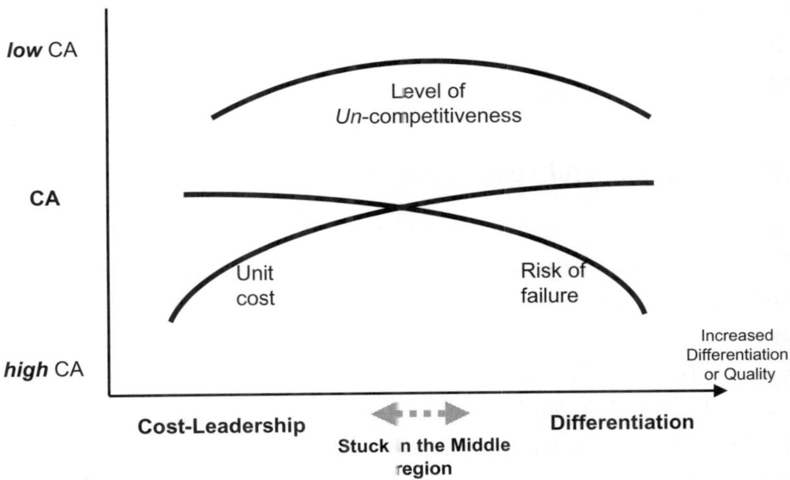

Figure 11.1 Generic cost and differentiation strategies viewed as trade-offs.

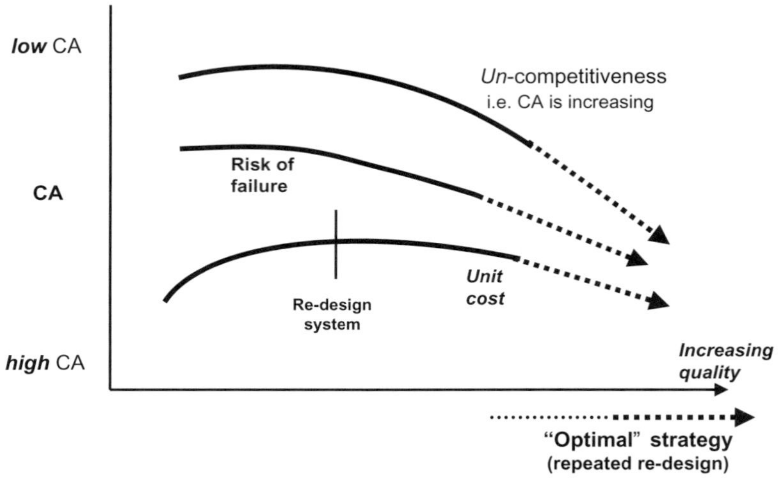

Figure 11.2   Cost and differentiation as complements.

expectations of quality at a low price steepened the risk line. The optimal strategy became re-conceptualised as involving low cost and high quality, located somewhere off the graph to the right, the so-called "happy hunting ground" (e.g. Lewis *et al.*, 1993). In the automobile industry, for example, Honda products moved from a position of low cost to a position of low cost and high quality in the 1980s and beyond. At the same time, other producers (e.g. Volvo) moved to reduce cost whilst retaining their high quality.

11.2.2 Environmental Compliance Cost and Risk

By the late 1980s, concerns for the natural environment had become a major strategic issue for manufacturing industries. Many firms have since settled upon an environmental strategic position or level of greenness. Figure 11.3 represents a widely employed conceptual model of this problem (e.g. *Bulletpoints Weekly*, 1995). First, it is understood that the so-called brown (i.e. polluting) strategies carry increased business risks, including risks of regulation, litigation by competitors, boycotts by consumers, exclusion from specialised equity-funds, de-motivation of employees and so on. Next, it has been assumed in these cases that green business

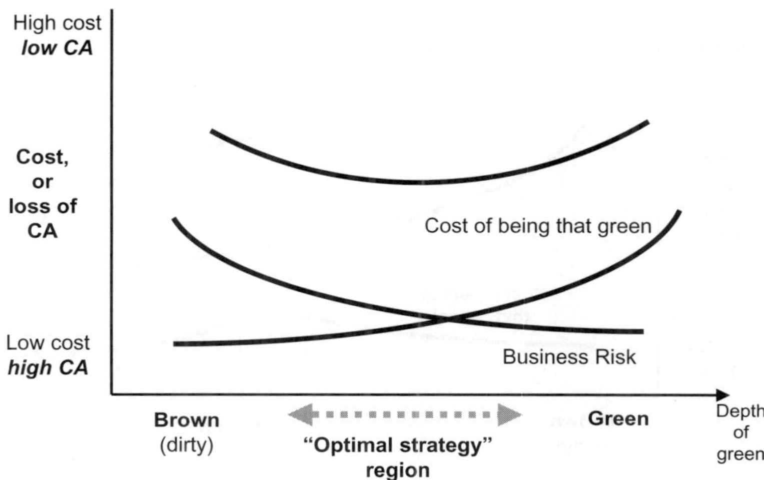

Figure 11.3 Environmental compliance costs and depth-of-green as trade-offs.

is necessarily more expensive. According to the conceptual model, the optimum (minimum cost position) is once again located somewhere in the middle of the graph, indicating that strategy should be somewhat reactive (i.e. pale brown) or else somewhat pro-active (pale green), but definitely not deep green.

Around 1990, the situation depicted in Figure 11.3 changed again. For example, strategies based upon environmental engineering, such as manufacturing for re-use, or design-for-disassembly (DFD), made manufacturing more environmentally benign, and it often saved on product and process costs. This application of design technology brought motivational and other market related benefits to many manufacturing organisations. In the 1990s, Xerox alone was reported to have saved around US$50m per annum in this way. To give but one further example, the highly networked mining industry in Australia redesigned its smelting processes, making them at once more efficient and less toxic (e.g. Grabosky, 1995).

In the re-conceptualised model (Figure 11.4) the environment–cost trade-off has been eliminated so that the optimal strategy shifts off to the right, to an even happier (and healthier) hunting ground. The basic principle in all of these examples is that constraints might be overcome by

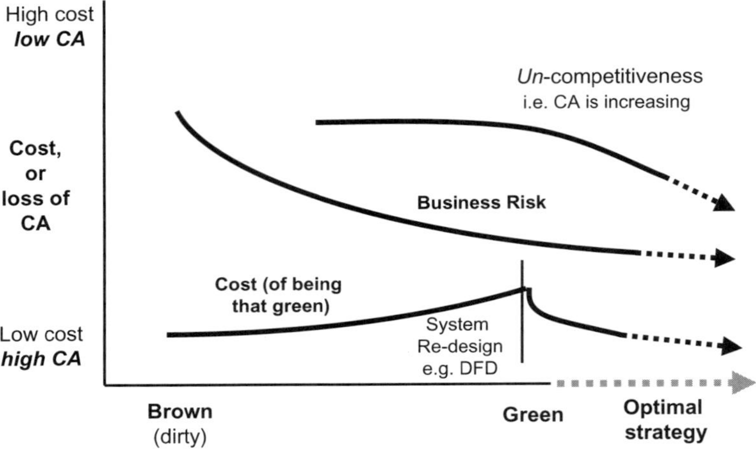

Figure 11.4 Environmental cost and depth-of-green viewed as complements.

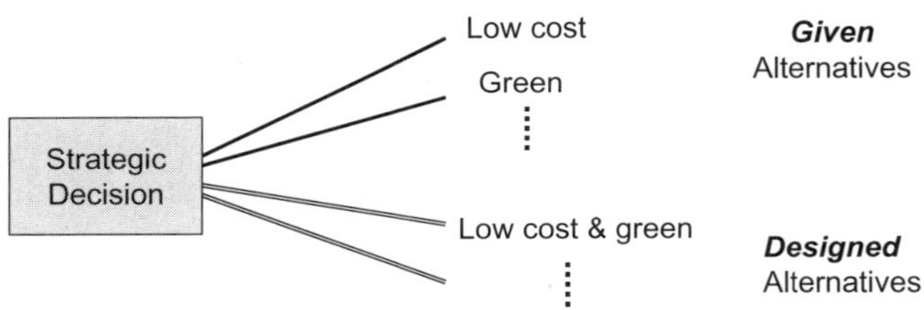

Figure 11.5 Decision analysis and strategy.

directing attention and resources to the process of re-designing the relevant system, thus creating new strategic alternatives, rather than selecting from a list of given ones.

11.2.3 Decision Analysis

This distinction between given strategic alternatives (low-cost, etc.) and the re-designed ones (featuring low cost and high quality) can be represented on a simple decision-tree (Figure 11.5). Generic strategic alternatives (plans or proposals) such as cost-leadership, differentiation, pale-green, etc., are each branches of the tree. The strategies specifically involving re-design are then represented as a second set of branches (the double-lines in Figure 11.5). Each of the latter combine the more salient properties of the so-called generic strategies. Examples are producing high-quality and cheap cars, or installing efficient and green processes. Although Figure 11.5 is extremely simple, it is nonetheless important, for it can be adapted to become a conceptual model that incorporates all of the many forms of optimality (refer to Section 11.6).

11.3 Optimality

Formal *de novo* programming models with their associated concept of trade-offs-free business strategies also serve to remind us that optimality itself is neither a single nor a fixed idea. It is becoming apparent that concepts of optimality themselves change over time, as new technologies, understandings and societies emerge. For example, the idea of optimisation through creative re-design can be contrasted with the idea of making choices from given alternatives. Compared with the classical instrumental rationality associated with strategic planning, or with traditional analytic maximisation of a scalar function (Appendix 11.1), it is quite a significant and distinctive idea for strategic management.

11.3.1 Generic Optimalities

It is not the only significant distinction. Over 40 years ago, Churchman (1994, p. 108) declared that "in the perspective of another age to come... we do not know the meaning of optimum". Since then, it has become apparent that optimality is "a far more profound and elusive state of affairs than can be derived from the most powerful mathematical proofs" (Mason, 1994, p. 70) and that "there can be no absolute definition of optimality" (Zeleny, 1994,a,c, 2005). In sum, (i) concepts of optimality change over time, (ii) there are many forms of optimality (Tables 11.1 and 11.2) and (iii) while some of these can be defined mathematically, others require some natural-language statements to complete their definition.

The same is also true of strategy; yet this is surely no coincidence. Table 11.1 gives us an indication of how a systematic study of optimality per se might richly inform strategy (i.e. strategic management). Certainly,

Table 11.1 Forms of optimality with strategy concepts.

	Form of Optimality	Strategy Concept(s)	Source Discipline
EOS	Maximisation	Classical rational model, DA	Economics
	Cybernetic	Management by exception, Management by objectives	Engineering
	Evolutionary	Environmental fit, Market-rationality	Biology
Boundary of EOS/SEO	Inherent	Organisational dynamics, dissipative systems	Chaos and complexity
SEO	Optimal Design	Management without trade-offs	Production-management, OR/MS
	Multi-criteria	Stakeholder model, multiple objectives	OR/MS
	Systemic	Plural rationality, embeddedness (within culture)	Sociology
	Ethical	Social responsibility, moral agency	Philosophy

optimality, when broadly defined, can be readily invoked as an epistemological organising principle (Keren, 1993) in order to restructure current thinking and soul-searching in the latter discipline (e.g. Bettis, 1991; Schoemaker, 1991; Mahoney, 1993; Whittington, 1993; Prahalad and Hamel, 1994; Hosmer, 1994). Moreover, the reverse is also possible, as further research in strategic management can potentially stimulate and refine ideas about optimality.

11.4 Two Classes of Optimal Strategy

The forms of optimality listed in Tables 11.1 and 11.2, with their corresponding strategy concepts, fall into two broad classes under the metaoptimal criterion of *Elusiveness* versus *Capture* (Singer, 1991 and Chapter 2). This refers to whether or not the specified form of optimality can be adequately captured as maximisation of a single parameter, like utility or profit, at least for some

Table 11.2   Descriptions of some forms of optimality.

Maximising: Maximisation is a measurement and search process (e.g. Zeleny, 1994a,c, 2005). Formally, we are given a set of objects of choice (alternatives), with a function mapping the set onto another well ordered set. We search for the elements that are mapped onto the maximum or supremum. In the case of utility maximisation, the optimal state is often described as the most preferred state. In strategic management, "maximisation", thus defined, is linked to the overall contribution from neo-classical economics, with profit-maximisation goals. Maximisation is also implicit in the classical model of strategic planning and in traditional decision analysis.

Cybernetic: The cybernetic form of optimality is a context for maximisation (or minimisation) of a parameter (like utility). However, it also specifically refers to a state of a system that is controlled by an actual homeostatic device. For example, one talks about an optimal temperature of a room, or an optimal depth of a lake (e.g. Schoemaker, 1991). Corresponding strategy concepts include management-by-exception, management-by-objectives, and statistical-quality-control methods. In each case, one part of the system controls another, or evaluates another with reference to a fixed measure.

Evolutionary: This form of optimality refers to a state produced by a "mindless" algorithm that offers guaranteed results (Dennett, 1995, p. 51). Moreover, such algorithms or rules are located in the environment of the strategic entities. The corresponding concepts of strategy are environmental-fit and market-rationality (Whittington, 1993). With this perspective, the rules of corporate (business) strategy are seen to be located in the competitive market environment. An optimal strategy is then conceptualised as a structure–behaviour combination that minimises costs within a given environment (with the meaning of "costs" somewhat fudged). With this model, strategy is slowly realised, by accident (Mintzberg and Waters, 1985).

Inherent: The inherent form of optimality is associated with the complexity and chaos paradigm. It is an evolutionary form (Harvey and Reed, 1994), as it occurs in biological systems in which there is a cumulative selection process; but it is also elusive, in that it cannot be represented as any maximising equilibrium point (hence the overlap of EOS and SEO, in Table 11.1). Dissipative systems import energy from their environment and transform it into their own complex internal structure. Put differently, they "work to maintain themselves against entroptic breakdown" (Miller, 1991, p. 228). There is an ongoing optimisation process that maintains the system in a mathematically defined state at the edge of chaos and far from equilibrium (Miller, 1991; Stacey, 1993). In this state of inherent optimality, adaptation (like creative change) proceeds at the fastest rate. In the complexity-and-strategy paradigm, strategic entities are assumed to be dissipative structures (e.g. Zeleny, 1990; Stacey, 1993; Levy, 1994; Bettis and Prahalad, 1995). Optimality and strategy both come to include the ideas that entities can (i) re-make or

Table 11.2 (*Continued*)

re-produce themselves (autopoiesis), (ii) co-produce their future environment, (iii) perform best in a state of bounded instability and (iv) actively, deliberately, or intentionally transform the course of evolution (Harvey and Reed, 1994).

Systemic forms of optimality involve seeking *balance*. MCDM (vector optimisation) falls within this category, in that balance is sought amongst multiple criteria (either given or designed). The corresponding ideas in strategy include the stakeholder model, in which balance is sought amongst competing claims, together with the acceptance of multiple corporate objectives (e.g. cost and safety). More generally, systemic optimality concepts involve balance amongst plural rationalities. For example, in an optimal rationality problem stated nearly 30 years ago by Professor March (1978), strategic entities were reminded to seek a balance between traditions and prospects, i.e. backward-looking and forward-looking forms of rationality (Singer, 1991a,b, 1993a). More recently, Habermas (1989) forcefully prescribed the restoration of balance in the mix of rationalities in contemporary societies (cf. Jay, 1985). In similar vein, Huysmans (1994, p. 164) has commented that OR–MS analysts actually optimise the "balance between identifying assumptions (i.e. beliefs) and demonstrating their implications" (i.e. instrumental rationalities), or "between formulating and solving a problem" (1994, p. 159). In strategic management, the systemic perspective, which sees that all economic activity is embedded in culture(s) and tradition(s), has also been expressed in terms of plural-rationality (see Chapter 3).

Ethical optimality is based upon the fact that the etymology of optimal is "the best", the superlative of *good*. Accordingly, the ethical optimalities are concerned with the essential nature of the good, or goodness in human systems. In the earliest moral philosophy, goodness was regarded as the pre-eminent category of meaning. Plato's conception of the good referred to a *balance*, or harmony between spirit (i.e. motivation), desire and reason. Moreover, such harmony was thought to be good for individuals as well as the whole of society. Both Aristotle and Confucius were concerned with human-goods, especially the virtues of honour, courage, kindness and justice, with the latter involving *deliberations* about merit, need, status, equality and fairness. In contrast, the traditional paradigms of strategic-management, organisation-theory and economics have equated goodness with such things as efficiency and effectiveness, performance, productivity, competitiveness, or commercial-success (Shenhav *et al.*, 1994). More recently, however, this discourse has been broadened out again to include other moral forms of goodness (see Chapter 2, Hosmer, 1994; Shanks, 1993).

specified purposes. The first class, labelled here as the Economic Optimalities, includes utility maximisation itself, together with the notion of evolutionary fitness (variously defined), but also the cybernetic form of optimality. These forms are all implicit in the more traditional paradigm of strategy (e.g. Porter,

1980; Thomas and Pruitt, 1993; Shenhav *et al.*, 1994; Grabosky, 1995), and they are referred to here, collectively, as Economic–Optimal–Strategy (EOS). A second class, the Systemic-Ethical-Optimum (SEO), includes the more elusive (non–maximising) forms of optimality, such as optimal-design and vector-optimisation as well as the systemic and ethical forms. The two broad classes of optimality, EOS and SEO, may now be described more fully by using the language of strategy and systems, as follows:

11.4.1 Economic Optimal Strategy

The main components of an EOS (Figure 11.6) are (i) a strategic entity *A* viewed as an individual, a firm, a player, a strategic-group, an industry, or a nation; (ii) a competitive environment consisting of other similar entities; (iii) a current macroenvironment comprised of similar entities whose strategic behaviour is understood in terms of their interests and utilities, with categories that include politics, technology, economics, ecology and society (e.g. demography).

An EOS of a strategic entity *A* then involves selecting from a repertoire of strategic behaviours that includes (a) signalling to other players in the competitive environment, (b) sourcing or acquiring resource inputs and (c) producing and marketing outputs in both environments (buyers and

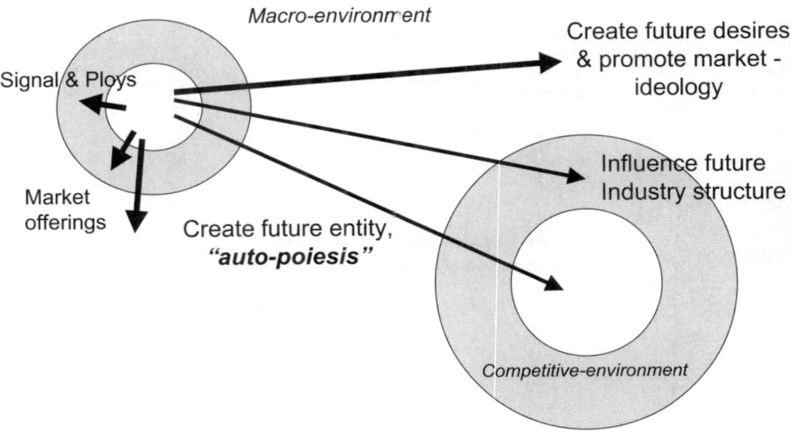

Figure 11.6   Strategic behaviour and economically optimal strategy.

consumers). This process is described (in natural language) as satisfying the needs, preferences or desires, of other entities. In addition, an EOS also involves a forward-looking dimension, or a vision of the future, that is commonly associated with strategic-planning and strategic-thinking (e.g. Venkataraman, 1989; Burgess, 1995). This involves (d) creating a future industry structure favourable to A, or a competitive space (e.g. Hamel and Prahalad, 1989) as well as (e) influencing preferences and creating desires amongst potential future buyers. Finally, EOS also involves (f) promoting or sustaining a market ideology within the political macroenvironment of A. To summarise, the entity intentionally co-produces a macroenvironment that is likely to sustain its strategy. In this sense, EOS involves self-production (autopoiesis) within a competitive utility-maximising economic system.

11.4.2 Systemic-Ethical-Optimum (SEO)

The basic components of an SEO (Figure 11.7) are somewhat different and can be described as follows: (i) a strategic-entity A viewed as any member of the entity-set, that is, an individual, team, alliance, network, competitive-complex, or abstractly defined system, (ii) a current *Local* environment consisting of other entities that are perceived as neighbours with reference to some metric of physical or psychological distance, (iii) a current *Global*

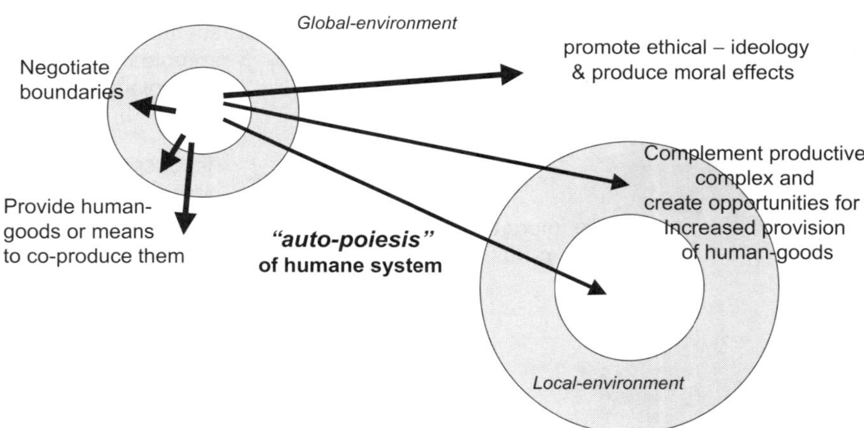

Figure 11.7 Conceptual framework for determining the systemic-ethical optimum.

environment, comprised of all types of strategic entity, whose strategic behaviour is mutually understood in terms of plural-rationality and the Platonic human-goods (e.g. justice, dignity, friendship, harmony, etc.).

With these categories in place, the SEO of *A* then involves the following strategic behaviours (which can be compared item by item with the above description of EOS). Behaviours (a) and (b) involve negotiating (discussing) the boundaries of a productive complex within the local and global environments; behaviour (c) involves producing (or co-producing) human goods, or else providing the means to co-produce them in those environments. In addition, an SEO (like EOS) also involves a forward-looking dimension, but it is associated with "transforming the course of evolution and forestalling unwanted outcomes" (Harvey and Reed, 1994, p. 400). This involves (d) complementing or completing a future productive complex that incorporates *A*, (e) creating opportunities for increasing the provision of human goods, as well as (f) promoting a Systemic-Ethical ideology in which expressed values prominently reflect the human goods. Put differently, *A* intentionally co-produces moral effects. In this sense, SEO involves the co-production (heteropoiesis) of other entities, including a productive complex that incorporates *A* but is itself embedded in a larger human system.

11.5 Metaoptimality

Which class of optimal-strategy is *better*? Attempts to answer this question lead directly into a philosophical and political swamp (e.g. Rosenhead, 1989) inhabited by notoriously slippery problems. These include (i) the proper scope of any optimality formulations (i.e. optimal for *whom*, or for which entities?), (ii) the ultimate reducibility of goodness (as in SEO) to betterness (as in EOS), and (iii) the proper relationship between facts and values.

11.5.1 Whose Optimality?

According to O'Keefe (1995, p. 202) "MS-OR has often provided *local* optimisation... (yet) it is necessary to concentrate on the whole". At the same time, many are now asking what is the whole? Until the 1970s, it made quite good sense to concentrate on individuals, firms and nations. For example, in ancient times, Plato talked about the proper conduct of individuals and the proper function of states. Since around 1980, however, as a result of technological and social changes, it has become more natural to talk about the optimal functioning of a team, a network, a virtual corporation, or an entire region. Indeed, there are a great many types of entity whose behaviour could be improved, or optimised. They include

> groups, coalitions and teams; families, clans and tribes; flex-firms, hollow or virtual corporations; TNCs and MNCs; strategic alliances; competitive complexes; networks; industries, learning communities, institutions corporations, cities, regions, blocs, societies, social classes and strata; species, populations, ecosystems

as well as abstract systems and entities such as players, cultures, cognitive systems, multiple selves, knowledge systems, social systems, living systems, dynamic systems and autopoietic systems. To accommodate this diversity of categories, but still remain useful, knowledge in the social and managerial sciences somehow needs to be re-mixed. The traditional disciplinary boundaries have become quite dysfunctional. As a result, many researchers and practitioners (too many to cite!) are now asking *who* or *what* is

- deciding, in various theories of decision-making,
- being rational, in rational-choice theory and economic models,
- being moral, in ethical theory,
- competing against and co-operating with whom and
- trusting or communicating with whom, in business and politics.

Accordingly, we must also now ask the three questions: who or what is optimising, with respect to which forms of optimality, and on behalf of whom? In particular, a network that collectively attempts to maximise profits on behalf of shareholders, or that seeks only to maximise levels of service to its paying customers, might be sweeping out too much so that its strategy is not optimal, at least in the SEO sense.

11.5.2 The Is–Ought Relationship

Despite standard objections to deriving values from facts (e.g. Moore, 1903), this actually happens quite often in modern management theory.

For example, the fact that "A few companies have proven themselves adapt at inventing new markets" (Prahalad and Hamel, 1990, p. 79) is used as a basis for a prescription, or claim, that they are the ones to emulate. Implicitly, one finds a conceptual model of EOS. However, with SEO in mind, an alternative claim can also be made: a few organisations have found ways of increasing the provision of human goods ... these are "the ones to emulate". Which is correct? It is possible that both are.

One reason for the blending and the confusion of is (fact) with *ought* (value) lies in a continuing enthusiasm for evolutionary metaphors in management theory, economics and ethics (e.g. Kadane and Larkey, 1983; Dennett, 1995), coupled with an inability to fully specify the actual cumulative selection mechanisms involved in the studied social and economic systems (e.g. Miller, 1991; Casti and Karqvist, 1994). It now seems quite possible that the complexity and chaos paradigm, which is already part of twinned discourses of strategy (see Chapter 9, Zeleny, 1990; Stacey, 1993; Levy, 1994; Bettis and Prahalad, 1995) and optimality (Miller, 1991; Stacey, 1993), could help to resolve this confusion.

11.5.3 Betterness and Goodness

A third metaoptimality problem concerns the relationship between betterness and goodness. Formally, "good" is a one-place predicate (Broome, 1993). That is, one can say that " _ is good", whilst betterness is two-place, i.e. "_ is better than _ ". Accordingly, only betterness is amenable to formal mathematical analysis (e.g. involving transitivity axioms, etc.), while good, like Zeleny's (1994a, p. 15) value-complex, can only be "articulated in imprecise and fuzzy language". Accordingly, in comparing betterness, as in EOS, with goodness, as in SEO, one must consider not only metatheoretic criteria such as analytic-tractability, but also the practical usefulness of talking about human goods.

Should the parallel conversation and discourse of strategy be restricted to utility, betterness, human-betterment (e.g. Boulding, 1978) and improvement? Or should it also accommodate specific forms of goodness? Some believe that economists "miss nothing" by reducing goodness to betterness (e.g. Broom, 1993). Others (e.g. Etzioni, 1988; Shanks, 1993) disagree, arguing that while preference is a a part of goodness, it surely needs filling out. This corresponds precisely to the position in strategic management that EOS is an important part of strategy, but it, too, needs "filling out". Put differently, the EOS conceptual framework sweeps out too much so that both the cultural dimension (e.g. Venkatraman, 1989; Burgess, 1995), and the moral dimension (see Chapter 2, Etzioni, 1988; Hosmer, 1994) should be swept back in.

11.6 Meta-Decision-Analysis

Given the ambiguity and incompleteness at the metalevel, it is inevitable that strategic decisions are often experienced as wicked messes. Yet, there remains a minimal or archetypal decision structure for the "mess" that is essentially an adaptation of Figure 11.5. In addition to the given and designed strategic alternatives, there are also several inter-related meta-decisions. Strategic entities must step back into the relevant metatheory (compare the term "roll-back" that is applied to expected values in the quantitative decision-tree analysis), in order to decide upon their forms of optimality, their forms of rationality, their models (see Chapter 9) and their preferred categories of language and meaning.

The first three meta-decisions can be supported by arguments of meta-optimality (Section 11.5), metarationality (Singer, 1991a,b and Chapter 2) and metamodelling (e.g. Van Gigch 1991, and Chapter 9). The fourth, choosing language, invites analysis of discourse and meta-cognition, that is, reflection upon current beliefs, categories of meaning, language use and its purposes. To illustrate this, one might consider the case of a US-based forestry manager, who once described a plan to cut down ancient Redwood trees as a strategy of "paying down the junk bond debt" of a forestry corporation (Poff, 1994, p. 440). In such cases, other descriptions, such as destroying ecological capital (e.g. Hawken, 1993), and other models (e.g. Bare and Mendoza, 1988; Shi, 1995), become an important part of a new and more enlightened form of strategic-decision-analysis.

By drawing attention to the four meta-decisions, the meta-decision-analysis (i.e. Figure 11.8 viewed as methodology) promotes or propagates a wider or augmented perspective on strategic choice in business. In MDA (as in Zeleny's comparable model of cognitive equilibrium), neither the alternatives nor the criteria are given. They must be re-designed and re-described. Accordingly, traditional maximisation is not possible. Instead,

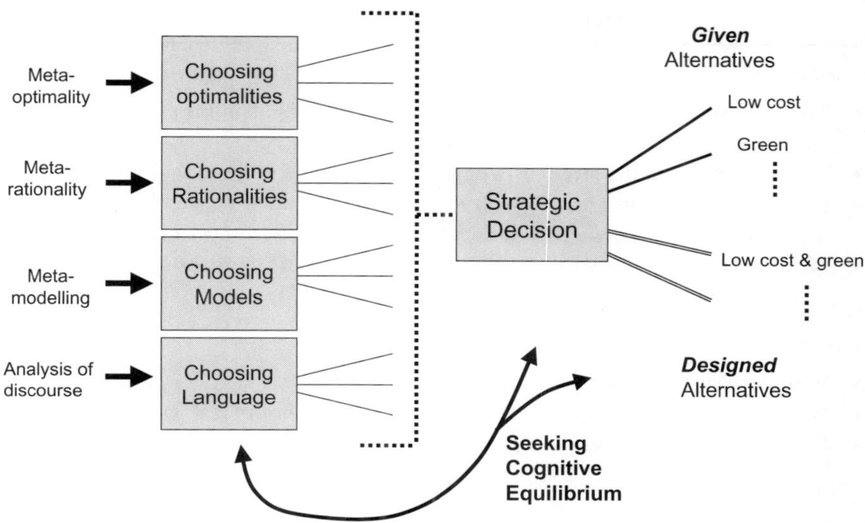

Figure 11.8   Meta–decision–analysis and strategic decision making.

strategic-entities must rely upon their processes of deliberation, reflection, persuasion, argumentation and inquiry (Table 11.3). Rather than a solution, one seeks a resolution or a settlement (e.g. Levi, 1986), or a dissolution (Zeleny, 1989, 1994a,c) of the strategic problem.

11.7 Transitions

Meta-decision-analysis is an augmentation or adaptation of the traditional decision analysis (Figure 11.6). It is but one example of how maximising models might be adapted[1] so that they become optimising in other distinctive senses (whilst also embodying other distinctively defined forms of rationality). Other examples of methodological adaptation along similar lines include (i) linear programming becoming *de-novo* programming, (ii) cash flow forecasting becoming *fake*-casting (Singer, 1994a,b), and (iii) games becoming Ultra-games (Chapter 10). In each case, existing models and behavioural repertoires of the entity are augmented, rather than forgotten, or extinguished. Such methodological adaptations can then become catalysts for *ideological transitions* (Figures 11.9 and 10.6). Whenever

Table 11.3   Optimalities and inquiries.

Maximisation

- To what extent do the axioms of utility maximisation (e.g. transitivity of preferences) reflect the empirical psychology of choice?
- To what extent are the preferences of an entity aligned with its overall well-being?
- Is utility maximisation a tautology? Is it an *ex-post* heuristic? (i.e. an observer assumes that something is maximised, then does he search for it, or construct it?)
- To what extent and for what purposes are other forms of rationality captured by utility maximisation?

Cybernetic

- Who or what is the controller?
- Who or what is best served by the system when it is in its optimal state?
- Can the entire system be re-designed to achieve even better outcomes?

Evolutionary

- What, exactly, is the algorithm, the cumulative selection process, that adopts particular entities (or products) in social and economic systems?
- What exactly is the meaning of cost, in this context?
- In what sense(s) is the optimal strategy (thus defined) *good*? (It could be the "*worst* viable solution"; Lea, 1991, p. 225).

Inherent

- In human systems, how developed is the capability to intentionally transform the course of evolution?
- How effective is the use of foresight, images of the future, in forestalling unwanted outcomes?

Systemic

- Which forms of rationality should apply to which entities (e.g. individuals, TNCs, alliances, etc.)? Equivalently, which rationalities should be used to prescribe strategy?
- What are the meta-rational arguments and criteria that apply to these plural forms?

Ethical

- Which forms of the good (wealth, justice, harmony, etc.) should be pursued by which entities? Why?

---

new models and methodologies are devised and popularised, new ways of thinking and new standards of behaviour are also co-produced and propagated (e.g. Rinnooy-Kan, 1991). Put differently, Rorty's idea (1982, p. 104) that human beings can "re-make themselves by re-making their

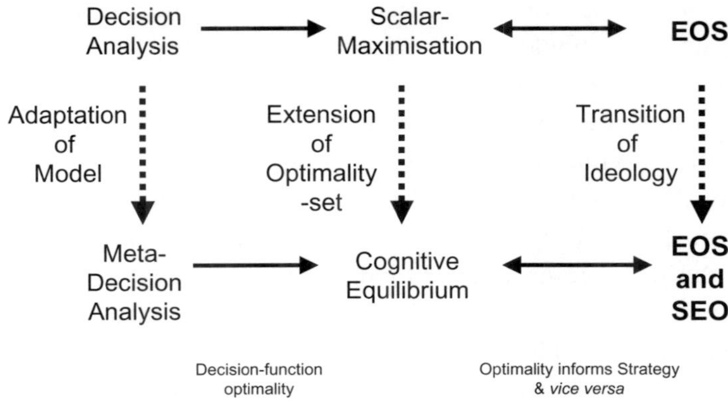

Figure 11.9   Methodological adaptations and ideological transitions.

speech" might be extended to refer to all strategic entities, with the "re-making" of their models and their language.

11.7.1 Decision-Function-Optimality

The implied relationship between methodologies and ideologies can itself be expressed more formally and concisely, by defining a mapping *Decision-Function-Optimality* whose domain is the set of optimising models (scalar maximisation, *de-novo* programming, MDA, etc.) and whose range is the set of distinctive forms of optimality, including those listed in Table 11.1. For example, "DA" maps onto traditional maximisation (Table 11.1 and Figure 11.9), which in turn corresponds (in the table linking strategy and optimality) with the mainstream ideology of EOS. Similarly, MDA maps onto multiple optimalities, but it also provides a framework that can be used to promote and propagate a more inclusive and augmented ideology, combining SEO and EOS.

11.8 Conclusion

It has often been suggested that management theory must be revitalised (e.g. Bettis, 1991; DeBono, 1992; Prahalad and Hamel, 1994), if it is to become a "proactive challenge and motivation to the world of practice"

(Zeleny, 1995c). But for what, exactly, should practitioners now be motivated to achieve? Should it be more efficiency and higher productivity on behalf of whoever, or whatever, provides the funds (and as noted in Chapter 4 are often not engaged in the business). Or should it be to increase the provision of the human goods (justice, autonomy, harmony and dignity) throughout the global environment? Since there are many specific situations where these achievements are not the same, nor even co-aligned, this has become a rather fundamental question.

To try yet again to answer it, let us first look back, then more closely at the present situation. The 1960s was the era of classical optimality and planning. In the 1970s, management theory placed more emphasis on the ongoing process of incremental change in organisations (e.g. Hamel and Prahalad, 1989; Whittington, 1993); but the 1980s then saw the ascendancy of evolutionary ideas. In each of these decades, the earlier perspectives were not forgotten. When one now focuses upon the present situation, strong cross-currents appear. The ideology of EOS undoubtedly prevails, yet systemic (sociological) perspectives are also evident, with a heightened concern in many entities for matters such as culture (e.g. Burgess, 1995), learning and development (e.g. Osterberg, 1994) and ethics. As industrial productivity has improved, many new desires and many inequities have been created (some deliberately, as depicted in Figure 11.7). Certainly, in the global co-production of the human goods (Figure 11.8), we are not doing so well, at present (although one could point to specific localised exceptions). Accordingly, it is likely that the systemic perspective will continue to gain ground, whilst the coming decades, indeed the 21st century, could see the emergence of a more inclusive and universalisable ideology of SEO and EOS. If this occurs, we will then have progressed beyond trade-offs-free strategic thinking, to a form of strategic-thinking-without-boundaries (Singer, 1996a). Put differently, universal humane ideals will have been swept back on to the agenda of productive strategic entities. Therefore, let us agree that optimality is worth arguing about and that strategy does matter.

Notes

1. Zeleny (1994a,c, 2005) has identified eight generic cases (or forms) of optimality that are somewhat different from the categories used here, but can be placed

relative to them. His "eight forms of optimality" can be thought of as comprising a set of intermediate steps on a path from Figure 11.5 (DA) to Figure 11.8 (MDA and cognitive equilibrium). Zeleny noted that in a linear-programming type of optimisation problems, the number of criteria can be either single or multiple and the decision alternatives can be either given (as in the upper half of Figure 11.5) or else "yet-to-be constructed" (as in the lower half of the figure). Furthermore, the (single or multiple) criteria themselves can also be given *ex ante*, or else "still to be selected" with reference to the "decision maker's value complex". This yields 2 × 2 × 2 = 8 cases, or forms. When neither the criteria nor the alternatives are given, the situation is essentially as depicted in Figure 11.8. The descriptions or representations of the problem, as well as the criteria and the identified "alternatives", are all understood to interact in the process of (strategic) decision making. For example, as Schick (1991) noted, "we value things under the descriptions we put on them". Zeleny (1989, 2005, p. 73) has also depicted this situation as a dynamic recursive (circular) process of "pattern-matching" or seeking cognitive equilibrium.

Chapter 12

SYSTEMS: Management Science and Business Ethics

Abstract: This chapter is an adapted version of AE Singer and MS Singer, "Management-science and business-ethics," *Journal of Business Ethics* 16, pp. 385–395, 1997. It is noted that many leading management scientists have advocated ethicalism: the incorporation of social and ethical concerns into traditional "rational" OR- MS techniques and management decisions. In fact, elementary forms of decision analysis can readily be augmented, using ethical theory, in ways that sweep in ethical issues. In addition, alternative conceptual models of decision-analysis, game-theory and optimality are now available, all of which have brought OR-MS and business-ethics into a closer alignment.

12.1 Introduction

Within the field of operations-research or management-science (OR–MS), there have been many developments in areas such as social systems, human systems and soft systems that appear to be directly relevant to the primary mission and concerns of the Business Ethics (BE) movement. However, up to the late 1990s these developments had received very little attention within the mainstream BE literature. In both fields, major changes have taken place. Accordingly, where it once appeared that OR-MS and BE had little in common, perhaps even to be opposed, they now share many similar themes and concerns. For example, several leading exponents of OR–MS have been systematically subsuming ethical and social issues, or at least urging their inclusion, into the more traditional forms of OR-MS. The purpose of this brief chapter is simply to locate such developments within the spectrum of the BE literature, at the same time pointing to some special points of convergence or potential synergies.

12.1.1 Sweeping Out

During the 1950s and 1960s, the ethos of OR-MS appeared quite firmly tied to that of economics, engineering and production-operations management, as generally understood at that time. With a few exceptions, rational analysis in these fields was equated with utility maximisation, whilst optimality and optimisation occurred within given problem contexts, or in problems defined by others (e.g. scheduling warplanes for a mission, selecting amongst defined investments, etc.). These rational disciplines were overwhelmingly mathematical in content and, with a few exceptions to be discussed shortly, emphatically *a-political*, or accepting of the *status quo*.

For example, a 1971 engineering text (cited in Checkland, 1989, p. 277) advised readers that "...engineers, planners and economists (must) recognise the legitimacy of the political process to decide social priorities". An expert in operations-management (cited in Zeleny, 1982, p. 497) noted that "efficiency in operations results from arranging conditions of work in such a way that human elements interfere to a minimum degree". Put differently, there used to be a quite broad consensus that OR-MS should *sweep out* the messy problems of social systems, human systems, strategy and policy, whilst its students and practitioners should "stick to their fields of facts and logic..." (Checkland, 1989).

There is a rather obvious parallel between all of this and the famous Friedmanite prescription concerning the proper goals for corporate management. Friedman's (1970) advocacy of the idea that "The social responsibility of business is to increase its profits" is undoubtedly familiar to anyone who is remotely interested in business ethics (or strategic management, for that matter). Indeed, it is a prescription that has been supported and followed by many, particularly during the 1980s, despite its having been systematically and thoroughly refuted (e.g. Goldman, 1980; Buchanan, 1985; Grant, 1991).

12.1.2 Sweeping Back In

Whatever the merits of the Friedmanite position, it has undoubtedly earned its Nobel prize-winning author pride of place in the rogues' gallery of business ethicists. Indeed, much of the energy driving the BE movement, from the mid-1970's to the present day, has been directed squarely against any narrow management ideology of calculated profit maximisation, with all that this entails in terms of practices, language — use, symbolism and social outcomes. Yet, largely unnoticed in the mainstream BE literature, a parallel and contemporaneous effort was also underway amongst the *doyens* of the OR-MS fraternity (e.g. Churchman, 1971; Beer, 1972; Mason and Mitroff, 1981; Zeleny, 1982; Boulding, 1978, to mention but a few).

More recently, as the influence of formal economic theory on business practice has receded (e.g. Kay, 1991; Kuhn, 1992), the level of interest in other theories has grown. This has particularly been the case with Philosophy, which, throughout the 1960's and 1970's, had been the "absent center of Anglo-American management theory" (Burrell, 1989). In 1989, an entire special issue of *Human Systems Management* was devoted to Philosophy and Management. More generally, across the entire spectrum of OR-MS, there has been gradual movement away from traditional "1950s and 1960s" techniques, with their given "hard" objectives (e.g. profit maximisation, cost minimisation, etc.) towards alternative approaches that involve systematic inquiry and problem structuring. Thus, the new OR-MS includes methodologies that are either non-optimising, or else optimising in some different and wider sense, with more of the system being swept in. Put differently, there has been a growth in "ethicalism".

The post-1980 push for alternatives in Management Science, exactly coincided with the flourishing of the BE movement. For example, journal *Human Systems Management* and the *Journal of Business Ethics* both date back to the very same year: 1981. At that time, in a definitive OR-MS text (Zeleny, 1982, p. 490), it was argued that "... criteria of equity and fairness, employment and education, energy and environment, personal privacy and self-reliance, ethics and beauty individual safety and security all are becoming the inner core".

In such phrases (for many others, see the1994 special issue of the TIMS-ORSA journal *Interfaces* 24(4), it has become ever more apparent that leading thinkers in OR-MS have, in effect, signed up with the BE movement. They too have campaigned passionately against the "sweeping out" of social concerns and admonished against the uncritical military-style acceptance of given objective(s). Accordingly, an opposing process of *sweeping in* social and human factors is now well and truly underway. The old OR–MS techniques are being steadily discarded and replaced with new ones (e.g. Mason and Mitroff, 1981; Linstone, 1984; Rosenhead, 1989) or else augmented or adapted (e.g. Singer, 1994b) in ways that reflect the ethical imperatives.

In the following section, three simple illustrations are set out, each indicating how elementary (1950s and 1960s style) OR–MS approaches to management decision analysis can quite readily be augmented, so that they come to incorporate ethical concerns. Following this, some other, more general conceptual and methodological adaptations are briefly outlined. Taken together, the underlying direction of theory development is unmistakable: it is one of convergence, with management science and business ethics becoming more closely aligned, complementary and synergistic.

12.2 Three Illustrations

The major themes of BE (e.g. caring for others, concerns for justice, devotion to self-knowledge and reflective thinking) may be quite readily swept in as augmentations to the more traditional OR–MS solutions. Accordingly, in the illustrations that follow, one may identify an old–style analytic approach, based upon utility maximisation (profit maximisation, cost minimisation), which is then simply augmented by a more pluralistic and ethical approach. The latter incorporates:

- plural forms of rationality and ethical reasoning,
- the creation or design of alternatives,
- the search for wisdom and self-knowledge,
- the commitment to human betterment (Boulding, 1978).

The three illustrations set out below involve (i) environmental concerns in a logging decision, (ii) personal well-being in a dealing decision (a PDG) and (iii) justice concerns in dividend decisions.

12.2.1 A Logging Decision

Many strategic business decisions simply involve one-off special profit opportunities. For example, a manager in a forestry business faced a decision about purchasing an area of developed woodland, with the intention of logging. The manager knew that for various reasons (environmental, recreational, aesthetic and spiritual) the trees should stay. He also knew that "if he were to refrain from felling these trees, *someone else would do it*", because there was undoubtedly a profit to be made. This is the commonly understood reality of business, the "facts and logic" of countless similar situations (as well as countless justifications to the media). A simple traditional decision analysis (DA) of this situation is set out in Figure 12.1.

This DA, which implicitly assumes (a narrow form of) utility maximisation gives a clear unambiguous prescription, a solution to the given problem: *start the chainsaws!* Until quite recently, this would have been a very fair description of how almost all people in business framed such decision problems (cf. Poff, 1994). By law, managers have a fiduciary duty to shareholders (institutions, pension funds, individuals or the managers themselves). They neither have any legal obligation to other stakeholders, nor, especially, to the trees. That ethos (and its legislative underpinnings) are now changing, in many parts of the world, resulting in changes to the calculated utilities in the DA (e.g. as fines are increased, the inequality $\pi - f \gg 0$ becomes reversed). At the same time, in the newer forms of decision analysis, such as multicriteria decision making (MCDM) with ethical decision making (EDM), to be elaborated shortly, much less emphasis is placed upon aggregated utilities and probabilities. Instead, the focus shifts towards (a) the creation of alternatives and (b) structuring reflective inquiry.

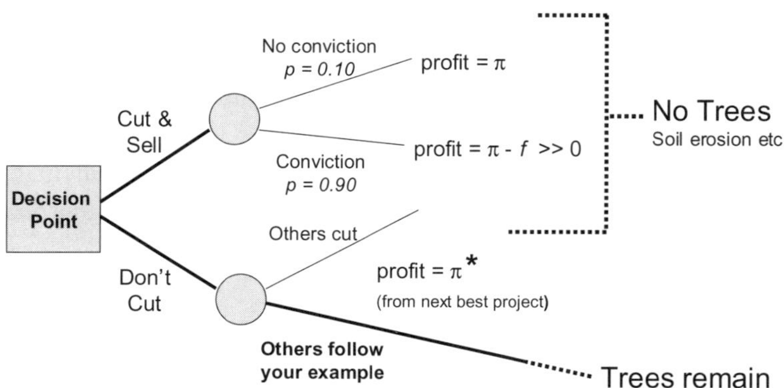

Figure 12.1   A decision-tree analysis of a logging decision.

Accordingly, these newer approaches sweep in business ethics; in particular, they inform the manager that he or she should

- *understand* that "If I don't do it others will…" is not a valid reason for action.
- *set an example,* remembering not to underestimate the influence of your behaviour on others.
- *lobby* governments, to pass laws with sufficient penalties and effective enforcement.
- *enlist support* from pressure groups and NGOs (e.g. Greenpeace, Friends of the Earth, etc.).
- *cultivate an image* of social responsibility to win over customers (Green marketing).
- *develop* new businesses and retrain employees (Green strategy).

Creating and selecting these strategic options, the designed objects of rational choice, then requires moral courage, or moral character (e.g. Solomon, 1992). Of course, such creative strategies are easy to write about, hard to implement (see concluding section). It is much easier for any manager to "cut them down and ship them out", increase profit, pay a dividend to shareholders, then move on to the next management position, taking with him/her a solid record of profit increases. According to Poff (1994), it is this very dynamic that has made the economy and the environment irreconcilable in practice. Churchman (1994) agrees, saying that "we ruin the environment… but don't know how to stop. Thus, it seems that we know that we should stop; but we do not know how to stop, by taking appropriate action, for we lack moral courage.

12.2.2 A Double-Dealing Decision

This illustration[1] involves game theory and the PDG. Imagine you are a consultant (in OR–MS or BE) advising a client. The client is, by his/her own admission, only minimally concerned with the welfare of others. In accordance with his/her personal outlook he/she has recently arranged a secret deal:

> He/she will go to a prearranged location, in a forest, leave a briefcase full
> of illegal drugs to be collected by a customer, then he/she will pick up

another briefcase full of cash, to be left by the "customer" in a different prearranged spot. After this big deal he/she plans to make a dash to Rio, equipped with a new secret identity.

He/she is seeking an opinion from you about an idea he/she has had: to leave her case empty, thereby keeping the drugs... and picking up the cash. This problem appears on the surface to have very little to do with business ethics. Nevertheless, you try to help him/her, by writing down a (traditional) rank-order payoff matrix (Figure 12.2).

This is the PDG, undoubtedly as familiar to business ethicists (e.g. Solomon, 1992) as to students of OR–MS. The client's ranking of the four possible scenarios found in the left-hand entries, in each cell of the matrix; the "customer's" rankings, you are quite sure, are those shown in the right-hand entries in each cell. You notice that whatever the "customer" does, your client will be better off, in his/her own terms, by choosing to leave his/her bag empty. To use the language of DA and GT, "empty" dominates "full", it is better under all contingencies, so, logically, one must choose "empty".

Of course, the customer, at the same time, faces an identical problem (in terms of the matrix), so it is equally "obvious" that he/she must leave his/her case empty as well. As a result, no deal will be done. But this outcome

		Customer decides to leave his bag...	
		full	**empty**
Client "should" leave her bag...	**full**	**2, 2** Deal as pre- arranged	**4, 1**
	empty	**1,4**	**3,3**

Key:
1 = highest ranked outcome, the best for that player
2 = next best
3 = not as good as 2
4 = worst outcome for that player

Figure 12.2   A rank-order payoff matrix for a dealing decision.

(i.e. no deal) is ranked lower by your client (3) than the prearranged deal (2). In sum, by prescribing the dominating option, your clients preferences will most surely be violated.

This hard-core paradox demonstrates a fundamental flaw in the idea, mentioned in the introduction of "logic and facts" in human systems. According to Rapoport (1991), a management scientist, the PDG provides a "rigorous rationale" for *Kantian ethics* (i.e. act only according to universalisable maxims). Fortunately, there are several quite workable approaches to living with the paradox, each of which is rather similar in spirit to the recommendations in the previous "logging" example. Each prescription represents good (rational and ethical) advice to the client, within the obvious limitations of the context!

- *Define the objects of choice more fully.* Your client is not really choosing "full bag versus empty bag", but (a) full with peace of mind versus empty-with-worry… about being tracked down later by a gang or (b) empty-with-guilt or remorse.
- *Judge motives and character and reveal prior intentions.* You should ask your client (a) to judge whether or not the customer is honest and trustworthy and (b) whether he/she herself always intended to cheat, right from the start. If he/she did, there is a good chance that the customer sensed this intention when the arrangement was made, earlier.
- *Consider the shadow of the future.* Your client should be advised that his/her behaviour will very likely influence the future behaviour of others. Your self-interested client must factor in the costs to himself/herself of (a) losing future deals and (b) helping to create a less trusting society.
- *Form worthwhile habits.* This is a fourth reason to co-operate. Forming the habit of keeping agreements requires practice. It involves short term sacrifices, but it serves you well in the long run… over your own lifetime.

As in illustrations (i) and (iii), the decision alternatives must be created or designed, whilst social and psychological dimensions of the problem must also be swept in. Each of the above approaches to "living with the PDG", moreover, represents a major pathway from the old OR–MS to the newer human system approach and hence to BE. Considerations such as learning, habit formation, culture, character and language must be introduced augmenting and complementing the older narrower ethos. Put differently, other forms of rationality (e.g. Kantian, systemic, constrained, deliberative and contextual forms) must be invoked in order to complement narrow utility maximisation in management decisions (e.g. Singer and Van der Walt, 1987; Singer, 1991b, *et seq.*).

12.2.3 A Dividend Decision

In recent years, several decisions have been taken to invest in setting up national lotteries (e.g. LOTTO, in NZ and UK etc.). The decision process for these large investments interacted with the dividend decision, i.e. the decision about the best way of distributing the statistically-guaranteed substantial profits from LOTTO. However, the understood nature of that interaction was very far removed from the analytic version of the interaction, found in many finance texts (e.g. Brealey and Myers, 1981).

Traditional OR–MS (statistical analysis, central-limit-theorem, etc.) informs us that the game, once set up, will almost certainly produce very high ROI, but will also contribute to an increase in economic inequality in the society. This is because (a) there are definitely more net losers than net winners and (b) because player's diminishing marginal utility for money implies that the less well off, as a group, have a stronger psychological incentive to play (and therefore, as a group, to make greater absolute losses). Traditional economic analysis (Pareto-optimality in the market, associated with utility maximisation) prescribes that the investment is indeed "worthwhile", it should go ahead; moreover, the profits from LOTTO should be returned to the providers of the capital (as with any other capital project), for they, in turn, must either spend it on their own consumption or else invest it in other assets that also have an appropriate (forecast) risk and return profile.

This analysis may be augmented and complemented, with one based upon *deliberative* rationality, associated with the veil-of-ignorance approach to ethical decision making (Rawls, 1972). The latter prescribes that resource allocations in society should conform to the principle that

> Inequalities of wealth in society are okay so long as they arise in a way that also benefits the least advantaged member(s) of society.

According to this principle, the investment in LOTTO is "worthwhile" *if and only if* the least advantaged members of society can be expected to receive net benefits. It could be argued (from the economic right) that these "net benefits" are adequately delivered as the *utility* (i.e. psychic pleasure) of checking LOTTO coupons, or watching the draw on TV. But if that seems doubtful compensation, it then becomes necessary to ensure that some part of the profit from the LOTTO goes directly to "benefit the least advantaged". It follows that in deciding about the investment, with the dividend policy, management is also implicitly choosing amongst alternative forms of rationality. Put differently, policy decisions for such investments lie in the metarational and metaethical domains. (This observation is elaborated in Chapters 2 and 13).

In practice, it turns out that in every actual case to date of such lottery investments, the deliberative form has been chosen over the utility maximising form, since significant dividend payments are being forwarded to charities, hospitals, social agencies, as well as the providers of the financial capital. Accordingly, one must now ask: why should any other commercial investment and dividend decision be any different? This is not a trivial question. One obvious answer concerns the current actual state of commercial law, which upholds a system that Churchman (1994, p. 110) described as the particular "form of capitalism we primitive humans have today".

12.3 From Decision-Analysis (DA) to Meta-Decisions (MDA)

The extension of economic rationality concepts is certainly nothing new to the BE discipline! For example, plural forms of rationality are already quite clearly manifested in the available published techniques of ethical decision making (EDM), as follows:

- Hosmer's (1991) "multiple analysis" uses economic, legal and moral forms of reasoning, in order to "make the right, proper or just decision more readily apparent". It is, he says, necessary to strike a *balance*.
- Goodpaster's (1988) "steps towards an ethical analysis in management" include a prescription to understand all the facts, including all the options, identifing the moral issues and then reaching for a synthesis.

- The EDM checklist at McDonnell Douglas Corporation (cf. Murphy, 1988, p. 913) also requires a search for "creative solutions", with an attempt to identify the option that "does the most to maximise benefits, reduce harm, respect rights and increase fairness".

It seems striking that each of the above techniques is so similar in its basic form and content even though each was developed quite independently. Thus, there appears to be a consensus, at least within BE, about the appropriate nature and scope of EDM techniques. Managers should engage in a structured and guided inquiry, one that inevitably sweeps in ethical issues and rational–ethical principles. Accordingly, in practice, checklists consisting mostly of questions (not answers) or partial structuring of client's "answers" are the best one can do, as technique.

Others within OR–MS agree. For more than a decade, they have also advocated similar approaches (e.g. Mason and Mitroff, 1981; Linstone, 1984; Ackoff, 1994). They have each devised decision aiding techniques that are inquiry-based, multi-principled and non-optimising. All such approaches, like those of EDM, reflect the realisation that education, including management education, "should be devoted more to learning how to raise questions, than to answering them" (Ackoff, 1994, p. 78).

12.3.1 *Problem Structuring*

In addition to the EDM and other multiple-perspective checklists, the need for other, different forms of "rational analysis" has also been recognised, in the new OR–MS. Throughout the 1970s and 1980s various problem-structuring methodologies (Rosenhead, 1989; Jackson, 1991) have been developed. For example, *cognitive mapping* involves recording a network of connected ideas provided by managers. Elicited meanings are then clarified by identifying a contrasting idea, and the meanings are recorded in ways that guide managerial actions. Such methods (often built into computer software) structure managerial inquiry, enrich the description of strategic alternatives and, especially, improve the conceptual models of managerial problems (e.g. Oral and Kettani, 1993). Yet, to the extent that all such problem structuring approaches in OR–MS foster a better understanding and a *clearer vision* of the world as it really is, these techniques also become directly identified with ethical decision making, for moral agents must always strive for the greatest possible clarity of perception and understanding (e.g. Murdoch, 1970).

12.3.2 Meta-Decision Analysis

The advance from DA through to EDM and problem structuring can itself be represented, quite usefully, as a metadecision analysis (e.g. Singer, 1994a). MDA recognises that all decisions have an archetype structure (Figure 12.3), a set of proposals, projects, or plans, however vaguely these may be perceived and described. Then, in contrast with the traditional DA which involves a (futile) attempt to predict cash flows with roll-back in order to calculate net present values, MDA steps backwards into the domain of the inter-related meta-decisions: decisions about descriptions, rationalities, models and optimalities.

(i)   Descriptions: In MDA, the choice of description, label or representation of strategic options is especially important. It is assumed that each strategic entity must settle upon whatever descriptions and whatever language it thinks fit. For example, in Poff's (1994) case study, a business selected a strategic option of "paying down junk bond debt to improve the capital structure and reduce bankruptcy risk"; yet the very same option could also have been re-described, most saliently, as "felling one of the last remaining privately owned old growth Redwood stands".

(ii)   Rationalities: Whereas the traditional OR–MS talked about "rational choice" with problematic subjective probabilities (e.g. Singer *et al.,* 1984), the new OR–MS, as in BE, the talk is more about "choosing rationalities, or ethics", in the sense illustrated in Figure 12.3. This is because, in OR–MS, it has long been understood (e.g. Zeleny, 1982, p. 491) that decisions based on probabilities and expected values (i.e. traditional DA) "... justify suffering in the name of random selection". Accordingly, alternative forms of rationality should also be taken into consideration.

(iii)   Formal models: Finally, in MDA, there is a metamodelling decision about whether or not to use any particular formal model (e.g. a DCF analysis. See also Chapter 9). This, in turn, is closely related to the

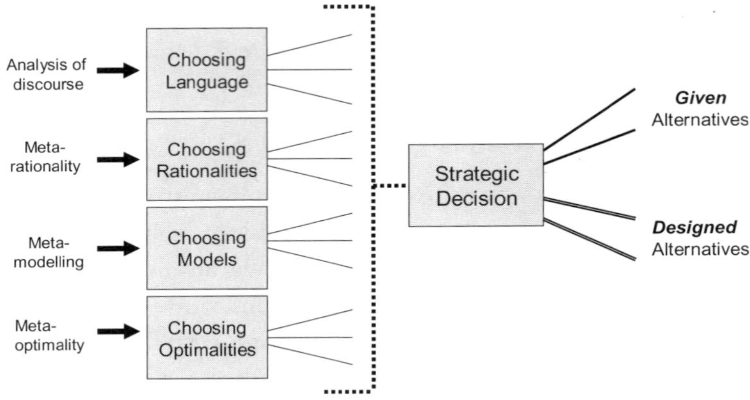

Figure 12.3 A meta-decision analysis of a strategic business decision.

choice of rationalities (Morecroft, 1983; Singer, 1991a; Van Gigch, 1991). For example, one should not use models that require quantitative parameter forecasts if one also knows, scientifically, that such forecasts are completely unreliable and "bound to be wrong" (Rosenhead, 1989).

The form of decision analysis depicted in Figure 12.3 symbolises an even more fundamental idea that is already very familiar in BE (e.g. Rawls, 1972; Rossouw, 1994) that decisions should be made, in practice, by processes of deep reflection and discussion. The outcomes of MDA can then be interpreted as an expression of the free-will of the various parties. All conflicts that arise at the metalevel... and these surely will arise as meanings clash... must be managed through conversation, until they become resolved, settled or dissolved, over time (e.g. Zeleny, 1989; Singer, 1994b).

12.3.3 Decision Errors

With MDA in mind, it becomes quite apparent that the concept of error, as it is commonly used in OR–MS and behavioural-decision-theory, can no longer be confined to experimentally demonstrated phenomena, such as misapplied cognitive heuristics (cf. Cohen, 1981). Such a narrow definition of "error" must be radically expanded until it includes the entire spectrum of improvable or suboptimal choices at the metalevel (e.g. Schoemaker, 1993). Whereas systematic biases affect judgements of probability in well-defined engineering-type projects, it is the poor choices of rationalities, models, language, or categories of meaning that can more readily create confusion, despair, disparity and resentment, in management decisions that involve complex human systems (e.g. Ibarra, 1995).

12.4 From Maximality to Optimalities

Each of the proposed EDM checklists (in Section 12.3) have invited managers to select an *optimum* solution to their strategic decision problem. But none said how. Managers are being urged to inquire about the potential conse-quences, the benefits and harm, with the rights and fairness implications of their proposals and alternatives; yet, no procedure for making any trade-offs amongst the multiple criteria has been set out, at least in EDM. The reason for this is quite simple: EDM techniques do not demand such trade-offs. The intention appears to be to encourage users to actively pursue all the objectives, to the very best of their ability. This often involves strategic action aimed at changing the constraints, the system, or the wider environment. Any balance amongst the criteria must then come from within the user, as a sense of bal-ance, harmony, or *cognitive equilibrium* (Zeleny, 1989). Such terms as "inner harmony" are certainly not new to philosophers and ethicists! Now, even in the OR–MS community, there is growing acceptance that decisional conflicts between opposing imperatives must be settled, resolved, or else dis-solved,[2] by continually reformulating problems, redesigning alternatives and taking incremental actions (e.g. Quinn, 1982; Zeleny, 1989; Singer, 1994b).

So what, then, has happened to the concept of optimisation (profit maximisation, cost minimisation, etc.) at the very heart of OR–MS? Half a century ago, Churchman (cf. 1994, p. 108) declared that "in the per-spective of another age to come… we *do not know* the meaning of "opti-mum". That new age has come now. What is known, now, is that the concept of optimality "is a far more profound and elusive state of affairs than can be derived from the most powerful mathematical proofs" (Mason, 1994c, p. 70). Moreover, according to Zeleny (1994c, p. 2), "there can be no absolute definition of optimality".

One can, however, identify, classify and even formalise multiple optimalities. Zeleny (1994c, 2005) has described eight distinctive forms of optimality and classified them on the basis of (i) single versus multiple criteria (e.g. cost and safety) and (ii) whether or not (a) alternatives and (b) criteria are given (as in traditional OR-MS programming problems), or have to be created or designed. In the case where neither alternatives nor criteria are given, according to Zeleny's analysis, a value complex is needed, but this consists of "mostly qualitative and difficult to measure principles, ethics and rules, best articulated in (natural) language". Thus, "optimality" in OR-MS has now come to be identified, quite explicitly with the concept of ethical optimum and the human goods.

12.5 From Games to Ultragames

Despite its early promise, formal game theory (GT) has been slow to solve managerial problems, in practice. In many ways, a very beautiful formal mathematical theory has been rather badly abused: it is sometimes invoked as "theoretical" justification for ethically questionable business practices (e.g. *Fortune,* Jan 9, 1995, p. 10; Solomon, 1999). On the other hand, if one looks to the natural language metatheory or conceptual models of business strategy as games, a strikingly different picture of theory use in management is revealed. The metatheory has been very thoroughly absorbed into the mainstream contemporary management ideology and language. Witness the tremendous popularity and influence of Michael Porter's works, based upon GT, with its related economic concepts.

12.5.1 Ultragames

If one accepts, in line with pragmatic philosophy, that metatheory or conceptual models can properly be termed "useful", then the same can surely be said of an extended conceptual model of a strategic interaction, seen as occurring between plurally rational entities rather than the utility-maximising players of the formal GT. The idea here, to paraphrase Solomon's text (1992, p. 56), is simply to get people to think about business differently. Such a conceptual model, an *Ultragame,* was proposed and elaborated in Chapter 10 (and in Singer, 1993b, 1995).

In Ultragames, each entity (player) is considered to be engaged in a search for success with reference to its plural rationality. Each entity is seen to operate in a complex and dynamic world, a multi-verse, constrained not only by its attentional limits, but also by its struggle for autonomy, its visions of its future and some concerns for human betterment. As with the "value complex" notion (mentioned in the previous section), it is not even necessary to formulate an Ultragame mathematically. Unlike formal GT, recipes for successful strategies, expressed in natural language, flow directly from the conceptual model (see Chapter 3). Moreover, necessary empirical support for the success of such "competitive" strategies is not at all hard to find (e.g. Uphoff, 1994; Ritzer and LeMoyne, 1991; Maruyama, 1992).

12.6 Conclusion

Simply outlining various ways in which OR–MS has reached into the domain of business ethics need not imply any superiority of one discipline over the other. The partitioning of new knowledge into old "disciplines" is quite obviously untenable and most certainly not optimal. Instead, the principle of complementarity manifestly applies to management theory itself, for we most surely need both approaches: the scientific and the ethical. Moreover, there are many potential synergies to be realised amongst the disciplines. Put differently, OR–MS can readily inform BE, and vice versa.

Take the question of *implementation*. In 1970, C. W. Churchman defined OR–MS as "the securing of improvement in social systems, by means of the scientific method". The first part of this definition would undoubtedly be welcome in any BE forum; but there would also be some dispute about the "means". However, as Ulrich (1994, p. 29), notes it is neither the means nor the ends, but the *securing* that really matters. Has BE, as a discipline, secured improvements? Certainly, as economists have often predicted, mere appeals on the basis of ethical principles have not worked particularly well. For example, at this very moment, trainee financial analysts are being indoctrinated in the "old" ideology: commanded to deliberately and consciously *sweep out* social concerns from their professional economic judgements. Yet it must also be said that the struggle to sweep such concerns back in to all commercial practices and management education has really only just begun. It may well be another 20 years or so[3] before the myopia of financial markets is perceived as a "passing of the buck" (i.e. responsibility for distributive justice and human rights) on a truly global scale.

Meanwhile, there are other ways, apart from appeals, of securing improvements (e.g. Murphy, 1988). One must not only use the new language, but also adapt the old methodologies, devise new symbols, develop new procedures and advertise sustainable ideologies. In sum, a logical-incremental approach is required, within the BE movement. Quinn's (1982) classic exposition of "logical incrementalism" was originally published in *OMEGA*... a journal of *Management Science!*... yet, it has become one of the most cited articles in the field of strategic management. The latter, in turn, is largely devoted to one main idea: implementation, or the "securing" of change. Has business ethics missed the boat? Not at all, for in the 1990s, business ethics and strategic management have also become one and the same.

Notes

1. This succinct story of the PDG was originally provided by another writer.
2. A problem is settled when a solution is arrived at, but some parties or constraints are not satisfied; yet they acquiesce (or a constraint is ignored). It is resolved when values and criteria have shifted or adjusted during the solution process to fit or match an available solution (and its representation). It is dissolved when a newly designed solution (or representation) overcomes the original constraints, so that in a sense there is no problem any more.
3. This was originally written in 1995, so it is only another "8 years or so", from the time of publication of this adapted version. Meanwhile, the business ethics and the CSR movement have definitely been gaining momentum, with several global initiatives (search for "corporate social responsibility" on the web!).

Part III: Contexts

Chapter 13

POVERTY: Business Strategy and Poverty Alleviation

Abstract: Corporations justify their strategic priorities with reference to wealth creation and innovation. They do not normally view the alleviation of global poverty as an explicit strategic goal. In this chapter, which is an adaptation of "Business strategy and poverty alleviation," *Journal of Business Ethics* 66, pp. 225–231, 2006. It is argued that if MNCs are going to contribute to the reduction of global poverty, their deliberate strategies will need to systematically take into account the known limitations of market based systems, many of which compound the effects of poverty. To achieve this, existing strategies can be augmented in ways that involve partnership with NGOs, governments and trans-governmental networks.

13.1 Introduction

It is often said that the best cure for poverty in any region of the world lies in stimulating more business activity and start up ventures. Others are inclined to a different view: that deeper systemic changes are a necessary prerequisite for poverty reduction. At the very least, a change of attitude, agenda, mindset or political philosophy is needed amongst the world's more influential actors, including corporations, lobbyists, governments and other international institutions.

Both viewpoints can draw upon credible support. Nobel laureate economist Gary Becker was reported in *Business Week* (2002) as saying that "the fraction of the world's population living at less than $2 a day fell by about 20% during the last three decades" (of rapid globalisation and the triumph of capitalism) and that since 1950 "real per capita income grew by about 2% per year around the world". At about the same time, another Nobel laureate economist, Joseph Stiglitz, reported that the poorest countries such as those in sub-Saharan Africa "became *worse off* at a rate of about 2% per year". Stiglitz also commented that "the basic issue is one of fairness", and this "is something that everyone can understand".

A rather similar level of ambivalence currently surrounds the empirical relationship between the social and the financial performance of corporations (e.g. McWilliams and Siegel, 2000; Margolis and Walsh 2003). Indeed the latter authors noted (p. 269) that the literature in this area "reinforces rather than relieves the tension surrounding corporate responses to social misery". Accordingly, they recommended "a systematic normative analysis of the imperative for corporations to do more to redress societal problems". Several other researchers have pointed to ways in which specific corporate strategies (e.g. to increase market power) can have both positive and negative effects on a variety of social conditions (e.g. Quinn and Jones, 1995; Prakash Sethi, 2003; Haksever *et al.*, 2003, to mention a few). In some cases, they have also made suggestions about ways of limiting the negative effects of those strategies.

Many of those "negative effects" relate to poverty, broadly conceived. However, by far the most common response to the ambivalent data and conflicting pronouncements is an insistence that, in the absence of the wealth-creating and job-creating activities of entrepreneurial businesses, the depth and extent of world poverty would be far greater. Not only is job creation widely viewed as the highest form of charity, but what many LDCs plainly need is more start-ups, more microcredit, more new business entries and more efficient financial institutions. It is argued here that this "more of the same" solution to global poverty is correct but partial, or incomplete. It proposes (in line with others, such as Freeman, 1998; Sen, 1999; Prakash Sethi, 2003, to mention a few) that if poverty is to be unambiguously reduced, a new mindset (or model, or expectation, or concern, or narrative, or paradigm, or political philosophy, or ideology) is also needed amongst producers all over the world that incorporates an actual intention (or mission, or goal, or deliberate strategy) to directly reduce poverty. Second, a global legislative and institutional framework is needed that actively responds to and promotes that mindset.

In the following section, some distinctive forms of poverty are identified, together with a classification of the positive and negative effects of entrepreneurial activity on each form. With poverty (like capital) thus construed as multidimensional, poverty alleviation is seen to require a multifaceted approach (e.g. Sen, 1999). It is argued that poverty alleviation under contemporary conditions requires (i) a constellation of partnerships amongst entrepreneurs, governments and other international agencies, but (ii) with each partner (and particularly businesses) *intentionally* pursuing multiple objectives that explicitly include poverty reduction.

13.2 Poverty

Normal language use attests to the multifaceted nature of poverty. The most obvious "facet" or form refers to lack of income or assets, but the notion of poverty as capability deprivation (lack of competence, confidence, disempowerment, etc.) has also gained currency. It is also quite common to speak of an "impoverished understanding", or culture, or spirit (Appendix 13.1). Each of these aspects or forms of poverty constitutes a distinctive condition that can be either ignored or changed by business entities and activities. Furthermore, this "change" can be either positive or negative at various locations[1] and at different times (Figure 13.1).

Although wealth creation does not necessarily imply poverty reduction, it is obvious that business activity alleviates some instances of *income* poverty, in several ways (e.g. Prahalad and Hammond, 2002; Ahmed and Werhane, 2004). When entrepreneurs successfully harness technology in order to coordinate production arrangements globally, the result can be a greatly increased supply of basic consumer items, many of which are newly

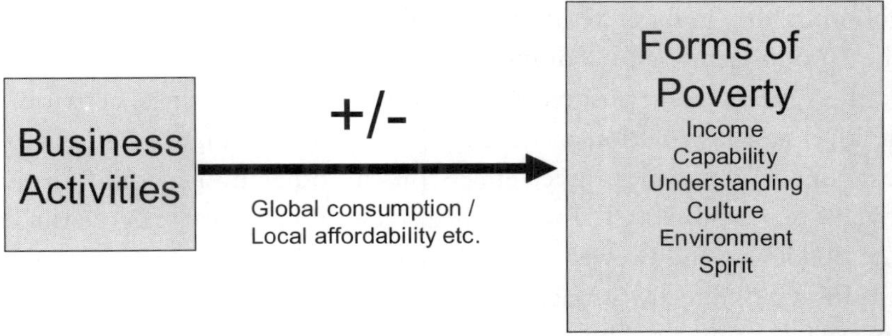

Figure 13.1   The effects of business activity on poverty.

affordable by those with low incomes. In LDCs, many people from rural villages make their way to supplier companies (nodes of the global network) in search of jobs. Although their wages are low, they alleviate income poverty and confer other benefits for the employees' families and villages. However, as discussed subsequently, this mainly occurs in situations where governments, NGOs and other entrepreneurs are all acting as partners against poverty, rather than remaining neutral or making matters worse.

On the other hand, business activity can sometimes have the effect of reducing purchasing power or access to resources for the least well off in a society. For example, locally grown crops and other natural resources can quickly become unavailable and unaffordable if they are exported (with the connivance of governments) to wherever in the world the ability to pay is higher. Thus, in many famines (e.g. Sen, 1999, p. 170), one finds coexistence of hunger with food exports. At the same time, in advanced economies where the prices of some basic needs can be high (e.g. Europe, US), workers can experience great reductions in their purchasing power as a direct result of narrowly focussed or deceptive corporate activity (e.g. the *Enron* case).

13.3 Ideology

The notion that business activities impact in both positive and negative ways on each distinctive form of poverty can be developed much further. Just about every example, claim or proposition concerning the effects of business on poverty reduction confronts a counter-claim, or counter-proposition (Table 13.1) that points to a corresponding negative effect (e.g. Dobson, 2001; Prakash Sethi, 2003; Haksever *et al.*, 2003 and Chapter 5). The "propositions" and "counters" can be classified as follows. First, there are the various direct positive and negative effects of business activities on the level and distribution of income (as depicted in Figure 13.1, above); next, one can consider direct effects on the other non-income forms of poverty (e.g. Hill, 2002). Two further classes of effect are via governments (e.g. Boddewyn and Brewer, 1994). Businesses influence governments in two broad ways: (i) directly through lobbying and (ii) indirectly through ideology, especially as propagated by corporate media, in ways that subsequently effect forms of poverty in a region for better or for worse (Figures 13.2 and 13.3).

Table 13.1 Classification of propositions and counters about business effects on poverty.

	Positive	**Negative**
Income-poverty	Provide jobs	Create sweatshops
	Increase global consumption	Decrease local affordability
Other forms	Create and share knowledge	Protect and conceal knowledge
Capability	Create new cultures	Destroy old cultures
Understanding	Restore environment	Damage environment
Culture and environment	Design ecologies	Destroy ecologies
Via governments	Pay tax	Avoid tax
	Lobby to update laws	Lobby for advantage, less tax
	Stabilise government	Support corruption or oppression
Via ideology	Keep dream alive	Frustrate with unrealistic goals
	Demonstrate mastery	Create slaves, colonise the mind
	Encourage value expression	Create alienation
	Engage in philanthropy	Reduce tax and improve image

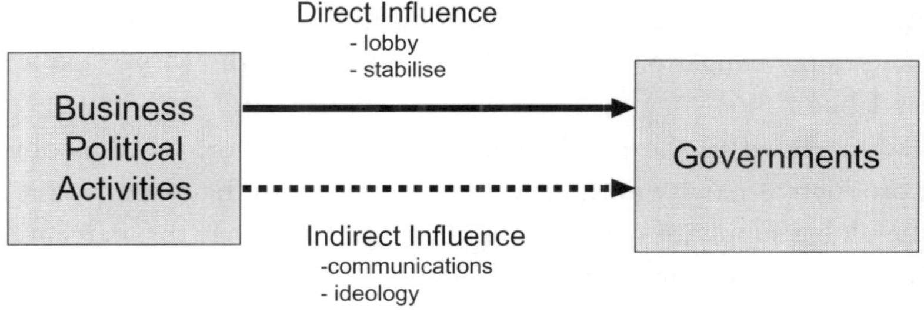

Figure 13.2 Two classes of effect of businesses upon governments.

The situation depicted in the figure differs from traditional accounts that cast government as a necessary constraint on business power and privilege. Newer "narratives" refer to the possibility of a reverse and benevolent influence exerted by enlightened business leaders upon uncaring or oppressive governments, or related actors (e.g. Freeman, 1998; Prakash Sethi, 2003).

13.3.1 Effects on Income-Poverty

Entrepreneurs create jobs whilst also increasing the supply of consumables to the market. Accordingly, they are often courted by governments to create

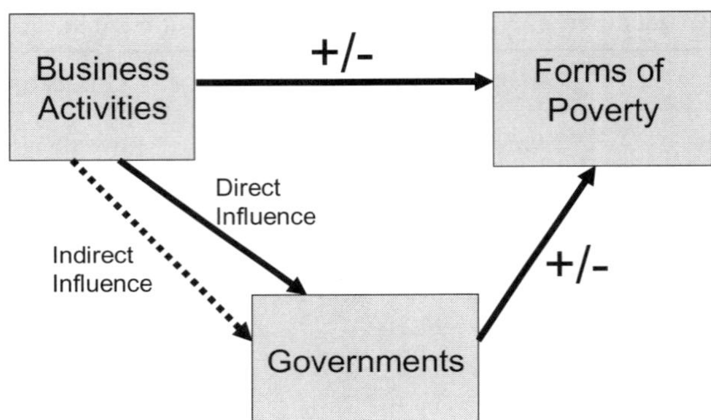

Figure 13.3　The combined effects of business activities and governments on poverty.

employment opportunities for constituents. Under recent political conditions, this has been well rewarded at the ballot box. In some cases, however, "job creation" can be re-described as the establishment of sweatshops, with oppressive work conditions. Oxfam, amongst others, has pointed to the danger of "equating" development with "MNCs exploiting cheap labour".

With regard to the purchasing power of the poor, it seems obvious that productive activity must have a positive effect to the extent that it adds to the global supply of consumable offerings. However, this perception is incomplete, or myopic. In the LDC context, for example, one must consider Sen's (1999) salient observation of famine and food exports. In developed regions and segments, one must also consider the quite widespread tendency to further reduce the purchasing power of the poor through predatory lending practices (e.g. Hill, 2002). In general, therefore, wealth creation through enterprise does not necessarily imply poverty reduction. The frequently deployed (but ideologically driven) metaphor that "a rising tide lifts all boats" is thus misleading. It downplays the systemic barriers to alleviation of income poverty, whilst it ignores the other forms.

13.3.2 Effects on Other Forms

The effects of entrepreneurial activities on non-income forms of poverty (i.e. capability, understanding, culture, environment, etc.) can be similarly stated in terms of propositions and counters (Table 13.2). For example, entrepreneurial activities have increased poor people's capability and understanding through up-skilling and the sharing of knowledge (know-how); but these benefits confront the fact that some corporations routinely protect or conceal their knowledge, in some cases privatising aspects of what were communal practices or public goods (e.g. Collier, 2000). Another grand claim is that businesses are creating a new global and technological culture; but this must also be balanced against the forms of impoverishment that accompany destruction of the old and the traditional, as well as the expected uses of the technology in ways that increase particular forms of poverty by pandering to peoples latent self-destructive or violent tendencies (i.e. impoverishment of health and spirit).

13.3.3 Direct Support for Governments

Businesses influence governments directly (Figure 13.2) by various means, towards the adoption of specific policies which can in turn effect levels of poverty. These "means", apart from paying tax, include lobbying (which can also include drafting of legislation), as well as political actions that protect or stabilise existing oppressive regimes. Other indirect influences are sometimes exerted within an electorate, at the level of ideology or political philosophy (e.g. Freeman, 1998).

For example, media-created entrepreneurial "leaders" often speak out in favour of tax reductions. This is entirely within traditional commercial-legal doctrine that permits active minimisation and avoidance of tax; but there is rarely any public acknowledgement of the very plausible idea that increased tax rates might enable governments to more effectively reduce poverty (e.g. by funding efficient providers of suitable services). It is obvious that tax enables governments to pay for programmes most likely to improve the security, opportunities and empowerment, upon which forms of poverty reduction (and much else) depends. In contrast, direct lobbying of governments by businesses is almost always for the sake of some business-specific or industry-wide advantage (e.g. Weber, 1996; Brooke-Hamilton and Hock, 1997; Altman and Vidaver-Cohen, 2000). Lobbying by powerful business interests is hardly ever directed towards the alleviation of poverty, with this goal in mind. Historically, in the *Wealth of Nations*

(1776), Adam Smith opposed lobbying by "merchants", seeing that it rarely served the "*public good*". In more recent times, many lobbying episodes have reflected industry opposition to public-good legislation.

The well-documented role of global corporations in supporting corrupt or oppressive governments can also be described in terms of propositions and counters. These political interventions might be for the sake of stability, or an ideological commitment to some form of capitalism; but they have also had negative consequences for some forms of poverty. For example, during the latter part of the apartheid era in South Africa, some corporations bravely violated the apartheid laws by having mixed-race facilities. Some provided jobs and recognised unions; yet, as has often been noted, they also directly supported the regime simply by maintaining a presence and therefore having to pay tax. In this way, they enabled the SA government to finance the apparatus of repression,[2] which increased the level of poverty-of-capability.

13.3.4 Ideological Support

Business communications can also influence entire electorates, indirectly, by promulgating an ideology. This is especially the case with contemporary for-profit media and entertainment industries. The result can be a shift in the attitudes of citizens towards the phenomenon of poverty, in its various forms and locations. In time, this attitude change alters the make-up of governments and their policies towards poverty. Typical persuasive messages or themes include keeping the dream alive, demonstrating mastery, encouraging self-expression and engaging in strategic philanthropy. The latter (e.g. scholarships, drug donation programs, and so on) typically facilitates human and social capital development, thereby directly alleviating forms of poverty in specific localised and demonstrable or photogenic ways. Yet at the same time it also increases the public acceptance of capitalism and corporate power, whilst implicitly suggesting that governments are incapable of alleviating poverty, should not be expected to try, or cannot be trusted to do so.

13.4 Partnership

If business activities are to become more effective in reducing global poverty, it is necessary for managers to first become aware of the oppositions

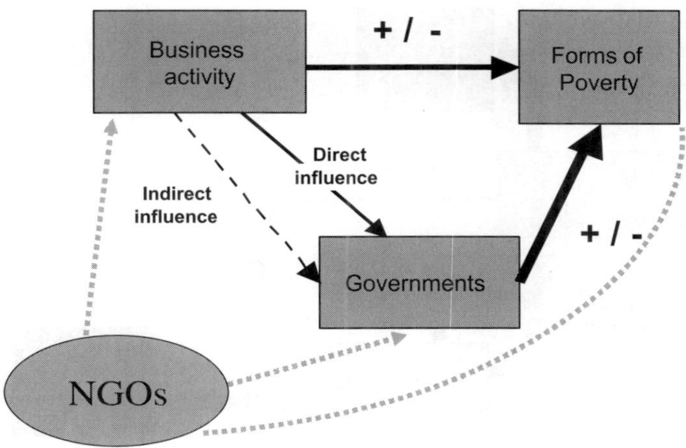

Figure 13.4   NGOs take direct action but also influence businesses and government.

or tensions set out in the above tables, then to deliberately and intentionally design ways of overcoming them; but it is also necessary to influence and co-opt other entities, especially governments and other institutions, including NGOs. The latter then work directly on the problem, but also jointly with businesses and governments (Figure 13.4). Similar approach has been indicated by Freeman (1998) who wrote of a "politics of conversion" towards the pursuit of joint interests, but also by Sen (1999) who described the need for simultaneous progress on different fronts, including different institutions that reinforce (rather than confront) each other. In the present context, this implies the *joint* and *direct* pursuit, by governments and businesses, of an explicit goal of reducing poverty in its various forms. Powerful and socially responsible corporations can attempt to influence governments directly and indirectly towards participating in such joint and synergistic solutions. NGOs and other entities that share the partnership vision can mediate and contribute to this re-alignment process.

13.4.1 Internationalisation

The entire process depicted in Figure 13.4 can be recast onto the global stage, simply by observing that all these participating entities are also pursuing strategies of internationalisation (e.g. Collier, 2000; Boatright, 2000;

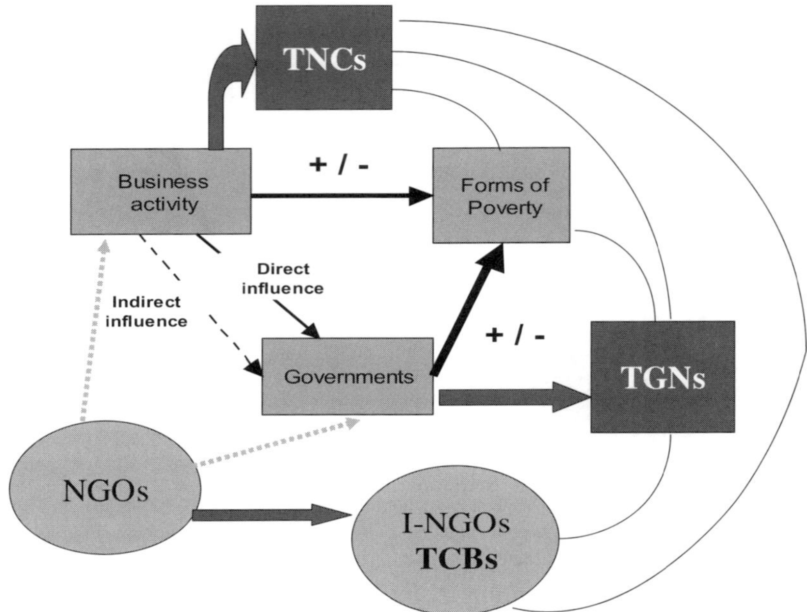

Figure 13.5 Internationalisation of the partnership against poverty.

Logsdon and Wood, 2002). Under this "strategy" (depicted by the heavy arrows, in Figure 13.5), national and local governments seek to participate in an ever increasing extent in trans-governmental networks (TGNs). Thus, corporations become multinational or transnational (TNCs), whilst many NGOs similarly expand their scope to become international (I-NGOs) or what Etzioni (2004) described as "transnational communitarian bodies" (TNCBs). Many of these entities envision a world "community" involving cooperative partnerships, and they adopt missions that embrace that community, but especially its poorer members. They accordingly operate at the transnational level (as indicated by the arcs in Figure 13.5).

In contrast with the above framework, there is a much more familiar conception of business–government relationships that simply involves profit maximisation by business with the delegation of the task of poverty reduction to the invisible hand of the market and the visible hand of governments. At the same time, business entities are assumed to confront and challenge the visible hand(s) in an adversarial mode. This industrial-age understanding reflects (and reinforces) the descriptions and expectations of merchants at the time of Adam Smith and Thomas Hobbes and has arguably been responsible for much contemporary poverty. An alternative and more contemporary concept of an international partnership against poverty in which all players remain educated about and mindful of the dialectic tensions set out earlier now appears to be the best way of reducing the overall level of poverty in the world.

13.5 Implementation

From the perspective of a business corporation, the "conversion" or "transition" towards a mission of partnership against poverty can be facilitated with reference to a suitable guide, or methodology (see Chapter 4). Several general approaches to implementing ethical business strategies have been devised by various authors (e.g. Sims and Brinkman, 2003; Roussouw and Van Vuuren, 2003; Waddock, 2004, to mention a few). Drawing upon the present analysis, one can simply review the current strategy and communications of any business, making explicit any previously implicit value priorities (core values) and political (systemic) understandings. This does not have to be done in a vacuum: it can be carried out with direct reference to the several known limitations of market based systems (KLMBS) such as monopolistic tendencies, lack of distributive justice, and so on. Each identified proposition about the various elements of the current corporate strategy then yields a "counter", or complement, which in turn becomes the focus of further deliberation and discussion. Augmentations of corporate strategy can then be designed with a view to overcoming or compensating for each limitation. In this way the strategic entity can be transformed, incrementally, into an active partner against poverty.

13.5.1 Example

The mission and strategy of an American consumer–credit company, Fingerhut, provides a good illustration (in a national rather than international context) of how compensatory strategies might be designed and implemented to deliberately help some poor people (cf. Fennel *et al.*, 2002). The company claims to have the image of an "ethical and socially conscious company". However, at the same time, it directly shares responsibility for the perverse fact that in many situations the poor actually pay more for a given product. Fingerhut supplies consumer goods tied in with expensive (high risk) credit financing.[3] Its target market is the lowest 40% by income in the US and in those who cannot obtain credit cards. The price paid for the goods-with-finance is usually far more than the cash price (according to the case-study, USD1029 versus 329 in one instance).

Fingerhut's market offerings are arguably helping the less-well-off in the specific sense that they enable customers to take immediate possession of consumer goods when they would otherwise have to wait and save. However, one might also say that Fingerhut's business involves desperate exchanges that make income poverty (and possibly other forms) worse, quite similar to the purchasing of expensive patented life-saving drugs by agencies and individuals in poor countries (Chapter 14).

There are several specific practical ways in which strategy at Fingerhut could be augmented (Table 13.2) in order for the company to live up to its "ethical and socially conscious" self-description in an authentic and credible way. First, the higher total cost to the customer can be clarified and clearly communicated (advertised) so that customers are more likely to make fully informed choices. This might also encourage a more general sense of competence and capability amongst customers, reversing the opposing tendency towards learned helplessness. The company can also actively encourage patience and saving (e.g. "it is worth the wait"), rather than trying to exploit customers' weakness-of-will. Such an approach relieves an aspect of spiritual poverty, because it can give people a worthwhile goal to focus upon, but it can also be viewed as a contribution towards optimising the overall level of consumer credit in the economy.

Table 13.2   Augmenting strategy at a consumer credit company.

Current Elements	Additional Elements
Obscure cost to customer	Clarify full cost
Exploit weakness of will	Encourage saving
Foster helplessness	Increase competence
Low-cost suppliers	Supplier engagement
Deal with agencies	Engage their clients

The company can also take steps to engage its suppliers (following the efforts of Levi Strauss in the early 1990s) and encourage good practices along the supply chain, rather than just searching for the lowest-price suppliers (and participating in a race to the bottom). Put simply, the company could deliberately pursue a mission of genuinely trying to helping people on low income in an enlightened way, rather than having to deal with personal bankruptcies and the troubled clients of social agencies.

13.6 Conclusion

Since the late 1970s, the unfolding political agenda of the New Right has been described by its detractors as a temporary aberration in a broader historic movement to a technologically enabled revitalisation of communities, social justice, human values and the natural environment. Since then, ironically, the visible hand of government almost everywhere has been preoccupied instead with security and with conferring increased market power upon profitable national businesses. If, at the same time, the absolute level of poverty in the world had noticeably decreased, then the overall approach might have been vindicated; but many studies and reports have attested to the contrary. The "invisible hand" thus remains, well, invisible. This is really not very surprising. Put simply, a combination of ideologies and practices that ignore the several causes of the several forms of poverty has accomplished what might logically have been expected, that is, an increase in poverty. To correct this, capable and influential business managers should adopt an explicit mission of deliberately reducing poverty, whilst also creating wealth.

Appendix 13.1

Some Non-Income Forms of Poverty

Capability

A recent World Bank (2001) report cited "opportunity, empowerment and security" as the main components of any poverty-reduction strategy. These are all to do with enabling or developing human capabilities.

Understanding

"Poverty of understanding" refers to an absence of the political awareness, practical know-how and scientific knowledge that can enable people to devise and implement solutions (with others) that improve their lives (e.g. Sen, 1999).

Culture

A culture is impoverished when it is oriented towards basic lower needs of survival and security. This distinction seems as relevant today as it was 2500 years ago, when Confucius wrote that "people will proceed to what is good only when in bad years they shall not be in danger of perishing" (Wu, 1967, p. 230).

Environment

Environmental poverty (desertification, loss of species, etc.) involves a loss of security and destruction of culture. Sen (1999) noted that "the demise of old species, even old trees, can be a source of great distress". This is especially the case for the income-poor who have extra reasons to value any remaining environmental public goods, such as free clean air and water.

Spirit

Setting aside issues of faith, the notion of "spiritual impoverishment" can be associated with any of the above forms of poverty, but especially with their combination.

Notes

1. This mixed effect was also noticed in a model of strategy and value creation devised by Haksever *et al.* (2003).

2. One US based automotive company responded to such pressures by spinning off its SA operation and selling it to local managers who were no longer bound by the Sullivan Code and accordingly resumed sales of vehicles to the SA police and military.

3. Fingerhut's strategy appears to contrasts with that of discount retail chains such as Dollar General, who also successfully target low-income consumers with low cash prices and a stated mission of " a better life for everyone" (e.g. Hill, 2002).

Chapter 14

HEALTH: Curing Strategic Myopia

Abstract: This chapter is adapted from "Curing strategic myopia: drug pricing and health care," *Human Systems Management* 23, pp. 161–168, 2004. Various elements of pharmaceutical corporate strategies are described and evaluated from a perspective that sees dialectical tensions at all levels of economic and social systems. Dialectical reasoning is applicable to the formulation and evaluation of corporate strategies in general, but it is especially relevant to strategies involving health (i.e. life and mind), where it also indicates the potential and suitability of business–government partnerships. Several ways of augmenting corporate and industry strategy and communications are indicated, accordingly.

14.1 Introduction

Pricing strategies for life-saving drugs have become increasingly controversial in the pro-patent era (e.g. Maitland, 2002; Perelman, 2002; Weatherall, 2002; Weber, 2002; Werhane and Gorman, 2005, to mention a few). The present paper traces out some implications of this controversy for corporate strategy, particularly in the pharmaceutical industry. The following section sets out some of the arguments that are commonly deployed by corporations in order to garner political support for drug patents, but also places these in correspondence with direct counter-propositions. Section 14.3 then sets out a wider view of the strategic activities of pharmaceutical companies, that is based upon the very same pattern of "proposition" and "counter", that is, dialectical reason and the complementarity of opposites. It is suggested that whilst this type of reasoning is generally applicable to the formulation and augmentation of corporate strategies (Chapters 1 and 6), it is especially relevant to strategies involving healthcare (Sections 14.4 and 14.5). Finally, various elements of corporate strategy in the pharmaceutical industry are re-examined in accordance with this perspective. They include business–government partnerships, as well as drug pricing in various market segments.

14.2 Patents

Intellectual property rights (IPR) policy has always been controversial, with a noticeable pattern of proposition and counter evident at every turn of the historical and continuing dialogue (e.g. NRC, 2000; Vaver, 2000; Watt, 2000). In support of drug patents, in particular, industry lobbyists have selected and deployed standard arguments from the economic theory of IPR (Table 14.1, column 1). However, a strategic silence is normally maintained by all of the more powerful stakeholders, regarding some equally "standard" counter-arguments (column 2).

For example, in support of patents, the Lockean notion of a person's natural right to the "fruits of their labour" is sometimes mentioned (e.g. Maitland, 2002), but without also mentioning that (i) most "persons" employed by today's pharmaceutical companies completely forgo that right, as they are in effect required to assign all intellectual property over to the corporation (e.g. Singer and Calton, 2001, and Chapter 15; Perelman, 2002); (ii) at quite the opposite end of the political spectrum, Marxist thinkers also championed the rights of "labour" to possess these "fruits". Even if Lockean and Marxists' notions of "labour" seem outdated in the modern biotechnology context, where knowledge management concepts referring to human, social and intellectual capital have currency (e.g. Zeleny, 1995a; Rastogi, 2002), the implied political and ideological tensions[1] remain firmly in place in the knowledge era; indeed, they are quite central to healthcare policies and strategies.

Table 14.1 Some propositions and counter-propositions about patents.

Proposition	Counter
Fruits of labour	IP is taken from labour
Pecuniary motives	Complex motives
Efficiency	Monopoly
Public domain	Privatisation of commons
Relations of power	Relations of care

With regard to innovative knowledge products, the observation that US-based for-profit pharmaceutical corporations lead innovation in drug design can also be set alongside a record of innovative companies that are apparently managed according to more complex motives (e.g. Collins and Porras, 1994; Sen, 1999). Perversely, the modern patent system can actually deter innovation (e.g. Heller and Eisenberg, 1998), whilst is can also promote wider inefficiencies as corporations are able to attain excessive global market power. It might be countered that the patent system serves the greater good by placing knowledge in the public domain, to the extent that it offers self-interested innovators an alternative to making costly arrangements for secrecy; yet the very same system very obviously privatises much of what might be public, because it excludes those who lack the ability to pay.[2]

Another rather salient tension or contradiction arises in connection with the theory of "property", when applied to drug patents. Resnick (2003) has noted the need to place general limitations of property rights if they are to be consistent with Rawlsian principles of distributive justice, whilst Werhane and Gorman (2005) have pointed out that property rights ought not to override the "right to life". More fundamentally, since property rights in general can be defined as "relations between people, with respect to things" (Munzer, 1990), the patenting of drugs, ostensibly to protect property, places relations of power (i.e. monopoly market power) directly above relations of care (i.e. care of the sick); yet in health services and in the medical profession, the exact reversal of this priority is often made explicit, even mandatory.

14.3 Complementarity and Dialectics

The vast majority of corporate strategies and communications express only the kind of "propositions" listed in the first column of Table 14.1; there is typically a silence, a failure to act upon, or perhaps even a failure to perceive the various direct "counters". However, it is not only possible to act on the basis of the latter, it is also possible that managers and policy makers can come to understand that the very pattern of "proposition and counter" (as indicated in the Table) is itself of much wider significance. Indeed, the logic of the dialectic and the principle of complementarity—both point to the fundamental wisdom of managing and acting with both sides in mind. Furthermore, in almost all strategic business decisions, two "sides" can be set out with systematic reference to the standard accounts of the known advantages and limitations of market-based systems: instrumental or manipulative treatment of others, preferences that reduce well-being, monopolistic tendencies, and so on.

14.3.1 Complementarity

Despite its long history and its 20th century scientific resurrection (in Physics), the principle of complementarity is only rarely invoked in contemporary business decision-making. Over 2000 years ago, Neo-Confucians first wrote about "the rectification of the one and the many" in mental life (e.g. Wu, 1967, p.140), with the associated idea that "harmony is achieved by affirming both, in the here and now". In quantum mechanics (unlike the Newtonian mechanics generally associated with the engineering view of economics, the neoclassical paradigm and the neo-liberal position on drug pricing), it became scientifically rational to believe in a dual reality and hence to act in the world "as if two things are going on at once" (cf. McCurdy, 2002, p. 528).

Since then, several writers have characterised the general relationship between profit-maximisation and the other goals of business in these "both-and" terms. For example, in discussing fairness and efficiency, Sen has noted the importance of taking note of each. In discussing the stakeholder model, Goodpaster (1991) wrote of managing with ethics and economics in mind. In describing so-called visionary companies, Collins and Porras (1994, p. 44) referred to "the tyranny of the *or*" with the accompanying need for managers to be "liberated with the genius of the *and*".[3]

14.3.2 Dialectics

As with the principle of complementarity, a dialectical analysis of any business problem sets out propositions and counters, or contrasting descriptions of the circumstances. An attempt at designing a synthesis follows, in which polar-oppositions and perceived tradeoffs are overcome, or a more inclusive narrative is crafted (e.g. Zeleny, 1994; Werhane, 1999a,b; Nagel, 2001).

Like complementarity, the notion of dialectics (derived from the Greek *dialektos* meaning debate) also originated over 2000 years ago. Plato (428–324 BC) used the term to refer to binary oppositions amongst ideas that advance from opposition towards synthesis, a process he considered as characterizing the progress of reason. In the modern era, Hegel (1770–1831) regarded the pattern of thesis–antithesis–synthesis as "the required approach for all significant *non-mechanical* problems" (cf. Reece, 1980). Later, Engels (1820–1895) described this same "approach" as embodying the "qualities of life and mind", thus hinting at its special relevance to the design of health systems, as discussed in the following section.

14.4 Health

The "dual reality" of complementarity and the contradictions within dialectics now appear especially relevant to the formulation of strategies involving health. This has been indicated earlier (e.g. McCurdy, 2002, p. 534; Weber, 2002), but there are some specific linkages between the abstract principles and the design of health-care systems have hitherto gone relatively unnoticed. These "linkages" involve (i) the visible hand, (ii) poverty, and (iii) general living systems.

14.4.1 The Visible Hand

Nowadays, the dialectic is often associated with totalitarian political regimes (cf. Fukuyama, 1992); yet this does not justify an exclusion of dialectical reason per se from strategic thinking in business (Chapter 5). More constructively, it points to the need for corporate strategists to remain mindful of the potentialities of governments and to continually re-consider ways in which the health-related activities of governments and businesses might be jointly optimised (Figure 14.1). In this calculation, almost every element of the strategies of pharmaceutical companies can be seen to yield a mixture of both positive (+) and negative (−) impacts on health, over various time horizons and across diverse market segments. For example, a skimming strategy for drugs (high price, low volume) can prevent access within some low-income segments (−), even as it quickly contributes funds (+) to the next corporate R&D effort. Expensive promotion strategies can yield efficiency

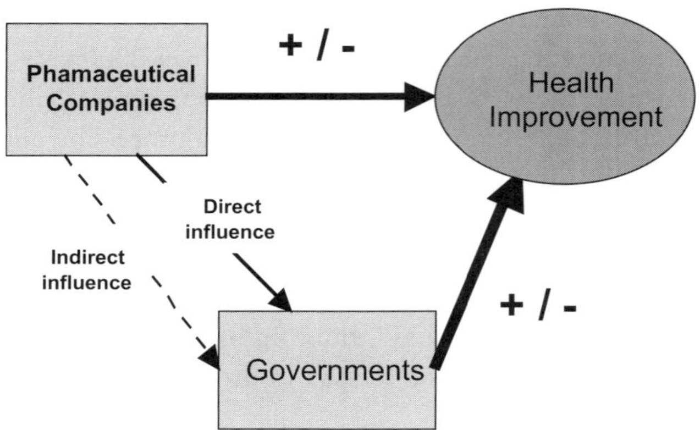

Figure 14.1 Pharmaceutical corporate strategies and health improvement.

gains from a heightened sense of competition (+), but can also have negative psychological effects.[4] Politically, corporations can directly influence governments (often via industry associations) at the trans-national, national, regional and city levels. This includes lobbying for specific regulatory changes, in areas such as tax, patents, subsidies, testing and imports, each of which, in turn, have a mixture of positive and negative effects.

Another level of corporate strategy, often overlooked or denied by those under the sway of the neoclassical paradigm, involves corporate communications that can undoubtedly have an ideological influence,[5] or an indirect political effect (Figure 14.1). For example, a pharmaceutical company might support an industry advertising campaign that includes fear-appeals, since it is also intended to broadly increase demand for private over public health services. This increase, in turn, might impact negatively on the public system and its overall political standing, thus affecting the future policies and compositions of governments.

14.4.2 Poverty

The dialectic is not only associated with the politics of poverty, due in part to the Marxist idea of class-conflict, but also the related idea that wealth-creation can be in tension with poverty reduction (i.e. the opposite of the "trickle-down" hypothesis). Yet it is the challenge of poverty alleviation, as much as health improvement that forms the macro-political context for understanding many strategic problems now faced by pharmaceutical companies. At the risk of stating the obvious, it is the inability to pay for expensive drugs that lies at the core of drug pricing controversies and political pressures on the companies. This "inability" currently extends to well over 1 billion people, most of whom live (or die) in LDCs.

To reinforce the underlying linkage between dialectics and strategies for health, one simply has to see that poverty-alleviation (broadly defined) and health-status improvement are almost equivalent, as goals or outcomes in a society. Poverty is not just an inability to pay for necessary market offerings, it is also a matter of capability-deprivation, of which life-threatening disease is undoubtedly the most extreme type. Furthermore, impoverished environments, cultures and understandings, each correspond directly to the known determinants of low health-status, as set out in Table 14.2.

In crafting policies intended to improve health, it is noteworthy that higher medical expenditure does not necessarily yield longer lives (Maitland, 2002). More broadly, health services including pharmaceutical offerings typically account for no more than 20% of any improvements in a population's health-status. The other known co-determinants include income-levels, water, sanitation and environmental factors, as well as food, lifestyle and social climate. At the same time, ordinary language use (e.g. "impoverished culture") and the literature on economic development (e.g. Sen, 1999) commonly describe "poverty" in almost exactly the same ways. Accordingly, if multinational pharmaceutical companies were to accept health improvements as an authentic part of their mission, they would also accept that they are deeply involved in the alleviation of poverty (within relevant populations, societies, market-segments or whatever). At that

Table 14.2 Health and poverty.

Determinants of Health	Forms of Poverty
Health services	Capability
Income	Income
Water and sanitation	Environment
Food, lifestyle and social	Cultural
Psychological condition	Understanding

point, business–government partnerships for health (Figure 14.1) become recast as partnerships against poverty, a re-description that seems particularly significant for MNCs operating in the LDC context.

14.4.3 Living Systems

There is yet another relatively un-noticed linkage between dialectics and health. Ever since the principle of binary oppositions amongst ideas was first articulated, it has been associated intuitively with progress in the sciences of life and mind. Yet this type of "progress" (bio-technology, info-technology) is precisely the core activity of today's major pharmaceutical companies. In the last decades of 20th century, these "intuitive" linkages between dialectics and life were often alluded to in connection with management practices (e.g. Hampden-Turner and Trompenaars, 1997) whilst mathematical advances and empirical discoveries in dynamic game theory and fractal geometry have forged formal linkages between "synthesis of opposites" and the patterns found in nature (Chapter 5).

14.5 Descriptions and Frames

In the description and analysis of health strategies and policies, one frequently encounters a "dual reality"; indeed there are often multiple descriptions and ways of framing almost every relevant issue. Generally, "we value things under the descriptions we place on them" (Schick, 1984), but this is especially the case in the economic and political arena, where descriptions and frames have a surprisingly large effect on individual's evaluations and wider public attitudes. For example, it has been shown (Thaler, 1985) that most people perceive it as "fair" for a small business to pass on its increased costs by raising prices, but they perceive it as "very unfair" for a local store to raise the price of a snow-shovel, during a snow-storm. The latter "very unfair" pricing strategy involves opportunism and desperate exchange, as do the high prices for patent-protected life-saving drugs.

Such effects of re-framing and re-description are especially pertinent to R&D investment decision-making in the pharmaceutical industry (e.g. Werhane and Gorman, 2005), where almost all proposals (90% by one estimate) are evaluated "strategically", that is, on the basis of documented descriptions. Accordingly, in crafting strategy, all statements about macro-environmental conditions, including such issues as who really bears the cost of health provision and who benefits, can readily be re-drafted and re-framed to support almost any given political position. Maitland (2002, p. 468), for example, wrote that the public (via taxation) "pay twice" for drugs because governments fund some research and also help some people to buy drugs; yet, one might just as well state that the public pays four times, since they also pay private insurers and other health-service providers. The point is simply that partial descriptions of the system are not only quite common, but are also misleading.

Attempts to strike a balance between R&D outlays and drug prices confront similar issues of problem-description and problem-formulation. A common formulation sees corporate R&D funding capability directly related to patent-protected prices (i.e. revenues are captured, profits are appropriated and ROI is secured, according to the strength of the relevant IPR regimes). It then becomes a matter of balancing prices against R&D funding requirements. A broader formulation sweeps in the entire range of potential R&D funding sources, especially public funds and ethical funds. The focus then shifts away from "balancing", towards strategic and political action aimed at re-design or re-shaping the wider system (as indicated in Figure 14.1). A more complete set and mixture of possibilities for R&D funding is then contemplated. It extends to public subsidies, tax-shields, grants and donations, as well as internally generated cash flows, loans and private capital. The latter, in turn, can reflect a variety of investor motives, instruments and entities, including ethical funds.

14.6 Strategies of Pharmaceutical Companies

Many specific elements of the strategies of pharmaceutical companies can be quite easily re-described. For example (Table 14.3), the options for pricing within selected market segments include a "zero" option (i.e. drug donation programs), "marginal pricing" (i.e. covering variable costs only) and a "focused strategy" (including skimming from price-insensitive buyers). At the political level, the elements include lobbying and corporate communications in relation to tax policy, patents and drug-testing, whilst

Table 14.3 Some levels and elements of pharmaceutical company strategy.

Levels	Elements
Market	zero, marginal, focus
Politics	tax, patents, testing,
Broader ideology	responsibility, public–private, subsidies, trade-barriers

Table 14.4 Dialectics and drug-donation.

Propositions	Counters
Philanthropy is Altruism	Philanthropy is strategy: PR; brand-awareness; avoiding "compulsory" license; undercutting local competitors; acquiring local knowledge; building political capital.
Multi-capital is formed	Multi-capital destruction (via political and ideological elements).
Pharm. Co. is role model	Pharm. Co. is constraining development of host industry.
Communities are supported	Disrupted with globalisation.

broader ideological elements of strategy extend to such matters as individual versus collective responsibility for health, private versus public provision of related services, as well as subsidies and related policies on tariffs and trade-barriers.[6]

Corporate drug donation programs (zero pricing) are often described as altruistic and idealistic (Table 14.4). They are portrayed, accurately in some cases, as building human and social capital and as supporting communities. The donor company is often duly upheld as a role model. Examples of communications in this vein include the account of Merck's programme to donate *Mectizan* (The Business Enterprise Trust, 2002) and Boehringer Ingelheim's account of its *Viramune* donation programme (e.g. Wecker, 2002). Such programmes can indeed inspire local governments, NGOs and UN agencies to become involved as partners for health, sometimes further stimulating the more general development of health-related infrastructures.

The programmes can also be described, with similar credibility and force, as corporate public relation instruments,[7] or as sources of potentially valuable knowledge to the company, or as possible means to undercut "unauthorised" local competition, or as ways of creating goodwill amongst host governments, irrespective of the nature of the regime. Furthermore, at the ideological level, they might serve to increase the acceptance and legitimacy of global capitalism (business-as-usual), in turn implying disruption and re-development of communities, within a cycle of creative destruction. If one then looks to the self-reported intentions of corporate decision makers, one finds they are increasingly being shaped by the kinds of consideration listed in Table 14.4 as "counters", rather than community, corporate citizenship or humane ideals.

Recent evidence (Saiia *et al.,* 2003) indicates a trend, in the USA at least, towards purely commercial motives for so-called corporate giving. In the context of the pharmaceutical industry, this trend is highly likely to be dysfunctional, because it implies a fragmented approach rather than an authentic and protracted commitment. For example, when BI donated *Viramune* in 34 LDCs, the incidence of mother-to child transmission of HIV in these poor countries was greatly reduced. Yet the treated mothers often later died from AIDS because they lacked the ability to pay for the patented non-donated AIDS drugs "cocktail", leaving uninfected but orphaned and impoverished children, on the streets. These children are at extremely high risk of becoming involved in prostitution, though coercion and desperation, thus becoming infected anyway. Such circumstances are reportedly far from uncommon (e.g. Leeper, 2003).

A similar mixture of positive and negative health outcomes, with varied commercial consequences, are yielded by a strategy of pricing at close to marginal cost, in selected geographic segments. Typically, this strategy is a result of negotiations with governments and NGOs within the TRIPS framework. With reference to alliances, or partnerships for health, such a strategy can be accurately described as a "public health service" or as "foreign aid". Werhane and Gorman (2005) noted that when health businesses forge alliances with NGOs, social marketing organisations and governments to enable drug distribution and set up a network for user-education, they are not only distributing more than just the product, they are also distributing (rather than avoiding) the many risks and responsibilities.

On the other hand, low pricing for LDCs has also been described (e.g. Maitland, 2002, p. 466) as "free riding" (i.e. by the recipients of drugs at below fully-allocated cost), or even as "mooching", but it is not only those things. As indicated throughout, when both descriptions enter into the public and managerial discourse, not to mention corporate communications and messages, the chances of optimising the overall system are surely raised. To give but one example, pharmaceutical companies would probably become less-inclined to hold back on the development of drugs for diseases in LDCs out of concerns such as "the product would just be grabbed by international agencies and private sector copycats" (2002, p. 461).

Turning finally to the strategy of geographic focus (Table 14.3), most of the marketing and promotional effort in this case goes into the wealthier countries and regions (e.g. Europe or USA), with prices set at whatever the buyers (i.e. individuals, private and public insurance schemes, etc.) are willing to pay. This has been described (again myopically) as "gouging" of the public, but within wealthier national markets, the strategy can be augmented by government policy (in turn influenced by the industry position) to ensure access for those who lack the ability to pay.

In the USA, for example, there are many who currently have to make fairly desperate choices between needs such as medicines and rent. Their plight is somewhat alleviated by cross-border shops or e-businesses that re-import generic drugs that were originally supposed to be supplied at marginal-cost-plus to LDCs (i.e. at discounts of 20%–80%). The associated controversy provides yet another example of the need for a wider view. Parallel importing is obviously a service to public health in the here and now, yet it has been described by its detractors only in technical and political terms as "broadening the channel of imports" and as "compromising safety".[8] Once again, constructive action becomes more likely to the extent that all parties (corporations, governments, stakeholders) re-describe and re-frame the strategy and policy options according to a dual reality, whilst remaining mindful of the concept of partnership for health.

14.6.1 *Political and Ideological Elements*

The notion of differential pricing of drugs, according to the ability to pay, necessarily involves some form of subsidy or wealth transfer from rich to poor. Therefore, its evaluation as a corporate strategy is very firmly in the political arena, where it immediately confronts the standard objections to any form of corporate involvement or meddling in social issues (e.g. Friedman, 1970).

However, despite these objections, pharmaceutical companies already do routinely and substantially influence governments on "social issues" (Figure 14.1), directly through lobbying and indirectly through corporate communications, particularly on matters that relate to wealth distribution, such as patenting and taxation. Put simply, many corporations, including those that espouse ethics and engage in strategic philanthropy, go far beyond prudent tax avoidance: they actively lobby through industry associations for further reductions in tax.[9] Within the partnership framework, it becomes more rational to lobby for tax policies that are expected to increase the overall effectiveness of the relevant public–private partnerships. Such policies would involve a mixture of targeted tax-shields, perhaps compensating for upward adjustments to other taxes or rates. The founding director of the Institute of Molecular Medicine at Oxford University advocated exactly this approach recently:

> Pharmaceutical companies have shown themselves reluctant to deal with the problems of developing countries, which offer little promise of financial return. We in the developed World need to persuade our governments to provide incentives to the companies, through tax exemptions for example, to put their money into this kind of work. Governments themselves will have to provide much more realistic levels of aid to developing countries (Weatherall, 2002, p. 15).

Other broader political-level elements of strategy, such as corporate lobbying in the areas of patents,[10] drug-testing[11] and subsidies, can also be more richly described and re-evaluated, within the partnership framework. Finally, with regard to general ideological issues, such as the extent of individuals' lifetime responsibilities for their own health, or the proper level of governments' support for international trade barriers, pharmaceutical and other corporations can review and augment all their political donations, public communications and promotional strategies in accordance with this wider view.

14.7 Conclusion

It is sometimes said that we cannot have a view of the world that does not reflect our own interests and values (e.g. Putnam, 1990). Yet, strategists, communicators and policy makers can quite easily accommodate the diverse stakeholder perspectives, which reduce in almost all cases to a basic thesis–antithesis polarity. Corporations do not then necessarily face an either/or choice: they can understand and frequently act upon both "poles". To the extent that all players develop this type of double vision, with the corresponding habits of thought, there is every chance that a more efficient and effective health system can be designed and implemented, both nationally and internationally. Indeed, such an exercise is likely to prove quite effective for solving a variety of strategic, political and social problems, not just the pricing and marketing of life-saving drugs.

Notes

1. The knowledge management discourse is quite political. For example, a view from the right (e.g. Rutledge, 1997; cited in O'Conner, 2000, p. 370) sees the concept of intellectual capital as "A potential Trojan horse for those who want stakeholders, not stockholders to control our companies". A view from the left sees that "IC" language is an attempt to capture all human knowledge production in dollar terms, thus essentially disregarding intrinsic values (cf. Singer and Calton, 2001, p. 21).
2. Although corporate communications have opposed "attacks" on patent rights, individuals within the industry have privately admitted that the patent system could be weakened, perhaps even abandoned, provided that a mixture of other policies and strategies are adopted in its place.
3. These authors believed (p. 48) that Merck's well-documented decision to invest in a cure for Riverblindness (e.g. The Business Enterprise Trust, 2002) involved a mixture of corporate ideals and pragmatic action. Several subsequent reports of the *Vioxx* episode seemed to cast the company's motives in a less favourable light.
4. Drug promotions create desires, manipulate perceptions and constrain autonomy, creating a gap between expressed preference and well-being, whilst making it harder for individuals to understand their own health (and other) needs and hence construct solutions (e.g. Crisp, 1987; Sen, 1999; Weber, 2002).
5. This critique of the ideological effect of corporate communications is a micro-level counterpart of an historical critique of Economic theory (political-economy) that refers to the "teaching" or "insinuating" of an ethic of self-interest (Coleman, 2002, p. 143).
6. According to Oxfam, trade barriers "rob developing countries of vital opportunities to create employment" (www.maketradefair.com). Global companies

have the power to work with governments and others towards re-describing and re-assessing these measures, thus breaking the current deadlock and contributing to the common good.

7. For example, "Pfizer Inc. in December agreed to give away its antifungal drug *Diflucan* to certain AIDS patients in South Africa, rather than lower its price and reveal the scope of its profit". *Wall Street Journal* (April 23, 2001, A1) as cited in Perelman (2002, p. 140).

8. Accordingly, in some cases, a logo has been placed on exported drug packages, so that customs authorities can, at considerable cost, prevent this particular "service to health".

9. It might be claimed (i) that this falls within fiduciary duty (the legal embodiment of the neoclassical paradigm), or (ii) that tax reductions actually lead to a larger tax take, ultimately benefiting the poor, or that (iii) corporate philanthropy is more effective than tax, in relation to health-status goals. Proposition (ii) is believed by just 2% of Americans, according to a recent CNN poll; proposition (iii) encounters another "free-rider" objection.

10. The pro-patent era of the last 20 years can be described as the resultant of political lobbying, driven by narrow industry interests (e.g. Singer and Calton, 2001; Perelman, 2002). Whereas some see patents as "society's commitment" or "gift", to the industry (Maitland, 2002, p. 464), others see strong patents as the spoils of victory. Shorter patents, conditional patents, or selective overriding of patents can be re-evaluated accordingly.

11. Currently, about half of the (fully-allocated) USD500 million cost of a new drug is spent on the regulatory process. To save costs, testing might be re-located or informed patients might be permitted in specified circumstances to use partly-tested products.

Chapter 15

KNOWLEDGE: Meta-Theory and Intellectual Property

Abstract: This chapter is an adaptation and extension of (i) "Dissolving the digital dilemma: meta-theory and intellectual property," *Human Systems Management* 20, pp. 19–33, 2001, by A.E. Singer and J.M. Calton and (ii) "Profit without copyright," *Small Business Economics* 16(2), pp. 149–156, 2001 (Special issue on Networks, Internationalisation and Policy), by A. E. Singer, J. Calton and M. Singer. It analyses the contemporary worldwide dissensus and dilemma concerning the nature and enforcement of intellectual property rights, particularly copyrights and software patents, indicating that the debate can be informed by metatheory. Intellectual Property Rights (IPR) policy can be depicted as a resultant of narrowly defined interests of stakeholder groups. It can also be described in terms of rational deliberations that span scenarios and strategies, but are informed by social science theories and metatheories. When these are considered together, the case for weaker IPR policy regimes (e.g. much shorter patents) becomes quite compelling. A wider potential for contributions from meta-theory to public policy and business strategy is also indicated.

15.1 Introduction

Napster, Versity and *Amazon* are but a few of the dot-com names associated in the 1990s with the dissensus surrounding Intellectual Property Rights (IPR). Amidst claims of "unfair" copying made by some of the world's richest individuals and most powerful lobby groups, many other scientists and policy advisors have used words like absurd, ludicrous, or crazy, when describing some of the wider effects of current IPR regimes. For an indication of what is at stake, a spokesperson for a not-for-profit research team stated "it would be a major blow for science and humanity if the human genome became a piece of commercial property". The dissensus and complexity surrounding IPR law and policy now has to be taken into account and managed pragmatically, by today's business strategists.

It is also quite apparent, to say the least, that new conceptual frameworks and philosophical understandings are needed to guide policy, in this area. The present paper attempts to fulfil that need. In the following section, IPR policy is described and depicted as a resultant of narrowly construed interests of various stakeholder groups. Policy formation is then re-described (Section 3) in terms of rational deliberations and discussions. These span applied considerations, such as scenarios, generic strategies and business models (Sections 4 and 5), as well as deeper theoretical and meta-theoretical frameworks (Sections 6 and 7). It turns out that the latter can quite richly inform IP policy (Section 8), first by recasting the problem in terms of an ecology of knowledge, then prescribing cautious intervention in that ecology, in ways that uphold human ideals and developmental goals.

15.2 Stakeholder Analysis

For several years, particularly in Europe and US there has been a great deal of well-financed political lobbying activity directed at the strengthening and coordinating (or "harmonising") of IPR regimes (e.g. Vaidhyanathan, 2006). Specifically, powerful stakeholder groups have lobbied for stronger and more universal copyright and patent laws, with the necessary enforcement mechanisms. These "groups" include professional legal associations, accountancy institutes, media and related industry associations (Figure 15.1) as well as security and defence-related industries and organisations.

Numerous arguments and reasons for strengthening IPR regimes have been deployed (e.g. WIPO, 1993, *et seq.*) in a protracted campaign to justify stronger regimes and to persuade the key players. Some of the arguments are briefly set out below. In appraising these, one has to be mindful of biases that are inevitably present to the extent that "as human beings we cannot have a view of the world that does not reflect our interests and values" (Putnam, 1990, p. 178). Then, in similar spirit to the recently published National Research Council (US) report (which appeared after this chapter was first drafted), several counter-arguments are set out. When

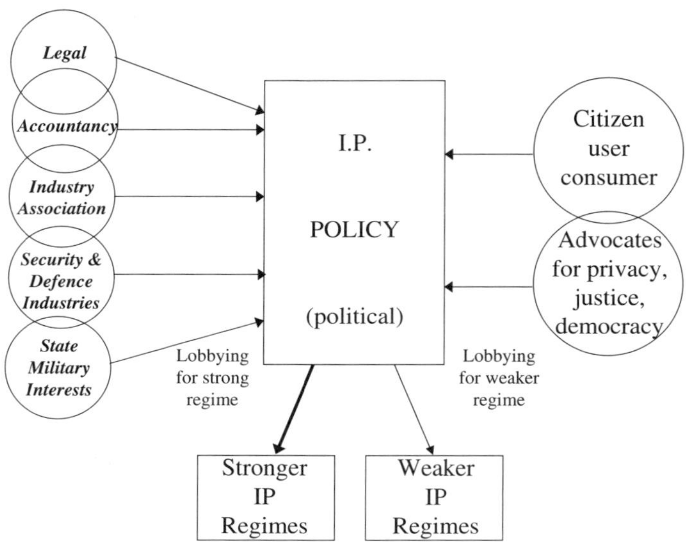

Figure 15.1   Stakeholders in IP regimes.

these are placed in the context of an exposure of the strategic interests (and hence also the likely biases) of the various stakeholder groups, the result is a much more critical account of strong regimes.

15.2.1 Legal Groups

The legal profession can be depicted as a major stakeholder in strong regimes (Figure 15.1). Several recent accounts of the history and philosophy of intellectual property (e.g. Granstrand, 1999; Watt, 2000; NRC 2000) have seriously questioned whether current IPR legislation can be attributed to lawmakers' desire to increase the overall well being of whole societies, or economies. For example, according to Vaver (2000) we have now arrived at a situation where 'Intellectual property has become more an end in itself, than a means to the end of stimulating desirable innovation'.[1] To the extent that the legal profession can be viewed collectively as a self-sustaining and self-interested entity (rather than public-interest-oriented) the language of business strategy can be invoked. Legal groups can be described as attempting to shape the future of cyberspace, so that it becomes a future competitive space. Strong regimes are advocated, since these can be expected to create a vast potential "space" for litigation. Indeed, in the US they have already spawned "a set of firms devoted to nothing more than harvesting patents for later exploitation" (Vaidhyanathan, 2006). The seriousness of this becomes apparent when one considers that that great many business and social activities, indeed all forms of communication in cyberspace, potentially lie within the ambit of strong IPR laws.

As with other grand strategies, the strategic shaping of cyberspace involves the deliberate promulgation of an ideology. In this case, it is a variant of capitalism, that retains and expands the traditional spectrum of property rights, including IPR (e.g. Munzer, 1990; Handy, 1997). Accordingly, in policy forums, stronger IPR regimes have been justified with reference to the need for capital accumulation and financial returns from investment–intensive products (e.g. high first-copy cost programmes). Reference has also been made to the benefits that users (misleadingly called consumers) allegedly derive from these products.

These ideological arguments can be countered in quite standard ways that refer to market limitations, imperfections, inefficiencies or failures. These include externalities and public goods, but also involve the entire economics–ethics nexus involving justice, social relations, alienation development and poverty alleviation (e.g. Sen, 1987, 1992). Counterarguments of this more general type (discussed further in Section 15.6) have only rarely been voiced in policy forums on IPR.

15.2.2 Accountancy Institutes

The accountancy profession, when viewed as a self-sustaining entity, is in a rather similar strategic position. Their "future competitive space" is mainly for valuation activity, rather than litigation. In the last 20 years or so, a gap has opened up between business asset valuations based upon historic costs (or realizable values) and the much higher total market capitalisation. The greater the information intensity, or level of embedded knowledge within a business entity the greater the gap. The existing gap or space has already been filled by a variety of market offerings, as accounting firms have produced differentiated and highly priced methodologies for valuing intangibles.

The ideological dimensions of this strategy become quite apparent when one considers alternative feasible accounting practices that might serve the public interest more directly. For example, financial reporting can still be based upon historic costs, whilst intangibles such as leadership, knowledge, capacity to innovate and other competencies (the so-called intellectual capital of a business) can be described in plain natural language that everyone can understand. This would be perfectly adequate for public reporting, strategic analysis and investment guidance. Furthermore, if this were normal practice, capital markets might arrive at fundamental valuations of knowledge-based entities that incorporate a more detached and balanced (less biased) view of the macro-environment. Most significantly, in the present context, any such "view" would incorporate a range of possible futures for IPR regimes, including those likely to best serve the public interest. In practice, this level of detachment and objectivity in business valuation is rare. More commonly, there is a myopia, induced by ideological blinkers that people might not even realise they are wearing (cf. Section 7).

15.2.3 *Producers and Distributors*

Industries such as music, software, broadcasting and pharmaceuticals have lobbied for stronger IPR regimes. In addition to the arguments deployed by the various professional groups (e.g. concerning investment intensity, product quality, etc.) they have also expressed some specific managerial and operational concerns. These include the effect of (currently illegal) replications on dilution of trademark, product-management and relationship marketing.

These "concerns" incorporate a rather obvious element of gamesmanship. For example, faults in replicated software packages, sometimes purchased at less than 1% of the full retail price, are vastly more likely to be attributed to the "pirate" provider, than to the original producer. With regard to the management and marketing practices, producers and distributors are overlooking or ignoring the potential benefits to themselves and others from weaker IPR regimes. For example, if producers forced themselves to accept weak IPR regimes, they would have to become more innovative at the level of their management practices and marketing strategies

(Section 3). This increased competence in turn might serve their longer term and broader interests quite well. Accordingly, producers of digital works face a problem of rational self-control, or weakness of will, as in the classical story of Ulysses who deliberately bound himself to the mast of his ship to avoid the temptation of the Sirens' song.

15.2.4 Military and Security Interests

Military and security interests also have a stake in IPR policy. Innovation, particularly in the area of information technology, increases a state's military power and especially its intelligence capability. Accordingly, military forces of nation states have an interest in policies that maximise the rate of technological innovation. This "interest" does not by itself indicate any particular direction of lobbying with respect to strong versus weak IPR regimes. This is because, the effect of regime strength on the rate of innovation per se remains ambiguous. The open source software movement and the public science genome projects, to mention just two examples, indicate how weak regimes might be conducive to rapid high-quality innovation.

However, military and security related industries have a more specific interest in particular types of innovation: those that can be directly applied to activities of command and control, security and surveillance. Strong IPR regimes can be expected to increase the market demand for exactly these types of technological innovations (so that compliance with the IPR law can be monitored and controlled). It is far from clear, to say the least that a focus on this particular type of innovation is in the public interest. It is not necessarily conducive to quality of life, or even to economic development, to the extent that important individual freedoms are also at stake (e.g. Sen, 1999).

15.2.5 The Public Interest

To date, commercial and security interests have dominated the policy-making process (Figure 15.1). There has been an inevitable downplaying of concerns about user privacy, monitoring and surveillance. For example, traditional public-interest arguments that support copyright, such as ensuring "variety and dissemination" of literary and artistic works (books), are no longer deployed by the above stakeholder groups, since they have obviously lost force in the context of contemporary technologies such as the internet. Furthermore, the news media, who are themselves major producer-stakeholders, have tended to either ignore the "digital dilemma", or else they have simply broadcast industry adverts that support strong regimes. As a result, the issue has not been presented to the wider public as being particularly contentious. Certainly, IPR issues have never been prominent in any (mediated) public election campaign.

This situation might change. At the grassroots level, so to speak, some not-for-profit/public-interest groups have recently proclaimed a mission to make the voice (or interests) of users and citizens heard, on this matter. Meanwhile, popular movies such as *Enemy of the State* might have also raised awareness of some related public policy issues. At the level of policy experts, an article in *Harvard Business Review* (Thurow, 1997) called for a new system of IPR several years ago. More recently, the report of the US National Research Council (2000) stated that "the average citizen... will surely be incredulous, as lawyers descend with cease and desist orders as they learn to program" (thereby infringing software patents).

More generally, there are signs of a worldwide public re-awakening to the potential dangers of totalitarian corporatism (e.g. MacPherson, 1985; Handy, 1997) that might accompany the growth of the global knowledge economy. Within developing nations in particular, advocates for development and distributive justice (e.g. Shiva and Holla-Bhar, 1996) have been increasingly willing to express concerns about the exploitation that is made possible by strong IPR regimes, not to mention more general concerns about distributive justice in the global context.

15.3 Rational Deliberations

The various arguments deployed by stakeholder groups, together with the counter-arguments, can be developed further with reference to business practices such as scenario building and design of new business models, as well as available social science theories and meta-theories (Figure 15.2). These are set out in the following sections.

In contrast to the political process depicted in Figure 15.1, the extended rational or deliberative process depicted in Figure 15.2 appears to support the case for weaker IPR regimes, particularly with respect to the

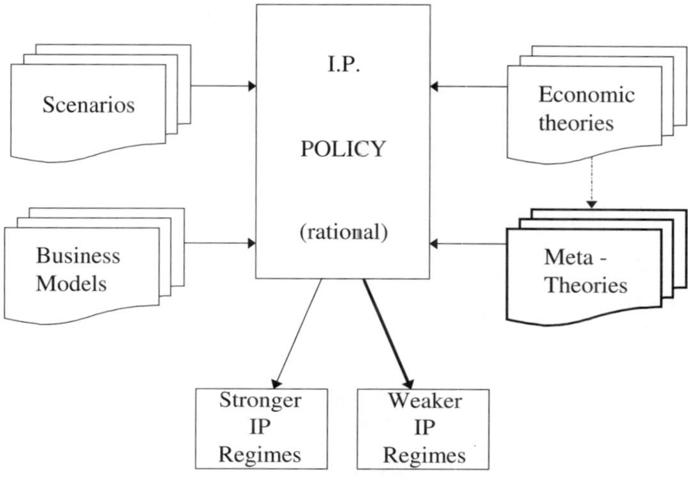

Figure 15.2   Rational IP policy.

copyrighting and patenting of digital sequences (DS's). For example, various scenarios (Section 15.4) indicate the basic feasibility and common sense aspects of weak regimes, in which the property rights are restricted. The "business models" (Section 15.5) then represent various ways in which business can capture revenue and appropriate profit in the presence of competition, but in the absence of copyright and patent protection. Other limitations of traditional economic and legal arguments for having strong IPR regimes (e.g. incentives for innovation, capital formation, quality works, etc.) are then briefly set out in Section 15.7, followed by the distinctive contributions from meta-theory. The latter enables us to recast the digital dilemma in terms of ecology of knowledge, in which cautious regulatory intervention shaped around human ideals can be of universal benefit. Several policy recommendations then follow.

15.4 Scenarios

The design of IPR regimes requires creative thinking and the generation of new alternatives. Scenarios and heuristics are often used for this purpose. They can also serve to challenge and disrupt historically determined attitudes, mental models, frames and discourses (a necessary first step towards establishing a

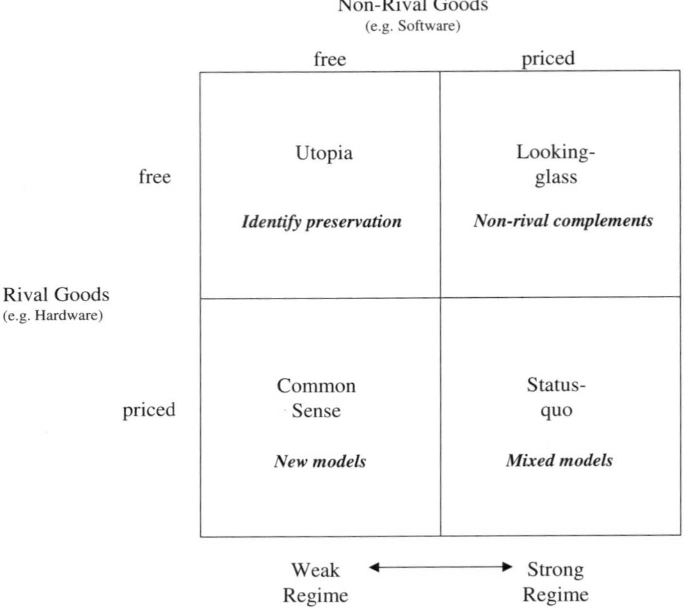

Figure 15.3   Non-rival goods, prices and strategies.

subsequent contribution from meta-theory). One simple set of scenarios can be constructed by envisioning possible worlds in which co-produced rival and non-rival goods are variously priced to users at (a) zero, or (b) greater than zero (Figure 15.3). Rival goods such as hardware and in-person services, are like a cake that must be divided up. Non-rival goods like software are such that their use by one entity does not necessarily have to deprive another. For both types of goods, their availability (i.e. the total size and quality of the "cake") can depend on the way that it is in fact divided up and used. The four resulting scenarios are described below, where they are referred to as: (i) *status quo*, (ii) looking glass, (iii) common sense and (iv) Utopia. Each scenario corresponds with some distinctive business strategies, or business models.

15.4.1 *Status quo*

Current IPR regimes motivate a varied mixture of business strategies. For example, a small business that co-produces or co-transforms a non-rival good (co-transformer seems a more accurate description) such as digital music or a software program, might adopt a promotional strategy that focuses on geographic segments that are within strong IPR jurisdictions. A business with particularly high first–copy costs (movies, high-end software) might pursue a hyper-competitive strategy, or other "new" strategies (Section 15.5) that capture revenue without any IPR protection, whilst they might simultaneously lobby through industry associations for the expansion (globalisation, harmonisation, etc.) of stronger regimes to support their own strategy (even though it might oppose the public interest).

15.4.2 Common Sense

Here, non-rival goods (e.g. a digital download) are free, but rival goods (e.g. hardware) are priced, so they can be efficiently allocated, subject to standard limitations. This is essentially the world according to Napster. It is "common sense", insofar as an average three-year-old child can quickly grasp the "no-deprivation" aspect of the replication of non-rival goods. (By this age, the concept of object-permanence, is quite well understood, with the social benefits of sharing, soon following on.) At a more sophisticated level, natural rights arguments of the type asserted by John Locke (regarding rights over land) dictate that once a non-rival good has been produced and is not held as a private secret, it should then be freely available to all those entities that can make constructive (productive) use of it. Within this common sense (or "natural") scenario, any business entity that produces or transforms a DS would need to use "new" business models, or design even newer ones, in order to capture revenues and appropriate profit. For example, contractual arrangements can be made involving priced physical (rival) complements (Section 15.5). Profits would then depend upon the time-based and competency-based advantages of the producer entity.

15.4.3 Looking Glass

In this scenario, the role of money and prices seemingly oppose "common sense". Hardware is given away free, with profits flowing from the software. This is in line with a prediction, reportedly made over 20 years ago, by a spokesperson at the Apple Computer Company. The prediction has not quite become a reality, but it remains intriguingly feasible, especially if stronger regimes do continue to develop. Rival goods (hardware) become so cheap, due to economies of scale and scope in physical production and distribution, that it becomes worthwhile to create an installed base that is free to the user. Again, profits are appropriated from rival complements. High-tech hardware (and even rival services) thereby becomes part of a public good infrastructure. This strategy of rival/non-rival reversal can also work within weak regimes, by using the new models, but it is risky, because the time-based advantage is seriously eroded by reverse engineering of the installed base. It is therefore quite dependent upon strong regimes.

During the last 20 years or so, many producers of digitalisable works have followed a "looking glass" type of strategy. They have installed an affordable base of hardware that leverages the value of their produced DSs. IPR laws have been invoked and advertised to help the businesses to maximise the capture of downstream revenues. The spectacular success of this strategy has been described as a miracle, yet others see it as "a con trick of global proportions": a description that Noam Chomsky has applied to the new capitalism as a whole.

15.4.4 *Utopia*

In Utopia, all goods are free. Robots tirelessly produce and distribute every conceivable type of product, service and sequence, satisfying human material and informational needs and desires. Radically different institutional structures and productive relationships can then develop. In particular, traditional priorities for exchange give way to concerns about identity[2] and self-expression, as well as in-person social relations. Accordingly, those IP rights that specifically serve to uphold identity, reputation and integrity take on a renewed priority. These include the moral rights of authorship, protection against the dilution of identity-related symbols (that we currently think of as "trade" marks) and against the disruption of social communications.

Taken together, the four scenarios serve to challenge and disrupt the traditional frames and discourses associated with IPR legislation. The balance between capital accumulation (needed for investment-intensive works) and the provision of public goods has already shifted during the pro-patent era, but these scenarios suggest that it is likely to continue to change. It is becoming quite apparent that the dynamic nature of technological innovation demands an equally kinetic response by legislators and by businesses. The next section indicates how the latter might be achieved in practice.

15.5 Business Models

The common-sense and utopian scenarios envision weak IPR regimes, but they are made quite feasible within a variant of capitalism by the existence of various methods for capturing revenue from co-produced DSs, that depend on market forces and new technologies, rather than IPR regulations. In Table 15.1, these methods (models, strategies, etc.) are listed, together with some examples. The particular principles of revenue capture and profit appropriation, together with the limitations of each method, are also briefly mentioned. For example, the excludability strategy that involves encryption works for an interval of time before counter-measures become available (if sought), but it also reduces share of mind. Extreme customisation reduces the demand for any re-distribution, but the strategy itself is easily copied. A business-to-business sale or license can result in a situation where the user (business entity) has an incentive not to re-distribute, and so on.

The methods or models based upon rival complements (basically, physical products that piggyback on DSs) are potentially the most significant. Here, revenues are captured from rival (material, service) goods that complement the co-produced DS. Such strategies might become very common in future. Given some anticipatory planning, co-producers of DSs can still appropriate profits (as distinct from super-profits in the global winner-take-all markets), despite the inevitable widespread replication and re-distribution of the sequence. This is because the original producer of a digital work often retains at least two competitive advantages: (i) a unique early-mover advantage, and (ii) a distinctive competence in the shape of a more thorough understanding of the digital product and how it might be used and complemented. The strategy is similar in some respects to that adopted by some European car manufacturers in the 1980s who lobbied for tougher environmental laws while at the same time designing greener

Table 15.1 Business models in weak regimes.

Strategy or "Model"	Example	Captures Revenue by	Limitation on Revenue Stream
1. *Excludability*	Encryption.	Interval of time before counter-measures devised.	Retards shadow diffusion and share of mind. Consumer resistance.
2. *Exclusivity*	Position as a status good.	Remove incentives to re-distribute.	Rarely feasible.
3. *Mass/extreme customisation*	Personalised newspaper, collection of music tracks.	Reduces demand for re-distribution.	Strategy is easily copied.
4. *Niche in industrial markets*	Audio (encoder sold to radio station).	B2B sale (or license), broadcaster increases advertising revenues.	Listeners can re-package, remove adverts, etc.
5. *Information*	CAD–CAM program for automated factory.	B2B sale or license.	Can be replicated for collaborating businesses, or sites.
6. *Target inelastic segment*	Sell high-end software to businesses that want immediacy, quality and service.	Value added in the segment.	Short time window.
7. *Low price/mass market*	Cheap CDs.	Easier to buy than to copy. Low margin/high volume.	Competition, "normal" profits from commodity.
8. *Hyper-competitive, disruption and cannibalisation*	Free version, sell upgrade(s).	Combination of other methods (e.g. immediacy).	Combination of other limits, but these are side-stepped.
9. *Rival complements*		——— See Text ———	

products. The digital variant can be seen as an attempt to co-produce (or restore) ecology of knowledge, in service of society.

Rival complement strategies are essential to the "common sense" and "utopia" scenarios, but they also have wider implications concerning the feasibility of a new and more advanced form of knowledge capitalism: one that is upheld by weak IPR regimes (e.g. short patents, more stringent criteria). In this form, efficient markets for rival goods (material, personal service, public event, etc.) exist at a super-structure level where money and price are used to mediate exchanges (of rival goods), but the co-production of non-rival goods takes place within an underlying ecology of knowledge that subsumes a vast pool of readily accessible and free digital patterns (including programs and algorithms) as well as human minds.

15.5.1 Innovation

Fortunately, there are several variants of the rival complement business model (see Appendix 15.1). To generate these in any given business context (and perhaps discover new ones) heuristic devices can be used to stimulate creativity. For example, in the matrix depicted in Figure 15.4, each type of market offering (i.e. digital download, material good, service, or

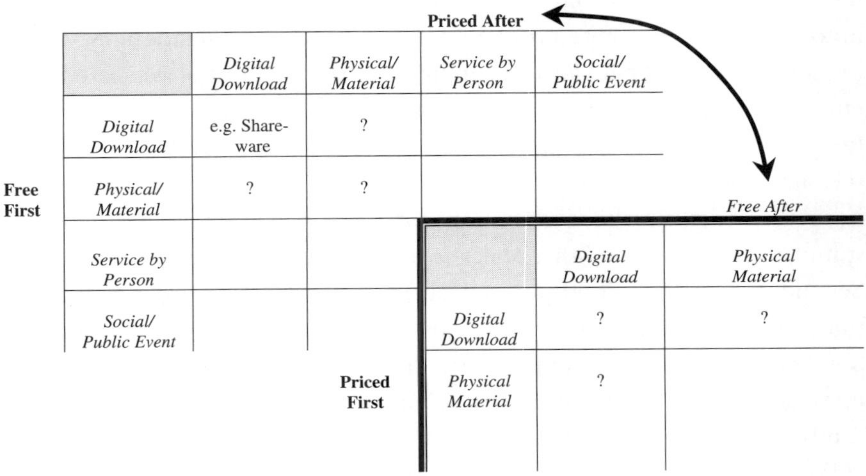

Free First / **Priced After**

	Digital Download	Physical/ Material	Service by Person	Social/ Public Event
Digital Download	e.g. Shareware	?		
Physical/ Material	?	?		
Service by Person				
Social/ Public Event				

Priced First / **Free After**

	Digital Download	Physical Material
Digital Download	?	?
Physical Material	?	

Figure 15.4 A business model generator.

social/public event, etc.) is paired off with each possible type of complement, under various possible pricing strategies. The exercise of filling in the cells of the matrix (here left to the reader) then generates new combinations of strategy attributes.

The business model generator is a morphological analysis tool,[3] of the type more commonly used to identify novel combinations of product attributes (e.g. size, colour, etc.). This heuristic fosters innovative thinking at the abstract level of business methods, as distinct from the level of the market offering itself. Weak IPR regimes actually increase the incentives for this type of innovation in an economy. Looking further ahead, as technology inevitably progresses towards the production of powerful virtual reality and biological (nanotech) systems, the distinction between behaviour of producer and behaviour of product, as well as the distinction between the various categories of product in the matrix, will become increasingly blurred. This, in turn, will necessitate continual renewal and innovation at the level of business practices and regulatory policies (e.g. Hunt and Mehta, 2006).

15.6 Economics

Stakeholders in strong regimes have deployed standard economic arguments to advance their interests in various policy forums. They refer to (i) innovation, (ii) corporate profitability and capital accumulation, as well as (iii) aggregate-level benefits or economic welfare outcomes, associated with efficient markets. It is then claimed, with the support of selected theory (e.g. Teece, 1998) that strong regimes can contribute positively to all of these measures. With regard to innovation, the claimed effect can be challenged in several ways. As already mentioned, weak IP regimes are also likely to stimulate innovation, with respect to new business models and methods. Secondly (as NRC, 2000 pointed out) entrepreneurs and designers routinely stimulate and direct their creative efforts by perusing patent records, but strong IPR regimes can provide a dis-incentive for this, because knowingly duplicating an invention (e.g. a software process, or business process) can be a more costly legal violation, at least in the US (as noted in NRC, 2000). Thirdly, there has been abundant innovation by public interest oriented entities, such as the networked open source software movement and the human genome project. This success, in turn, might be explained with reference to the diversity of motives and contexts that foster human creativity and productivity (e.g. Kao, 1996).

With regard to capital formation and aggregate welfare, systematic counter-arguments are readily available from standard critiques of neoclassical economic models (e.g. Sen, 1987). Further support for weak regimes flows from alternative models and theories of how markets for information-intensive goods can operate (e.g. Deardorff, 1992; Helpman, 1993; Arthur, 1996; Kelley, 1999, to mention a few). The critiques and models refer to factors such as (a) the effects of externalities, particularly positive network externalities created by the connectivity premium (e.g. the more the copies of a program, the more useful each one becomes) and the sociality premium (e.g. people like to discuss the product); (b) the widespread use of strategies whose purpose is to create and then exploit market imperfections; (c) monopolistic tendencies, with the associated distributive justice concerns (e.g. Calton, 1999; Donaldson, 1999; Werhane and Gorman, 1995). These are acute, given the increasing returns and winner–take–most phenomena that are quite common in markets for information-intensive products.

Finally, there is a broad and fundamental need for regulations that prevents tragedies-of-the-commons and that ensure the reasonable availability of public goods. Here, it is obvious that strong regimes can be expensive to administer (socially inefficient) and that to the extent that information dispersion is constrained, or that access to existing knowledge is in any way limited, the overall rate of production of new knowledge can be retarded (e.g. Heller and Eisenberg, 1998).

15.6.1 Information Economics

Theories and models of information economics which formalise some of the above concerns about IPR have only rarely been invoked in the context of policy forums and political lobbying (e.g. Dempsey, 1999). When they have been discussed (e.g. within the NRC, 2000), the result has been nothing more than an appeal for empirical data to indicate how to best manage the various tradeoffs that are expressed in those models. For example, it might be possible to quantify the lost contribution from unauthorised replications and compare this with the contribution gained indirectly from the resulting increased share of mind, in various markets. Similarly, the costs and benefits of maintaining additional trade secrets (including the loss of employee freedom, etc), might be estimated and compared with the cost of IPR litigation.

Although this research approach is benevolent and aimed at informing policy, it also confronts several rather fundamental limitations. First, there is a standard critique of all such cost–benefit analysis approaches (e.g. Kelman, 1981). Next, there is an inevitable or a priori bias in the behaviour of the researcher, as discussed in the following section. Finally, policies that attempt to strike a balance between various sets of costs and benefits also have to take into account the dynamic and chaotic patterns of change in the system. To summarise, those who attempt to measure the effects of IPR policies are not only standing on a shaky and contested platform, they are also aiming at an erratically moving target. A possible way of managing these higher level or meta-theoretic constraints is set out below.

15.7 Meta-theories

A variety of interdisciplinary meta-theories can now richly inform IP policy and business practices. These include (i) representative practices (Alvesson and Deetz, 1998); (ii) synergy-oriented frameworks (see Chapter 1); and (iii) ecological systems (e.g. Bateson, 1972). These are briefly outlined below, followed by their policy implications.

15.7.1 Representative Practices

This meta-theory[4] sets out a way of classifying research programmes within social science disciplines. It can be applied, in a spirit of pragmatism, to any type of knowledge creation process, including those falling within the ambit of current IP law. The meta-theory describes and depicts the types of knowledge as claims made by social communities. It does not focus upon the explicit patterns of information or DSs. For example, the situation depicted in Figure 15.1 can be re-described as a process involving knowledge claims made by the various stakeholder communities, but specifically referring to the possible effects of stronger IPR regimes.

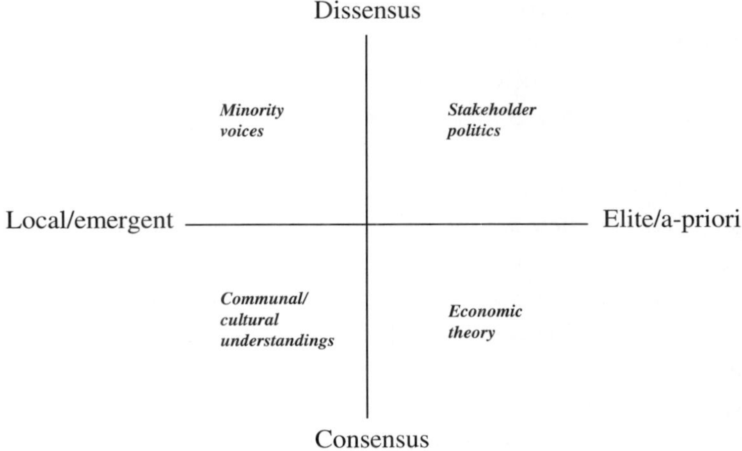

Figure 15.5 Representative practices and IP policy.

The classification scheme in the meta–theory (Figure 15.5) involves two dimensions: consensus versus dissensus and local versus elite. The consensus pole locates knowledge production practices that advance a dominant discourse. The adoption of traditional IP laws with reference to neoclassical economic ideas belongs here. The "dissensus" pole, in contrast, locates knowledge production practices that are oriented towards disruption, or replacement of a dominant discourse. Here we find newspaper articles that mockingly report some of the more comical aspects of strong IPR enforcement (such as prosecuting suppliers of plastic lemons, or cakes decorated with cartoon characters, etc.), or web chatrooms on the subject of copyleft and open source, as well as academic critical management theories and accounts like this current chapter.

The "elite/a-priori" pole locates knowledge claims that rest upon socially privileged insights. Closed door meetings where managerialist and legal language is readily deployed belong here. The resultant claims, or the outcomes of such meetings, are not only biased, but the bias is a priori that is, it is built in before the discussions even begin. Finally, the "local/emergent" pole locates forms of knowledge that have arisen entirely within an identifiable community. Traditional indigenous (tribal) knowledge about medicinal qualities of local fauna (cf. Shiva and Holla-Bar, 1996), localised constellations of property rights that incorporate duties of care,[5] such as those conferred on canoe owners, by Yurok Indians (Munzer, 1990), as well as distinctive cultural schemata such as the Chinese understanding of ideas being "in the air" (quoted in NRC, 2000, p. 57), all belong near this pole of the meta-theory.

The two axes of the system (Figure 15.5) create a conceptual space in which to locate four distinctive research approaches, or knowledge-production practices. These are the normative (e.g. economic theory), the critical (e.g. critical management theory), the dialogic (e.g. minority and radical voices) and the interpretive (i.e. communal understandings). The overall contribution of the metatheory to IP policy formulation is then similar to its contribution to academic sociology. First, it draws attention to the various types of knowledge, making it quite apparent that there are indeed many alternatives to the dominant discourse. Secondly, it places the four poles (and the four quadrants) on an apparently equal footing. Minority voices, local knowledge and distinctive community-wide understandings do not have to be excluded or discarded as the products of some less developed minds or cultures. Given the rather explicit limitations of the dominant theoretical discourse, as well as the manifest exclusivity of the mainstream stakeholder discussions and forums, the alternatives are now seen to be an important component of any comprehensive and responsible rational policy deliberations, all the more so if the policy is genuinely intended to foster economic, social and human development (cf. Sen, 1999).

15.7.2 Synergy Orientation

Synergy orientation refers to a generic pattern observable at the level of streams of theory and research in the social and managerial sciences (see Chapter 3). The pattern reveals how a single concept, such as utility maximisation (or economic capital formation, or shareholder value, etc.) is typically challenged by an alternative account that involves multiplicity, such as plural rationality (or the multi-capital framework, or the multi-fiduciary stakeholder model, etc). Next, the relationships or meta-relations, between the singular and plural approaches become the focus of yet further theory development. Typically, at this stage, tradeoffs are specified. Finally, new approaches to theory and practice are outlined (Table 15.2), involving some type of synthesis or synergy. Amongst the various "synergy-oriented"

Table 15.2 Synergy orientation and intellectual property.

Synergy-oriented Framework	Basic Components or Elements	Synergy or Synthesis Component	Implication for IP Policy: Regimes Should...
Plural rationality	Utility-maximisation, expressive, reflective, deliberative, sociality and Weberian forms.	Hyper-rationality (i.e. synergy-seeking)	... foster utility, identity, sociality, justice and the advance of science and ethics.
Multi-capital framework	Economic, human social, ecological.	Designed multi-capital synergies	... foster accumulation of all the forms of capital.
Multiple optimalities	Economic and systemic-ethical forms of optimality; alternatives, representations, values and criteria	Optimal-design, cognitive-equilibrium, super-optimum	... design ways top overcome perceived tradeoffs, co-produce profit, human-goods, and the future-system of knowledge creation.
Systemic and holistic themes and methods	Dialectical inquiry Moral imagination, Stakeholder — synthesis, generative discourse	New synthesized possibilities, generated alternatives	... encourage re-descriptions, create and design synergistic options, avoid premature closure, keep discussion open.

frameworks, multiple-capital, plural rationality and stakeholder learning dialogues (e.g. Calton, 1999; Isaacs, 1999) can be selected for application to IP policy, as briefly indicated below.

The claim by some stakeholders that strong IPR regimes encourage economic capital formation can be challenged by an alternative account that explores the effects of IP regimes on social, human and ecological forms of capital (e.g. Chapter 3). Social capital refers to communities, trust and identity (e.g. Zeleny, 1995a); human capital is the knowledge and capabilities embedded within individuals and collectivities; ecological capital refers to the nature-produced inputs to all types of productive processes. The dominant discourse has implicitly assumed that the goal of IP policy is to increase the level of economic capital (although exactly how to do that remains contested), but it also appears to assume that the levels of the other forms of capital will increase as a consequence, or afterwards. Furthermore, this subsequent increase will at least compensate for any temporary reduction in the other forms of capital caused by the limitations or market failures mentioned in the previous section (e.g. externalities, increased litigation costs, etc.). A synergy-oriented approach seeks ways of adding simultaneously to all the forms of capital, even in mutually reinforcing ways. According to the multi-capital framework, this is the approach that should be adopted when designing IP policy.

A similar prescription flows from the general theory of rationality. A rational utility-maximising entity engages in the limited and constrained behaviours described earlier (Section 15.6). In contrast, a hyper-rational entity (in the sociological sense of the term) is one that continually seeks and designs new patterns and structures that enable a synthesis of the distinctive forms of rationality (Chapters 2 and 3). Such an entity is engaged in formulating a hyper-strategy: it attempts to designs ways of generating income (utility), whilst also maintaining identity (expressive rationality), promoting distributive justice (deliberative rationality) and improving social relations (sociality). The plural rationality framework indicates that IP policy should be designed with a view to fostering and encouraging this type of synergy-seeking strategic behaviour.

The generic pattern of synergy orientation is once again evident within a general theory of optimality and optimisation (e.g. Chapter 13). There are many distinctive forms of optimality, each of which can be associated with particular strategic behaviours. For example, an economically optimal strategy, such as the strategies of the stakeholder groups described earlier (e.g. creating future markets, promulgating ideology, etc.) can be distinguished from a systemic ethical strategy that aims to directly increase the level of co-production of (classical) human goods, such as health, friendship, justice and wealth. An optimally designed IP policy would therefore foster attempts to synthesise these two classes of strategy.

Finally, there are several qualitative accounts that emphasis the desirability of synergy-oriented behaviour. They include moral imagination (e.g. Werhane, 1998) and stakeholder learning dialogues (e.g. Isaacs, 1999). The latter describes how the position of a single stakeholder group leads onto a discussion involving multiple stakeholders, exactly as depicted in Figure 15.1. Here, political interests prevail. Such discussions are often settled by premature closure (such as the pushing through of strong IPR laws), leaving some stakeholders muted and perhaps resentful. An alternative account re-casts this discussion as an interaction of disembodied propositions, in which stakeholders are replaced by their respective points of view, so that power-relations are (seen to be) held in abeyance. Thus far, this is very similar to the Habermasian ideal speech situation. However, according to Isaacs' recent account, the next step is towards a generative discourse, or a learning dialogue. New alternatives, descriptions, understandings and solutions are created and designed. It is claimed that participants in a "generative discourse" can sometimes experience a psychological sense of flow, commonly associated with high levels of human performance.

The primary contribution to IP policy of the synergy-oriented meta-theories lies in the emphasis that they all place on continually designing policies that foster the synergies, or overcome the tradeoffs. This is a rather similar message to that conveyed by Paul Hawken in the books *Ecology of Commerce* (1993) and *Natural Capitalism* (1999), but those works referred to the production of rival (physical material) goods, associated with the degradation and restoration of the natural environment or biosphere.

15.8 Recursivity

It is perhaps no coincidence that in telling the above story of generative discourses (in the info-sphere) Isaacs (1999) invoked metaphors of ecology. The theories, meta-theories, meta (meta-(theories)), and so on that are about social and communicative systems are themselves unfolding at ever higher levels of generality, mutual support and integration. At the meta-level, the synergy-oriented frameworks are not only similar to each other (despite quite different lineage), but can also be placed relative to each other. At the "theory" level, economic capital and utility-maximisation correspond with the "economic" element of the representative practices framework. In addition, the meta-theories can be directly deployed in practice, as aids to creative design, or for stimulating moral imagination and generative discourse. Thus, recursivity (self-reference) has now become quite apparent in almost all research approaches aimed at understanding human social and economic systems (see Chapter 9).

This is significant for policy makers. As information technology continues to advance, political interventions in systems of production, exchange and transformation will increasingly have to confront the many kinds of paradox that are associated with recursivity and self-reference. This has already happened, as the distinction between digital products and digital processes (variously copyrightable and patentable under strong regimes) has already become highly problematic.[6] It is also likely that the more fundamental and traditional distinction, between a product and a productive entity, will increasingly become blurred. As abstract patterns co-produce other patterns, with the intervention of human minds, they generate a partly abstract ecology that grows ever more complex. At a more concrete level, produced nano-replicators themselves take over productive and reproductive tasks (e.g. Hunt and Mehta, 2006). In contrast, strong IPR regimes have been shaped with traditional (industrial age) economic forms of rationality in mind (preference relations amongst rival objects of choice), coupled to tradition public policy concerns (such as quality and dissemination of works). It is not surprising that attempts to enforce these regimes now create confusion and injustice, invite incredulity and mockery and are being described as crazy, absurd and ludicrous.

15.8.1 Ecology

The metaphor or theme of ecology is also detectable within the above meta-theories. For example, in the multi-capital framework, the concepts of ecological and economic production are synthesised by a process that involves the exercise of moral imagination and design. Also, the human capital component incorporates individual and collective minds, that can be seen, or see themselves, as part of an ecology that encompasses mind and nature (e.g. Bateson, 1972, 1979). Finally, the stakeholder learning dialogue is described (Isaacs, 1999) as a process from which new meanings unfold, like a tree unfolds from a seed, or indeed, like a computer image (of a tree) that unfolds from a mathematical "seed", used in fractal image de-compression technique. Recursive relationships are thus the fundamental bridge between contemporary theories in the social or managerial sciences and the new co-produced biosphere.

It seems increasingly likely that ecology will become the next grand narrative, or meta-(meta-(theory)) of strategy, ethics and policy. The term is already quite used widely in business practice, where phrases like "product ecology" have quickly gained share of mind amongst consultants, but it might also now be poised to displace (and inform) economic theories, so that it becomes the new dominant discourse. This would provide timely guidance to political and judicial elites involved in the period re-design of IPR regimes. If this happens, recursivity will have replaced utility as the foundation (or seed) from which enlightened policies and practices eventually unfold. Gregory Bateson tried to encourage (but failed to achieve) the same ideological transition, about 40 years ago.

15.9 Policies

An IP regime that intervenes (from above) in the ecology of knowledge can be likened to a deliberate intervention in a natural ecology by gardeners, farmers, breeders and bio-engineers. These entities breed crops, inform products, design AIDS drug cocktails, produce and distribute GM rice, and so on. Such activities can, in turn, be conceptualised in at least two distinctive ways:

(i) as an *intrinsic* part of a larger ecology, that is, the practices are part of a macro-level ecological system that subsumes all human minds and nature.

(ii) as *transcending* ecologies and operating from a vantage point of dominion over nature, in ways that are distinctively human, moral, or spiritual (rather than natural).

With the latter interpretation, issues such as justice, freedom and truth-telling (i.e. the concerns of citizens) become distinctive policy goals, representing the viewpoint that humans are indeed above the beasts. This, in turn, carries some specific implications for "human" or humane IPR policies, as described in the following sections.

15.9.1 Justice and Freedom

Strong IP regimes tend to shift power from citizens to corporations, from labour to capital (when a company claims copyright over a creation of an employee, cf. Calton, 1999) and from poor to rich (e.g. LDCs versus Hollywood). It is not surprising that governments of some LDCs worry about being marginalised or excluded from the so-called new economy. Strong regimes also tend to increase the motivation and the capabilities of states and corporations to monitor the private behaviour of citizens, thus creating the spectre of totalitarian corporatism. To the extent that individual freedom is a constitutive part of development (e.g. Sen, 1999) strong regimes are thus profoundly limiting. In contrast, weaker regimes are likely to contribute to distributive justice, as well as a more democratic political climate, without necessarily retarding development and efficiency.

15.9.2 Moral Rights

Weak regimes can uphold the moral rights of identification of authors and the collective or corporate producers of digital works. If an entity simply replicates a digital work, it ought not to pose as, nor claim to be, the original producer. Original producers should be identified and cited as necessary (as, for example, in this article). The essence of these "moral rights" is the upholding of the identities of human individuals, groups and corporations (i.e. expressive rationality), rather than narrow instrumental forms of rationality. In a world in which boundaries are continually shifting, enforcement of these moral rights is highly likely to gain popular acceptance and respect, in contrast to the contempt and frustration frequently demonstrated towards the aspects of strong regimes. Put differently, weaker IPR regimes would also be more democratic.

15.9.3 Education

Programmes of copyright education (or mis-education) have been advocated in several countries in order to persuade citizens to comply with strong IP regimes. These have included appeals to citizens and workers to "protect their ideas". Yet it seems far more humane, ethical and desirable to project one's ideas, that is, to try to help, educate, enlighten and entertain others. More generally (cf. Vaver, 2000) one might well ask, "why should any culture bother to protect the ideas of the human mind?" To say the least, the notion seems odd to anyone whose professional life has been spent attempting to educate others. More importantly, the public appeal to restrict access to ideas plainly violates the spirit of the moral precept against placing a stick in the path of the blind.

Accordingly, such programmes can be seen as a rather blatant attempt to impose an elite consensus (Section 15.7) that is not only highly ideological, but also manifestly opposes common sense (Section 15.2). Not many people were amused in the late 1990s by TV images of clowns dressed up in animal costumes and stomping heavily on perfectly good "pirated" music CDs in a foreign city square. Such attempts at persuasion or indoctrination of young people are unlikely to succeed, given that most children already know that (i) copying someone else's work and then changing the name of the author is wrong, but that (ii) replicating a work with the author's name still on it, say, in a school newsletter, is a good and moral thing to do. It obviously honours and dignifies the author, without causing any deprivation. On the other hand, some children might be pleased indeed by the idea that teaching some mathematical algorithms or programming techniques might be judged illegal under some strong regimes, as these activities might infringe some digital patent.

15.9.4 Truth-Telling

Strong IPR regimes tend to strengthen the position of large media corporations (hence the lobbying, as depicted in Figure 15.1). Such entities offer *edu-tainment* (and perhaps eventually some form of interactive job training and assessment), but they can also offer subtle ideological propaganda, misleading statements and re-written histories. To the extent that weaker regimes make it easier to disrupt the winner-take-most market structures in the broadcasting industry, the risks posed by combining excessive market power and political power (or political capital, as it is sometimes called) would be reduced. To the extent that governments seek to uphold truth in its varied forms, a network of publicly funded public-interest oriented entities might serve as an accreditation agency for broadcast content. Such an entity might assess and critique the information, especially by invoking alternative frames and mental models, upholding minority points of view, or by appealing to other scientific, evidential and pragmatic truth criteria.

15.9.5 Language

Rorty (1979) wrote that a primary role of philosophy is to help people and society to "break free from their outworn vocabulary and attitudes". If this is accepted, IPR policy represents a perfect arena for assessing the effectiveness of that discipline. For example, in popular communications, one finds routine deployment of words like "theft", "stealing" and "piracy" when referring to nothing other than the replication of DSs. Yet, to constrain photocopying, or to restrict the availability of any digital works that enlighten or foster human development can hardly be described as "breaking free". Such usage of language carries an awful lot of ideological baggage. They might be more fully understood as a powerful battle tactic in a political campaign. Vaver (2000) made this point succinctly when he noted that "neither the 'intellectual' nor the 'property' part (of IPR) is persuasive as description". He further observed how "property language helps tip the balance against other rights, such as freedom of expression". Charles Handy (1997) also referred more bluntly to the contemporary language of property as "an insult to democracy".

An alternative description of copying might refer to imitating, replicating, or learning from others, whereupon it becomes no more apparently criminal or anti-social than a stroll through a forest that one did not plant oneself, or simply reading a book. One might also speak of stewardship of a digital work, or of having a stake in it. More generally, business (and educational) systems might be re-described with reference to productive strategic entities whose repertoires include the co-production of digital patterns (Figure 11.3). Such deployments, in turn, might serve to stimulate a re-thinking of IPR policies and business practices, with ethics and economics in mind. Put differently, if we re-invent language in this particular contested domain we can become more impartial and less biased with respect to the narrow stakeholder interests mentioned earlier, whilst more clearly perceiving the overall public interest and global well-being.

15.10 Conclusion

Current political interventions in the ecology of knowledge appear to be the resultants of lobbying activities motivated by quite narrow self-interest. They have been justified in ways that are myopic and rather ideological. A more enlightened self-interest, coupled to human concerns for justice, freedom and development, provides a deliberatively rational justification for weaker IPR regimes. In the short term, there is indeed an opportunity for profit-seeking businesses to be players in a tragedy of the electronic and biotech anti-commons, or to "ride the crazy horse until it drops", as one manager recently put it. In the longer term, it might be possible to co-produce a vast and accessible knowledge ecology, cultivated with human ideals and ethics in mind. A more traditional economy of rival goods can continue to exist, as a super-structure of exchanges. The present state of affairs, which has been variously described as crazy, absurd, ludicrous and incredulous, might turn out to be nothing more than a brief but remarkable historical aberration, like the era of the alchemists, or the Spanish inquisition. But, there is certainly no guarantee. As a first step, visionary ethical business leaders can quickly invoke the new business models. At the same time, concerned citizens can voice support for weaker regimes, whilst enlightened legislators can design and re-design cautious interventions, as prescribed and justified in the meta-theories outlined in this paper and many other like-minded works.

Appendix 15.1

Some Business Strategies for Profit in Weak IPR Regimes

Generic business strategies for profit in the absence of patent and copyright (but with moral rights of identification retained) include the following:

Excludability

This relies upon technical copy-protect features, such as software that self-destructs, or that can be copied just a few times. The protection creates an interval of time in which early adopters might be willing to pay for a digital sequence (DS), but they cannot re-distribute it.

Status good

A DS might be positioned as a status good, so that excludability becomes a value-added feature, reflected in a higher price. The buyer has a disincentive to re-distributing it. However, most DSs have the opposite qualities due to network externalities such as the connectivity effect and the sociality premium.

Non-rival niche

Here, a special-purpose DS is either contracted in advance, or else aimed at a niche market. A good example of this strategy is found in the MP3 player produced by *Real Audio* corporation (RA) in the 1990s. (a) RA sells a Digital Encoder system (software) to a Broadcaster (B). (b) B makes digital recordings of its own broadcast music, which reside on B's hard disk. (c) Listeners (radio audience) download the de-coder for free onto their (the listeners') hard disks. (d) Listeners access B's website to download previously broadcast and now-encoded program of their choice, so that they can listen to it anytime (or anywhere). Listeners can even give it away to others. The return on investment comes to B via the increased share of mind, or audience penetration.

Disruption

Players can only make profit by sustaining a momentum of varied strategic moves over time, including moves that disrupt the market. These include entering new product markets and segments (invasion), or cannibalisation of existing offerings. At any one time, several generations of a DS can be prepared for timely launch.

Rival complements

The financial incentive for the original production of innovative DSs now comes from the prospect of revenues and profits from these rival good complements. Profits can be expected, because the original producer of the DS has at least two competitive advantages, a unique early-mover advantage, and a distinctive competence in the form of a complete understanding of the DS/work. There are several variants of this strategy, as follows.

Manuscript

A novelist could attempt a variant of this strategy. First, the novelist (DS producer) earns a reputation for the ability to produce works with market appeal, simply by posting a manuscript on the web. Then, the novelist sells information (a form of trade secret) about the next planned novel, to interested producers of rival complements, such as games, toys, movies, but especially traditional books.

In-formation

Here, a design (description, picture, program, instructions) is sold under prior contractual arrangement to an industrial customer who incorporates it into the production of material (rival) goods, such as cars. Here, the DS simply "informs" a material product (cf. Zeleny, 1998), but the revenue is ultimately captured for the whole system when someone pays for the car, which is a rival good.

Pre-emption

Producers of DSs and their fixations (like CDs, microchips, pharmaceuticals) sell at a high price only to the early adopters of the DS, since it is soon copied, or reverse-engineered. However, the original producer entity has a unique advantage, in being able to foresee and plan all manners of pre-emptive moves in the market for the complementary goods and services, such as user-support, books and manuals, toys, health products and services, etc.

Services

In the case of complementary services (rival goods), the previous strategy has been made quite famous by the open source software movement. *Linux* (an operating system) and *Sendmail* (an email administering program) were produced by voluntary collaboration, but companies quickly emerged to sell related services and other support materials.

Piggybacking

The "open source" type of arrangement might also work in reverse. New DSs can be composed that piggyback on existing rival goods. Suppose that someone produces an engaging image of a Barbie Doll. The producers of the "meat space" Barbie, far from demanding a slice of the action (there is not much), might offer to pay this image producer (artist) to do further similar works. The artist thereby earns a retainer fee based upon reputation, whilst the producer of the material Barbie benefits from the increased share of mind.

Notes

1. Vaver (2000, p. 623) also noted with irony that in the US, written court opinions do not have copyright, yet "as many good opinions issue from American courts as from courts (in other jurisdictions) where copyright of opinions does exist. In this case at least, intellectual property is irrelevant as an incentive for creation".
2. In a world without patents and copyrights, the related moral rights of identification (of author/producer) remain important. Policies that preserve the identity and authenticity of individuals and corporations in the world of free non-rival

goods should find support amongst any well-informed electorate. This includes trademarks with their misrepresentation or dilution. However, this "protection" needs to be balanced against the right to criticize, mock or parody.

3. Over 700 years ago, Ramon Lull devised the idea of identifying all the salient attributes of a system and then exploring their possible re-combinations. He designed a matrix of 16 attributes of God and Nature, in order to generate new arguments for the purpose of converting non-Christians to Christianity. According to Gardner (1958), this work (*Ars Magna*) was the precursor of the morphological analysis techniques used since the 1960s to identify new combinations of attributes for production and marketing purposes.

4. Professor Jerry Calton indicated to the author the relevance of the meta-theory of representative practice to IPR policy and knowledge management.

5. Munzer (1990) defined property as "a relationship between people with respect to things". He noted the case of canoe ownership in the Yurok Indian tribe, which conferred a duty on the owner of the "property" to ferry any passing stranger across the river. This is a very different relationship between people from that implied by intellectual property. Put simply, one is human and ethical, the other is not.

6. The NRC report on intellectual property in the digital age (2000, p. 205) specifically recommended that the traditional concept of "publication" should be "re-conceptualised".

Chapter 16

DIVESTMENT: Corporate Conscience and Foreign Divestment Decisions

Abstract: This chapter is based on "Corporate conscience and foreign divestment decisions," *Journal of Business Ethics* 6, pp. 543–552, 1987, by A. E. Singer and N. T. van der Walt. It discusses the notion that the rational-agent frame of reference for the analysis of all types of corporate strategic decision-making might be expanded to a moral-agent perspective, whereby decision content is seen as comprising commercial, strategic and ethical factors. The relevant "factors" in any strategic decision can be classified on the basis of commercial, strategic and ethical decision principles to which they relate: rational-egoism, self-referential altruism or deontology. This approach is illustrated with reference to the paradigm case of strategic divestment: MNCs operating in South Africa, during the era of Apartheid.

16.1 Introduction

Corporate strategic decision-making processes may be analysed using a variety of theoretical "frames of reference". Some of these emphasise behavioural phenomena, whilst others focus on forms of normative rationality and decision content. However, contemporary efforts to construct a synthesis of various behavioural and normative theoretical approaches, in order to improve the analysis and support of strategic decisions, have generally overlooked ethical considerations as mediators of corporate acts (e.g. Pennings, 1985).

There are historical and pragmatic reasons for this theoretical oversight. Philosopher Jaki (1978) has commented on a historical "failure to integrate ethics with normative decision theory", whereas the latter is prescribed for business decision support. Jaki also contrasted the neglect that befell Adam Smith's "*The Theory of Moral Sentiments*" (1759) with the fame and influence of *"The Wealth of Nations"* (1776) by the same author. Moreover, this historical and theoretical neglect is compounded by the fact that, for practitioners, the introduction of ethical issues into questions of corporate strategy can have the unwelcome effect of transforming messy strategic problems into "hopelessly messy" ones (cf. Chapter 8).

16.2 A Moral Gap

Unfortunately, this moral gap between "corporate consciousness" and "corporate conscience" (i.e. between strategy and ethics) may actually be growing at the present time (i.e. in the 1980s) both in theory and in practice. Contemporary developments in the academic field of "strategic management", in which the corporation is cast as a rational agent, are open to serious and obvious objections from a moral point of view (e.g. Gilbert, 1986). In essence, progress in this field has involved the repositioning of microeconomic theory so that it provides practicing managers with more easily understood guidelines for the pursuit of corporate self-interest. The goal of the new strategist is then to achieve "competitive advantage" for a given corporation (Porter, 1985), but without regard for wider issues of social progress, nor wider economic gains (see also Chapters 4 and 5 of this book).

On this point, economist Teece has remarked that the principle focus of the new theory of strategic management is "not to increase consumer welfare... but... to increase profit (of a given corporation)... by containing or restricting competition" (1985, p. 44, parentheses added). The clearly implied ethic is an extreme form of egoism, on the part of the corporation *qua* moral agent (cf. Chapter 2).

Other analytic frames of reference do little to furnish any corrections to this ethical myopia in strategic management theory: behavioural descriptions and explanations of organisational strategy tend to be amoral. Psychologists focus on the development of paradigms, the synthesis of competing behavioural models and on problems of research methodology. Meanwhile, practical managerial applications of psychological research are directed at solving problems of functional-level management, rather than at problems of MNC corporate strategy. The dominant concern is to "get things done" (cf. Knight, 1936) or to "produce action" (cf. Gladstein and

Quinn, 1985 and Chapter 5). Thus, in sum, it is apparent that contemporary efforts directed at defining the content and explaining the process of corporate strategic decisions have been made without particular regard to ethical norms, or ethical content.

16.3 A Classification of Factors

According to the "rational agent" frame of reference, corporate strategic decisions are seen to be the result of the systematic identification of all relevant factors (e.g. market shares, etc.) coupled to an evaluation (in relation to corporate goals) of the consequences of various strategic options (e.g. divestment). Yet, this "rational-agent" frame of reference may easily be enlarged to one in which the corporation is viewed as a *moral* agent, so that norms of morality complement or displace norms of rationality as the basis for decision support and decision analysis (i.e. corporate consciousness is expanded to corporate conscience). The resulting "moral agent" frame of reference may then be adopted by analysts or decision makers in appropriate contexts. As a first step towards constructing an expanded decision analysis, the "relevant factors" which comprise strategic decision content may be classified as follows:

1. "*Direct commercial factors*" (*egoist*): decision factors that are considered to directly effect corporate valuation and business prospects in the short to medium term;
2. "*Stakeholder long-range factors*" (*self-referential altruist*): semi-commercial decision factors that are considered to affect the environment for business in the longer term and therefore to indirectly affect valuation;
3. "*Other moral factors*" (*deontological*): considerations such as corporate obligations, which are unrelated (or even negatively related) to commercial gain.

These three classes of factors roughly correspond to traditional divisions within ethical and economic theory. Thus, arguments about the validity of this classification and the normative importance of factors in each class will tend to parallel arguments about alternative principles of morality and systems of moral and economic reasoning. Yet, the exercise of corporate conscience requires that each class of factors is somehow taken into account in the decision-making process. Put differently, ethics should be "swept in" to business.

16.4 Divestment Decisions by MNCs

A "moral agent" frame of reference can be enlightening in the context of multinational corporate divestment decisions. First, divestment entails the termination of activities (by the particular organisation concerned), so that behavioural considerations of "producing action" are less relevant to divestment planners; second, divestment decisions, especially by MNCs, almost always have a conspicuous ethical dimension. These decisions are frequently surrounded by moral and political controversy, whilst they are widely recognised as being amongst the more "difficult" problems encountered by corporate management (see Chapter 8). In the following sections, the various factors (or issues) that can mediate divestment decisions by MNCs are briefly described and classified using the above criteria (Figure 16.1). Each "factor" corresponds with a question or line of inquiry that can (and arguably ought to) support the strategic decision (Table 16.1). The final section of the chapter then offers some thoughts on how the several factors, or answers to the questions, might be combined in order to guide the strategic decision.

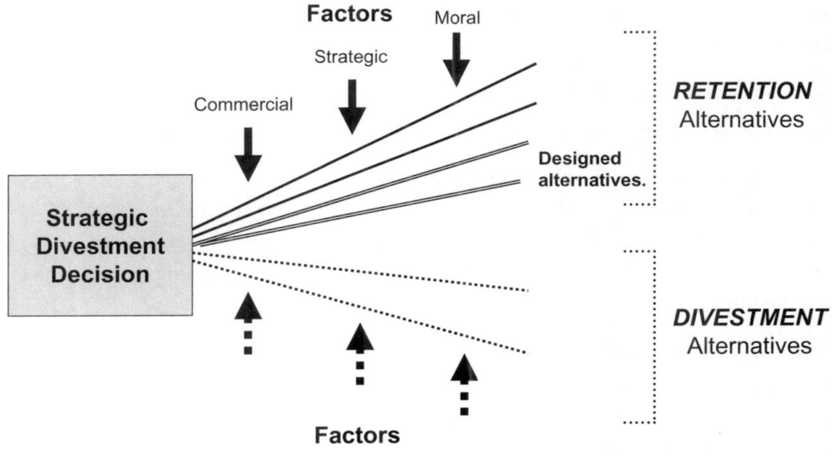

Figure 16.1

Table 16.1   Questions corresponding to the three classes of factors in strategic divestment decisions.

Direct commercial factors: rational-egoist ethic

What is the broader business outlook?

Does the market structure favour continued participation?

What are the likely actions of other industry participants?

Do we have any internal demand for funds that may be released by the divestment?

Does this operation have sales substitutions or synergies with other businesses in the corporate portfolio?

Do we have alternative markets for the outputs of upstream units?

Do we have alternative sources for downstream corporate activities?

Should we license our technology to unaffiliated companies that remain in the host?

Does the candidate serve as an important risk-hedge against other operations?

If retained, to what extent can the risks of this operation be controlled through insurances, currency hedges and other means of protection?

Can we obtain further equity and debt capital, or refinancing for the operation at acceptable rates and from acceptable sources?

Are there any financial-risk factors that could seriously impact net cash flows for reinvestment and repatriation?

Is there a suitable potential buyer for the subsidiary?

Does this subsidiary investment act as a deterrent, or invitation to takeover at the corporate level?

How will share price respond to this divestment?

What are the costs and benefits arising from home political pressures?

How committed are the various contributors?

Do we want to retain a strategic window, or foothold in the area?

What went wrong?

Stakeholder and long-range factors: self-referential altruist ethic

What is the likely impact of the proposed strategic alternative (such as divestment) on

- the actions and reactions of other corporations
- investor confidence in the host economy and other related economies
- social and political developments in the host and its neighbours, and
- international politics, i.e. the global arena in which the organisation expects to operate in the future

Other moral factors: rights and obligations

Should we wash our hands of the host's problems?

Can it be ethical to facilitate a violent revolution?

Should the host society be judged using different ethical criteria?

What are the detailed implementation plans?

16.4.1 Direct Commercial Factors: Rational-Egoist Ethic

(i) *Macroenvironmental forecasts*

"What is the broader business outlook?" Forecasts of "social, economic, political and technological" developments may include consideration of labour relations and wages, exchange and interest rates and specific "political" risks in the host nation. The analysis may also extend to global political and economic developments that potentially affect industry structure.

(ii) *Product-market characteristics and competitor analysis*

"Does the market structure favour continued participation?" The structural characteristics of the market that support the candidate for divestments are considered. For example, a declining overall market might be "favourable for continued participation" where there are only few committed, direct competitors, or where the remaining demand is insensitive to price (cf. Porter, 1980). In other cases, divestment and liquidation of some corporate capacity may be profitable if it serves to reduce overall industry capacity, so that price increases generate a net financial gain for the corporation, at least in the short term.

"What are the likely actions of other industry participants?" Forecasts of the likely actions of other participating corporations are often relevant in strategic decision making. In some cases, divestment from one market or host country might influence corporate competitors' behaviour in other arenas.

(iii) *Corporate portfolio effects*

(a) Funds: "Do we have any internal demand for funds that may be released by the divestment?" This question is important to the extent that the corporation may not wish to raise external finance. Sometimes, even profitable units are divested for this reason (Duhaime and Grant, 1984). Corporate management may also consider whether in the event of continued operations, the forecast cash flows fit well with the projected funds requirements of other operations (Singer, 1986).

(b)   Sales: "Does this operation have sales substitutions or synergies with other businesses in the corporate portfolio?" Such synergies or substitutions may reflect ordinary market forces, or they may be mediated by the actions of politically motivated consumer groups who advocate divestment. (The likely actions rather than the motives and morals of such groups are relevant to "egoist" principles.)

(c)   Vertical integration: "Do we have alternative markets for the outputs of upstream units?" The candidate unit may represent a major or sole buyer of the outputs from upstream operations owned by the corporation. If so, then divestment means loss of control or influence in that market. This might have repercussions for all stakeholders in the upstream operations (possibly involving the home government).

(d)   Sourcing of supplies: "Do we have alternative sources for downstream corporate activities?" In the case of a divestiture candidate that serves a downstream link in the chain of corporate activity, the availability and cost of alternative supplies to that downstream unit may be a critical factor. If the candidate unit serves downstream activities in a special or unique way (e.g. through host country comparative advantage), then the level of corporate commitment to those downstream operations may also become a key issue in the divestment decision.

(iv) *Proprietory technology*

"Should we license our technology to unaffiliated companies that remain in the host?" Where the candidate unit makes use of special proprietery technology or managerial know-how, it is generally profitable for the corporation to retain ownership of the unit and "protect" the technology, rather than to allow its uncontrolled diffusion (Teece, 1985, p. 58).

(v) *Portfolio aspects of risk reduction*

"Does the candidate serve as an important risk-hedge against other operations?" The candidate for divestment may be an important component of a co-varying portfolio of corporate investments, for example, where the corporation conducts business with both sides of a political or military conflict. Such policies generally protect corporate management against excessive downside risks, rather than the shareholders, who may achieve risk reduction through capital market transactions. Thus, it is managerial rather than shareholder interests that dictate the handling of this issue.

(vi) *Direct risk reduction*

"If retained, to what extent can the risks of this operation be controlled through insurances, currency hedges and other means of protection?"

(a) Insurances: The risks associated with foreign direct investment can generally be reduced through commercial insurances and hedging in the foreign exchange markets.

(b) Market power: The level of protection against forced divestment by a hostile (self-interested) host government is also important. This again entails considerations of vertical integration, or "degree of inter-relatedness" of the candidate unit. Where alternative outlets for upstream operations and sources for downstream operations are available, expropriation may be an acceptable risk for the corporation. On the other hand, if the corporation controls (or otherwise has influence over) these alternative suppliers and buyers, a government's threat of expropriation can be directly countered by a threat to isolate the candidate unit.

(c) The level of risk may also be affected by the ownership structure of the affiliated unit, as discussed below.

(vii) *Finance and ownership*

"Can we obtain further equity and debt capital, or refinancing for the operation at acceptable rates and from acceptable sources?" The continuing availability of external finance for continued investment in the unit is obviously an important factor. The identity of equity participants as well as the overall capital structure of the subsidiary and parent may also be important. These factors influence the threat of takeover of the foreign subsidiary (and possibly the parent), as well as political relations with the host government and community.

(viii) *Financial risk*

"Are there any financial risk factors that could seriously impact net cash flows for reinvestment and repatriation?" Capital structure changes arising in conjunction with a divestment, or from continued investment, can directly influence net cash flows and reported profits corresponding to a projected operating-income stream. For MNCs, these effects are mediated by macroeconomic factors such as exchange and inflation rates. Tax policies (or agreements with the subsidiary) in either country may change in ways that affect net cash flows to the parent and reinvestment in the subsidiary, although the corporation may be able to protect itself against these "threats" through adapting its transfer pricing practices and using third countries as tax havens.

(ix) *The market for corporate ownership and control*

(a) "Is there a suitable potential buyer for the subsidiary?" Sometimes, a special opportunity to sell a business or assets at a favourable net price can be the principal motive for a divestment, particularly where assets are specialised. More generally, divestment is effected through the selling of shares held by the parent in the subsidary, or by dilution of holdings in the subsidiary through a rights issue of shares in the subsidiary. In these cases, capital market opinion and "sentiment" are important factors influencing the feasibility and profitability of the divestment option.

(b) "Does this subsidiary investment act as a deterrent, or invitation to takeover at the *corporate* level?" If another corporation wishes to invest in the host country, it may attempt to do this indirectly through seeking a controlling interest in the parent corporation, a move that may affect shareholders and managers (separately) for better or worse. On the other hand, the subsidiary may function as a "political poison pill" deterring takeover because of a potential raider's unwillingness to risk association with the host country. (A further byzantine possibility is that the subsidiary invites corporate suitors intending to initiate subsequent divestment from the host in order to appear as a "moral crusader".)

(x) *Stock market perceptions of corporate prospects*

"How will share price respond to this divestment?" In normative finance theory, equity value is the supreme management objective. In practice, a focus on equity values serves corporate and managerial interests for a variety of reasons. To a considerable extent, the effect of divestment on corporate equity valuation will depend on the market's assessment of the corporate prospects with and without the candidate unit. There are several issues to consider:

(a) The role of "ethical" investment funds: corporate shares may become attractive to a wider range of investors as a result of divestment from an "offending" host.

(b) Shareholder activism regarding operations in the "offending" host: if management can succeed in creating the perception that it is "hassle free" and able to concentrate on other operations, this may affect share price. On the other hand it may serve to encourage activists to focus on other aspects of corporate operations that they do not like.

(c) Perceptions of management strength: divestment is sometimes seen as a signal of failure. Management may be seen as inconsistent, or be called upon to justify the original entry decision. However, managers may be able to shape these perceptions through carefully worded public statements.

(d) "Balance sheet optics": In the short term, capital market reaction may also be mediated by the impact of a divestment on the corporate balance sheet. This must be considered as a seperate factor, because consolidated accounts do not necessarily reflect the underlying economics of a change; yet the accounts are closely monitored by investors. In some cases, divestment of a business may substantially alter market analysts' perceptions (or business–classification) of the corporation as a whole.

(xi) *"Outgroup" perceptions: home country politics*

"What are the costs and benefits arising from home political pressures?"

(a) Pressure from home politicians: politicians may put pressure on a company to withdraw from a politically "offending" host country.

They might use a combination of inducements (regarding future concessions and rewards) and threatened punishments. In addition, the collective action of the home political process may result in binding legislation on the issue, e.g. political sanctions against the host.

(b) Imminent sanctions: forecast political developments in the home country may include legally binding sanctions which *inter alia* force a form of withdrawal from the host. In this case, the proactive, self-interested, strategic alternatives are either prevention or pre-emption.

Prevention: This entails influencing the home political process through negotiation with politicians, possibly including efforts to alter constituency opinion (cf. Kilpatrick, 1985). The key criterion dictating the adoption of this preventative approach is the calculation (taking all remaining factors into account) that continued operation in the host, in the absence of sanctions, or with reduced pressure from home country pressure groups, would actually serve corporate objectives.

Pre-emption: An alternative response is rapid divestment. Where the answer to the above question is negative (e.g. forecasts clearly show a deteriorating economic outlook in the host in the absence of threatened or actual sanctions), the immediate divestment becomes the rational alternative. This move gives the appearance of voluntary withdrawal. It therefore serves to maintain a useful, corporate sense of autonomy (or "illusion of control") amongst corporate personnel and external observers, at the same time securing the approval of the divestment lobby (conferring the above-mentioned, market-related benefits).

(xii) *Organisational and managerial factors*

(a) Motivation and commitment: "How committed are the various contributors?" In the case of divestment by MNCs, the existence of a high level of commitment or motivation amongst contributors to the host operation, or to the host country itself, is an important positive factor in favour of retention. Conversely, preferences for leaving the host country or lack of commitment to the operation almost guarantees unacceptable economic performance.

(b) Corporate control system integrity: In general, continued investment in a unit that has been returning below the target ROI (and divestment of high performers) potentially undermines the integrity of the internal control system, with damaging consequences for morale in other business units.

(xiii) *Maintenance of strategic options*

"Do we want to retain a strategic window, or foothold in the area?" Pure strategic considerations of this sort cannot be subsumed into any of the above categories, because they are concerned with unspecified future possibilities. Yet, the desire to keep future options open is an important criterion for rational strategic choice (e.g. Gupta and Rosenthal) so that a divestment decision may be mediated by a desire to retain:

(a) A strategic window: operations in the host that serve as a conduit for information about developments in the host region.

(b) A strategic foothold: operations at a low level that may serve as a base for future expansion as conditions change. Such a presence need not be entirely passive, since, by remaining in the region, management may be able to develop relations with potential future power groups in the host region.

(xiv) *Link to original entry or acquisition*

"What went wrong?" The divestment decision making process often entails an awareness of past strategies and past mistakes. At the same time, these factors strongly indicate poor future prospects for managing the candidate unit within the corporate portfolio. Typical examples of this pattern of "retrospective" rationalisation are

(a) an excessive price paid for original acquisition of the unit, resulting in an unacceptable corporate debt burden;

(b) an asset or operation originally acquired as part of a now-abandoned strategy (e.g. an aborted takeover attempt);

(c) an undervalued asset acquired for the sole purpose of subsequent resale or liquidation.

Each of the above factors potentially influence calculations of the effect of divestment on corporate equity valuation. However, most contemporary organisations also profess to have objectives other than valuation, profitability and growth. Yet, these "non-financial" objectives can often be interpreted as ultimately relating to corporate financial interests. Thus, according to Thomas (1986), "… whatever the weight given to… political and social pressures… (these)… are most commonly subsumed into an appreciation of market opportunities on an essentially commercial basis". The implications, for the ethics of divestment, of this interpretation of multiple-goal structures are explored in the following section.

16.4.2 Stakeholder and Long-Range Factors: Self-Referential Altruist Ethic

Advertised or explicit corporate goals such as "serving the customer" (employees, community, etc.) have questionable significance. Formally, a multiple-goal problem is isomorphic to one having multiple constraints. In practice, satisfying these constraints is generally regarded as a practical requirement for achieving "commercial" ends of profitability and growth. Accordingly, acknowledgement and awareness of stakeholders' interests is "good" management, in the sense that it reflects an ability to think through the longer-term consequences for the corporation of stakeholder neglect. Thus, the existence of multiple corporate objectives corresponds roughly, in practice, to a corporate ethic of self-referential altruism.

This interpretation is not necessarily cynical. Recent advances in game theory and evolutionary biology have highlighted the role of self-referential altruism as an explanation for a wide range of apparently "moral" behaviours (e.g. Mackie, 1982; Axelrod, 1984). These developments emphasise the good consequences that can emerge when the possibilities for future interactions with other parties are included in the teleological calculation (Axelrod's "Shadow of the future"). Rational self-interest dictates a consideration of the impact that any strategy may have on the overall future environment. Therefore, a corporate ethic of self-referential altruism entails an assessment of the impact of any proposed corporate strategy (such as divestment) on

(a)   the actions and reactions of other corporations,
(b)   investor confidence in the host economy and other related economies,
(c)   social and political developments in the host and its "neighbours" and
(d)   international politics, i.e. on the global arena in which the organisation expects to operate in the future.

A narrow or short-term conception of corporate self-interest, one that overlooks these wider processes of social and political evolution, is irrational. In the first place, it compromises MNC corporate "ideals" such as "The Global Marketplace"; second, it reflects a failure to take all relevant factors into account. It is also likely to be *unethical*, because it does not even meet the relatively weak moral requirements of (corporate) self-referential altruism. Yet, even a strategy that is selected after the most comprehensive assessment of consequences (for the corporation and its environment) is not necessarily an ethical strategy. The issue here is whether any form of consequentialist reasoning can generate morally correct solutions to problems of strategy. A vigorous defence of the morality of self-referential altruism has been constructed by Mackie (1982) who argues, *inter alia* that the "pure altruism" embodied in Christian moral teachings is flawed because, in practice, it allows selfishness to prosper amongst others. On the other hand, powerful challenges to the employment of any consequentialist ethic have also been mounted. These alternative (Deontological) principles concern notions of rights, duties, obligations and the intrinsic morality of a proposed course of action.

For managers, the possibility of limits to consequentialism (and *a fortiori* to self-referential altruism) is sobering. In practice, it means that ethical issues might not be entirely "subsumed into commercial calculations", no matter how far-sighted or accurate these calculations may be. It suggests that, for truly ethical decisions, separate consideration should be afforded to the intrinsic morality of corporate acts.

16.4.3 Other Moral Factors: Rights and Obligations

After all commercial considerations have been taken into account, there remain several issues of potentially over-riding importance as determinants of a morally correct strategic choice. For divestment by MNCs, these might include the question of active participation and reform (of host country practices) versus "clean hands", the problem of ethical relativism (in making moral judgements about the host) and, in some cases, the morality of facilitating political violence, or revolution (in the host country). Each of these issues is briefly considered below:

(i) *The ethic of engagement, participation and reform, versus "clean hands"*

"Should we wash our hands of the host's problems?" If it is believed that host country policies and practices are immoral, there may be several conditions influencing the morality of a continuing corporate presence in that offending host. The first of these conditions is whether the business activities associated with the corporate presence primarily serve those committing the moral violation ("the oppressors"), or those on the receiving end ("the oppressed group") in the host society.

Corporate activities that broadly indicate "serving the oppressed" in a host society include

(a)   "affirmative action" programmes such as the provision of housing, social services, direct legal and financial support to employees (or others) whose rights are being violated within the host society;

(b)   payment of wages at some "high enough" level (e.g. Berleant, 1982);

(c)   attempts by corporate management to persuade or otherwise pressure the violating host government (or some other party) to change its policies. One way of exerting leverage is through public statements and another (ironically) may be through the *threat* of withdrawal from the host, because this signals disapproval. In general, the efforts of one (moral) agent to persuade another to cease acting immorally seem to be praiseworthy.

Corporate activities that broadly indicate "serving the oppressor" include

(a)   payment of taxes to the host government;
(b)   making available other resources to the government that might assist them (e.g. technology and arms components);
(c)   compliance with the dictates of an "immoral" host government (cf. Elfstrom, 1983).

Where activities of this latter sort are dominant, the ethics of participation seem fairly clear-cut: the lending of direct or tacit support to a moral evil is itself surely immoral, suggesting that the corporation should withdraw or otherwise change its strategy. In the first case, however, the ethics of participation are far less clear. The decision to withdraw or divest then appears to offend against several moral precepts: first, a moral agent has duties arising from its past commitments and the relationships that it has established with stakeholders, particularly employees in the host society. This has been widely recognised and accepted in other, similar contexts (e.g. Kavannagh, 1979). Any corporation that ignores these duties towards unrepresented stakeholders usually provokes widespread contempt, as well as hostility from the directly affected parties. Second, it may be argued that anyone is entitled to receive assistance when in serious difficulty; the corporation has a duty to relieve the suffering of others (cf. James, 1982; Margolis and Walsh, 2003) and to avoid acting in ways that may seriously harm others (e.g. Kamm, 1986). Such duties would extend to all stakeholders, including people in other "societies" (e.g. neighbouring countries) who might be harmed by corporate withdrawal.

(ii) *The ethics of revolution*

"Can it be ethical to facilitate a violent revolution?" Harm can take many forms, the most obvious involving physical violence, whilst the option of corporate divestment may be linked (accurately or not) to a scenario of revolutionary or violent change in the host country. This association could then be regarded by corporate decision makers as a moral justification for a policy of continued operations in an offending host. However, according to Marcuse (1966, p. 135), violent revolution may be ethically justified in some cases:

> ... to claim an ethical and moral right, a revolutionary movement must be able to give rational grounds for its chances to grasp real possibilities of human freedom and happiness, and it must be able to demonstrate the adequacy of its means for obtaining this end.

If Marcuse is right, the onus falls on the corporate decision maker to be fairly specific about the likely path of political change in the host nation and then to ethically evaluate this scenario, using Marcuse's criteria. Thus, it may be inadequate to construct a moral defence of a strategy purely in terms of its role in preventing (or facilitating) revolution in the host country.

However, a view that conflicts with Marcuse has been expressed by Marsh (1980). He argues that ethical criteria simply do not apply at all, in some decision contexts: "There is a point...", he says, "... at which all morality ceases". One such point, he says, is where violence is contemplated as a remedy for other violence. In such cases, according to Marsh, "We have been brought into a situation in which no act can be moral". Unfortunately, Marsh does not provide the decision maker with a general rule for discriminating between situations which are "beyond morality" and those that are not; he thus avoids a crucial issue that governs the relationship between business ethics and business strategy.

(iii) *Ethical relativism*

"Should the host 'society' be judged using different ethical criteria?" This question frequently arises in relation to aspects of the MNC conduct. The mere existence of different laws and customs is far from sufficient to prove the relativist position. Moreover, even if a relativist position is assumed, it must then be established which morality applies in any given situation. (For example, in the case of South Africa, relativists would have to consider whether the position of oppressed groups should be evaluated using "Western morality" or "African morality".)

Nor is there total agreement concerning universal moral laws, although the notion of "Structural Universals" (Berleant, 1982) might provide a useful basis for establishing the immorality of certain practices in any society, whilst Donaldson's (1985) algorithm (and later work on hypernorms) may also provide welcome guidance in some cases. However, in the context of divestment decisions where host society practices are a factor, the moral violations are generally of an extreme sort that would be outlawed under any plausible ethical code. Thus, the relativism issue may be of only minor importance in this context.

(iv) *Ethical issues surrounding implementation*

"What are the detailed implementation plans?" The evaluation of any strategy interacts with the way in which that strategy is implemented. (For example, a decision to relocate within the same country may be justifiable using utilitarian arguments, but the manner of implementation determines the extent of the avoidable harm inflicted by the move.) Divestment by MNCs has many forms (Figure 16.2), including liquidation or abandonment, selling of shares in the host subsidiary, ownership dilution through rights issues in the subsidiary, asset-swaps, management buy-outs, franchises and management contracts (e.g. Coyne and Wright, 1986). Divestment through abandonment has different direct consequences from mere dilution of corporate ownership in an operating subsidiary; although, both may have harmful effects. Divestment through the transference of power and ownership raises the question of the motives and intentions of the new owners. For example,

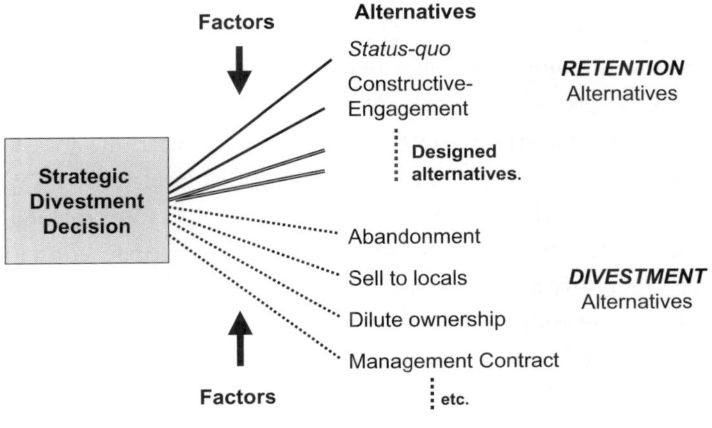

Figure 16.2

if a company that is operating to "support the oppressed" is sold to one that intends to abandon the supportive programmes, then the morality of the divestment is questionable on both utilitarian and deontological grounds.

16.5 Combining the Factors

Once all of these factors are "on the table", how can an ethical agent (e.g. a management group) combine them in order to determine the morally right strategic alternative? The absence of any agreed procedure for doing this lies at the heart of the failure of normative decision theory and ethics to provide effective decision support to corporate policy makers and strategists.

This failure may be traced to disagreements about principles of ethical reasoning, as well as to an absence of shared ideals, or ultimate values, from which valid decision procedures might be derived. No satisfactory synthesis has been achieved between competing systems of moral reasoning, whilst the conflict between the different ideals of various rational–moral agents cannot be resolved by debate. No super-ordinate criterion exists that might function to rank the different ideals.

Therefore, decision aids (as depicted in Figures 16.1 and 16.2) are bound to be inadequate and incomplete as a guide to business policy and strategic decision making. Quantification may inspire confidence in the wisdom of a strategic choice, but this impression is frequently only an illusion. In discussing the relationship between ethics and formal decision theory in business, Jaki (1978) has reminded us that... the Cartesian distinction between objective and subjective is a fallacy... That is, even the most "objective" mathematical entities are ultimately subjective. Following the work of Godel (1931) even the "God-given" integers might be regarded as the creation of men's minds; following Heisenberg (1930) even rigorous scientific measurements may be flawed. These newly discovered conceptual limitations of "quantity" re-affirm the ultimately human nature of the policy decision-making task.

Thus, for divestment decisions by MNCs, "corporate consciousness" can serve to identify and organise all the relevant factors and issues, but the final response can only be formulated and decided upon by engaging in a higher level search for cognitive equilibrium (as in the meta-decision analysis of Chapter 13) and by plumbing the depths of the human soul, the conscience of the individual.

Chapter 17

CORRUPTION: Management Decision and Political Action

Abstract: This chapter is a development of "Reducing corruption in international business: behavioural managerial and political approaches," *Journal of Economic and Social Policy* 10(2), pp. 3–24, 2006, by A. Roy and A. E. Singer. It sets out some approaches to managerial decision making in corruption-related contexts. These include structuring the generic consequences of bribery for individual decision makers and incorporating principle-based reasoning into decision models, or guides. It is argued that the reduction of corruption ultimately depends on corporate support for NGO anti-corruption initiatives, as well as a plausible consensus at the political level.

17.1 Introduction

Until quite recently, very few articles about corruption and corporate crime have appeared in mainstream academic journals on business and management. Instead, the burgeoning literature on corruption and corrupt practices has been classified under "politics", criminology or legal studies (e.g. Rose-Ackerman, 1978; Noonan, 1984; Klitgaard, 1988; Elliot, 1997; Raunch, 1997; to mention but a few). However, since the turn of the millennium, that situation has changed rather quickly, with articles by Schnatterly (2003) and Robertson and Watson (2004) appearing in the *Strategic Management Journal* and a call for "interdisciplinary" papers on corruption in international business by the *Academy of Management*. The academic business ethics journals had also picked up on the importance of corruption in business slightly earlier, with about 25 articles appearing in the *Journal of Business Ethics* after 1999 (plus a few before that), whilst six out of a total of eight articles on corruption in *Business Ethics Quarterly* appeared between 2000 and 2005.

Not one of these recent works has approached the question of bribery payments specifically as a *management decision making* problem. This is surprising, because that is an extremely common approach in the broad fields of strategy and systems, where decision trees and structured guides abound. Furthermore, within the business ethics literature, generic ethical decision making (EDM) approaches have often been proposed. Accordingly, in the present chapter, some new approaches to making decisions and formulating policies in the context of corruption and bribery are considered. Distinctive forms of bribery are identified; then (in Section 17.3), two different ways of analysing and structuring corruption-related decisions are proposed. A brief discussion then follows on the wider politics of corruption.

17.2 Corruption

Corrupt business activities have often been classified by their context, purpose and magnitude (e.g. Elliot, 1997; Raunch, 1997), suggesting that each form merits a distinctive prescription. Some typical examples are

(i)   a facilitating payment to secure preferential treatment from a public servant (e.g. Motorola in Russia, as described in Donaldson *et al.*, 2002),

(ii)   a bribe to secure a competitive advantage, in an otherwise legal transaction, (a) of a public official (e.g. Lockheed in Japan, in the 1970s), or (b) an officer of another business corporation (e.g. Argandona, 2003),

(iii)   an act of extortion (e.g. a demand for payments for the return of kidnapped persons),

(iv)   a bribe to have an illegal activity performed in (a) a legitimate regime (e.g. bribing a jailer to free a convicted murderer), or (b) an oppressive regime (e.g. a bribe to free a prisoner from a concentration camp, as described in Rose-Ackerman, 1978).

When assessing managerial responses to these types of situation, one can further distinguish between active bribery (i.e. offering or soliciting bribes) versus passive bribery (e.g. Roy, 2006; Weber and Getz, 2004), which means responding to solicitations. In addition, one can and should consider whether or not any particular payment is reasonably expected to result in subsequent violations of human rights, harm to relevant stakeholder communities, or damage to the natural environment. Indeed, in situations where harms and violations seem genuinely unlikely, the ethicality and advisability of acceding to solicited bribe payments in order to secure significant and otherwise legitimate business can be quite finely balanced, especially where there is no practical alternative.

17.2.1 Systemic Effects

According to Sen (1999, p. 275) corruption is "a major stumbling block in the path to successful economic progress" as it tends to undermine competition and draw investment away from productive pursuits. Sen also noted that consequences of corruption include the fostering of violent organisations. However, it is quite uncommon to see public documents that refer to the serious social, environmental and moral consequences of corruption, as distinct from its economic consequences. These "social" consequences include serious violations of human rights, extreme distributive injustices and various forms of oppression, whilst corruption is also closely associated with harm to the natural environment. Indeed, the Environmental Sustainability Index (ESI) 2001, which ranked the environmental performance of 122 countries, found a rank correlation of (0.75) with Transparency International's Corruption Perception Index (CPI) 2000. Despite this, the issues of environmental and stakeholder interests and the protection of human rights have remained essentially implicit in almost all recent policy discourse and documents, even though all these rights and interests are very vulnerable, indeed shockingly vulnerable to corruption-related activities by corporations operating in the LDC context.

17.3 Reducing Corruption

The apparently straightforward notion of "reducing corruption" has many distinct meanings, depending on the levels of the nexus of corrupt activities that one is considering (Table 17.1). At the transnational level, for example, one is essentially dealing with grand ideals and the prospects for

Table 17.1 Levels of analysis and necessary transitions.

Level	Nature of the Transition
Transnational	Moral progress of humanity
Nation–state	Change of government or policy, enlightenment of leaders
Corporate	Implanting ethics, augmenting strategy
Individual	Developing integrity, reflecting on consequences

moral progress of all humanity. At the level of particular nation–states, one can consider corruption reduction with regard to specific legislative instruments and processes, but also political ideologies and the nature of leadership. Corporations, in particular, can contribute to corruption reduction by augmenting their strategies and policies (as suggested throughout this book) so that they more directly and intentionally support the "common good" (the changes that appear to have taken place at Royal Dutch Shell in the period 1996–1997 are a possible example of this). Finally, individual managers can contribute to positive change simply by becoming more mindful of the intrinsic value of their own personal integrity, whilst also paying more attention to the negative consequences of corruption, for the decision maker and for others.

Various researchers have outlined general approaches to controlling corruption at the political level (e.g. Klitgaard, 1988; Elliot, 1997). The present chapter, in contrast, suggests some specific approaches to managing corruption at the levels of the individual and the organisation, or corporation. However (refer to Section 4), it cannot be forgotten that changes at all of these levels are interdependent and intertwined with general politics and ideology: on the one hand it is hard for an individual to act with integrity amidst a nexus of corruption; but it is also possible for political and business leaders to explicate (act in accordance with and appeal to) humane ideals, thus "enabling individuals … to feel the spark of life" (Kale, 2004, quoting Gandhi).

17.3.1 The Individual Level

There have been surprisingly few attempts in the literature and the media to draw attention to or publicise the typical personal and business consequences of bribery. Furthermore, these consequences are hardly ever made explicit in managerial codes, guides and policies (e.g. Gordon and Miyake, 2001; Roy, 2006). Yet, from an ethical point of view, consideration of the likely consequences of an action is often seen to be the first and most fundamental of steps on the path towards moral progress. Indeed, according to Freeman (1999, p. 235)

> "Hardin (1988) has argued persuasively that if we take bounded rationality and a through-going uncertainty about the world seriously enough, consequences may be all that our moral apparatus can handle".

Although most general-purpose ethical decision making tools for management seem to be intended to augment consequentialist reasoning, it seems that a more elementary phase of considering consequences is also necessary, in practice. Accordingly, where guidelines, codes of practice, or decision making models (akin to popular and ubiquitous strategy "models") are used to assist managers in corruption-related situations, they should first and foremost set out in full the generic consequences of bribery and corruption.

At the level of the individual decision maker, there is no doubt that powerful psychological factors come into operation in any corruption-related context. For example, the securing of a single contract or a bid may be crucial for a particular manager's career advancement, the company's performance, or even its survival (as indicated in the famous 1970s Lockheed case testimony). Furthermore, managers confronting demands for bribe payment are often under pressure of time and immersed in a generally negative psychological field or ambience. In such circumstances, decisions by individuals are often based on a narrowing of perception, akin to panic. They are thus unlikely to be based on a thorough consideration of the consequences of bribery, or the more reflective and deliberative forms of rationality associated with business ethics and humane ideals.

For any individual confronting a decision to pay a bribe, some of the personal consequences can be expressed quite systematically, in terms of positive and negative psychic utilities and then placed within a simple pre-constructed decision tree (Figure 17.1). This approach might not only forestall "panic" in practice, but also enlarges the usual notion of decisional

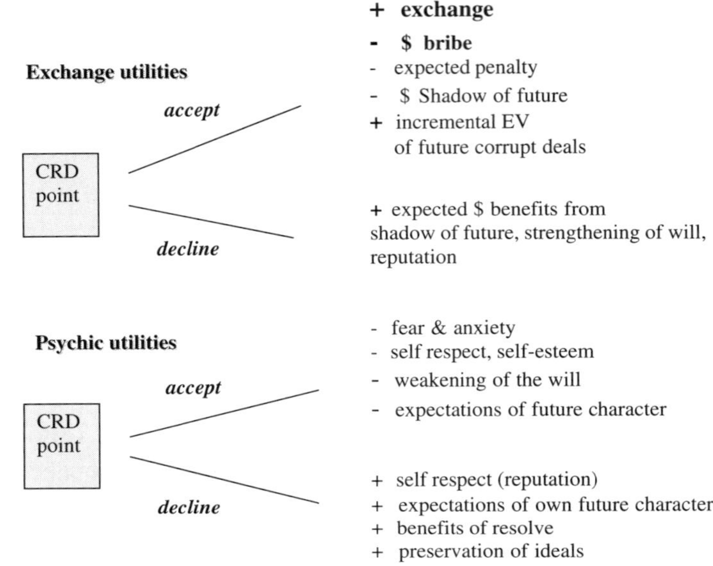

Figure 17.1   The personal and business consequences of bribery.

"consequences" in a way that any reflectively rational individual really ought to consider, but rarely does (see Chapter 12). The "psychic utilities" associated with accepting bribery (either passively or actively) arise *inter alia* from personal fears and anxieties about possible discovery and prosecution, an expected loss of self esteem, a weakening of the will, a sense of resignation and a likely loss of idealism (indicated as a cost or "–" in the lower half of the figure). Typically, all of these consequences are foreseeable, but they are also amplified by the reflective individual's realisation that each corrupt act makes future corrupt acts by the same people, with their net consequences, more likely to occur; that is, they involve changes in the decision makers' expectations of their own future behaviour. Conversely, the psychic consequences of declining involvement in bribery include *inter alia* expectations of future personal resoluteness and the willingness to uphold ideals (indicated as a "+").

In addition to personal consequences, an individual manager can also consider the typical categories of business and financial consequences of a typical decision to pay a bribe. These include the net business benefits from the exchange or business deal in question (indicated as a benefit, or "+" in Figure 17.1), together with an increased likelihood of net benefits from future similar business deals (net of their bribe payments). Set against this, there are the expected legal penalties and reputation effects associated with the possible discovery of the bribe (as in the Lockheed case, for example), together with the expected long-run dollar benefits from non-payment, due to (a) recognition by other honest players and (b) a general strengthening of the individuals' will. Finally, there is a marginal (second order) "shadow of the future" effect, in that every act of bribery, together with expected copies of that act by others, damages the overall business system.

17.3.2 Organisational and Managerial Level

Many companies have apparently sincere ethics policies and codes of conduct. Most of these address some forms of corruption. Even in LDCs, many local and international businesses already have written codes prohibiting bribery (e.g. Roy and Singer, 2006). However, as Weber and Getz (2004, p. 703) noted, there is "little evidence that... executives truly believe in putting down a marker indicating that bribery is no longer tolerated". More fundamentally, these codes often do not seem to really attempt to influence managers' hearts and minds; they typically provide nothing more than a list of "do-nots" Such a proscriptive approach to managing corruption is not only unsatisfactory from the point of view of moral psychology, but also quite naïve and questionable on ethical grounds. The nature of the ethical problem is indicated in the following example involving a decision about a passive facilitating payment (that falls within the personal experience of one of the authors).

Company X is a fruit importer and distributor with a clearly worded corporate policy of "no bribes". It opens up a new branch in country Y where customs officials always expect a facilitating payment to clear every consignment. The assigned manager learns that their consignments of fruit will not be cleared without a facilitating payment. The company has a clear choice of either permitting the fruit to rot and lose money, or to pay the customs officials.

In some situations like this, a manager might be well advised to give in to the solicited bribe or facilitating payment, not only as a matter of commercial prudence, but also, arguably, as a matter of moral principle. The manager must consider the possibility that an initiator of a "facilitating payment" in such situations might be in a condition of severe poverty, or that the payment in question might have no expected adverse consequence for human rights and the environment: indeed, rotting food can be an immediate hazard and is the near-certain consequence of non-payment.

On the other hand, many thoughtful managers remain uncomfortable with making such facilitating payments, perhaps noting that they might reinforce the dynamic of corruption in the wider society. Typically, written codes do seem to be mindful of the latter "dynamic", but they ignore the immediate pragmatic (and ethical) concerns. Therefore, in practice, managers often need to know *when to break the rules*. Indeed, according to Molyneaux (2003, p. 142), "knowing when to break the rules appropriately may be a sign of real respect and understanding of them". This type of knowledge (or meta-rules) is constituted by the concepts and principles of philosophical ethics.

For example, in passive bribery-related decisions like the one mentioned above, the ethical principle of double effect (PDE) finds a direct application. In general, the PDE deals with decisions in which harmful side effects are expected to occur (e.g. Bomann-Larsen and Wiggen, 2003, p. 4). In the case of bribe payments, the "harmful side effects" (HSE's) can include the reinforcement of the dynamic of corruption in the societies involved, but more importantly, some bribes can lead quite directly to serious human rights violations and environmental damage (these are labelled "Type B" in Figure 17.2, with "Type A" referring to payments that do not carry these expectations of harm).

According to the PDE, any action with an HSE is not morally blameworthy, provided that the following five conditions hold:

(i)   the main ends and means are good, or neutral,
(ii)   the HSE is not part of the ends, nor used to achieve the ends,
(iii) the intended good outweighs the harm of the HSE,
(iv) the HSE is unavoidable if the main good is to be achieved,
(v)   the actor (e.g. a manager) has taken steps to minimise the HSE.

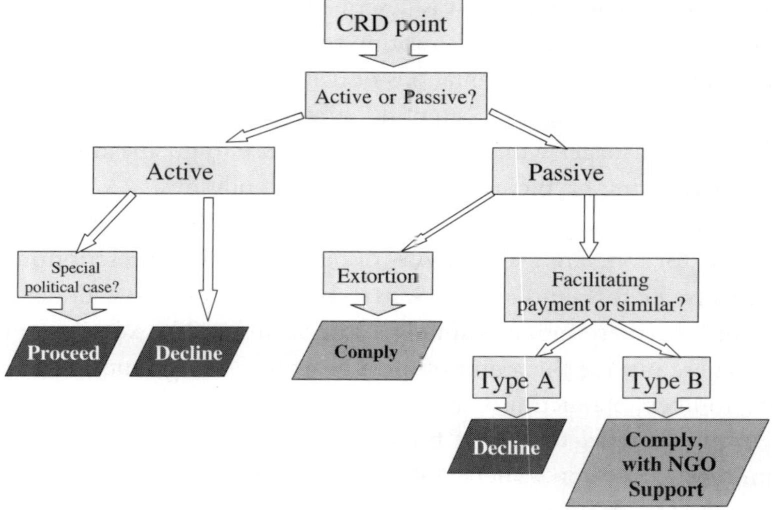

Figure 17.2 Forms of corruption with prescriptions for managers.

A passive facilitating payment in which there is no expectation of human rights violation nor environmental harm (i.e. Type A) does indeed meet the first four of these conditions. In the case of the "fruit on the dock", we can see that (i) the main ends and means are offloading the fruit and getting it to market, which are indeed good; (ii) the HSE (the strengthening of the dynamic of corruption) is certainly not part of the ends, nor is it used per se to achieve those ends; (iii) by almost any reasonable estimate, the intended good (marketing the fruit) outweighs the HSE harm (an abstract and almost negligible increment in corruption); (iv) the HSE is also likely to be inescapable and unavoidable if the good is to be achieved: if you do not pay the bribe, as a matter of fact, the fruit will rot (although there ought to be an effort to seek or design a feasible alternative).

Finally, the fifth condition of the PDE (i.e. taking steps to minimise the HSE) can be met, simply by having the company engage in an ongoing programme of corporate support of wider anti-corruption initiatives. Several such initiatives have been undertaken by NGOs (e.g. Transparency International) and by good governments. They are explicitly aimed at disrupting the dynamic of corruption and protecting human rights. This general notion of "corporate support" was described earlier, in relation to poverty alleviation and more generally in relation to partnership strategies for overcoming the several known limitations of market based systems. In the corruption related context, the "support" strategy can now also be seen as providing the manager with a useful moral license to go ahead with questionable facilitating payments, in the specified conditions.

The other forms of corruption that were identified earlier (active bribery, extortion, etc.) also invite distinctive ethical prescriptions for managers (refer to Figure 17.2). Where active corruption is under consideration, the prescription is simply "do not proceed", except in special cases that are outside the ambit of most business dealings, such as offering a bribe to liberate a victim of an oppressive regime. The ethical principle here is quite simple: the act of bribery might *initiate* or set in motion a dynamic of corruption, where none existed before.[1] Next, in those passive corruption decisions where there is indeed a likelihood of human rights violations (i.e. Type A in the figure), the ethical prescription is once again "do not proceed", since one ought not to be instrumental in such violations. The remaining case is that of passive extortion (involving threats of violence, or blackmail, etc.). In these circumstances, compliance with extorted payments might be ethically endorsed, provided that the payment is essentially unavoidable; that is, there is no known alternative way of securing the deal (e.g. payment in exchange for the safe return of a kidnapped person).

17.4 Politics and Ideology

As already indicated (in Section 17.3), approaches to corruption reduction cannot be very effective in isolation. Older definitions of corruption in the political literature have conservatively referred to "inducements to alter conduct from normal" (Noonan, 1984), "deviations from norms" (Nye, 1967; Scott, 1972), or behaviours that are "destructive of a system of public civic order" (Rogow and Lasswell, 1970). None of these referred to the important possibility that the system itself might be corrupt or unethical. Put differently, they have not really challenged any particular "order" or "norm". Other descriptions of corrupt activity have referred to "violations of common interest for special advantage"

(Rogow and Lasswell, 1970) or "undue influence for private gain" (Leff, 1964).

These descriptions of corruption can be read as applying to both private-to-public and private-to-private business arrangements. The characterisations in terms of private gains at the public expense then also appear to describe many of the behavioural "norms" of international business, as well as the current world "order" of global capitalism. One only needs to consider, for example, the extremely common practices of lobbying[2] for special privileges in ways that are arguably against the public interest (e.g. Brooke-Hamilton and Hock, 1997; Weber, 1996; Oberman, 2004) or payments of inflated fees within interlocking business directorates, not to mention "improper use of 'old boy' networks" (Ryan, 2000, p. 334). More generally, any business practice that deliberately exploits market power or other known limitations of markets with respect to the common good is *prima facie* "corrupt" in precisely the above-mentioned senses (Chapter 4).

This aspect of corruption can be illustrated quickly with reference to a few well-documented historical episodes of international business (Table 17.2). The cases of Lockheed, Motorola, Enron and Shell, for example (cf. Donaldson *et al.*, 2002; Gini, 2005), all indicate that the above descriptions of corruption involving public officials can reasonably be applied to the other types of "violation of the common interest" that happen to be quite "normal" elements of corporate strategy (and are often taught prescriptively in business schools).

Table 17.2 Business cases and forms of corruption.

Case	Type of Violation of Common Interest
Lockheed	Grand corruption, anti-competitive, passive bribe solicited by agent of foreign government
Motorola	Passive facilitating payment, normal business development, apparently no direct harms
Enron in India	Rewards to politicians who permitted human rights violations, environmental damage, anti-competitive deals
Shell in Nigeria	Resources contributed to oppressive military regime. Human rights violations and extreme injustices ignored, environment damaged, profits repatriated

17.4.1 Political Leanings and Prescriptions

Any proposed changes at the societal level to improve the situation, whether local, national or transnational, have to be considered in relation to the current advance of global capitalism as an ideology and as a set of practices. It follows that any prescription for reducing corruption will be contingent upon the political attitudes and leanings of those in a position to implement and foster them. At the risk of simplifying the categories, even moderate right versus left political leanings (see Chapter 1) yield contrasting prescriptions for reducing the level of corruption. From the far-right, one sees that the best way of eliminating corruption, at least in the public services, would be to eliminate the public sector. At the opposite extreme, one observes brutal state executions for anyone "found" to be involved in bribery.

A more moderate right-leaning position (e.g. Bardhan, 1997) sees that facilitating payments to government officials can improve economic efficiency and help growth in cases where regulation is obviously excessive and processes are slow or costly (as described, for example, in Moorthy *et al.*, 1998). However, when viewed from the left, these same "regulations and processes" appear to be legitimate responses to the known limitations of markets. From a neutral (or upright) position, e.g., Jacoby *et al.* (1977) have noted that, other things being equal, bribes are more likely to be offered in circumstances where (a) regulations are complex and (b) their application is uncertain; but (c) there is a high level of profitable business opportunity; whilst public officials are more likely to accept or solicit bribes (a) when there is political instability, (b) when their remuneration is low or (c) when they exercise a high level of discretion.

Each analysis of the problem (from the left, right and centre) thus yields prescriptions for reducing corruption. From the right we have recommendations to

(i)   reduce the scope and intrusiveness of the public sector (less government),

(ii) ensure that public sector is generally supportive of profitable ("worthwhile") private initiatives,

(iii)   pay public servants adequately but also ensure that they are properly motivated,

(iv)   reduce political patronage and cronyism,

(v)   ensure that the reputation of public servants matters in the long term, so have a vigilant (right-leaning) press,

(vi)   create cultures of business efficiency, competitive wealth creation,

(vii)   increase monitoring, accountability and the awareness of the legal consequences.

From the left, we have a corresponding but somewhat contrasting set of prescriptions, as follows:

(i)   increase the scope of the public sector in order to dilute the known limitations of markets,

(ii)   reduce privileges in society that are based on non-earned income,

(iii)   create a culture of wealth distribution by merit and need, not cronyism, nepotism and unfair inheritances,

(iv)   create a stronger sense of community, with less selfishness,

(v)   ensure that the reputation of corporations matters long term, so have vigilant (left-leaning) press,

(vi)   emphasise intrinsic and care-based motives, with a general awareness of consequences for self and others.

Finally, a third set of prescriptions from the centre represents a balance, with a reasonable chance of acceptance across much of the political spectrum. Furthermore, this "balanced" set is broadly consistent with (a) the limited available empirical evidence on corruption and (b) the several other prescriptions for integrating ethics with strategy that have been set out in this book. They are as follows:

(i)   Public and private sectors should adopt communication/propaganda strategies that raise general awareness of the various consequences of corruption (cf. Section 17.3.1).

(ii)   Business entities should respond to market limitations and regime weaknesses by lending ongoing support to programs of corruption reduction, as well as agencies that promote human rights and environmental improvement (cf. Section 17.3.2 and Chapter 4 *et seq.*).

(iii)   The private sector should sustain a liberal and individualistic culture, but augment it so that it has dual vision (e.g. Molyneaux, 2003, p. 141) that include moral commitments, protection of human rights, care of stakeholders and the environment (cf. Chapter 1).

(iv)   The public sector should combine a public-good mission with adequate pay funded by taxation (cf. Chapter 5).

17.5 Conclusion

Sen (1999, p. 279) once wrote that the success of capitalism depends in part on "business honesty in the face of contrary temptations". It also depends on similar types of honesty and forthrightness in the public sector, not to mention at the national and transnational political levels. It is plainly far beyond the capacity of any one actor to significantly reduce the overall level of corruption in the world. Instead, a multifaceted approach is needed (as with poverty) involving individual managers, corporations, NGOs and governments. However "honesty and forthrightness" is perhaps most pressingly needed with respect to the known limitations of market based systems and the current order. Certainly, the historical quest to link production distribution and property rights more directly to human rights, social justice and environmental protection is very far from over.

The currently fashionable right-leaning individual accountability approach to reducing corruption, together with the enduring justice and care orientation on the left, ultimately shares the same type of mission: both are driven by a commitment to some form of general moral progress. At this point, what seems most necessary is an attempt at all levels to heighten awareness of the consequences of corruption, to improve understanding of some of the applicable ethical principles and to cultivate an ethos in business and in politics that incorporates authentic moral commitments, human rights and environmental concerns.

Notes

1. The distinction between active and passive forms of bribery swings on this "initiation". For example, in the Motorola-in-Slovenia case (Moorthy *et al.*, 1998) a small facilitating payment was offered by a manager, suggesting "active bribery". However, there appeared to be many prior indications that the dynamic of corruption was already in place such that payments were quietly being invited, rather than overtly demanded.

2. Weber and Getz (2004, p. 696) noted that "A prototypical bribe transaction involves a firm or its agent making a payment to a government official so that the official will make a decision in the firm's interest rather than in the public interest". Yet, much of what is called "business lobbying" answers to that very same definition, except perhaps that the "payments" are not made directly to officials for their personal use. To the extent that corporate political activity constrains the level of democratic participation by ordinary individual citizens, this type of lobbying also curtails human rights (Donaldson, 1989). Furthermore, when endemic is in a society, it can be a "form of oppression" (Ryan, 2000, p. 337).

Chapter 18

JUSTICE: Preferential Hiring and the Dualism

Abstract: This chapter is an adapted version of "Justice in preferential hiring," *Journal of Business Ethics* 10, pp. 91–97, 1991, by M. S. Singer and A. E. Singer. It describes empirical studies of perceptions of preferential selection. Preferential selection is widely perceived as unfair. Indeed, the level of perceived unfairness is directly related to the discrepancy in candidates' test scores on job-relevant tests. Furthermore, the provision of particular "ethical" or "legislative" justifications for the selection decisions increased the perceived level of unfairness. The question of preferential hiring, far from being an esoteric and annoying HR issue, can be thought of as representative of the larger "strategy versus ethics" question. It is only when people take the time and make the effort to fully contemplate and discuss all the arguments on both sides of the issue that they can reoccupy the centre.

18.1 Introduction

Practices such as preferential hiring or affirmative action are a significant part of the HR strategy in many organisations; yet they are seen by some as annoying distractions from the big issue of distributive justice and poverty alleviation on a global scale. A contrary viewpoint is revealed in this chapter: preferential hiring (which involves efficiency and justice from both sides of the dualism framework) is a kind of paradigm case, an acid test, whose proper study can also lead people to think differently about those "bigger issues". It is only necessary that enough time be taken to contemplate and discuss the many arguments on both sides of the divide, hence arriving at some point of balance between healthy egoism and universal concerns.

18.1.1 Arguments For and Against

The issue of preferential hiring has received considerable attention in both the ethics and psychology literatures on personnel selection. In the literature of ethics, theoretical analyses of the rights and wrongs of preferential hiring have been quite well documented. Several major justifications have been put forward (Table 18.1). First, preferential hiring obeys some compensatory justice principles and is a form of compensation to minorities for past discriminations they have suffered (e.g. Minas, 1977; Taylor, 1973; Thomas, 1973). Second, preferential hiring is a means to promote social welfare and to achieve distributive justice in future employment opportunities (e.g. Fiss, 1976; Nagel, 1973; Sher, 1975). Together these yield the "rectification" argument (row 4 of the table), whereby preferential selection is seen as imposing a *temporary* moderate injustice (on the majority) in order to rectify a long-term severe injustice to the minority. The metaphor of "straightening a bent branch of a tree" is sometimes used. It can also be argued that the ethical principle of role integration, whereby work life and community life ought to be governed by similar principles, seems to imply that the workplace ought to have a "group" composition that is representative of the larger community in which it is embedded.

Another set of pro-preferential selection arguments involves considerations of economic efficiency. Preferential hiring avoids wastage of minority abilities and helps to broaden the talent pool of organisations (Shaw, 1988). In businesses that involve in-person service, especially on personal matters such as health, hiring customer-service personnel based on ethnicity can be a straightforward response to customer-preferences for dealing with someone of a particular ethnicity or language ability. In practice, this can be an important way of improving social services for minority communities, hence arguably also increasing the general welfare of society (e.g. Kennedy, 1986; Nagel, 1973; Nickel, 1975). Finally (Table 18.1, row 9), where a minority group is known to have been disadvantaged (e.g. poor schools), but a minority candidate scores well on merit-based tests, this indicates probable higher future performance by the candidate, because they have demonstrated the personal ability to overcome the "disadvantage".

Table 18.1 Arguments for and against preferential selection.

PRO-Preferential Selection		ANTI-Preferential Selection	
Justice-based			
Compensation	Compensates for past discrimination	**Infliction** (counter-point)	Such compensation should be levied against those (individuals) who actually inflicted the harm
Verification (counter-point)	Individuals' claims or allegation of past injustices to themselves are often difficult or expensive to verify in practice	**Harming** (individuals)	Compensate individuals, not a group, based on the specific harm each one suffered. Some employers do this as charity; but it can be difficult
Distribution	Increases distributive justice (assumed to benefit society)	**Discrimination**	Discriminates against current majority
Rectification	PS/AA imposes a moderate but *temporary* injustice on the majority, to rectify a long-term severe injustice to the minority ("straightening a bent branch")	**Race-based**	Directly violates equality by using race or gender as an explicit criterion
Efficiency-based			
Validity (counter-point)	Doubtful validity of job-related and merit-based tests	**Merit**	Use merit-based and job (task)-relevant criteria in order to increase performance, efficiency and competitiveness
Waste	Avoids wastage of minority group's talents	**Side-effects**	Unintended adverse effects: denigration and downgrading of "selected" candidates' job-related achievements, lowering of self-esteem

Table 18.1   (*Continued*)

PRO-Preferential Selection		ANTI-Preferential Selection	
Variety	Broadens talent pool of organisation (ecology metaphor)	**Inferiority**	Confirms (admits, signals) that the target group (Minority) needs help, hence implying inferiority
Preferences	Responds to customers' preferences for specific ethnicity or language in personal-service contexts	**Well-being** (counter-point)	The customers' preferences may not reflect their own long-term well-being (a KLMBS)
Overcoming disadvantages	If a minority group is known to have been disadvantaged (e.g. poor schools), but a minority candidate then scores well on merit tests, this suggests higher future performance	**Overcoming disadvantages** (counter-point)	In some cases, minority groups have received extra help throughout the school system. If an individual is known to have suffered some disadvantage, but then scores well on merit tests, this suggests higher future performance. Employers do recognise this, case by case

Opponents of preferential selection have argued against the practice on several grounds. First, selection should be based on job-relevant merits or qualifications, rather than on irrelevant factors such as sex or ethnic origin (e.g. Garrett and Klonoski, 1986). Merit-based selections result in greater efficiency in terms of the utility of human resources in organisations (e.g. Black, 1974; Schmitt and Noe, 1986). Second, compensation for past ills should not be required from all members of majority groups, nor should reparation go to all members of minority groups. A principle of compensatory justice[1] requires that reparation be paid only to those injured by the very ones who inflict the injuries (e.g. Goldman, 1975; Karst and

Horowitz, 1974; Nickel, 1974). Third, preferential hiring itself violates the principle of equality (rows 3 and 4, right column) by being explicitly race-based and by discriminating against white males (e.g. Cohen, 1975; Newton, 1973). Fourth, preferential hiring may have unintentional adverse effects on minority members, in that it implies minorities are inferior, hence are in need of help (e.g. Goldman, 1976), that it causes people to denigrate real achievements of minorities (e.g. Shaw, 1988) and that it lowers self-esteem (see below).

Yet another set of (secondary) arguments are direct counter-points to some of the above arguments. For example, in response to the principle of compensating individuals (rather than whole groups), it must be said that allegations of past injustices to individuals are often difficult and expensive to verify or prove (Table 18.1, row 2). In response to the strongly held belief in merit-based appointment (row 5), it can be pointed out that many job-related and merit-based tests (including educational qualifications in many cases) are of doubtful validity, or are themselves inherently biased against minorities due to linguistic and cultural factors. In response to the "customer preference" argument (row 8) one can yet again invoke a known limitation of market-based systems (Chapter 4), that expressed preferences do not generally align with well-being (e.g. the customer's long-term well-being might be better served if they themselves learnt to deal equally with all groups, etc.). Finally (row 9), in response to the argument that "overcoming limitations imply better future performance", it can be pointed out that in some cases, minority groups have, on the contrary, received extra help throughout the school system (so if anything there should be a reversal of the preferential concession in job recruitment). Furthermore, if any individual is known to have suffered some past disadvantage, but then scores well on merit based tests, this indicates high performance; yet, smart (and ethical) employers already try to recognise this, case by case, and in the absence of any imposed program.

18.2 Empirical Studies

The psychological literature on preferential hiring provides empirical evidence on two related issues: the utility of preferential hiring in terms of organisational productivity (economic efficiency), and the social psychological consequences of the program. The latter include consideration of distributive justice, which is often operationalised in such studies as "perceived fairness" (e.g. Greenberg, 1987). Several studies (e.g. Cronbach *et al.,* 1980; Schmitt *et al.,* 1984; Schmitt and Noe, 1986) have attempted to estimate in dollar terms net economic gains or losses associated with preferential hiring. The overall conclusion was that the efficiency-related goal of optimising organisational productivity and the "social" or justice goal of preferential hiring were almost certain to be in conflict with each other.

Several studies have demonstrated that preferential hiring may have adverse social and psychological consequences for individuals. Jacobson and Koch (1977) found that gender based preferential hiring had a negative impact on subordinate's judgements of leaders' performance. Chacko (1982) reported that women managers' commitment, satisfaction and stress were adversely associated with their belief that their own selections were gender based. Heilman and Herlihy, 1984 and Heilman *et al.,* 1987 found that women's jobs were devalued (by self on others) when their selection was thought to be based on preferential treatment. These and other studies are convergent in suggesting that preferential hiring may harm the very people it was intended to benefit (e.g. Sowell, 1978).

18.2.1 *Effects of Score-Discrepancy and Justification*

In the late 1980s we identified what appeared to be a quite surprising gap in the empirical literature. There had been no previous investigation of how the level of "perceived fairness" varied as a function of the level of "preference" in a preferential-selection program. If you hire a minority member with a considerably worse job-relevant or merit-based score (under preferential selection), is that likely to be perceived as much *more* "unfair" than if the applicants' scores were quite close? Accordingly, we carried out two empirical questionnaire based studies that examined the perceived fairness of preferential selection under various hypothetical scenarios. This section briefly summarises those studies.

A questionnaire was used to obtain data from over 200 respondents. Two independent samples of respondents[2] were given the questionnaire, with varied information about the "candidates". Each item referred to a hypothetical case of selection involving two candidates for a training course (see below). For each item, the trainability scores of the two candidates (A and B) were given. Respondents were told that A belongs to a majority group, B to a minority. Respondents then rated the "fairness" of the decision on a 7-point scale. The independent (horizontal axis) was the discrepancy (difference) between the trainability scores.

> *Preferential* selection was represented by five questionnaire items that described selection of B when B had a lower trainability score.

> *Conventional* discrimination was represented by five questionnaire items that described selection of A (the majority member) when B had a higher trainability score.

> *Merit-based* selection was represented by the other items, within an overall carefully balanced experimental design.[3]

18.2.2 Results

All the mean ratings, except for those having "0" discrepancy scores, were significantly lower than a null mean of 4, which represented the neutral point (neither fair nor unfair) on the 7-point scale. Thus, preferential hiring based on either sex or ethnicity was perceived as *unfair*. In addition, the degree of perceived unfairness was directly associated with the score discrepancy between the two hypothetical candidates: the less "qualified" the candidate, the more the selection was seen as unfair (Figure 18.1). The results were quite symmetrical for conventional discrimination and preferential selection (in other words, in all cases it was the score not the ethnicity that influenced the fairness judgements).

18.2.3 Study 2

A limitation of study 1 concerned the use of a within-subjects design. We were concerned that the two sets of findings might be in part due to respondents making direct comparisons among the outcomes of the 22 hypothetical cases, some of which involved ethnicity, some gender. Accordingly, in a second study, a between-subjects design was used, in which respondents were required to evaluate the fairness of only one case of preferential selection. One purpose of the study was to cross validate the

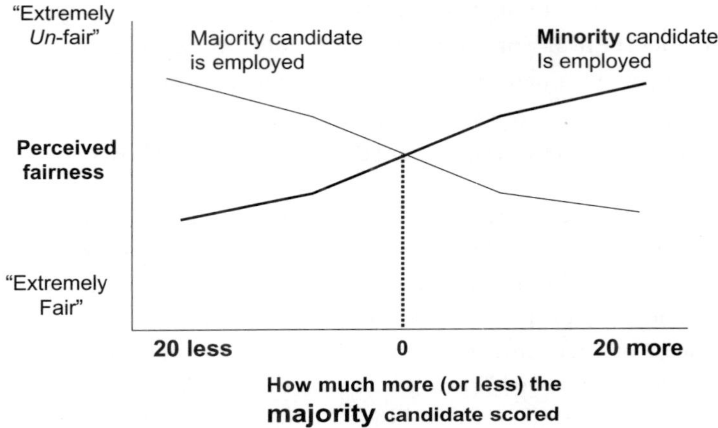

Figure 18.1   Mean ratings for perceived fairness of preferential selection, as a function of score discrepancy on merit-based test (schematic representation of study 1 results).

findings of study 1. In addition, study 2 also aimed to ascertain whether the *provision of explanatory justifications* for the preferential selection (in the hypothetical scenarios) would have an effect on fairness perceptions.

Bies (1987a, p. 304) had previously argued that perceptions of justice are the product of "*a process of argumentation or persuasion*" and they are influenced by the provision of a social account (explanation, justification) for the outcome. Bies further argued that perceptions of injustice associated with various unfavourable outcomes (events) are primarily due to the inadequacy or absence of justifications (i.e. communicated explanations). Significantly in the present context he concluded from several experimental studies (Bies, 1987a,b; Bies and Shapiro, 1988) that, in contrast to the present study, when adequate justifications are provided, feelings of injustice would be significantly reduced.

In study 2, two types of justification for preferential selection were used: "ethical" and "legislative". As discussed earlier, supporters of preferential selection have deployed reasons (listed in the left column of Table 18.1) involving justice and efficiency, such as "correcting past ills", "to promote fair distributions of employment" and "to utilise minority talents". Many organisations, in contrast, simply note that their a preferential selection program is required by legislation. According to Bies, either type of justification, the "ethical" or "legislative", would be expected to reduce the level of perceived unfairness in the experimental context when compared to study 1, in which no justification was provided.

A hypothetical case was designed for study 2, as follows:

"This case concerns the recruiting practice of a large computer consultancy firm. The firm advertised a position for a computer programmer. All candidates were required to sit for the computer programmer aptitude test (CPAT). Previous research had shown that the test is a valid predictor of later job performance. The top 10 scorers on the CPAT were then interviewed. Their names with their CPAT scores were John H (95), Fu-Tuk S (90), Bruce N (86), Jerry T (81), Alan B (75), Chie-Min R (72), Don T (67), Rob A (61), Paul P (56) and Sandy D (50). All candidates were between 21 and 23 years of age, with B.Sc. and similar academic records. All had some previous working experience, but none had worked as a computer programmer or in a related job. The position was offered to Fu-Tuk S".

One group of respondents also received "ethical justifications" of this hypothetical selection decision, as follows:

"In justifying the decision, the personnel department wrote in a letter to all rejected candidates that the firm had been concerned with the very small number of ethnic minority members currently working as computer programmers. Because, historically, they have been disadvantaged, the firm is interested in correcting such ills. The firm is also committed to promote a fair distribution of employment opportunities and to broaden the overall talent pool by actively seeking qualified minority employees".

Respondents receiving "legislative justifications" were given this information:

"In justifying the decision, the personnel department wrote in a letter to all rejected candidates that in recent years there has been an increasing number of ethnic minority graduates who majored in computer programming. Equal employment legislation stipulates that ethnic minority candidates be given equal employment opportunities without discrimination. The firm therefore feels obliged to actively seek qualified minority programmers to join its staff".

Table 18.2   Fairness ratings under three types of justification.

Score Discrepancy	Type of Justification		
	None (*N* = 72)	Ethical (*N* = 72)	Legislative (*N* = 72)
2	5.26 (1.99)	4.48 (1.62)	3.56 (1.68)
4	4.89 (1.92)	5.30 (2.32)	4.19 (1.72)
7	3.35 (1.07)	3.06 (1.91)	3.65 (1.85)
10	3.98 (1.36)	2.98 (1.56)	2.32 (1.35)

A null mean of 4 represents the neutral point (neither fair nor unfair). Lower numbers indicate more unfairness. Type of justification is a significant main effect (std. devs. in parentheses).

The mean fairness ratings under the "no-justification", "ethical-justification" and "legislative-justification" conditions are set out in Table 18.2. The cell means were 4.42 (none), 3.96 (ethical) and 3.43 (legislative), that is, where no justification was given, the minority-hire decision was judged as fair. But when ethical justification was given, it was considered unfair. Finally, when legislative justification was given, it was considered the most unfair (amongst these three conditions). Thus the provision of justification in the context of a questionnaire-based study, rather than reducing any perceived injustice (as one might expect and in accordance with the several earlier studies by Bies), actually exacerbated the overall sense of injustice associated with preferential selection.[4]

18.3 Discussion

The two studies provided convergent evidence, based on hypothetical scenarios and questionnaires, that preferential selection is broadly perceived as unfair, regardless of whether it was based on the candidate's ethnic origin or gender. Overall, the less "qualified" the minority candidate as compared with the majority candidate, the more the selection was perceived as unfair. Also, as just described, the provision of either an ethical or a legislative justification actually exacerbated the perception of injustice in this experimental context rather than reducing it. This was against prior expectations and seemingly inconsistent with earlier psychological studies that showed a reduced level of perceived injustice when justifications were given for an "unfavourable" outcome (e.g. Bies, 1987b; Bies and Shapiro, 1988).

18.3.1 Psychological Explanations

Two explanations of the experimental anomaly seem plausible. The first involves the "winner effect"; the second, which also seems to have wider implications, refers to the phenomenon of psychological reactance (e.g. Brehm, 1966) or what might be called a "knee-jerk effect". In earlier experimental studies of perceived injustice, the "unfair" outcome did not actually involve an individual winner (like the selected candidate in the present study). For example, in a study by Folger (1983), subjects (respondents) were told that the "rules of the game" had changed so that no one had won a staged competition. In the absence of a winner as a reference point, this left everyone in the same boat. In that situation, a social (legal or ethical) justification of the bad outcome was probably more readily accepted by the subjects, or assimilated into their current mental set, schemata, or script. In the present study, the "justifications" provided to respondents might have been seen as missing the point (as they saw it), or to be touching upon uncomfortable prejudices and fears. (History is replete with incidents of tension due to "foreigners" taking employment opportunities away form "locals"). It seems reasonable to suggest that in the experimental context the "justifications" elicited an emotional reaction, or reactance, rather than an openly rational or deliberatively rational process.

18.3.2 Sustaining Reflection

In contrast to the above studies, but more in line with the earlier experimental studies by Bies *et al.*, it has been the authors' personal experience over many years of discussing this issue with groups of university students, that an open and prolonged consideration of all the arguments on both sides of the debate (in a class or lecture situation) does indeed lead people to moderate their position on the preferential selection or affirmative action issue. Most participants in a protracted and well-managed discussion of the issues, aided by Table 18.1 or similar, do indeed tend towards the centre. Indeed, several students have actually changed their position on a forced-choice "pro- versus anti-" vote, on this matter.

18.4 Conclusion

Far from being a minor and somewhat annoying "human resource management" issue, preferential hiring can thus be considered to be representative of (even central to) the entire strategy–ethics relationship. In particular, the differences in responses to (a) an experimental questionnaire requiring immediate responses, and (b) an informed, protracted and open debate probably have much wider significance for integrating business strategy and ethics in practice.

When using Table 18.1 in classroom discussions of preferential selection we have found a moderation of positions. This is also quite likely to be the case for when something like Figure 1.1 (the dualism framework for ethics and strategy in Chapter 1) is used to discuss business ethics in general. Irrespective of a person's ideology or culture, people everywhere can understand and appreciate both sides of the strategy–ethics dualism, provided only that they are able to take the time and effort to learn the arguments on both sides. Each point and counter point needs to be considered and discussed openly and slowly, in the presence of the other argument (or person). Then, to the extent that ideology per se can be defined as "a framework of ideas used to explain values", any such protracted process has a really good chance of producing a modest shift in ideology, a transition towards the political centre by both parties.

In the narrow experimental context, but also in the contemporary media treatment of issues like preferential selection and business ethics, one almost always observes precisely the opposite: deployment of words as weapons, breathless hurried responses, incomplete information and narrow or provocative framing of the crucial issues. As our experiment suggests, all of this does indeed attract peoples' attention, elicits emotional audience responses and evidently tends to polarise opinions. It is perhaps no coincidence that in the US as elsewhere the political centre is currently being shunned and vacated.

On the "polarising" issue of preferential selection, most people who have taken the time to canvas all the arguments on both sides thoroughly and completely have generally become more willing to countenance some type of temporary affirmative action program. On the wider issue of integrating strategy with ethics, or accommodating ethics into the schemata and ideology of global business (and indeed politics), a similar phenomenon might now reasonably be anticipated. Views on the relationship between corporate strategy and ethical behaviour can be pretty extreme. Accordingly, it is hoped that the present collection of essays, not to mention the many current efforts of like-minded institutions and academics all over the world, will promote a more fully informed reflection and dialogue, hence paving the way for a more settled and integrated society.

Notes

1. This principle of compensatory justice is also relevant to the moral responsibility and blameworthiness component of the corporate moral agency (CMA) debate (Chapter 2). It argues *prima facie* that specific individuals are morally responsible for any harms caused by "corporate" activities (e.g. a CEO, or a specific senior management team that functions as the effective brain of the firm).

2. Respondents in sample 1 were used to assess fairness perceptions of "*ethnicity* based" selection. They were 108 (39 males and 69 females) Europeans. All were undergraduate psychology students with a mean age of 20 years and 6 months. All were told that candidate A was a European and that candidate B was a member of an ethnic-minority group. Sample 2 was used to collect data on fairness perceptions of "*sex* based" selection. The respondents were a different group of 44 male and 70 female undergraduate psychology students, with a mean age of 20 years and 11 months. They were instructed that candidate A was a male and candidate B was a female.

3. For details of the design, samples, results and statistical analysis in studies 1 and 2, refer to Singer and Singer (1991).

4. In study 2, mean fairness ratings with low score discrepancy (2, 4) were mostly above the neutral point (i.e. fair). This contrasted with study 1.

Bibliography

Ackoff, R. L. (1983). An interactive view of rationality. *Journal of the Operational Research Society*, 34(8), pp. 501–515.

Ackoff, R. L. (1974). *Redesigning the Future*. John Wiley and Sons.

Ackoff, R. L. (1994). Higher education and social stratification. *Interfaces*, 24(4), pp. 73–82.

Ackoff, R. L. and F. E. Emery (1972). *On Purposeful Systems*. Tavistock Publications.

Ahmed, A. and P. Werhane (2004). Hindustan Lever case. *International Journal of Entrepreneurship and Innovation Management*, 4(5), pp. 460–465.

Allison, G. (1971). *The Essence of Decision*. Boston: Little Brown.

Altman, B. and D. Vidaver-Cohen (2000). A framework for understanding corporate citizenship (introduction to a special issue). *Business and Society Review*, 105(1), pp. 1–7.

Alvesson, M. and S. Deetz (1998). Critical theory and postmodern approaches to organisational studies. In *Handbook of Organisational Studies*, London: Sage Publications, pp. 191–217.

Andrews, K. R. (1980). *The Concept of Corporate Strategy*. Homewood, IL: Irwin.

Ansoff, H. I. (1965). *Corporate Strategy*, New York: McGraw Hill.

Ansoff, H. I. (1991). Critique of Henry Mintzberg's 'The design school: reconsidering the basic premises of strategic management'. *Strategic Management Journal*, 12, pp. 449–461.

Appley, L. A. (1963). *The Management Evolution*. American Management Association, Inc.

Argandonna, A. (2003). Private to private corruption. *Journal of Business Ethics*, 47(3), pp. 253–267.

Argyris, C. (1977). Double loop learning in organisations. *Harvard Business Review*, Sept–Oct, pp. 115–125.

Armstrong, P. (2005). *Critique of Entrepreneurship: People and Policy*. UK: Palgrave, Macmillan.

Arrow, K. (1963). *Social Choice and Individual Values*, 2nd ed. NY: Wiley.

Arthur, W. B. (1996). Increasing returns and the new world of business. *Harvard Business Review*, July–Aug, pp. 100–109.

Axelrod, R. (1984). *The Evolution of Cooperation.* NY: Basic Books.

Badaracco, J. L. (1991). *The Knowledge Link: How Firms Compete Through Strategic Alliances.* Boston: HBS Press.

Baier, K. (1995). *The Rational and Moral Order: The Social Roots of Reason and Morality.* LaSalle, IL: Open Court Publishing.

Bardhan, P. (1997). Corruption and development. *Journal of Economic Literature,* 36, pp. 1320–1346.

Bare, B. and G. Mendoza (1988). A soft optimization approach to forest land management planning. *Canadian Journal of Forest Research,* 18, pp. 545–552.

Barney, J. B. and M. M. Hansen (1994). Trustworthiness as a source of competitive advantage. *Strategic Management Journal,* 15, pp. 175–190.

Barney, J. B. (1994). Beyond individual metaphors in understanding how firms behave: A comment on game theory and prospect theory models of firm behaviour. In *Fundamental Issues in Strategy: A Research Agenda,* R. Rumelt, D. Schendel and D. Teece, eds. Boston, MA: HBS Press, pp. 55–70.

Bateson, G. (1972). *Steps to an Ecology of Mind.* NY: Chandler.

Bateson, G. (1979). *Mind and Nature: A Necessary Unity.* London: Wildwood.

Bauman, Z. (1998). *Globalisation: The Human Consequences.* NY: Columbia University Press.

Beer, S. (1972). *The Brain of the Firm.* Allen Lane: Penguin Press.

Bell, D. (1973). *The Coming of Post-Industrial Society: A Venture in Social Forecasting.* NY: Basic Books.

Bennett, P. G. and C. S. Huxham (1982). Hypergames and what they do: A 'soft OR' approach. *JORS,* 33, pp. 41–50.

Berleant, A. (1982). Multinationals, local practice and the problem of ethical consistency. *Journal of Business Ethics,* 1, pp. 185–193.

Bettis, R. and C. K. Prahalad (1995). The dominant logic: retrospective and extension. *Strategic Management Journal,* 16, pp. 5–14.

Bettis, R. (1991). Strategic management and the straightjacket: An editorial essay. *Organization Science,* 2(3), pp. 315–319.

Bies, R. J. and D. L. Shapiro (1988). Voice and justification: Their influence on procedural fairness judgements. *Academy of Management Journal,* 31, pp. 676–685.

Bies, R. J. (1987a). The predicament of injustice: The management of moral outrage. In *Research in Organisational Behaviour,* Vol. 9, L. L. Cummings and B. M. Staw, eds. Greenwich, CT: JAI Press, pp. 289–319.

Bies, R. J. (1978b). Beyond voice: The influence of decision maker justification and sincerity on procedural fairness judgements. *Representative Research in Social Psychology,* 17, pp. 3–14.

Binmore, K. (1999). Game theory and business ethics. *Business Ethics Quarterly*, 9(1), pp. 31–35.

Binmore, K. (1987). Modelling rational players. *Economics and Philosophy*, 3, pp. 179–214.

Birnbaum, J. (1993). *The Lobbyists*. NY: Times Books.

Boatright, J. R. (2000). Globalisation and the ethics of business. *Business Ethics Quarterly*, 10(2), pp. 1–6.

Boddewyn, J. and T. Brewer (1994). International business political behaviour: New theoretical directions. *Academy of Management Review*, 19(1), pp. 119–143.

Bolton, B. K. and J. L. Thompson (2004). *Entrepreneurs: Talent, Temperament and Technique*, 2nd ed. Oxford: Elsevier.

Bomann-Larsen, L. and O. Wiggen (2003). *Responsibility in World Business: Managing Harmful Side-Effects of Corporate Activity*. Policy Brief, International Peace Research Institute, Oslo and UN University Press.

Boulding, K. E. (1978). *Human Betterment*. Sage Publications.

Bourgine, P. (1989). *Homo economicus* is also *homo cogitans*. *Theory and Decision*, 27, pp. 1–6.

Brandenburger, A. M. and B. J. Nalebuff (1996). *Co-opetition*. NY: Doubleday.

Brealey, R. and S. Myers (1981). *Principles of Corporate Finance*. McGraw Hill.

Brehm, J. W. (1966). *A Theory of Psychological Reactance*. NY: Academic Press.

Brenkert, G. (1998). Trust, morality and international business. *Business Ethics Quarterly*, 8(2), pp. 293–317.

Broekstra, G. (1998). An organisation is a conversation. In *Discourse and Organisation*, D. Grant, T. Keenoy and C. Oswick, eds. London: Sage Publications, pp. 152–176.

Brocklesby, J. and S. Cummings (1996). Designing a viable organisational structure. *Long Range Planning*, 29(1), pp. 49–57.

Brooke-Hamilton, J. and D. Hock (1997). Ethical standards for business lobbying: Some practical suggestions. *Business Ethics Quarterly*, 7(3), pp. 117–130.

Broome, J. (1993). Goodness is reducible to betterness: The evil of death is the value of life. In *The Good and the Economical*, P. Koslowski and Y. Shionoya, eds. Berlin: Springer-Verlag, pp. 70–84.

Buchanan, A. E. (1985). *Ethics, Efficiency and the Market*. NJ: Rowman and Allenheld.

Buchholz, R. A. and S. B. Rosenthal (2002). Technology and business: Rethinking the moral dilemma. *Journal of Business Ethics*, 41(1), pp. 45–50.

Bulletpoints Weekly, 3(19), May 1995. Published by *AT Kearney* Inc. Chicago.

Burgess, K. (1995). Prospering in a global economy. *Journal of the Operational Research Society*, 46, pp. 553–561.

Burrell, G. (1989). The absent centre: The neglect of Philosophy in Anglo-American management theory. *Human Systems Management,* 8, pp. 307–311.

Calori, R. (1999). Philosophising on strategic management models. *Organisation Studies,* 19(2), pp. 281–306.

Calton, J. M. (1999). Who owns the knowledge creation processes of learning organisations? A pragmatic ethical exploration. Paper Presented at *IABS* 1999 Paris.

Camerer, C. F. (1994). Does strategy research need game theory? In *op cit.,* R. Rumelt *et al.,* eds. pp. 195–220.

Casson, M. (1982). *The Entrepreneur, an Economic Theory.* London: Gregg Revivals.

Casson, M. (1998). An entrepreneurial theory of the firm (manuscript). University of Reading, England.

Casson, M. C. (1997). *Information and Organisation: A New Perspective on the Theory of the Firm.* Oxford: Clarendon Press.

Casti, J. L. (1994). *Complexification.* London: Abacus.

Casti, J. L. and A. Karlqvist, eds. (1994). *Cooperation and Conflict in Evolutionary Processes.* Wiley.

Chacko, T. L. (1982). Women and equal employment opportunity some unintended effects. *Journal of Applied Psychology,* 67, pp. 119–123.

Chatterjee, K. and G. L. Lilien (1986). Game theory in marketing science, uses and limitations. *International Journal of Research in Marketing,* 3, pp. 79–93.

Checkland, P. B. (1989). Soft systems methodology. *Human Systems Management,* 8, pp. 273–288.

Churchman, C. W. (1970). Operations research as a profession. *Management Science,* 17(2), pp. B37–B53.

Churchman, C. W. (1971). *The Design of Inquiring Systems.* NY: Basic Books.

Churchman, C. W. (1982). *Thought and Wisdom.* Seaside, CA: Intersystems Press.

Churchman, C. W. (1994). Management science: Science of managing and managing of Science. *Interfaces,* 24(4), pp. 99–110.

Cockroft, L. (2003). Tackling corruption: A question of leadership www.iofc.org.

Cohen, C. (1975). Race and the constitution. *The Nation,* 8 Feb. 1975.

Cohen, J. (1981). Can human irrationality be experimentally demonstrated? *The Behavioral and Brain Sciences,* 4, pp. 317–370.

Coleman, W.O. (2002). *Economics and Its Enemies: Two Centuries of Anti-Economics.* NY: Palgrave.

Collier, J. (2000). Globalisation and ethical global business. *Business Ethics: A European Review,* April, pp. 71–76.

Collins, J. C. and J. I. Porras (1994). *Built to Last: Successful Habits of Visionary Companies.* NY: Harper Business.

Colman, A. (1982). *Game Theory and Experimental Games*. Pergamon Press.

Coyne, J. E. and M. Wright (1986). *Divestment and Strategic Change*. Oxford: Phillip Allan.

Crisp, R. (1987). Persuasive advertising, autonomy and the creation of desire. *Journal of Business Ethics*, 6, pp. 413–418.

Cronbach, L. J., E. Yalow and G. Schaeffer (1980). A mathematical structure for analyzing fairness in selection. *Personnel Psychology*, 33, pp. 693–704.

Cudd, A. (1993). Game theory and the history of ideas about rationality. *Economics and Philosophy*, 9, pp. 101–133.

D'Aveni R. (1994). *Hyper-competition: Managing the Dynamics of Strategic Manoeuvring*. NY: Free Press.

Danley, J. R. (1984). Corporate moral agency: The case for anthropological bigotry. In *Business Ethics: Readings and Cases in Corporate Morality*, Hoffman and Moore, eds., McGraw Hill, pp. 172–179.

Davis, J., F. Schoorman and L. Donaldson (1997). Towards a stewardship theory of management. *Academy of Management Review*, 22(1), pp. 220–247.

Davis, P. J. and R. Hersch (1981). *The Mathematical Experience*. Boston: Birkhauser.

Dawkins, R. (1976). *The Selfish Gene*. Oxford: OUP.

Deardorff, A.V. (1992). Welfare effects of global patent protection. *Economica*, 59, pp. 35–51.

DeBono, E. (1992) *Sur/petition: Going Beyond Competition*. London: Harper Collins.

DeGeorge, R. T. (1990). *Business Ethics*, 3rd ed. New York: Macmillan.

Dempsey, G. (1999). Revisiting intellectual property policy: Information economics for the information age. *Prometheus*, 17(1), pp. 33–40.

Dennett, D. (1995). *Darwins Dangerous Idea*. Simon and Schuster.

Derkenderen, F. G. J. and R. Crum (1979). *Project Set Strategies*. Boston: Martinus Nijhoff.

Derry, R. (2001). Seeking a balance: A critical perspective on entrepreneurship and the good society. *Business Ethics Quarterly (Ruffin Series No. 3), Ethics and Entrepreneurship*, pp. 197–208.

Dhammananda, K. Sri (1999). *Food for the Thinking Mind*. Taipei: Buddha Educational Foundation.

Di Benedetto, C. A. (1987). Modelling rationality in marketing decision making with game theory, *Journal of the Acad Marketing Science*, 15(4), pp. 22–32.

Dobson, J. and J. White (1995). Towards the feminine firm: an extension to Thomas White. *Business Ethics Quarterly*, 5(3), pp. 463–478.

Dobson, J. (2001). The battle in Seattle: 2 world views on corporate culture. *Business Ethics Quarterly*, 11(3), pp. 403–413.

Doktor, R. H. (1969). On the commonality of creative products in the arts and sciences. *Journal of Creative Behavior*, 13(2).

Doktor, R. H. and D. H. Bloom (1977). Selective lateralization of cognitive styles related to occupation as determined by EEG alpha asymmetry. *Psycho-Physiology*, 14(4).

Donaldon, T. and W. Dunfee (1999). *Ties That Bind: A Social Contracts Approach to Business Ethics.* Boston: HBS Press.

Donaldson, T. (1985). Multinational decision-making: Re-conciling international norms. *Journal of Business Ethics*, 4, pp. 357–366.

Donaldson (1989). *The Ethics of International Business*, NY: OUP.

Donaldson, T. and L. Preston (1995). The stakeholder theory of the corporation: Concepts, evidence and implications. *Academy of Management Review*, 20(1), pp. 65–91.

Donaldson, T. (1999a). Staking and ethical claim to intellectual property. Paper presented at *IABS* 1999, Paris.

Donaldson, T. (1999b). Values in tension: Ethics away from home. In *Ethical Issues in Business: A Philosophical Approach*, 6th ed. T. Donaldson and P. H. Werhane, eds., NJ: Prentice Hall, pp. 431–441.

Donaldson, T. P. Werhane and M. Cording, eds. (2002). *Ethical Issues in Business: A Philosophical Approach*, 7th ed., NJ: Prentice Hall.

Dryzsek, J. S. (1995). Democracy and environmental policy instruments. In *Markets, The State and the Environment: Towards Integration*, R. Eckersey, ed., Melbourne: Macmillan.

Duhaime, I. M. and J. R. Grant (1984). Factors influencing divestment decision-making: Evidence from a field study. *Strategic Management Journal*, 5, pp. 301–318.

Earl, P. E. (1992). The evolution of cooperative strategies: Three automotive industry case studies. *Human Systems Management*, 11, pp. 89–100.

EFMD (2005). *Globally Responsible Leadership: A Call for Engagement.* European Foundation for Management Development. www.GloballyResponsible Leaders.net.

Eigen, P. (2002). www.transparency.org.

Eisenhardt, K. M. and D. C. Galunic (2006). Co-evolving: At last a way to make synergies work. *Harvard Business Review*, Jan–Feb, pp. 91–101.

Elfstrom, G. (1983), On dilemmas of intervention. *Ethics*, 93, pp. 709–725.

Elliot, K. A. (1997). *Corruption and the Global Economy.* Washington, DC. Institute for International Economics.

Elster, J. (1986). *The Multiple Self.* Cambridge: CUP.

Engleberg, E. (1972). *The Unknown Distance.* Harvard University Press.

Etzioni, A. (1988). *The Moral Dimension: Towards a New Economics*. NY: Free Press.

Etzioni, A. (1986). The case for a multiple-utility conception. *Economics and Philosophy*, 2, pp. 159–183.

Etzioni, A. (2004). *From Empire to Community*. NY: Palgrave, Macmillan.

Evans, P. and T. Wurster (2000). *Blown to Bits: How the Economics of Information Transforms Strategy*. Boston: HBS Press.

Fischoff, B. and B. Goiten (1984). The informal use of formal models. *Acadamy of Management Review*, 9(3), pp. 505–512.

Fiss, O. M. (1976). Groups and the equal protection clause. *Philosophy and Public Affairs*, 5, pp. 150–151.

Folger, I. L., O. Rosenfeld and T. Robinson (1983). Relative deprivation and procedural justifications. *Journal of Personality and Social Psychology*, 45, pp. 268–273.

Fortune, Feb. 6, 1995.

Freeman, R. E. (1999). Divergent stakeholder theory. *Academy of Management Review*, 24(2), pp. 233–236.

Freeman, R. E. (1998). Poverty and the politics of capitalism. *Business Ethics Quarterly*, (Special issue) 1, pp. 31–35.

Freeman, R. E. (1984). *Strategic Management: A Stakeholder Approach*. Boston: Pitman.

Freeman, R. E. (1994). A stakeholder theory of the modern corporation. In *Ethical Theory and Business*, T. L. Beauchamp and N. E. Bowie, eds. NJ: Prentice Hall, pp. 66–76.

Friedman, M. (1970). The social responsibility of business is to increase its profits. *New York Times*, Sept. 13.

French, P. (1984). *Collective and Corporate Responsibility*. NY: Columbia University Press.

Fukuyama, F. (1992). *The End of History and the Last Man*. London: Hamish Hamilton.

Fumerton, R. A. (1990). *Reason and Morality: A Defence of the Egocentric Perspective*. Ithaca: Cornell University Press.

Garrett, T. M. and R. J. Klonoski (1986). *Business Ethics*, 2nd ed. Englewood Cliffs, NJ: Prentice Hall.

Gauthier, D. (1990). *Moral Dealing*. Cornell University Press.

Geanakoplos, J. and D. Pearce (1989). Psychological games and sequential rationality. *Games and Economic Behavior*, 1, pp. 60–79.

Giddens, A. (1998). *The Third Way: The Renewal of Social Democracy*. Malden, MA: Polity Press.

Gilbert, D. Jr. (1996). The Prisoners' Dilemma and the prisoners of the Prisoners' Dilemma. *Business Ethics Quarterly*, 6(2), pp. 165–178.

Gilbert, D. R. (1986). Corporate strategy and ethics. *Journal of Business Ethics*, 5, pp. 137–150.

Gilboa, I. and D. Schmeidler (1988). Information-dependent games: Can common sense be common knowledge? *Economics. Letters* 27, pp. 215–221.

Gladstein, D. and J. B. Quinn (1985). Making decisions and producing action: The two faces of strategy. In *Organisational Strategy and Change*, J. M. Pennings and Associates. San Francisco: Jossey-Bass.

Goldman, R. and S. Sapson (1994). Advertising in the age of hyper-signification. *Theory, Culture and Society*, 11, pp. 23–54.

Goldman, A. H. (1980). Business ethics: profits, utilities and moral rights. *Philosophy and Public Affairs*, 9(3), pp. 260–286.

Goldman, A. H. (1975). Limits to the justification of reverse discrimination. *Social Theory and Practice*, 3, pp. 110–113.

Goldman, A. H. (1976). Affirmative action. *Philosophy and Public Affairs*, 5, p. 187.

Goodpaster, K. (1985). Ethical frameworks for management. In *Policies and Persons*, J. B. Mathews, K. Goodpaster and L. Nash, eds., NY: McGraw Hill. pp. 507–552.

Goodpaster, K. (1991). Business ethics and stakeholder analysis. *Business Ethics Quarterly*, 1(1), pp. 53–73.

Goodpaster, K. (1996). Bridging East and West in management ethics: Kyosie and the moral point of view. Paper presented at Reitaku University, Chiba, Tokyo.

Gordon, K. and M. Miyake (2001). Business approaches to combating bribery: A study of codes of conduct. *Journal of Business Ethics*, 34(3/4), pp. 161–173.

Grabosky, P. (1995). Governing at a distance: Self-regulating green markets. In *Markets, the State and the Environment: Towards Integration*, R. Eckersley, ed., Macmillan.

Granstrand, O. (1999). *The Economics and Management of Intellectual Property: Towards Intellectual Capital*. Cheltenham, UK: Edward Elgar.

Grant, C. (1991). Friedman fallacies. *Journal of Business Ethics*, 10, pp. 907–914.

Greenberg, J. (1987). A taxonomy of organisational justice theories. *Academy of Management Review*, 12, pp. 9–22.

Grubel, H.G. and L. A. Boland (1986). On the efficient use of mathematics in economics. *Kyklos*, 39, pp. 419–442.

Guth, W. D. and R. Taguiri. (1965) Personal values and corporate strategy. *Harvard Business Review*, 43(5), pp. 123–132.

Habermas, J. (1981). *Theorie des Kommunikativen Handelns*. Frankfurt: Suhrkamprankfurt; McCarthy, T. (trans.) (1984). *The Theory of Communicative Action*. Boston: Beacon Press.

Haksever C., R. Chaganti and R. Cook (2003). A model of value creation: Strategic view. *Journal of Business Ethics*, 49(3), pp. 291–305.

Hambrick, D. C. and P. Mason (1984). Upper echelons: The organization as a reflection of its top managers. *Academy of Management Review*, 9, pp. 195–206.

Hamel, G. and C. K. Prahalad (1990). The core competence of the corporation. *Harvard Business Review*, May–June.

Hamel, G. and C. K. Prahalad (1989). Strategic intent. *Harvard Business Review*, May–June, pp. 63–76.

Hampden-Turner, C. and F. Trompenaars (1997). *Mastering the Infinite Game. How East Asian Values Are Transforming Business Practices*. Oxford: Capstone.

Handy, C. (1997). The citizen corporation. *Harvard Business Review*, September–October, pp. 26–28.

Hardin, R. (1988). *Morality within the Limits of Reason*. Chicago: U. Chicago Press.

Hargreaves-Heap, S. (1989). *Rationality in Economics*. Oxford: Blackwell.

Harries-Jones, P. (1995). *A Recursive Vision: Ecological Understanding and Gregory Bateson*. Canada: University of Toronto Press.

Harsanyi, J. C. (1968). Games with incomplete information played by Bayesian players, III. The basic probability distribution of the game. *Management Science*, 14, pp. 486–502.

Harvey, D. and M. Reed. (1994) The evolution of dissipative social systems. *Journal of Social and Evolutionary Systems*, 17(4), pp. 371–411.

Hawken, P. (1993). *The Ecology of Commerce*. London: Wisenfield and Nicolson.

Hawken, P. (1999). *Natural Capitalism*. London: Wisenfield & Nicolson.

Hayek, F. A. (1945). The use of knowledge in society. *Economica*, pp. 33–45.

Hayes, R. and G. Pisano (1994). Beyond world-class: The new manufacturing strategy. *Harvard Business Review*, p. 77.

Hayes, R. H. (1985). Strategic planning — Forward in reverse. *Harvard Business Review*, November–December, pp. 111–119.

Heath, J. (2006). Business ethics without stakeholders. *Business Ethics Quarterly*, 16(4), pp. 533–557.

Heilman, M. E. and J. N. Herlihy, (1984). Affirmative action, negative reaction? Some moderating conditions. *Organizational Behavior and Human Performance*, 33, pp. 204–213.

Heilman, M. E., M. C. Simon, and D. P. Repper, (1987). Intentionally favored, unintentionally harmed impact of sex-based preferential selection on self-perceptions and self-evaluations. *Journal of Applied Psychology*, 72, pp. 62–68.

Heller, M. A. and R. S. Eisenberg (1998). Can patents deter innovation? The anti-commons in biomedical research. *Science*, 280, pp. 698–701.

Helpman, E. (1993). Innovation, imitation and intellectual property rights. *Econometrica*, 61(6), pp. 1247–1280.

Hendry, J. (2001). Missing the target: Normative stakeholder theory and the corporate governance debate. *Business Ethics Quarterly*, 11(1), pp. 159–176.

Higgins, R. B. (2002). *The Search for Corporate Strategic Credibility: Concepts and Cases in Global Strategy Communications*. Westport, CT: Quotum Books.

Hill, R. P. (2002). Stalking the poverty consumer. *Journal of Business Ethics*, 37(2), pp. 209–219.

Hirshleifer, J. (1976). *Price Theory and Application*. NJ: Prentice Hall.

Hitt, M. A. and B. B. Tyler (1991). Strategic decision models: Integrating different perspectives. *Strategic Management Journal*, 12, pp. 327–351.

Hofstadter, D. R. (1979). *Gödel, Escher, Bach: An Eternal Golden Braid*. England: Harvester.

Hogarth, R. M. and S. Makridakis (1981). Forecasting and planning: An evaluation. *Management Science*, 27(2), pp. 115–137.

Hosmer, L. (1995). Trust: The connecting link between organisational theory and philosophical ethics. *Academy of Management Review*, 20(2), pp. 379–403.

Hosmer, L. (2001). Ethics and economics: Growing opportunities for joint research. *Business Ethics Quarterly*, 11(4), pp. 599–622.

Hosmer, L. T. (1994). Strategic planning as if ethics mattered. *Strategic Management Journal*, (Summer Special Issue), 15, pp. 17–34.

Hosmer, L. T. (1991). *The Ethics of Management*. Homewood, IL: Irwin.

Howard, N. (1971). *Paradoxes of Rationality: Theory of Games and Political Behavior*. Cambridge, MA: MIT Press.

Hunt, G. and M. D. Mehta (2006). *Nanotechnology: Risk , Ethics and Law*. London: Earthscan.

Huysmans, J. (1994). Using the systems approach to increase Management Science impact on business. *Interfaces*, 24(5), pp. 152–164.

Ibarra, E. (1995). Strategic analysis of organizations: A model from the complexity paradigm. *Human Systems Management*, 14(1).

Isaacs, W. (1999). *Dialogue and the Art of Thinking Together: A Pioneering Approach to Communicating in Business and in Life*. NY: Currency.

Jackson, M. C. (1991). *Systems Methodologies for the Management Sciences*. Plenum.

Jacobson, M. B. and W. Koch (1977). Women as leaders: Performance evaluation as a function of method of leader selection. *Organizational Behavior and Human Performance*, 20, pp. 149–157.

Jacoby, N., P. Nehemkis and R. Eells (1977). *Bribery and Extortion in World Business: A Study of Corporate Political Payments Abroad.* NY: Macmillan.

Jaki, S. L. (1978). In *Trends in Business Ethics: Implications for Decision-Making,* C. van Dam and L. M. Stallaert, eds., Boston: Martinus Nijhoff.

James, S. (1982). The duty to relieve suffering. *Ethics,* 93, pp. 4–21.

Janis, I. L. and L. Mann, (1977). *Decision Making: A Psychological Analysis of Conflict, Choice and Commitment.* NY: Free Press.

Jawahar, I. M. and G. L. McLaughlin (2001). Towards a descriptive stakeholder theory: An organisational life cycle approach. *Academy of Management Review,* 26(3), pp. 397–414.

Jay, M. (1985). Habermas and modernism. In *Habermas and Modernity,* R. Berstein, ed., MIT Press.

Jaynes, J. (1976). *The Origin of Consciousness in the Breakdown of the Bicameral Mind.* Houghton Mifflin Co.

Jones, T. and A. Wicks (1999). Convergent stakeholder theory. *Academy of Management Review,* 24(2), pp. 206–221.

Kadane, J. and P. Larkey (1983). The confusion of is and ought in game theoretic contexts. *Management Science,* 29(12), pp. 1365–1379.

Kaku (1996). Address on Kyosie and Canon's strategy. In *World Congress of Business Ethics and Economics.* Reitaku University, Chiba, Tokyo.

Kale, B. (2004). The clay and the spark. www.iofc.org.

Kamm, F. M. (1986). Harming, not aiding and positive rights. *Philosophy and Public Affairs,* 15(1), pp. 3–32.

Kant, I. (1956). *Critique of Practical Reason,* L. W. Beck, (trans.). Indianapolis: Bobbs-Merrill.

Kao, J. (1996). *Jamming: The Art and Discipline of Business Creativity.* Harper Collins.

Kao, R. (1997). Defining entrepreneurship: Past, present and future. *Creativity and Innovation Management,* 2(1), pp. 22–35.

Karlsson, C., B. Johansson and R. Stough, eds. (2005). *Entrepreneurship and Dynamics in the Knowledge Economy.* Routledge.

Karst, K. L. and H. Horowitz (1974). Affirmative action and equal protection. *Virginia Law Review,* 60, pp. 955–974.

Kavanagh, J. P. (1979). Ethical issues in plant relocation. In *Ethical Theory and Business,* Beauchamp and Bowie, eds., NJ: Prentice Hall.

Kay, J. (1991). Economics and business. *The Economic Journal,* 101(401), pp. 57–63.

Kekes, J. (1983). Wisdom. *American Philosophical Quarterly,* 20(3), pp. 277–286.

Kelly, K (1999). *New Rules for the New Economy.* London: Fourth Estate.

Kelman, S. (1981). Cost-benefit analysis: An ethical critique. *Regulation*, Jan.–Feb., pp. 74–82.

Kennedy, P. (1986). Persuasion and distrust: A comment in the affirmative action debate. *Harvard Law Review*, 99, pp. 1327–1334.

Keren, G. (1993). Optimality as an epistemological organizing principle. *Behavioral and Brain Sciences*, 16(3), pp. 622–623.

Kervern, G. Y. (1990). Au coeur des strategies. *Entreprise la Vague Ethique*. Paris: Assas Editions, pp. 49–54.

Kilpatrick, J. A. (1985). Corporate response to social pressures: A typology. *Journal of Business Ethics*, 4, pp. 493–501.

King, S. R., T. J. Carlson and K. Moran (1996). Biological diversity, indigenous knowledge, drug discovery and IPR. In *Valuing Local Knowledge*, S. B. Brush and D. Stabinsky, eds. pp. 167–185.

Kleijnen, J. and W. Van Groenendaal (1992). *Simulation: A Statistical Perspective* (trans.). Chichester: Wiley.

Klitgaard, R. (1988). *Controlling Corruption*, Berkeley: University of California Press.

Kloppenberg, J. and T. Gonzales (1994). Between state and capital: NGOs as allies of indigenous peoples. In *IPR for Indigenous Peoples*, T. Greaves (ed.) Oklahoma, USA: Society for Applied Anthropology, pp. 165–178.

Knight, F. H. (1936). *The Ethics of Competition*. Woking: Unwin Bros.

Koslowski, P. (2001). *Principles of Ethical Economy*. Dordrecht: Kluwer.

Krugman, P. (1994). Competitiveness: A dangerous obsession. *Foreign Affairs*, 73(4), pp. 28–44.

Kuhn, L. W. (1992). Ethics in business: What managers practice that economists ignore. *Business Ethics Quarterly*, 2(3), pp. 305–315.

Laing, R. D. (1969). *The Politics of the Family*. Toronto: Canadian Broadcasting Corp.

Landry, M. and M. Oral, (1993). In search of a valid view of model validation for operations research. *EJOR*, 66(2), pp. 161–167.

Lane, H. W. *et al.* (1999). Living and working in Bahrain. In *Ethical Issues in Business: A Philosophical Approach*, 6th ed, T. Donaldson and P. H. Werhane, eds.

Lea, S. (1991). Why optimality is not worth arguing about. *Behavioral and Brain Sciences*, 14(2), p. 225.

Leeper, M. A. (2003). Ethics, capitalism and HIV/AIDS. Keynote address at the *Society for Business Ethics Annual Meeting*, Seattle, July 2003.

Leff, N. H. (1964). Economic development through bureaucratic corruption. *American Behavioral Scientist*, 8(3), pp. 8–14 (Reprinted in Heidenheimer, A. J. ed. (1970). *Political Corruption*. New Brunswick, NJ: Transaction Books, pp. 510–520).

Leibenstein, H. (1976). *Beyond Economic Man: A New Foundation for Microeconomics.* MA: Harvard University Press.

Levi, I. (1986). *Hard Choices: Decision Making Under Unresolved Conflict.* Cambridge, MA: CUP.

Levy, D. (1994). Chaos theory and strategy: Theory, application and managerial implications. *Strategic Management Journal,* 15 (Special Issue), pp. 167–178.

Lewis, G., A. Morkel and G. Hubbard (1993). *Cases in Australian Strategic Management.* Prentice Hall.

Linstone, H. A. and Z. Zhu (2000). Towards synergy in multi-perspective management: An American-Chinese case. *Human Systems Management,* 19, pp. 25–37.

Linstone, H. A. (1984). *Multiple Perspectives for Decision Making.* NY: Elsevier.

Lodge, G. C. and E. F. Vogel (1987). *Ideology and National Competitiveness: An Analysis of Nine countries.* HBS Press.

Logsdon, J. and D. Wood (2002). Business citizenship: From domestic to global level of analysis. *Business Ethics Quarterly,* 12(2), pp. 155–187.

Luce, D. and H. Raiffa (1957). *Games and Decisions: Introduction and Critical Survey.* NY: Wiley and Sons.

Lutz, M. A. and Lux (1988). *Humanistic Economics.* N.Y: Bootstrap Press.

Mackie, J. (1978). The law of the jungle, moral alternatives and the principles of evolution. *Philosophy,* 53, pp. 455–464.

Mackie, J. L. (1982). In *Game Theory and Experimental Games: The Study of Strategic Interaction,* A. Colman, ed., Pergamon Press.

MacPherson, C. B. (1985). *The Rise and Fall of Economic Justice.* Oxford University Press.

Mahoney, J. T. (1993). Strategic management and determinism: Sustaining the conversation. *Journal of Management Studies,* 30(1), pp. 173–191.

Maitland, I. (2002). Priceless goods: How should life saving drugs be priced? *Business Ethics Quarterly,* 12(4), pp. 451–480.

Manning, R. (1988). Dismemberment, divorce and hostile takeover. *Journal of Business Ethics,* 7, pp. 639–643.

Manning, R. C. (1984). Corporate responsibility and corporate personhood. *Journal of Business Ethics,* 3, pp. 77–84.

March, J. G. (1978). Bounded rationality, ambiguity and the engineering of choice. *Bell Journal of Economics,* 9, pp. 587–608.

Marcuse, H. (1966). Ethics and revolution. In *Ethics and Society,* R. T. DeGeorge, ed., N.Y: Anchor Books.

Margolis, J. and P. Walsh (2003). Misery loves companies: Rethinking social initiatives by business. *Administrative Science Quarterly,* 48(2), pp. 268–306.

Marsh, P. D. V. (1980). *Business Ethics*. London: Associated Business Press.

Maruyama (1992). Lessons from Japanese Management failures in foreign countries. *Human Systems Management*, 11(1), pp. 41–48.

Mason, R. O. (1969). A dialectical approach to strategic planning. *Management Science*, 13, pp. 403–414.

Mason, R. O. (1994). Securing: One man's quest for the meaning of therefore. *Interfaces*, 24(4), pp. 67–72.

Mason, R. O. and I. I. Mitroff (1981). *Challenging Strategic Planning Assumptions*. Wiley, Interscience.

Mathews, J. B., K. Goodpaster and L. Nash (1985). *Policies and Persons*. McGraw Hill.

Maturana, H. and F. J. Varela (1980). *Autopoiesis and Cognition: The Realisation of the Living*. Boston: Reidel (orig. 1970).

McClennen, E. (1990). *Rationality and Dynamic Choice; Foundational Explorations*. Cambridge: CUP.

McCurdy, D. B. (2002). But is it a business? (Review of L. J. Weber *op cit.*). *Business Ethics Quarterly*, 12(3), pp. 527–538.

McWilliams, A. and D. Siegel (2000). Corporate social responsibility and financial performance: Correlation or mis-specification? *Strategic Management Journal*, 21(5), pp. 603–609.

Miller, G. (1991). Two dynamic criteria for validating claims of optimality. *Behavioral and Brain Sciences*, 14(2), pp. 228–229.

Minas, A. C. (1977). How reverse discrimination compensates women. *Ethics*, 88, pp. 74–79.

Mintzberg, H. (1976). Planning on the left side and managing on the right. *Harvard Business Review*, July–August.

Mintzberg, H. and J. Waters (1985). Of strategies deliberate and emergent. *Strategic Management Journal*, 6, pp. 257–272.

Mintzberg, H. (1987). The strategy concept: Five P's of strategy. *California Management Review*, 30(1), pp. 11–24.

Mintzberg, H. (1988). Ideology and the missionary organisation. In *The Strategy Process*, J. B. Quinn, H. Mintzberg and R. James, eds., Prentice Hall.

Mintzberg, H. (1990). The design school: Reconsidering the basic premises of strategic management, *Strategic Management Journal*, 11, pp. 171–195.

Molyneaux, D. (2003). Saints and CEO's: An historical experience of altruism, self-interest and compromise. *Business Ethics: A European Review*, 12(2), pp. 133–143.

Moore, G. E. (1903). *Principia Ethica*. Cambridge: CUP.

Moorthy, R. S., T. Donaldson, W. Ellos, R. Solomon and R. Textor (1998). *Uncompromising Integrity: Motorola's Global Challenge: 24 Global Case Studies with Commentaries.* Motorola University Press. (Reprinted in *op. cit.*, Donaldson T., P. Werhane and M. Cording, eds., pp. 429–431.

Morecroft, J. (1983). Rationality and structure in behavioral models of business systems. *Proc. Int. Syst, Dyn. Conf.*, MIT, MA.

Moss-Kanter, R. (1991). Transcending business boundaries: 12000 World managers view change. *Harvard Business Review*, May–June, pp. 151–164.

Munzer, S. R. (1990). *A Theory of Property.* Cambridge Studies in Philosophy and Law. Cambridge: CUP.

Murdoch, I. (1970). *The Sovereignty of the Good.* London: Routledge.

Murphy, P. B. (1988). Implementing business ethics. *Journal of Business Ethics*, 7, pp. 907–915.

Nagel, S. (2001). *Handbook of Win-Win Policy Analysis.* Nova Science Publishers.

Nagel, T. (1973). Equal treatment and compensatory discrimination. *Philosophy and Public Affairs*, 2, pp. 348–363.

Narveson, J. (2003). The invisible hand. *Journal of Business Ethics*, 46(3), pp. 201–212.

National Research Council (2000). *The Digital Dilemma: Intellectual Property in the Information Age.* Committee on Intellectual Property Rights and the Emerging Information Infrastructure. Washington: (U.S.) National Academy Press.

Newton, L. H. (1973). Reverse discrimination as unjustified. *Ethics*, 83, pp. 308–312.

Nickel, J. W. (1974). Classification by race in compensatory programs. *Ethics*, 84, pp. 146–150.

Nickel, J. W. (1975). Preferential policies in hiring and admissions: A jurisprudential approach. *Columbia Law Review*, 75, pp. 534–558.

Nielsen, R. P. (1988). Cooperative strategy. *Strategic Management Journal*, 9, pp. 475–492.

Noonan, J. T. (1984). *Bribes.* NY: Macmillan.

Nye, J. S. (1967). Corruption and political development: A cost-benefit analysis. *American Political Science Review*, LXI(2) (Reprinted in Heidenheimer, A. J. (1970). *Political Corruption.* New Brunswick, NJ: Transaction Books, pp. 564–578.

O'Conner, M. A. (2000). Comment on Bassi *et al.* In *The New Relationship: Human Capital and the American Corporation*, M. M. Blair and T. A. Kochan, eds., Washington DC: Brookings Institution Press.

Oberman, W. (2004). A framework for the ethical analysis of corporate political activity. *Business and Society Review*, 109(2), pp. 245–262.

O'Keefe, R. (1995). OR-MS enabled system design. *Operations Research*, 13, March–April, pp. 199–207.

Oral, M., A. E. Singer and O. Kettani (1989). The level of international competitiveness and its strategic implications. *International Journal of Research in Marketing*, 6, pp. 267–282.

Oral, M. and O. Kettani (1993). The facets of modelling and validation in Operational Research. *European Journal of Operations Research*, 66(2), pp. 216–234.

Oral, M. (1986). An industrial competitiveness model. *IIE Transactions*, 18(2), pp. 148–157.

Orlitsky, M., F. Schmidt and S. Rynes (2003). Corporate social and financial performance: A meta-analysis. *Organisational Studies*, 24, pp. 403–411.

Osterberg, R. (1994). *Corporate Renaissance*. Nataraj Press.

Paine, L. S. and J. P. Katz (1999). Levi Strauss and Co: Global sourcing. In. *op cit*, T. Donaldson and P. Werhane, eds.

Partridge, E. (1999). Holes in the cornucopia. In *op cit*, T. Donaldson and P. Werhane, eds. pp. 574–591.

Patel, S. J. (1996). Can the IPR system serve the interests of indigenous knowledge. In *Valuing Local Knowledge*, S. B. Brush and D. Stabinsky, eds., Washington DC: Island Press, pp. 305–323.

Pennings, J. M. (1985). *Organisational Strategy and Change*. San Francisco: Jossey-Bass.

Perelman, M. (2002). *Steal This Idea: Intellectual Property Rights and the Corporate Confiscation of Creativity*. NY: Palgrave.

Poff, D. C. (1994). Reconciling the irreconcilable: The global economy and the environment. *Journal of Business Ethics*, 13(6), pp. 439–447.

Porritt, J. (2005). *Capitalism as If the World Mattered*. England: Earthscan.

Porter, M. E. (1980). *Competitive Strategy*. N.Y: Free Press.

Porter, M. E. (1985). *Competitive Advantage*. N.Y: Free Press.

Porter, M. E. (1990). *The Competitive Advantage of Nations*. London: Macmillan Press.

Potter, N. S. (1996/9). The BMW acquisition of the Rover Group. In *Exploring Corporate Strategy*, G. Johnson and K. Scholes, eds. Europe: Prentice Hall, pp. 738–745.

Prahalad, C. K. and A. Hammond (2002). Serving the world's poor, profitably. *Harvard Business Review*, September, pp. 48–57.

Prahalad, C. K. and G. Hamel, (1994). Strategy as a field of study: Why search for a new paradigm? *Strategic Management Journal*, 15(Special Issue), pp. 5–16.

Prahalad, C. K. and G. Hamel (1990). The core competence of the corporation. *Harvard Business Review*, May–June, pp. 79–91.

Prakash Sethi, S. (2003). Globalisation and the good corporation. A need for pro-active co-existence. *Journal of Business Ethics*, 43(1), pp. 21–31.

Preece, S., C. Fleisher and J. Toccacelle (1995). Building a reputation along the value chain at Levi Strauss. *Long Range Planning*, 28(6), pp. 88–98.

Prescott, J. E. and J. H. Grant (1988). A manager's guide for evaluating competitive analysis techniques. *Interfaces*, 18, pp. 10–22.

Pucik, V. and N. Hatvany (1983). Management practices in Japan and their impact on business strategy. *Advances in Strategic Management*, Vol. 1, JAI Press, pp. 103–131.

Putnam, H. (1990). *Realism with a Human Face*. Cambridge, MA: Harvard University Press.

Quinn, D. and T. Jones (1995). An agent morality view of business policy. *Academy of Management Review*, 20(1), pp. 22–42.

Quinn, J. B. (1982). Managing strategies incrementally. *OMEGA*, 10, pp. 613–627.

Quinn, J. B. (1977). Strategic goals: Process and politics. *Sloan Management Review*, Fall, pp. 21–37.

Rankin, N. L. (1987). Corporations as persons: Objections to "Goodpaster's Principle of Moral Projection". *Journal of Business Ethics*, 6, pp. 633–637.

Rapoport, A. (1991). Prisoner's Dilemma. *The New Palgrave: The World of Economics*. Macmillan.

Rastogi, P. N. (2002). Knowledge management and intellectual capital as a paradigm of value creation. *Human Systems Management*, 21(4), pp. 229–240.

Raunch, J. E. (1997). Bribery in awarding government contracts. In *op cit.*, K. Elliot, ed., pp. 113–116.

Rawls, J. (1972). *A Theory of Justice*. Oxford: Clarendon Press.

Reece, W. L. (1980). *Dictionary of Philosophy and Religion: Eastern and Western Thought*. NJ: Humanities Press.

Rescher, N. (1988). *Rationality: A Philosophical Inquiry into the Nature and Rationale of Reason*. Oxford: Clarendon Press.

Resnick, D. B. (2003). A pluralistic account of intellectual property. *Journal of Business Ethics*, 46(4), pp. 319–335.

Reynolds, S. J. (2003). A single framework for strategic and ethical behavior in the international context. *Business Ethics Quarterly*, 13(3), pp. 361–379.

Rice, E. F. (1958). *The Renaissance Idea of Wisdom*. Cambridge: Harvard.

Richter, F. J. (1994). Industrial organizations as knowledge systems. *Systems Practice*, 7(2), pp. 205–216.

Ridley, M. (1999). *Genome: The Autobiography of a Species*. London: Fourth Estate.

Rinnooy-Kan, A. (1991). Optimality as a prescriptive tool. *The Behavioral and Brain Sciences*, 14(2), pp. 230–231.

Ritzer, G. and T. LeMoyne (1991). Hyperrationality: An extension of Weberian and *Neo*-Weberian theory. In *Metatheorising in Sociology*, G. Ritzer, ed., MA: Lexington Books, pp. 93–115.

Robertson, C. J. and A. Watson (2004). Corruption and strategy. *Strategic Management Journal*, 25(4), pp. 385–396.

Robertson, C. J. and W. C. Crittenden (2003). Mapping moral philosophies: strategic implications for multinational firms. *Strategic Management Journal*, 24(4), pp. 385–392.

Rogow, A. and H. Lasswell (1970). Power, corruption and rectitude. In *Political Corruption*, A. J. Heidenheimer, ed., New Brunswick, NJ: Transaction Books, pp. 510–520.

Rorty, R. (1986). Science as solidarity. In *The Rhetoric of Human Science*, J. Nelson, A. Megill and D. McCIosky, eds., Madison: Univ. Wisconsin Press.

Rorty, R. (1982). *Consequences of Pragmatism*, Minneapolis: Univ. Minnesota Press.

Rose-Ackerman, S. (1978). *Corruption: A Study in Political Economy*. NY: Academic Press, Inc.

Rosenhead, J. ed. (1989). *Rational Analysis for a Problematic World*. Chichester: Wiley.

Rossouw, G. J. and L. J. van Vuuren (2003). Modes of managing morality: A descriptive model of strategies for managing ethics. *Journal of Business Ethics*, 46(4), pp. 389–402.

Rossouw, C. J. (1994). Rational interaction for moral sensitivity: A postmodern approach to moral decision making in business. *Journal of Business Ethics*, 13(1), pp. 11–20.

Roy, Achinto and A. E. Singer (2006). Reducing corruption in international business: Behavioural managerial and political approaches. *Journal of Economic and Social Policy*, 10(2), pp. 3–24.

Roy, Achinto (2006). Corruption related decision making. Doctoral thesis, University of Canterbury, NZ.

Roy, Arundhati (2005). The checkbook and the cruise missile. (Sydney peace prize acceptance speech, Nov. 2004) Alternative Radio, Boulder, CO. www.alternativeradio.org.

Roy, B. (1993). Decision science or decision-aid science? *EJOR*, 66, pp. 184–203.

Rugman, A. and A. Verbeke (1998). Competitive strategy and environmental regulation: An organising framework. *Strategic Management Journal*, 19(Special Issue), pp. 363–375.

Rumelt, R. P., D. Schendel and D. J. Teece (1991). Strategic management and economics. *Strategic Management Journal*, 12(Winter Special Issue), pp. 5–29.

Russell, T. and R. Thaler, (1985). The relevance of quasi-rationality in competitive markets. *American Economic Review*, 75, pp. 1071–1082.

Ryan, L. V. (2000). Combating corruption: The 21st century ethical challenge. *Business Ethics Quarterly*, 10(1), pp. 331–338.

Sagoff, M. (1998). *The Economy of the Earth*. Cambridge University Press.

Saiia, D., A. Carroll and A. Buchholtz (2003). Philanthropy as strategy. *Business and Society*, 42(2), pp. 169–201.

Saloner, G. (1994). Game theory and strategic management: Contributions, applications and limitations. In *op cit.*, R. Rumelt *et al.*, eds.

Sandoz, P. (1997). Canon: global responsibilities and local decisions. In *Japanese Business: The Human Face*. London: Penguin.

Schendel, D. (1991). Editor's comments on the winter special issue. *Strategic Management Journal*, 12(Winter 1991), pp. 1–3.

Schick, F. (1984). *Having Reasons: An Essay on Rationality and Sociality*. Princeton University Press.

Schmitt, N. and R. A. Noe (1986). Personnel selection and equal employment opportunity. In *International Review of Industrial and Organizational Psychology*, C. I. Cooper and L. T. Robertson, eds., NY: Wiley.

Schmitt, N., R. Z. Gooding, R. A. Noe and M. Kirsch (1984). Meta-analyses of validity studies published between 1964 and 1982 and the investigation of study characteristics. *Personnel Psychology*, 37, pp. 407–422.

Schnatterly, K. (2003). Increasing firm value through detection and prevention of white collar crime. *Strategic Management Journal*, 24(7), pp. 587–614.

Schoemaker, P. J. H. (1991). The quest for optimality : A positive heuristic of science? *Behavioral and Brain Sciences*, 14(2), pp. 205–245.

Schoemaker, P. J. H. (1993). Strategic decisions in organizations: rational and behavioural views. *Journal of Management Studies*, 30(1), pp. 107–129.

Schumpeter, J. A. (1934). *The Theory of Economic Development: An Inquiry into Profits, Capital, Credit, Interest, and the Business Cycle*, translated by Redvers Opie. Cambridge, MA: Harvard University Press.

Schutte, H. (1994). *The Global Competitiveness of the Asian Firm*. Macmillan.

Schwenk, C. R. (1984). Cognitive simplification processes in strategic decision making. *Strategic Management Journal*, 5, pp. 111–128.

Scott, J. C. (1972). *Comparative Political Corruption*. NJ: Prentice Hall.

Sen, A. (1977). Rational fools: a critique of the behavioural foundations of economic theory. *Philosophy and Public Affairs*, 6, pp. 317–344.

Sen, A. (1987). *On Ethics and Economics*. Oxford: Blackwell.

Sen, A. (1993). Does business ethics make economic sense? *Business Ethics Quarterly*, 3(1).

Sen, A. (1996). Economics, business principles and moral sentiments. *Business Ethics Quarterly*, 7, pp. 5–16.

Sen, A. (1997). Economics, business principles and moral sentiments. *Business Ethics Quarterly*, 7(3), pp. 5–15.

Sen, A. (1999). *Development as Freedom*. Oxford University Press.

Shanks, M. (1993). Human goods in ethical business. In *The Good and the Economical*, P. Koslowski and Y. Shiona, eds., Berlin: Springer-Verlag, pp. 147–171.

Shaw, B. (1988). Affirmative action: An ethical evaluation. *Journal of Business Ethics*, 7, pp. 763–770.

Shenhav, Y., W. Shrum and S. Alon (1994). Goodness concepts in the study of organizations: A longitudinal survey of four leading journals. *Organizational Studies*, 15(5), pp. 753–776.

Sher, G. (1975). Justifying reverse discrimination in employment. *Philosophy and Public Affairs*, 4, pp. 159–170.

Shi, Y. (1995). Studies on optimum-path ratios in multicriteria De Novo programming problems. *Computers and Mathematics with Applications*, 29(5), pp. 43–50.

Shiogi, K. and C. Nakano (1999). Japanese philosophical traditions and contemporary business practices. In *Business Ethics in Theory and Practice: Contributions from Asia and New Zealand*, P. Werhane and A. E. Singer, eds. Dordrecht: Kluwer, pp. 167–176.

Shiva, V. and R. Holla-Bhar (1996). Piracy by patent: The case of the Neem tree. In *The Case Against the Global Economy*, J. Mander and E. Goldsmith, eds. Sierra Club Books, pp. 146–159.

Shrivastava, P. (1995). Environmental technologies and competitive advantage. *Strategic Management Journal*, 16(Special Issue, Summer), pp. 183–200.

Shrivastava, P. and H. Scott (1992). Corporate self-greenewal: Strategic responses to environmentalism. *Business Strategy and the Environment*, 1(3), pp. 9–21.

Simon, J. L. (1999). Scarcity or abundance? In *op cit.*, T. Donaldson and P. Werhane, eds., pp. 565–573.

Simon, H. A. (1987). Rationality in psychology and economics, In *Rational Choice*, R. M. Hogarth and M. W. Reder, eds. University of Chicago Press, pp. 25–40.

Simpson, W. and T. Kohers (2002). The link between corporate social and financial performance: Evidence from the banking industry. *Journal of Business Ethics*, 35(2), pp. 97–109.

Sims, R. and J. Brinkman (2003). Enron ethics (or culture matters more than codes). *Journal of Business Ethics*, 45(3), pp. 243–256.

Singer, A. E. (1981). Taking "right minded" decisions. *Accountancy*, October.

Singer, A. E. (1984). Planning, consciousness and conscience. *Journal of Business Ethics*, 3, pp. 113–117.

Singer, A. E., J. Davies and M. Huang (1984). Talking about probabilities: A logical problem for OR-MS. *Decision Sciences*, 15, pp. 488–497.

Singer, A. E. (1985). Strategic and financial decision-making processes in New Zealand public companies. *New Zealand Journal of Business*, 7, pp. 33–46.

Singer, A. E. (1986). A classification of factors in corporate investment decisions. *Management Research News*, 9(4), pp. 16–19.

Singer, A. F. and Van der Walt (1987). Corporate conscience and foreign divestment decisions. *Journal of Business Ethics*, 6, pp. 543–552.

Singer, A. E. (1988). Book review of 'The Evolution of Cooperation' by R. Axelrod, *Journal of MacroMarketing*, 8(1), pp. 59–61.

Singer, A. E. and R. Brodie (1990). Forecasting competitor's actions: An evaluation of alternative ways of analysing business competition. *International Journal of Forecasting*, 6, pp. 75–88.

Singer, A. E. (1991a). Meta-rationality and strategy. *OMEGA: International Journal of Management Science*, 19(2), pp. 101–110.

Singer, A. E. (1991b). Strategy as rationality. *Human Systems Management*, 11(1), pp. 7–21.

Singer, A. E. (1993a). Strategy with Sunk Costs. *Human Systems Management*, 12(2), pp. 97–114.

Singer, A. E. (1993b). Plural rationality and strategic intelligence. In *Global Perspectives on Competitive Intelligence*, J. Prescott and P. Gibbons, eds., Alexandria, VA: SCIP.

Singer, A. E. (1994a). Strategy as moral philosophy. *Strategic Management Journal*, 15, pp. 191–213.

Singer, A. E (1994b). DCF Without Forecasts. *OMEGA: International Journal of Management Science*, 22(3), pp. 221–235.

Singer, A. E. (1995). Competitiveness as hyper-strategy. *Human Systems Management*, 14(2), pp. 163–178.

Singer, A. E. (1996a). Optimality and strategy. *International Journal of Operations and Quantitative Management*, 2(2), pp. 111–126.

Singer, A. E. (1996b). Strategic thinking without boundaries: Meta-decisions and transitions. *Systems Practice*, 9(5).

Singer, A. E. (1996c). Metatheory, hyperstrategy and ultragames. In *Management, Marketing and the Competitive Process*, P. E. Earl, ed. Aldershot: Edward Elgar.

Singer, A. E. (1996d). *Strategy as Rationality: Redirecting Strategic Thought and Action.* Avebury Series in Philosophy. Aldershot: Avebury.

Singer, A. E. and M. Singer (1997). Management science and business ethics. *Journal of Business Ethics*, 16, pp. 473–484.

Singer, A. E. (1997a). Game theory and the evolution of strategic thinking. *Human Systems Management*, 16, pp. 63–75.

Singer, A. E. (1997b). Education without tradeoffs. In *Business Education: A Value-Laden Process*, S. M. Natale and G. Hayward, eds., Lanham and Oxford: University Press of America. pp. 67–79.

Singer, A. E. (1999a). Transforming managers and their mental models: The case of hyper-competition versus stakeholder theory. *Proc. I.A.B.S.*, Paris, 1999.

Singer, A. E. (1999b). Synergy orientation and intellectual property. In *On the Threshold of the Millenium*, S. M. Natale, A. F. Libertella and G .Hayward, eds. Lanham and Oxford: University Press of America, pp. 67–79.

Singer, A. E. (1999c). Synergy-orientation and the third way. In *Business Ethics: Contributions from Asia and New Zealand*, P. Werhane and A. Singer, eds., Dordrecht: Kluwer Academic.

Singer, A. E. and J. Calton (2001). Dissolving the digital dilemma: Meta-theory and intellectual property. *Human Systems Management*, 20(1), pp. 19–33.

Singer, A. E., J. Calton and M. Singer (2001). Profit without copyright. *Small Business Economics*, 16, pp. 149–156.

Singer, A. E. (2001a). Metamodelling. In *Encyclopedia of Life Support Systems*, M. Zeleny, ed., Paris: UNESCO. EOLSS.

Singer, A. E. (2001b). Recursivity and strategy (under review).

Singer, A. E. (2002). Global business and the dialectic: Towards an ecological understanding. *Human Systems Management*, 21(4), pp. 249–265.

Singer, A. E. and M. Singer (2002). Intellectual property and moral imagination. *Journal of Economic and Social Policy*, 7(1), pp. 1–22.

Singer, A. E. (2003). Enterprise action for the common good: Market limitations as strategic problems. *Journal of Enterprising Culture*, 11(1), pp. 69–88.

Singer, A. E. (2004). Strategy and poverty. *International Journal of Entrepreneurship and Innovation Management* 4(5), pp. 426–449 (Special Issue on entrepreneurship and poverty, edited by L. P. Dana and A. E. Singer).

Singer, A. E. (2006). Business strategy and poverty alleviation. *Journal of Business Ethics*, 66, pp. 225–231.

Singer, A. E. ed. (2007). *Business Ethics and Strategy*. Vols. I and II. The International Library of Public and Private Ethics, T. Campbell, CAPPE Canberra, series ed. England: Ashgate (forthcoming in 2007).

Solomon, R. (1999). Game theory as a model for business and business ethics. *Business Ethics Quarterly*, 9(1), pp. 11–29.

Solomon, R. C. (1992). *Ethics and Excellence: Cooperation and Integrity in Business*. Oxford University Press.

Soule, E. (2002). Management moral strategies: In search of a few good principles. *Academy of Management Review*, 27(1), pp. 114–124.

Sowell, T. (1978). Are quotas good for blacks? *Commentary*, 65, pp. 39–43.

Sperry, R. W. (1979). Consciousness, free will and personal identity. In *Brain, Behaviour and Evolution*, D. A. Oakley and H. C. Plotkin, eds., Routledge: Kegan & Paul.

Stacey, R. (1993). *Strategic Management and Organisational Dynamics*. Pitman.

Starkey, K. and A. Crane (2003). Towards green narrative: Management and the evolutionary epic. *Academy of Management Review*, 28(2), pp. 220–237.

Stock, G. (1993). *Metaman*. London: Bantam Press.

Tarnas, R. (1996). *The Passion of the Western Mind: Understanding the Ideas That Have Shaped Our Worldview*. NY: Ballantine Books.

Taylor, C. (1989). *Sources of the Self*. Cambridge, MA: Harvard University Press.

Taylor, P. W. (1973). Reverse discrimination and compensatory justice. *Analysis*, 33, pp. 177–182.

Teece, D. J. (1998). Capturing value from knowledge assets: The new economy, markets for know-how and intangible assets. *California Management Review*, 40(3), pp. 55–79.

Teece, D. J. (1985). Applying concepts of economic analysis to strategic management. In *op. cit.*, J. M. Pennings, ed.

Thaler, R. and H. Sheffrin (1981). An economic theory of self-control. *Journal of Political Economy*, 89, pp. 392–406.

Thaler, R. (1985). Mental accounting and consumer choice. *Marketing Science*, 4, pp. 199–214.

The Business Enterprise Trust (2002). Merck and Co. Inc. Re-printed in T. Donaldson and P. Werhane, *Ethical Issues in Business: a Philosophical Approach*, 7th ed. Prentice Hall.

The Economist (1998). Asian values revisited: What would Confucius say now? July 25, 1998, pp. 23–25.

Thomas, H. and M. Pruitt (1993). Perspectives on theory building in strategic management. *Journal of Management Studies*, 30(1), pp. 3–10.

Thomas, J. J. (1973). Preferential hiring, *Philosophy and Public Affairs*, 2, p. 381.

Thomas, R. E. (1986). Parent-to-parent divestment. In *op. cit.*, Coyne and Wright, eds.

Thurow, L. C. (1997). Needed: A new system of intellectual property rights. *Harvard Business Review*, Sep.–Oct., pp. 95–103.

Toffler, A. (1980). *The Third Wave*. Bantam.

Toffler, A. (1990). *Power Shift*. Bantam.

Tomer, J. F. (1987). *Organizational Capital: The Path to Higher Productivity and Well-being*. NY: Praeger.

Trompenaars, F. (1993). *Riding the Waves of Culture*. London: Nicholas Brealey.

Tsoukas, H. (1994). Refining common sense: Types of knowledge in management studies. *Journal of Management Studies*, 31(6), pp. 761–780.

Ulrich, W. (1994). Can we secure future-responsive management through systems thinking and design? *Interfaces*, 24(4), pp. 26–37.

Uphoff, N. (1994). Catalysing self-management capabilities: A post-Newtonian perspective. *Human Systems Management*, 13(3), pp. 171–181.

Vaidhyanathan, S. (2006). Nanotechnologies and the law of patents: A collision course. In *Nanotechnology: Risk, Ethics and Law*, G. Hunt and M. Mehta, eds. London: Earthscan.

Van Gigch, J. P. (1991). *System Design Modelling and Metamodelling*, NY: Plenum.

Vaver, D. (2000). Intellectual property: The state of the art. *The Law Quarterly Review*, 116, pp. 621–637.

Venkatraman, N. (1989). Strategic orientation of business enterprises: The construct, dimensionality and measurement. *Management Science*, 35(8), pp. 942–962.

Vogel, E. F. (1987). In *op. cit.*, G. C Lodge and E. F. Vogel, eds., pp. 301–323.

Von Neumann, J. (1959). On the theory of games of strategy. In *Contributions to the Theory of Games*, Vol. IV, A. Tucker and R. Luce, eds., (first ed. 1928), pp. 13–42.

Waddock, S. (2004). Creating corporate accountability: Foundational principles to make corporate citizenship real. *Journal of Business Ethics*, 50(4), pp. 313–327.

Waddock, S. A. and S. B. Graves (1997). The corporate social performance–financial performance link. *Strategic Management Journal*, 18, pp. 303–319.

Walliser, B. (1989). Instrumental rationality and cognitive rationality. *Theory and Decision*, 27, pp. 7–36.

Watt, R. (2000). *Copyright and Economic Theory: Friends or Foes?* Cheltenham, UK: Edward Elgar.

Weatherall, D. (2002). Health for all? *Oxford Today*, 15(1), pp. 13–15.

Weber, J. and K. Getz (2004). Buy bribes or bye-bye bribes: The future status of bribery in international commerce. *Business Ethics Quarterly*, 14(4), pp. 695–711.

Weber, L. (1996). Citizenship and democracy: The ethics of corporate lobbying. *Business Ethics Quarterly*, 6(2), pp. 253–259.

Weber, L. J. (2002). *Business Ethics in Healthcare: Beyond Compliance.* Medical Ethics Series Vol. 23, D. H. Smith and R. M. Veatch, eds., Bloomington: Indiana University Press.

Wecker, J. (2002). Boehringer Ingelheim GnbH. The Viramune donation programme; hope in the battle against HIV/AIDS (US Congressional Briefing). www.viramune-donation-program.org.

Wensley, R. (1981). Strategic marketing; betas, boxes or basics? *Journal of Marketing*, 45, pp. 173–182.

Werhane, P. (1998). Moral imagination and the search for ethical decision making in management. *Business Ethics Quarterly* (Special Issue), pp. 75–98.

Werhane, P. H. (1999a). Environmental business and the Rashomon effect. In *Business Ethics in Theory and Practice: Contributions from Asia and New Zealand*, P. H. Werhane and A. E. Singer, eds., Dordrecht: Kluwer.

Werhane, P. H. (1999b). *Moral Imagination and Management Decision Making*, NY: Oxford University Press.

Werhane, P. H. and M. Gorman (2005). Intellectual property rights, moral imagination and access to life-enhancing drugs. *Business Ethics Quarterly*, 15(4), pp. 595–613.

Whittington, R. (1993). *What is Strategy and Does it Matter?* London: Routledge.

Williams, B. (1985). *Ethics and the Limits of Philosophy.* Cambridge University Press.

WIPO (1993). Worldwide symposium on the impact of digital technology on copyright and neighbouring rights. Harvard University, 1993 (*et seq.*).

Wu, J. C. (1967). Chinese legal and political philosophy. In *The Chinese Mind*, C. A. Moore, ed., Hawaii: East-West Center Press.

Yawata (1994). Sociocultural background of competitive management and technology in the Western pacific Rim. In *The Global Competitiveness of the Asian Firm*, H. Schutte, ed., London: Macmillan.

Young, J. Z. (1978). *Programs of the Brain.* Oxford University Press.

Zeleny, M. (1977). Self organisation and living systems: A formal model of autopoiesis. *General Systems*, 4(1), pp. 13–28.

Zeleny, M. (1981). *Autopoiesis: A Theory of Living Organisation*, NY: North Holland.

Zeleny, M. (1982). *Multiple Criteria Decision Making*. NY: McGraw Hill.

Zeleny, M. (1986). Optimal system design with multiple criteria: de novo programming approach. *Engineering Costs and Production Economics*, 10, pp. 89–94.

Zeleny, M. (1988). Beyond capitalism and socialism: Human manifesto. *Human Systems Management*, 7(3), pp. 185–188.

Zeleny, M. (1989). Cognitive equilibrium a new paradigm of decision making. *Human Systems Management*, 8(3), pp. 185–188.

Zeleny, M., (1990). Chaos and self-organization in companies. *Human Systems Management*, 9(4), pp. 201–202.

Zeleny, M. (1992). Governments and free markets: Comparative or strategic advantage? *Human Systems Management*, 11, pp. 173–176.

Zeleny, M. (1994a). In search of cognitive equilibrium: Beauty, quality and harmony. *Journal of Multicriteria Decision Analysis*, 3(3), pp. 3–13.

Zeleny, M. (1994b). Towards tradeoff-free management. *Human Systems Management*, 13, pp. 241–243.

Zeleny, M. (1994c). Six concepts of optimality. Presented at *TIMS-ORSA* Joint National Meeting, Boston, 24–27 April.

Zeleny, M. (1995a). Human and social capital: Pre-requisites for a sustained prosperity. *Human Systems Management*, 14(4), pp. 279–282.

Zeleny, M. (1995b). Trade-offs-free management via de novo programming. *International Journal of Operations and Quantitative Management*, 1(1), pp. 3–15.

Zeleny, M. (1995c). Editorial commentary. *Human Systems Management*, 14(2), pp. 1–2.

Zeleny, M. (1996). Rethinking optimality: Eight concepts. *Human Systems Management*, 15, pp. 1–4.

Zeleny, M. (2005). *Human Systems Management: Integrating Knowledge Management and Systems*. NJ and Singapore: World Scientific.

Zeleny, M. (2006). Knowledge-information autopoietic cycle: Towards wisdom systems. *International Journal of Management and Decision Making*, 7(1), pp. 3–18.

Subject Index